CW01191593

The Defence
of Sevastopol
1941-1942

The Defence of Sevastopol 1941-1942

The Soviet Perspective

Clayton Donnell

Pen & Sword
MILITARY

First published in Great Britain in 2016 by
Pen & Sword Military
an imprint of
Pen & Sword Books Ltd
47 Church Street
Barnsley
South Yorkshire
S70 2AS

Copyright © Clayton Donnell 2016

ISBN 978 1 78346 391 6

The right of Clayton Donnell to be identified as the Author of this Work has been asserted by him in accordance with the Copyright, Designs and Patents Act 1988.

A CIP catalogue record for this book is available from the British Library

All rights reserved. No part of this book may be reproduced or transmitted in any form or by any means, electronic or mechanical including photocopying, recording or by any information storage and retrieval system, without permission from the Publisher in writing.

Typeset in Ehrhardt by
Mac Style Ltd, Bridlington, East Yorkshire
Printed and bound in the UK by CPI Group (UK) Ltd,
Croydon, CR0 4YY

Pen & Sword Books Ltd incorporates the imprints of Pen & Sword Archaeology, Atlas, Aviation, Battleground, Discovery, Family History, History, Maritime, Military, Naval, Politics, Railways, Select, Transport, True Crime, and Fiction, Frontline Books, Leo Cooper, Praetorian Press, Seaforth Publishing and Wharncliffe.

For a complete list of Pen & Sword titles please contact
PEN & SWORD BOOKS LIMITED
47 Church Street, Barnsley, South Yorkshire, S70 2AS, England
E-mail: enquiries@pen-and-sword.co.uk
Website: www.pen-and-sword.co.uk

Contents

Acknowledgements vi
Author's Notes vii
Introduction 1

Chapter 1 The Descent into Crimea – September to October 1941   10

Chapter 2 The Fortress of Sevastopol   23

Chapter 3 The First Assault – October to November 1941   43

Chapter 4 The Second Assault – 17 December 1941 to 1 January 1942   86

Chapter 5 January to June 1942   104

Chapter 6 The Third Assault (1) – The Bombardment of 2 to 6 June 1942   129

Chapter 7 The Third Assault (2) – 7 to 16 June 1942   140

Chapter 8 The Third Assault (3) – 17 to 23 June 1942 – Fall of the North   172

Chapter 9 The Third Assault (4) – 24 June to 16 July 1942 – The End of the Road   198

Chapter 10 Conclusions   230

Notes 236
Bibliography 243
Index 244

Acknowledgements

This book could not have been written without the assistance and guidance, over an eighteen-month period, of Alexander Nemenko, a writer and historian from Sevastopol. His research is impeccable and his knowledge of the subject is second to none. This book is dedicated to Alexander. I would also like to thank my brother James for his unceasing encouragement to me at some of the bleakest moments during this extremely difficult and trying work. He always gave me the little push I needed to keep going. I want to thank John Calvin who created the website www.wwii–photos–maps.com, an amazing source of aerial imagery from the Second World War. I want to thank my daughter Erin for helping once again with the images. Thanks to my wife for her extraordinary patience with me over nearly a two-year period.

Author's Notes

The large bay that is the location of the Sevastopol Naval Base is called Severnaya Bay in several accounts, including Manstein's. It will be referred to as Sevastopol Bay in this account.

In 1941 and 1942, the villages surrounding Sevastopol were referred to by their Crimean Tatar names. For the purposes of this account the original name is used throughout and in the first instance the modern name is cited in parentheses. For example, Alma Tamak (m. Pishchane).

Sevastopol was attacked by both German and Rumanian forces, however, in general, they will typically be referred to as Germans unless a specific Rumanian unit is mentioned.

The Chornaya River will be translated into the English 'Black' River.

The *Sturmgeschütz* III Assault Gun is often referred to as a 'tank' by Soviet writers. The terms 'assault gun' and 'tank' may be used interchangeably, however, 'assault guns' refer to the StuG III.

The term 'Soviet' is used rather than 'Russian', since there were non-Russian combatants at Sevastopol. Some accounts call the German opponents Russians but that is not technically correct, therefore we will use the umbrella term 'Soviet'.

Introduction

In ancient Greek, *Sevastopolis* means 'venerable' or 'honourable'. It is the Greek equivalent of the Roman honorific for *Augustus*, 'the August city'. History shows that Sevastopol became a symbol of courage and perseverance, undergoing two lengthy defensive struggles within a ninety-year period. The Russians call 'The Crimean War' of 1854–55, the 'First Defence'. The Crimean War, in particular the siege of Sevastopol by the French, British and Turks, was fought under appalling conditions – difficult terrain, brutal combat, ceaseless bombardments, disease and a shortage of food and supplies. The siege lasted 349 days. The allies had superior numbers of men and equipment but the Russian defenders had their backs to the sea behind a strong line of fortifications. During the 'Second Defence' of 1941–42 the Soviets were once again cut off from the mainland and surrounded on three sides by the enemy, this time the Germans and Rumanians. The Second Defence lasted for more than 250 days under the same appalling conditions, if not worse.

German and Rumanian forces reached the outer perimeter of Sevastopol's defences on 31 October 1941. In the West it was All Hallows Eve, a Christian feast, also called Halloween – the time of year when the days grow shorter, the nights colder and the rains begin to fall. Halloween is also associated with dark things and as such it was the perfect opening page to one of the darkest chapters in military history. The invasion of Crimea by the German Eleventh Army was an eight-month long nightmare of death and destruction that turned a proud Soviet city blessed with factories and collective farms, schools, museums and theatres, and a bustling naval base into a smoking, empty ruin.

The Black Sea coast from Balaklava to the Belbek River valley can easily be compared in beauty to a Mediterranean coastal resort. In the summer it is a land of sun, green mountains and picturesque, fruit-filled valleys dotted with ancient ruins and a vista of high cliffs overlooking a blue sea. But from the end of October 1941 to the beginning of July 1942, the Riviera of the Black Sea was a slaughterhouse. For eight months thousands of bombs fell, turning it into a lunar landscape. The many no man's lands between Soviet and German trenches were littered with rotting corpses and the entire area was filled with the smell of death, sulphur and cordite, like one of the nine circles of hell in Dante's *Inferno*. The ground shook like a series of continuous earthquake aftershocks. Fires burned everywhere and at night the sky was lit by multi-coloured tracer bullets and searchlights hunting for German night flyers. The men and women who fought there and the citizens of the city who lived like moles in underground caverns, would more than likely have preferred to be in Antarctica.

Adolf Hitler ordered the capture of Crimea in July 1941. This was an amendment to Army Group South's original objective to pursue retreating Soviet forces to Rostov. General Erich von Manstein was ordered to split Eleventh Army's forces, one part to pursue Soviet forces towards Rostov and the other to capture Crimea. During the planning of the invasion of the Soviet Union the peninsula was not seen as a main objective. The Germans would keep an eye on Crimea and conduct mopping-up operations later. Plans changed in July when Soviet bombers flying from Crimea struck the Rumanian oil fields of Ploesti, threatening German oil supplies. The Germans could not afford any such threat and Hitler ordered Eleventh Army to capture Crimea. At the time, Soviet forces defending Crimea consisted of IX Corps with two rifle and one cavalry division, plus a small number of sailors guarding the Black Sea Fleet's base at Sevastopol.

Prior to the Second World War most people were familiar with the names of places like Paris, London, Tokyo, Rome and Berlin. After 1 September 1939 Warsaw, Rotterdam, Narvik, Coventry and the Maginot Line appeared on newspaper front pages. In 1941 Europe descended into total chaos and the world learned of Leningrad, Smolensk and Kiev – and then later, but in smaller headlines – Crimea and Sevastopol. Upon reading the name Sevastopol one might have asked oneself, 'Haven't I heard that name before?' They may have harkened back to their school days, remembering a few lines from the famous Alfred Lord Tennyson poem:

> Half a league, half a league,
> Half a league onward,
> All in the valley of Death
> Rode the six hundred.

The poem was written in December 1854 and recounted the story of the charge of the British Light Cavalry Brigade against Russian gun batteries in the valley between the Fedyukhiny Heights and the Semyukhiny Causeway near Balaklava in the Crimea. It is one of the saddest chapters of the Crimean War of 1854–55. The Russian batteries were placed on the southern slopes of the Fedyukhiny Heights and on top of the line of Turkish Redoubts. The charge was a frontal assault against well-prepared Russian artillery batteries in which 110 British cavalrymen were killed and 161 wounded. It was later transformed into a romantic tale of courage but it was anything but. The truth was that the Light Brigade's charge was a terrible mistake – a suicidal cavalry charge headlong into an artillery

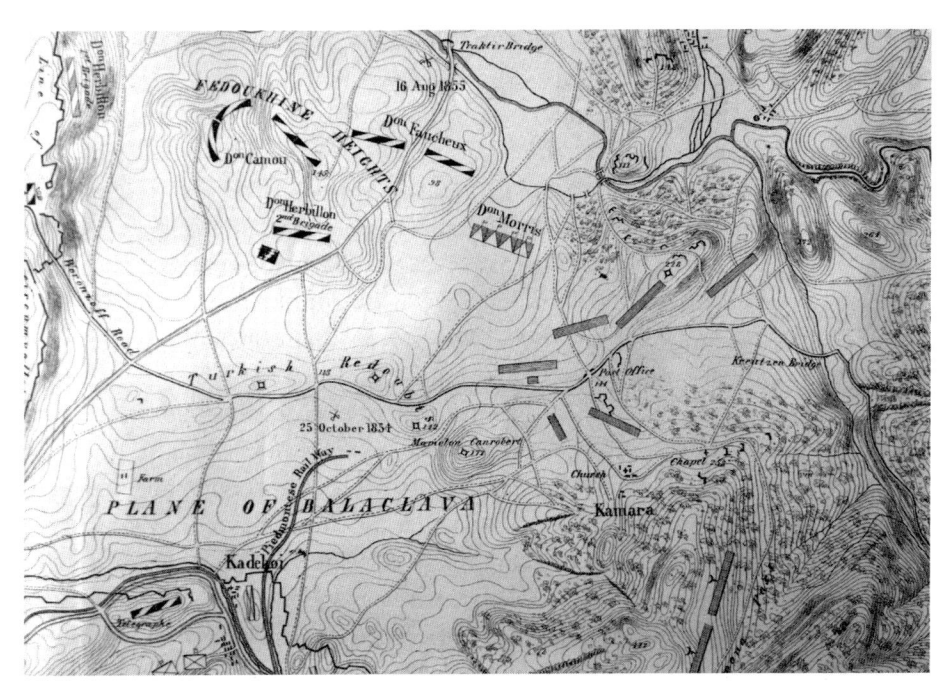

A section from the map Theatre of the War in Crimea in 1854-55. *From General Niel's journal of the Siege of Sebastopol, prepared by Major Delefield for Jefferson Davis, Secretary of War.* (Author's collection)

battery.[1] A frontal assault against a well-defended position violates the most basic rules of war yet, in 1941, the Germans launched similar frontal attacks against well-prepared Soviet defences, into what became many of their own Valleys of Death. They faced rifle bullets, bayonets, fists, knives, grenades, machine guns, minefields, tanks, anti-tank guns and artillery. Unfortunately, as things went, they didn't have much choice.

The deadly valleys of Second World War Sevastopol bore the names Bakhchisarai, Kacha, Belbek, Black River and Kara-Koba. The Germans attacked the Mekenzievy Mountains, the heights of Inkerman, Sapun Ridge, the Turkish Redoubts guarding the Yalta Highway and the heights of Balaklava. These valleys and heights, graveyards for the British, French and Russians in 1854–55, became graveyards for thousands of Soviet, German and Rumanian soldiers in 1941 and 1942. It took more than 250 days from the beginning of the First Assault on Sevastopol on All Hallow's Eve for German troops to cross Sevastopol Bay and finally set foot on the soil of Sevastopol City. When it was all over, it was expected that the victorious Eleventh Army would follow German forces east to capture Stalingrad. Instead, the army was disbanded and Manstein, recently promoted to Field Marshal, returned to Leningrad to pick up where he left off the previous year.

In 1955, after spending four years in prison for war crimes, Manstein published his memoirs, *Verlorene Siege*, translated into English as *Lost Victories*. His book included an account of the operations in Crimea, including Sevastopol. It was written in an even-toned, matter-of-fact style, devoid of anything more than strategic objectives and general details and in it he makes no boastful claims. This is not the case with other writers. Manstein is boldly described by Benoît Lemay as *Hitler's Master Strategist* and by Mungo Melvin as *Hitler's Greatest General*. The Second Defence is described as a 'German Conquest' and a 'triumph'. Are these true and fair accounts of Manstein or was he no more a conqueror or master strategist than Erich von Ludendorff was the Hero and Conqueror of Liège? Was he a legend or was he a myth? Was the final outcome of the Battle of Sevastopol worthy of being called a 'conquest' or a 'triumph?' Did he succeed where most others would have failed or was Sevastopol one of his lost victories?

In September 1941 General von Manstein was commander of LVI Panzer Corps, on the march towards Leningrad, when he received a message informing him that Adolf Hitler had appointed him commander of Eleventh Army, part of Army Group South now operating in southern Ukraine. So far Eleventh Army's exploits were notable but nothing approaching the achievements of Guderian's or Hoth's Panzer Groups that were moving at full speed across the flat, dry wasteland of Ukraine. Manstein was being sent south to take over a massive army tasked with the capture of the Crimean Peninsula.

Manstein arrived at Eleventh Army headquarters at Nikolaev in the Ukraine in mid-September. His predecessor, General Eugen Ritter von Schobert, was killed when his plane, for unknown reasons, came down in a Soviet minefield and was blown up. His death provided Manstein with the opportunity to achieve greatness. Eleventh Army was given the dual mission of pursuing Soviet forces towards Rostov and capturing Crimea, including the fortress of Sevastopol, the main naval base of the Black Sea Fleet. Manstein knew he did not have enough troops to complete both missions and voiced his concerns to Field Marshal von Rundstedt. After the Battle of the Sea of Azov, which exposed Eleventh Army's vulnerabilities, Manstein received permission to attack Crimea only. The campaign was launched against the narrow borders of Crimea in late September 1941; against Perekop, Chongar, Arabat and the Ishun Lakes, narrow strips of land that crossed over swamps, canals and lakes. From that point it took more than nine months to raise the Nazi flag over Sevastopol; 250 days of the most gruelling, frustrating, inch-by-inch fighting in harsh, unforgiving conditions. The Soviets consistently held the good ground, forcing the Germans to launch frontal attacks against heavily and expertly defended strongpoints, fighting through minefields, barbed wire and

A German Sturmgeschütz *III armoured vehicle with 75mm gun. Somewhere near Simferopol, Crimea, 1941.* (NARA)

trenches defended by sailors and soldiers and the crews of bunkers and artillery batteries determined to fight to the last man.

Against France, Manstein recommended modern tactics of shock, manoeuvre and surprise.[2] He attempted the same tactics against Sevastopol but they failed. When they did, he resorted to siege-like[3] tactics used by his predecessors against the forts of Belgium and France in 1914 – massive bombardment followed up by infantry attacks. To be fair, he did not have a massive mechanised force, with the exception of the *Sturmgeschütz* III (StuG III) assault gun, a 75mm gun mounted on a Panzer III chassis, and a fleet of armoured cars. However, after two failed attempts to capture Sevastopol (the First and Second Assaults), prior to the Third Assault in June 1942, Eleventh Army received what was arguably the most powerful force of artillery assembled in history, including the heaviest siege guns ever built. The army received the support of Baron Wolfram von Richthofen's VIII Air Corps with hundreds of the most advanced attack aircraft in the world. And yet the defence was just as stubborn as in October 1941. The capture of the base should have been a walkover. Instead it was a metre-by-metre battle of annihilation.

Manstein certainly underestimated his opponents, Vice-Admiral Filip Oktyabrsky, Major-General Ivan Petrov and Major-General Petr Morgunov, and he underestimated the Soviet soldiers and sailors, both men and women, that his troops fought. The Soviet commanders, especially Petrov, were like master chess players hunched over a chequered board, moving pieces from one square to another, plugging gaps at the last minute when defeat was imminent, checking the opponents' every threat. Petrov, with the forces at his disposal, was incapable of mounting anything more than a defensive, attritional strategy of knocking off one piece at a time while sacrificing his own pieces. Despite the odds against them, the Soviets launched a number of their own offensives and hundreds of tactical counteroffensives. In the end it was Petrov's pawn against Manstein's queen and the Soviets were worn down to a final, inevitable collapse.

Sevastopol Naval Base was a tremendously hard nut to crack, even though it was defended in the beginning by sailors, cadets, technicians, office workers and women.[4] The city of Sevastopol, the harbour and the naval base were in the centre of the circle of defences. There were only six routes into the city over the main roads and railways of the Sevastopol, Bakhchisarai and Balaklava Districts: the Kacha road along the Black Sea coast; the highway and railway along the Belbek Valley from Simferopol and Bakhchisarai; the Kara-Koba Valley from the east; the Black River Valley; the Yalta Highway; or by sea. The Kacha road was blocked by the Aranci strongpoint. The Belbek Valley was guarded by the Duvankoi strongpoint. The Kara-Koba Valley passed through the chokepoint and bunkers of Shuli and Cherkez-Kerman. The Black River Valley passed by the Chorgun strongpoint and the defences of Mount Gasfort. The Yalta Highway passed below the Balaklava Heights and was blocked by the modern defences set up on the old Turkish Redoubts, near the location of the Light Brigade's charge. Beyond all of this was the long and wide harbour of Sevastopol, called The Great Harbour, Sevastopol Bay and Severnaya or North Bay. The Sapun Ridge formed the eastern rampart of the city. The battlefield was a natural citadel of mountains, hills, ravines and valleys covered by dense thickets. There was not a single approach to Sevastopol that did not force the Germans to attack uphill into the face of withering Soviet rifle or machine-gun fire while being pounded by shells from mortars, field artillery, warships and distant Soviet coastal gun batteries. Finally, for all but the last few days of the Second Defence, the Black Sea belonged to the Red Navy.

A journey around Sevastopol using Google Earth's© street-level view shows just how difficult a challenge it was to capture the base. In two respects, this was not Liège or Antwerp. Sevastopol was not ringed by permanent, detached forts, but the hilltops and ravines were heavily fortified and well defended. With the exception of Battery 30 (Fort Maxim Gorki I) and Battery 35 (Fort Maxim Gorki II), there were no revolving steel gun turrets. Sevastopol's defences were not like the Maginot Line's with deep underground tunnels connecting barracks and magazines by train to powerful artillery and infantry combat blocks on the surface. Most of the fortifications of Sevastopol were earthworks, concrete bunkers or earth and timber[5] machine-gun emplacements, masterfully hidden in the rocky hills. The coastal batteries, built during the time of the Tsars and into the 1930s, were made of concrete with bomb-proof connecting tunnels and magazine. The

Battery 19 at Balaklava. German guns are shown under camouflage to the right. (Nemenko Collection)

naval guns were located in open gun platforms, the gunners exposed to incessant shelling from German guns and bombs dropped from Luftwaffe bombers.

The reason Sevastopol was not surrounded by a ring of detached forts was that the Soviets believed the enemy would attack by sea or from the air. The landward threat only became a reality when the Germans invaded the USSR. Even then the Soviet command, in particular the Black Sea Fleet, wavered between strengthening the land or the coastal defences or both. Work began on a landward defence perimeter covering the main access routes but this was put on hold to bolster the coastal defences. Work on the land defences was only partially completed when the Germans and Rumanians approached Crimea.

The Soviet fear of an amphibious or airborne landing was both warranted and unwarranted. In May 1940, German *Fallschirmjäger* stormed Fort Eben-Emael in Belgium by landing on top of the fort. They conducted airborne operations in the Netherlands, Denmark and Norway in 1940. Large-scale airborne operations were conducted against Crete in 1941, and amphibious operations were carried out against Norway and Greece. However, in June 1941, the Germans did not have any amphibious or airborne assets that directly threatened Sevastopol, or so it seemed. The Black Sea was 1,200km from Germany and the German naval presence in the Mediterranean or even that of Germany's allies, for that matter, was minimal. Plus the Turks were neutral and did not allow the passage of ships through the straits into the Black Sea. When Soviet intelligence agents received reports indicating the presence of submarines and landing craft in Rumania, this caused a panic at the Admiralty and construction of the landward perimeter was halted to work on defences against an amphibious landing. The rumours were dispelled, but the Soviets remained nervous about possible landings, even as late as June 1942 when Admiral Oktyabrsky hesitated to send reserves into battle that were guarding the coast.

Manstein seemed to do all of the right things, given the forces he had at his disposal. He successfully won the initial argument against splitting his forces and was given full control of the operation against Crimea in September 1941. Yet it took the Germans thirty-five days just to cross Crimea's northern border, to get through the badly undermanned, poorly-trained and poorly-equipped Soviet rifle and cavalry divisions guarding Perekop. To be fair, Eleventh Army was drawn away for more than two weeks to rescue Rumanian forces from two Soviet armies during the Battle of the Sea of Azov. The army battled from mid- to late September and then from 18 to 30 October to break through into Crimea. Manstein did the next thing right by sending motorised units quickly south to seize and block the major roads to Sevastopol and to cut off Soviet forces retreating towards the city, but he didn't expect to run into the hornet's nests occupied by the naval cadets on the Alma River or 8th Marine Brigade and the Guards Regiment on the Plateau of Kara-Tau or the 40th Cavalry Division east of Balaklava. Equally, by the time his main forces reached the gates of Sevastopol, he also didn't expect to find that regular Soviet army units had escaped overland or been shipped in by sea to the city, including entire rifle divisions from the Caucasus and the Coastal Army from Odessa. After eighteen days of fighting in November, his exhausted troops rested and concentrated their land and air forces for the Second Assault in December, which was interrupted by the Soviet counteroffensive at Kerch and Feodosia. The next pause lasted from January to May. The Third Assault was launched in June after a massive five-day air and artillery bombardment, at the time the most powerful in history. Only then did things begin to work as expected, but only after another gruelling month during which thousands more men were killed and wounded and the Soviets finally ran out of steam.

The Battle of Sevastopol of 1941 to 1942, called 'The Second Defence' by the Soviets, could not have ended any other way, but was it truly the great German victory it has been depicted as? Was the final breakthrough to Sevastopol Bay on 24 June celebrated in Hitler's bunker at Rastenburg or at Eleventh Army headquarters? I'm sure it was, in a sense, but it was a hollow celebration. When German troops knelt down and splashed water from Sevastopol Bay into their sweating, dust-caked faces and when the forces of XXX Corps punched through the Sapun Ridge and gazed out on Cossack Bay, they were standing where Lord Raglan's and General Canrobert's men stood when they *began* the Siege of Sevastopol in 1854; a siege that lasted 347 days. The only difference was that, at this point, the Soviets were finished. They had already fought Eleventh Army at Perekop and Ishun, along the Alma and the Kacha Rivers and the Belbek Valley. They were being steadily pushed back into the dead city of Sevastopol, where the inhabitants lived underground like moles, and their lifeline to the sea was slowly being choked off. The Germans had total control of the air and started moving light naval forces to ports along the Crimean coast. When they ramped up their anti-shipping activities the Soviets were no longer able to bring in food, ammunition and fresh troops. The Germans finally broke through the defences on the north side of the bay, cut all communications between forward units and command and trapped the remnants of Soviet units into isolated pockets or pushed their backs to the bay. On 29 June the German XXX Corps and their Rumanian allies captured the defences on the Sapun Ridge and German troops landed by boat on the south shore of the bay. When that happened, it was over.

A great military leader wins a great victory through extraordinary or unexpected means. The fall of Poland and France and the encirclement of vast Soviet armies in Ukraine in 1941 were great victories, but the Battle of Sevastopol was not. If it had ended in early November 1941 then it would have been. There was no single tactic or action of Manstein or his corps commanders that caused the German forces to capture Sevastopol by any means other than what the Light Brigade had done eighty-eight years before; by rushing headlong into the Valley of Death (the exception being the amphibious assault across Sevastopol Bay by 22nd and 24th Infantry Divisions in the early hours of 29 June). No *Blitzkriegs* took place. No encirclement of vast armies resulting in mass surrender. No checkmate in three moves.

The Battle of Sevastopol was, or should be considered, a very sad and dark chapter in the history of the German army. It was a hollow, lost victory. It was the action of one opponent wearing down the other until it made no sense for the defender to hold out any longer. The Germans did not have the pleasure of accepting a Soviet surrender. When it was over there were no parades through the streets of Sevastopol. The remnants of the Soviet army and navy continued to fight, holding smaller and smaller pieces of ground, hiding out in caves and tunnels, until they were eventually killed or captured or escaped to join the partisans. The commanders – Oktyabrsky, Morgunov and Petrov and several dozen senior officers – fled in the night like rats from a sinking ship, leaving the citizens to suffer two years of terrible German occupation.

The Battle of Sevastopol was a victory in only one sense: that the Eleventh Army could finally move on to the Caucasus. But by then it was too late for them to have any effect on upcoming operations. It was, in a greater sense, a Soviet victory because it kept an entire army bogged down for over eight months and it had a direct effect on the greatest Soviet victory of all a few months later at Stalingrad.

Chapter 1

The Descent into Crimea – September to October 1941

The idea of Operation Barbarossa and the subsequent invasion of Crimea began long before the generals poured over maps of the Soviet Union, planning the movement of millions of troops. It began as an idea, a mission, a duty formulated in the mind of Adolf Hitler. The exact date and time of its origin is unknown. Perhaps the idea surfaced while Hitler the Corporal served as a runner on the Western Front or while he lay in a hospital bed, blinded by mustard gas. Or perhaps it originated in the mind of a young man sitting in a Vienna coffee house mesmerised by a speaker talking about Jews and the Master Race; or while Hitler wandered the streets of a decimated, post-war, post-imperial Germany, devising in his mind a plan that would raise him up from starving artist to the most powerful man in Europe.

His mission – his 'Struggle' – was to cleanse the Reich and the Aryan race from the culprits who caused its humiliating defeat in 1918 – Jews, Communists and *Untermenschen* – sub-humans. When he took power Germany would rearm, the Western Powers would be crushed and the Germans would eradicate Communists, Slavs and Jews from Germany and then from Eastern Europe. Ukraine would be cleansed of its population to create 'living space' – *lebensraum* – for Aryan families to farm and provide food for the population of the Thousand-Year Reich.

Hitler's concepts for racial and ethnic cleansing spilled out on the pages of *Mein Kampf*, a nonsensical but prophetic series of rants, written while he was imprisoned at Landsberg in Germany for his failed attempt in 1923 to overthrow the Bavarian government. To his dark credit, he told the world exactly what he was going to do and why and he then proceeded to do it. Hitler's eastern promise of *lebensraum* was fulfilled through Operation Barbarossa, the invasion of the Soviet Union.

Barbarossa was launched on 22 June 1941, all along the 2,100km Soviet border that stretched from the Baltic to the Black Sea. The invasion force was huge, the largest ever assembled:

- Three million men.
- 3,300 tanks.
- 7,000 artillery pieces.
- 2,770 aircraft.

The Descent into Crimea – September to October 1941   11

Hitler's Führer Directive 21, dated 18 December 1940, codenamed Operation Barbarossa, ordered a three-pronged attack in the direction of Leningrad, Moscow and Kiev. The German invasion force consisted of 136 divisions, including nineteen Panzer divisions. It was made up of the following:

- Army Group North was the smallest with thirty-one divisions. Its forces would move north-eastward from East Prussia into Lithuania, clear the Baltic States and capture Leningrad.
- Army Group Centre was the largest with fifty-seven divisions. It would attack north of the Pripet Marshes and move east in two parallel columns into Belorussia towards Smolensk and Moscow. When it reached Smolensk, it would divert its armour north to the Baltics and south to Ukraine.
- Army Group South, with forty-eight divisions, had two widely separated wings:
  ○ The northern wing would advance along the southern edge of the Pripet Marshes into Ukraine to target the Dnieper River and Kiev.
  ○ The southern wing with six divisions and 200,000 Rumanian troops would cross from Rumania and head towards southern Ukraine.

The Soviets had about 3.4 million troops, 22,700 tanks and 12,000 aircraft. The bulk of their equipment was outdated. The Soviets could call on a reserve of seventeen million men.

The invasion began shortly after 0300 hours on 22 June with a huge artillery barrage and bomber strikes against airfields and troop concentrations as far as 320km into Soviet territory. After that, the Panzer divisions moved forward, followed by infantry. By nightfall of the first day 1,800 Soviet aircraft were destroyed, thousands of prisoners taken and a dozen Soviet divisions encircled and destroyed. In the north, LVI Panzer Corps, led by Lieutenant-General Erich von Manstein, was moving through Latvia. He pushed his tanks 400km in just four days. The corps' objective was to open the road to Leningrad and cut off Soviet forces south of the Dvina River. Army Group South headed towards Kiev. On the right flank, the German Eleventh Army, commanded by General Eugen Ritter von Schobert, established bridgeheads across the Prut River, stopping there to oppose Soviet counter-attacks to seize the Rumanian oil fields at Ploesti.

Manstein's LVI Panzer Corps and General Georg-Hans Reinhardt's XLI Corps crept slowly towards Leningrad. By mid-August they were facing stiff Soviet resistance made worse by poor roads. Manstein's advance stalled near Luga, 140km south of Leningrad. However, the situation changed on 15 August when the Soviet Marshal Kliment Voroshilov, commander of the Leningrad Front, launched an attack with eight infantry divisions on Sixteenth Army's X Corps. This prompted General Fedor von Bock, commander of Army Group Centre, to send Manstein reinforcements that included XXXIX Panzer Corps from Hoth's Army plus the SS Totenkopf Division. On 19 August Manstein raced southeast and struck the flank of Voroshilov's forces, causing it to break up. By 8 September, the Germans were again closing in on Leningrad.

In the south, von Rundstedt made swift progress. Engineer and assault troops of Eleventh Army's 22nd Lower Saxon Division completed a pontoon bridge across the Dnieper River. The LIV Corps and Rumanian Third Army crossed the river and fanned out in the direction of Rostov and the Crimean Peninsula.

In July and September two events occurred in relation to Crimea that altered the fate of both Eleventh Army and Manstein. On 9 July Soviet bombers conducted an air raid against the Rumanian oil refineries at Ploesti. The first attack had very little effect but on 13 July six bombers attacked the refinery and struck oil reservoirs at Unirea, igniting 9,000 tons of oil that burned for five days. Eight more air raids were carried out on Ploesti in the following days, destroying another 2,000 tons of oil. The aircraft took off from the Soviet naval base of Sevastopol in the Crimea. The bombing of Ploesti caused the German High Command to order the capture of the peninsula to remove the threat to the oil fields.

The second event occurred on 12 September 1941. General von Schobert boarded a reconnaissance plane to inspect the battle area. The plane landed in a field near Nikolaev Ukraine that turned out to be a minefield. The reason for the landing is unknown. The plane was destroyed and the general and his pilot were killed. About 1,600km to the north, General von Manstein's corps was moving in the direction of Demyansk when he received a dispatch stating he had been appointed commander of Eleventh Army in place of von Schobert. Manstein quickly headed south and into history.

Historically, the Crimean Peninsula (hereinafter referred to as Crimea) had always been a key military position on the Black Sea that guarded the entire Soviet southern flank. Major sea routes were patrolled by ships and watched by gun batteries along its entire coastline. Axis ships operating in the Black Sea could be observed and interdicted from Sevastopol by aircraft, surface ships or submarines. Crimea, because of its flatness and openness, especially in the centre, was an ideal spot for air bases.

Prior to the war the Germans were aware of the geographic and military value of the peninsula, however, Barbarossa had not included Crimea as an objective. German planners assumed the area would be captured in mopping-up operations once the bulk of the Red Army was destroyed west of the Dnieper River. A supplement to Führer Directive Number 33,[1] dated 23 July 1941, stated: 'The primary task of the bulk of the infantry divisions is to seize the Ukraine, Crimea and the territory of the Soviet Federation to the Don.' Due to the attacks against

Rumania's oil refineries, suddenly Crimea found its way into the Wehrmacht's operational plans.

On 12 August the supplement to Führer Directive 34 ordered Army Group South 'to occupy the Crimean Peninsula, which is particularly dangerous as an enemy airbase against the Rumanian oilfields'. The seizure of Crimea would eliminate the threat to Rumanian oil supplies. In addition, it would deprive the Black Sea Fleet of a base from which the southern flank of German forces could be threatened. The captured ports could then be used by the Germans to resupply troops in the south and as a base from which to launch attacks. Finally, Crimea's Kerch Peninsula was an alternative route to Taman and the Caucasus oilfields.

The High Command of the German Army – *Oberkommando des Heeres* (OKH) – assigned Eleventh Army a dual mission: 1) push east along the coast of the Sea of Azov and pursue Soviet forces heading towards Rostov; and 2) break through into Crimea and capture the peninsula. Von Schobert knew he had to quickly seize Perekop, Chongar and Arabat, the main points of entry into Crimea, to move in behind Soviet forces and prevent them from falling back to Sevastopol. XXX Infantry Corps, commanded by General Hans Eberhard Kurt von Salmuth and the IL Mountain Corps, commanded by Brigadier-General Ludwig L. Kübler, were pursuing Soviet forces retreating east towards Rostov. LIV Infantry Corps, commanded by Lieutenant-General Erik Hansen, was moving south towards Perekop. The Third Rumanian Army, placed under German command, was still west of the Dnieper River, but heading east.

The Advance into Crimea

Eleventh Army's invasion of Crimea began with the assault on the Perekop Isthmus. In 1941, there were three main highways, two railway lines and several unpaved roads that crossed over narrow isthmuses of solid land into the peninsula. The widest entry point was only 9km across at Perekop Isthmus. Seventy kilometres to the east was the Chongar Isthmus, barely 2km wide at the top. Chongar opened out further south and led to several possible crossing points over the Siwash, a large body of water about 75km long. The Siwash, identified as a large lake or small sea, ran from a few kilometres east of Perekop to Chongar. Twenty-three kilometres east of Chongar is the Arabat Spit, a narrow and easily defensible coastal strip that ran along the Sea of Azov. The Litovsky or Lithuanian Peninsula, used by Red forces to cross into Crimea in 1920, was another possible crossing point. Swamps dotted with dams and canals to control the water lay in between. The border was quite long and complex and it required a large force to defend it.

The German Eleventh Army had seven infantry divisions plus the Rumanian Mountain Corps. The Soviet Fifty-first Army had four rifle and three cavalry

14   The Defence of Sevastopol 1941–1942

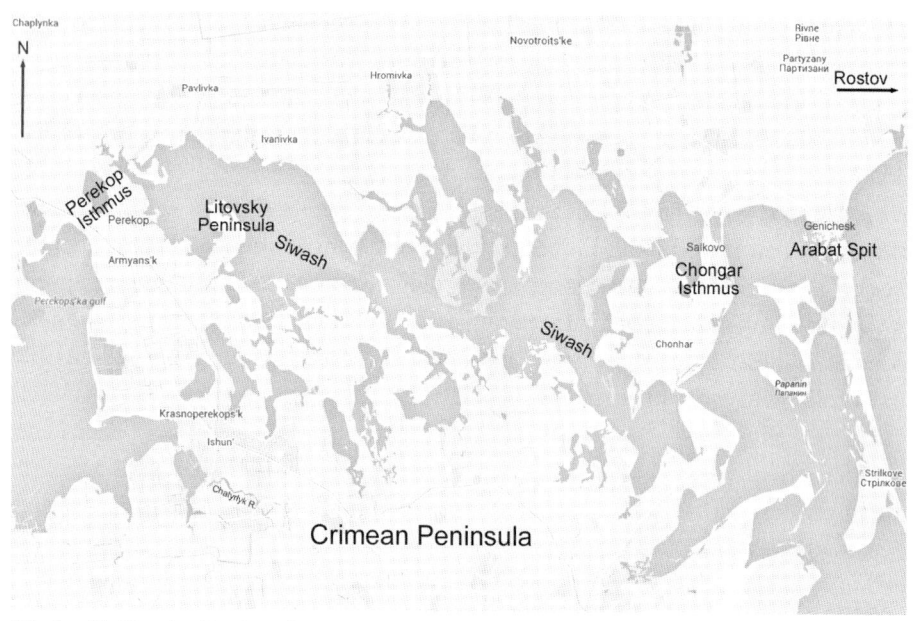

The land bridges leading into Crimea – Perekop, Chongar, Arabat. (© OpenStreetMap contributors, Author's collection)

divisions. Soviet units were undermanned, poorly equipped and the troops were mostly raw recruits with minimal training and even less combat experience, while Eleventh Army was made up mostly of hardened veterans with two years of combat experience in Western Europe, Poland and Ukraine.

Before the war the 156th Rifle Division was the main Soviet force in Crimea. The 32nd Cavalry Division was relocated there in August 1940. Military forces in Crimea (excluding sailors, marines, cadets of the Black Sea Fleet's training schools and other units located at Sevastopol) also included students from the Simferopol Quartermaster Military School, the Logistical School of Odessa Military District and the Kacha Red Army Aviation School. In May 1941 the 106th Rifle Division was transferred to Crimea from the North Caucasus, but the division arrived with only 2,500 men. These three divisions – 156th Rifle, 32nd Cavalry and 106th Rifle – were formed into IX Corps, commanded by General Ivan Batov.

On 1 July 1941 32nd Cavalry Division was moved to another sector of the front, leaving the two rifle divisions to defend the entire peninsula. The 106th defended the southwestern part of Crimea, a front of about 200km that ran from Ak-Metchet (m. Chornomors'ke) to Alma Tamak (m. Pishchane), on the border of the Sevastopol district. The division was tasked with building earthen fortifications and gun batteries along the coastline. These included Ak-Metchet, Cape Tarkhankut, Eupatoria and Mykolaivka (site of Coastal Battery 54). The 156th Rifle Division was centred on Simferopol. The Black Sea Fleet defended Sevastopol. Men of the older classes filled the ranks of about thirty-five local militia rifle divisions and construction and support units. In August 1941 the 48th Cavalry Division, commanded by Major-General Averkina, was sent to Crimea. The division had 3,000 horsemen.

The Soviet Fifty-first Army was formed on 14 August 1941 and placed under the command of General F. I. Kuznetsov. General Batov became his deputy because IX Corps units were placed under Kuznetsov's command. The army was tasked with the defence of Crimea from attack by land, sea and air, including the prevention of amphibious landings. In September 1941, Fifty-first Army consisted of the following components:

- 106th Rifle Division.
- 156th Rifle Division.
- 271st Rifle Division.
- 276th Rifle Division.
- 40th Cavalry Division.
- 42nd Cavalry Division.
- 48th Cavalry Division.

On paper, the defences of the Perekop Isthmus sounded formidable, not only in (apparent) numbers of military units, but also in the nature and depth of both field and permanent fortifications. Unfortunately for the Soviets, the defences collapsed within hours of the first attacks. General Kuznetsov[2] wrote on 28 August, two weeks before the first attack, that the defences were not prepared. However, when the first German forces arrived, the construction battalions had completed three lines of defence.

The field fortifications identified as the Chervony Chabad Strongpoint began 10km north of the Turkish Wall, also called the Perekop Ditch or Turkish Ditch or Turkish Wall.[3] The Chaplinka to Perekop road was blocked by a belt of anti-tank obstacles. These were made of railway track cut in pieces and embedded horizontally into the ground with remote controlled explosive charges buried throughout. From there to the east and south and west towards Siwash and Preobrazhenkia was a belt of mines, bombs and sea mines, located behind a barbed wire fence.

The second line was 5km beyond the first and consisted of a barbed wire obstacle and an anti-tank ditch 8m wide and 2–3m deep reinforced by anti-tank obstacles. Barbed wire was twisted around and between the beams. Behind these obstacles was a 15m-wide minefield with anti-personnel and anti-tank mines. Beyond that was another belt of barbed wire.

16   The Defence of Sevastopol 1941–1942

German aerial photograph showing the Turkish Wall south of Perekop. (Provided by John Calvin of www.wwii-photos-maps.com, altered by the author)

The third line was 2km from the Turkish Wall. It consisted of another anti-tank ditch 6.5m wide and 3.5m deep with vertical scarps. Once again there were anti-tank obstacles and barbed wire. Twenty-six remote-controlled flamethrowers were placed along the line. The next obstacle was the Turkish Wall itself. Concrete bunkers were placed along its earthen escarp. There were four bunkers equipped with 76mm guns and several machine-gun bunkers. Field guns were placed behind earthen ramparts. In total there were 13.5km of anti-tank ditches, 11,441 steel beams, fourteen concrete bunkers (two were still under construction), fourteen machine-gun positions, 14km of barbed wire and six earthen field artillery positions.

In addition, eight coastal batteries were constructed 10–15km apart along the Perekop and Chongar Isthmuses:

- Battery 121 (located by the dam near the village of Chiharu (m. Dzhantora) – four 152mm Kane guns taken from Sevastopol's Battery 12.
- Battery 122 (located 8km from Taganash – Salt Lake) – four 120mm Vickers guns taken from Sevastopol's Battery 13.
- Battery 123 (located at Tup-Djankoi) – four 130mm B13 series (guns removed from a refurbished destroyer).

The Descent into Crimea – September to October 1941   17

- Battery 124 (located on the Litovsky [Lithuanian] Peninsula) – four 130mm B13 series (guns removed from a refurbished destroyer).
- Battery 125 (located at Chongar) – four 100mm guns.
- Battery 126 (4km west of Ishun) – three 130mm Vickers guns from the reserve supply for the cruisers *Chervona Ukraina* and *Krasny Krim*.
- Battery 127 (located at Genichesk on Arabat Spit) – four 100mm guns.
- Battery 727 (located at Armiansk) – four 152mm Kane guns.

In conclusion, the Perekop defences were strong but they were not equal in strength to the Stalin Line or the Maginot Line. Their weakness lay in the lack of artillery and of operational reserves.

On 13 July 1941, Vice-Admiral Oktyabrsky, Commander of the Black Sea Fleet, informed General Tuleneva, Commander of the Southern Front, General Nikandr Chibisov, Odessa Military District and General Batov, IX Infantry Corps, of the possibility the enemy could attempt an amphibious landing in Crimea and recommended the strengthening of all coastal defences. General Batov sent a letter to the fleet indicating that the Germans did not have the capability to make an amphibious landing. At that time they lacked the shipping tonnage, cover and support from the sea. Batov's letter was ignored and forces in the peninsula were ordered to prepare to defend against German landings along the vast Crimean coastline. As German troops moved east and then south into Ukraine, elements of the Fifty-first Army were dispersed throughout the peninsula, leaving just three divisions to cover the north.

The Coastal Army was established on 18 July 1941 by the order of the Southern Front Command and was made up of elements of the Soviet Ninth Army's Coastal Group. On 1 August 1941, the Coastal Army was made up of the 14th Rifle Corps, 25th Rifle Division, 95th Rifle Division, the 1st Odessa Cavalry Division, the 265th Corps Artillery Regiment, the 26th, 175th and 504th Anti-Aircraft (AA) Battalions and the 69th Fighter Air Regiment. In September the 421st Rifle Division and 157th Rifle Divisions were sent as reinforcements.

The Coastal Army was commanded by Major-General Ivan Yefimovich Petrov. On 29 September, due to the deteriorating situation at Odessa, the Black Sea Fleet Military Council asked the Stavka (Soviet Supreme Command) to redeploy the Coastal Army to Crimea to strengthen its defences. The order was given the following day for the fleet to evacuate the Coastal Army from Odessa to Crimea. The operation began on 1 October and continued until the 16th.

In early September the Soviet Fifty-first Army lost contact with the Soviet Ninth and Eighteenth Armies and had no idea what was happening to the north. Kuznetsov sent out reconnaissance detachments from the 106th and 156th Rifle Divisions to locate the Germans. The search took them north of Perekop. The first sighting of enemy forces took place near the village of Chervona Polyana. The scouts spotted the 22nd and 72nd Infantry divisions and a Rumanian cavalry detachment and the next day the 170th and 46th Divisions. The Soviets decided to strike first and attacked the vanguard of 72nd Infantry Division of XXX Corps. It was a minor skirmish but the Germans were caught by surprise. The Soviet detachments pulled back towards Perekop but verified the presence of a large body of troops moving north of the peninsula.

On 11 September, the day before Eleventh Army was rocked by the death of von Schobert and von Manstein took command, units from German LIV Corps (46th and 73rd Infantry Divisions) attacked the 417th Regiment of the 156th Rifle Division at Chaplinka. On 12 September German reconnaissance units attacked along the Chaplinka–Armiansk road and at the village of Chervonyi Chabad. The 22nd Infantry Division headed along the north shore of the Siwash towards Salkova on the Chongar Peninsula. The 73rd Infantry Division ordered the reconnaissance battalion of the Leibstandarte-SS Adolf Hitler to drive through Perekop towards Ishun. The battalion approached Preobrazhenka and encountered strong Soviet resistance and trenches, an anti-tank ditch, machine-gun bunkers and field artillery. The Germans pulled back when they were fired on by armoured trains. They captured several Soviet prisoners who described the defences at Perekop to them and they decided that they were too strong to attack at that time.

Further east, the 276th Rifle Division was positioned along a line from Salkovo to Novo Aleksyevka to Genichesk. In the afternoon of 15 September the Salkovo railway station was attacked and captured by 22nd Infantry Division. The attackers included a motorised unit of the Leibstandarte-SS that was heading to Genichesk. Salkovo station was held by the 2nd Battalion of the 876th Rifle Regiment of 276th Division. Some of the 2nd Battalion troops fell back into the Chongar Peninsula. The 3rd Battalion, further to the north at Novo Alexeyevka, was attacked and surrounded. Both battalions were in the process of building defensive lines when they were attacked. German records show that part of 2nd Battalion of 876th Regiment was surrounded and captured. It appears that about half the division was killed or captured during this battle. The Germans also captured a Soviet supply train at Salkovo that was *en route* to Sevastopol. It carried eighty-six trucks, twenty-six tractors, two AA guns and large quantities of ammunition.

The 22nd Infantry Division attempted to move into Chongar across a pontoon bridge built by German pioneers. The SS headed towards Genichesk and then on to Gengorka on the Arabat. As both German units moved south, Coastal Battery 127's four 100mm guns opened fire, destroying several German assault guns. Three hours later reserve troops from the 276th Division moved up to stop the Germans. Three Soviet gunboats, the *Don*, *Rion* and *N4*, arrived and opened fire with five 130mm guns and the Germans were unable to move forward. They were also hit by Soviet air attacks.

Meanwhile, the 73rd and 46th Infantry Divisions of LIV Corps prepared to attack Perekop. The 73rd was ordered to break through the Perekop Isthmus while 46th Division attacked 10km east of Perekop on the Litovsky Peninsula to bypass Soviet forces at Perekop, which included the 417th, 361st and 530th Regiments of 156th Division, plus the 498th Artillery Regiment with 122mm and 152mm guns. The 397th and 442nd Rifle Regiments were positioned further east and the 276th Division was still at Chongar. On the night of 19 September Stalin received a report that eleven infantry divisions, one cavalry division and approximately 250 'tanks' were north of Crimea.

On 24 September the attack began on the first line of Perekop's defences. Units of 73rd Division attacked Chervonyi Chabad and after a bloody struggle, broke through the defences. The 46th also moved forward and around 1600 hours reached the anti-tank ditch on the outskirts of the village. In less than a day the 'formidable' defences of Perekop had fallen. The Soviets counter-attacked with two battalions of the 530th Rifle Regiment plus several tanks, trying to buy time to bring up reinforcements. German aircraft destroyed most of the armour but the attack succeeded in stopping the German advance. The German 213th Regiment's losses were high and their two battalions had to be amalgamated, while the 2nd Battalion of 170th Regiment was reduced to just one company.

The ditch of the Turkish Wall south of Perekop. (Nemenko Collection)

The attack continued on 25 September along the Chaplinka Road. The 417th Rifle Regiment's position was threatened when the Germans attacked the village of Kantemirovka. Soviet troops in the village retreated to the Turkish Wall. 442nd Rifle Regiment counter-attacked at Kantemirovka and allowed the 417th Regiment to escape to the Turkish Wall. On 26 September the Turkish Wall defences collapsed and the Germans advanced towards Armiansk. After a powerful artillery bombardment, the 213th Regiment and pioneers from 170th Regiment created a bridgehead on the northern part of the Turkish Wall. It was expanded to 700m in width. At 0720 hours the 3rd Battalion of the 213th Regiment moved 1,500m south of the ditch and seized a Soviet heavy artillery battery. The Soviets counter-attacked at Kullu with T-34 tanks but at 1300 the breakthrough at Perekop was complete.

Around 1000 hours on 27 September the German 72nd Infantry Division entered the battle and captured Armiansk, which changed hands several times over the next several hours. At 0500 hours the 42nd Cavalry and 271st Rifle Divisions, plus the 417th Regiment of 156th Rifle Division and 442nd Regiment of 106th Rifle Division, counter-attacked at Armiansk. At 0830 hours, after heavy fighting in the streets of the village, the Germans pulled out to the northern outskirts of Armiansk. Black Sea Fleet ships tried to provide gunfire support to the defenders but the water was too shallow to allow them to approach within firing range. Luftwaffe strikes took a huge toll on Soviet troops and equipment.

The Germans counter-attacked with a strong force of assault guns from the 190th Assault Gun Battalion and, by the end of the day, had driven the Soviets out of Armiansk. Around 0930 hours the 170th, along with 121st Regiment of 50th Infantry Division, launched an attack and captured the outskirts of Budanovka. In the early hours of 29 September the Soviet Military Council decided to withdraw the Fifty-first Army to the Ishun lakes.

The Germans continued to move south. The 213th Regiment was moving towards Ishun when news came that units were being pulled out of Eleventh Army, including the Leibstandarte-SS. A new threat was developing to the rear of the Eleventh Army. Since 26 September the Rumanian lines had been under heavy attack by the twelve divisions of the Soviet Ninth and Eighteenth Armies. By the morning of the 27th they had opened up a 15km gap in the German lines. Manstein was forced to put a halt to the Crimean offensive and diverted some of his forces to meet the new threat. Eleventh Army counter-attacked using XXXXIX Corps and elements of the 50th and 22nd Divisions and the Leibstandarte-SS. The First Panzer Army advanced into the rear of the Soviet armies. This double envelopment decided the battle, but not until 7 October.

The Battle of the Sea of Azov, as it was called, caused the German high command to re-examine their two-pronged strategy of simultaneous attacks by Eleventh Army on Rostov and Crimea. It proved that Eleventh Army did not have enough forces to conduct the two operations. As a result Manstein retained LIV and XXX

Corps to continue the Crimean operation. The Leibstandarte-SS was transferred to First Panzer Army for the attack on Rostov-on-Don. Manstein requested a further three divisions and more air support and was given the XXXXII Corps' 24th and 132nd Infantry Divisions.

From 30 September to 17 October the Soviets improved the defences at Ishun and brought in reinforcements. On 18 October the Germans resumed the Crimean offensive. 73rd Division was in the first line of attack on the right flank, 46th Division in the centre and 22nd Division on the left. They were reinforced by two regiments of the 50th and two regiments of the 170th Division. Regiments of the 73rd and 50th Divisions attacked Ishun, while the 46th Division plus the regiments from 170th Division attacked the dam at Old Lake (Stare Lake). The 22nd Infantry Division attacked between the Siwash and Red Lake in the vicinity of Krasnoperekopskiy. These bodies of water were referred to as the Ishun Lakes.

At 0525 hours on 18 October the 73rd Division began the offensive with an attack on Ishun between the Karkinitsky Bay and Old Lake. The Soviets were taken by surprise and the Germans quickly broke through the defences. At 0630 hours the 186th Infantry Regiment crossed the drainage canal that ran through the Isthmus but was stopped by Soviet artillery fire. The Soviets had well-prepared positions on the south bank of the canal, including barbed-wire obstacles. However, around 1300 hours the canal line was breached and the 122nd Regiment of 50th Infantry Division, kept in reserve, was brought up to assist the breakthrough.

The 530th Rifle Regiment of 156th Division, located on the left flank of Fifty-first Army at the Krasnoperekopsk Bromide Plant, was attacked by German assault guns and infantry from the 46th Infantry Division. The Soviets had turned the plant into a strongpoint. The Soviets set up machine-gun positions along one of the dykes that crisscrossed the isthmus near the plant. The buildings at the plant changed hands several times during the battle. A Soviet counter-attack around 2100 hours brought an end to the day's fighting. The Soviets were running out of heavy weapons and their counter-attacks were losing intensity.

At 0615 hours on 19 October the 170th Regiment of 73rd Infantry Division, supported by assault guns, artillery and aircraft, attacked Krasnoperekopsk in order to outflank Ishun (located 3km southeast of Krasnoperekopsk) and reach the Chatyrlyk River south of the village. Two main highways from Armiansk to Djankoi and Krasnoperekopsk to Simferopol converged in Ishun village. The North Crimean Canal ran northeast of the village and passed by the single-track railway line from Kherson to Djankoi, where heavy fighting took place. In the afternoon Soviet trucks brought in reinforcements to Ishun, but the Germans brought up the 173rd Anti-Tank Battalion and the 213th Regiment and by 1530 hours had driven the Soviets back, and about two hours later had captured Ishun. Fighting in and around Ishun continued for the next couple of days. Around 1600 hours on 20 October the 121st Regiment, using boats from the 903rd Assault Boat Battalion, launched an assault across the estuary of the Chatyrlyk River south of Ishun and on 21 October captured a small bridgehead by the mouth of the river.

On 22 October General Kuznetsov was relieved of command of the Fifty-first Army and replaced by Vice-Admiral Levchenko. The Coastal Army was ordered to send troops to shore up the defences at Vorontsovka south of Ishun. On 24 October the Coastal Army units arrived in the area of Vorontsokva. These included the 54th and 161st Rifle Regiments, 3rd Battery of 97th Anti-Tank Battalion, 90th Regiment, 2nd Battery of 97th Artillery Regiment and 241st Regiment. At 1000 hours Soviet artillery opened a barrage and 95th Rifle Division units advanced. The Soviets pushed the Germans back but the offensive soon stalled due to the strong German artillery and mortar fire. The Germans reported successes along the entire line, hardly mentioning the Soviet attack. At 0900 hours the 186th Infantry Regiment continued to move forward while the 46th Infantry Division took Chigir. During the night, the 213th Regiment successfully repulsed three Soviet counter-attacks against the position on the Chatrylyk and resumed their offensive in the morning to capture the bridge.

On 25 October the Germans broke through southeast of Chigir and the Soviets retreated. Gaps appeared in the Soviet defences that allowed the 50th Division to capture Vorontsovka. In the evening, 73rd and 46th Divisions moved through another gap and captured Novo Pavlovka and Yalantash. The troops of the Coastal Army tried but were unable to close the gaps. At this point the 132nd Infantry Division came into action. This was very bad news for the Soviets, who still lacked ammunition and artillery. The Soviet 25th Chapaevsky Division moved north but it was too little, too late. The Germans were now in a position to seize the Simferopol Road.

On 26 October German divisions began to spread out into Crimea and Manstein brought in new units, including the 'Ziegler Brigade'.[4] The 170th Regiment followed the Chatyrlyk River and reached Berdy-Bulat. The 213th moved west of Novo-Pavlovka. Their task was to clear the southern bank of the Chatyrlyk. 73rd Division advanced towards Yalantash. On 27 October the 213th Regiment continued its attack towards Novo-Pavlovka. The Soviets countered with artillery fire. The 186th Regiment was sent in as a reserve and the Luftwaffe carried out attacks against the Soviet guns at Dolinka.

The LIV Corps report for 28 October[5] was as follows: 'Enemy defences at Ishun completely broken. The enemy is retreating to the south and southeast with a rearguard covering the withdrawal of heavy artillery. The brunt of the attack fell on 73rd and 46th Divisions.'

The Soviet retreat became a rout. October 28th 1941 was given as the date for the end of the Battle of Perekop/Ishun. LIV and XXX Corps now began their pursuit of Soviet forces to the interior of Crimea and to Sevastopol, which they hoped to seize in a surprise attack.

Chapter 2

The Fortress of Sevastopol

The origins of the modern naval base of Sevastopol can be traced back to the eighteenth century. From 1768 to 1774 Russia was at war with Turkey. Crimea was ruled by the Crimean Khanate, vassals of the Turks. The capital was Bakhchisaray – 'Garden Palace'. The Russian victory over the Turks brought Ukraine, the North Caucasus and Crimea into the Russian Empire. The Treaty of Kucuk Kaynarca of 12 July 1774 granted independence to the Crimean Khanate and secession to Russia of two key Turkish seaports, Azov and Kerch. The Russian Navy now had direct access to the Black Sea and freedom to explore the Crimean coastline.

The Russian Navy had its eyes on a large harbour at the southwestern tip of the peninsula, first visited in the autumn of 1773 by Ivan Baturin.[1] He informed the Russian command of his discovery of the ancient ruins of Ackerman (Inkerman) with its well-preserved walls and towers and lots of caves in the mountains.[2] The bay west of Inkerman was deserted but on the north side Baturin found a small Tatar village called Akhtiar or Ak-Yar, meaning 'White Ravine' in Tatar. It was later described as '… a collection of miserable huts at the northeast corner of the harbour'.[3] The main bay was referred to as Akhtiar Bay.

In 1778 Lieutenant-General Alexander Suvorov (1729–1800), the Crimean Corps commander, brought ships and troops to Akhtiar Bay. Suvorov was the first to begin development of the bay.[4] In June 1778 he informed General Rumyantsev, Chief of the Russian Army: 'On the 15th of this month, the 3rd Battalion entered the harbour and began to build earthworks to defend it.'[5] Suvorov ordered the construction of eight earthen batteries with thirty-two field guns and five mortars as a defence against the Turks. Earthwork ramparts defended the rear of the batteries. He brought in two battalions of musketeers to defend the works. Local Cossacks patrolled the coast down to Balaklava since the Turks sometimes ventured near the harbour.

1783 was a pivotal year for the development of the new naval base. In January the government appointed Vice-Admiral Fedota Klokachev to conduct a more detailed survey of Akhtiar to determine if it could be used as a naval base for the Azov and Dnieper Flotillas, soon to be called the Black Sea Fleet. On 2 May 1783 Klokachev arrived and four days later he wrote to the Naval Minister, Count Chernyshev: 'At the entrance to the harbour I marvelled at the good position of

Akhtiar from the sea. Upon entering it I can say that in Europe there is no harbour such as this in relation to location, size and depth. It is possible to have here a fleet of 100 vessels.'[6] Klokachev claimed he could build a base to rival Kronstadt.[7]

Klokachev returned to St. Petersburg and left Rear-Admiral Thomas Mackenzie, the commander of the Black Sea Fleet, in charge of construction. British by birth, Mackenzie made an enormous contribution to the development of Sevastopol and its industry. Unfortunately, very little is known about him aside from his work at Sevastopol, which is attested to by the many appearances, even to this day, of places named after him: the Mackenzie (*Mekenzievy* in Russian) Mountains, Mekenzievy Mountain Station and the Mackenzie Farm.

Construction proceeded quickly. Workers used the vast resources of the Inkerman quarries to produce lime, bricks and tiles. Dozens of barracks buildings rose along the bay. In the fall of 1783, twenty vessels were stationed in the harbour. On 10 February 1784, by decree of Catherine the Great, the new port and settlement was named 'Sevastopol' after one of several Roman cities called *Sevastopolis* by Caesar Augustus, located in the area of modern Sukhumi, Thrace, Pontus or Myrna in Turkey. The name means 'magnificent city', 'worthy of worship'. In 1804 the Russian government officially declared Sevastopol the main military port of the Black Sea.

Sevastopol has always been known as a fortress. From the laying of the first foundation stone in 1783 until the German attack of 1941, the fortifications of Sevastopol were either in a continual state of improvement or neglected decay. The city's defences were oriented towards the sea to protect the base from an attack by enemy ships or amphibious landings. Therefore, throughout its history as a naval base, there was a constant evolution and devolution of the coastal gun batteries and infantry defences along the coast and the harbour cliffs.

The city of Sevastopol began as a small garrison town on the south coast of Akhtiar Bay. Over the years the town spread its boundaries but in essence continued to lie between two bays, Quarantine and Yuzhnaya or South Bay. The latter is one of a number of large and small bays and inlets located along the larger body of water originally called Akhtiar and later Great Harbour, Sevastopol Bay and Severnaya or North Bay (hereinafter referred to as Sevastopol Bay). It was about 7km long, 1.2km wide and 10 fathoms deep. The bay's access to the Black Sea was protected by two spits of land, Cape Alexander on the south and Cape Constantine on the north.

Several other key geographical landmarks were located south of the harbour and ran along the Black Sea coast. These included, from north to south: *Artyllereyskaya* or Artillery Bay; *Karantynnaya* or Quarantine Bay; *Petchánnaya* or *Pesochnaya* or Sandy Bay; *Streletskaya* or Musketeers' Bay; *Kroúglaya* or *Hrouglaia* or Round Bay; Abramov Bay; *Kamiesh* or *Kamyshovya* or Reed Bay, the French port during

The Bays of Sevastopol

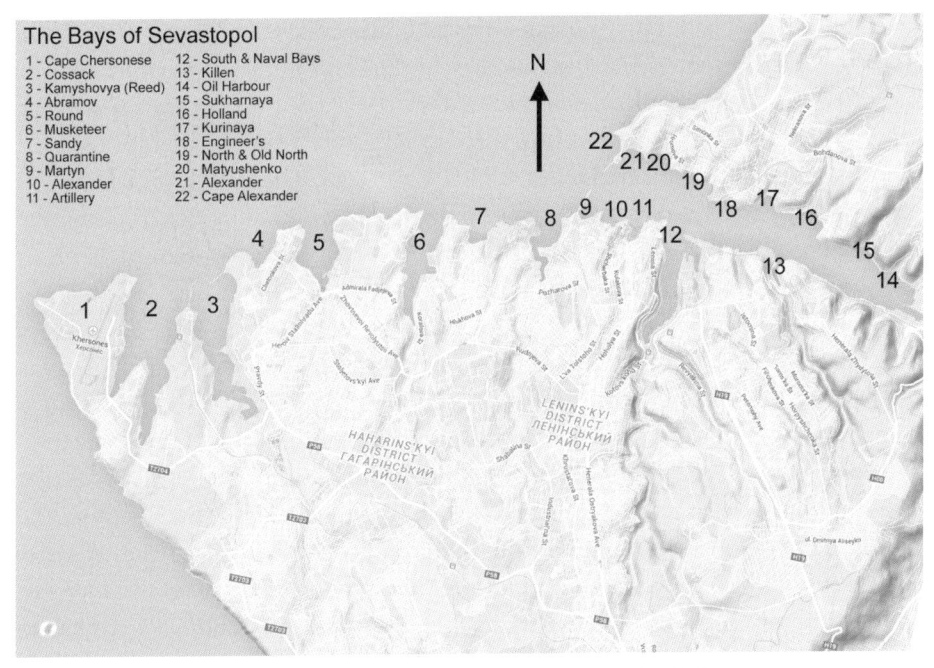

1 - Cape Chersonese
2 - Cossack
3 - Kamyshovya (Reed)
4 - Abramov
5 - Round
6 - Musketeer
7 - Sandy
8 - Quarantine
9 - Martyn
10 - Alexander
11 - Artillery
12 - South & Naval Bays
13 - Killen
14 - Oil Harbour
15 - Sukharnaya
16 - Holland
17 - Kurinaya
18 - Engineer's
19 - North & Old North
20 - Matyushenko
21 - Alexander
22 - Cape Alexander

The Bays of Sevastopol. (© OpenStreetMap contributors, Author's collection)

the Crimean War; and finally *Dvoynáya* (double) or *Kazachya* or Cossack Bay. Cape Chersonese was on the southern tip of the coastline.

The inner harbour included, on the south side, running west to east, Martyn Bay west of Cape Alexander, Alexander Bay, *Yuzhnaya*, *Korabelnaya* or Ship Bay and Killen (formerly Careenage) Bay. The *Chornaya* or Black River flows into the bay at its eastern end near Inkerman. This area was identified as the Inkerman swamps or marshes. On the north side of the bay are a series of small inlets that can hardly be called bays, but are identified as such. From east to west are the Oil Harbour near the fuel storage tanks on top of Lighthouse Mountain, *Sukharnaya* Bay, named for the former Naval Bakery and also called Rusks Bay (origin unknown), Holland Bay, *Kurinaya* or *Dokova* Bay, location of a dry-dock, the very small *Inzhenernaya* or Engineering Bay, *Severnaya* and *Staro-Severnaya* or Northern and Old Northern Bays, *Matyushenko* Bay and finally Constantine Bay east of Cape Constantine. It is a large and rather confusing list because of the change of names that took place over the years but each location is important in understanding the critical geography of the battle.

Sevastopol Bay is bordered by hills to the north and south. A series of strategic ravines plunge down from the tops of the plateaus into the bay. The mountain ranges and plateaus are separated by narrow river valleys. The Alma, Kacha and Belbek Rivers north of Sevastopol flow from the mountains into the Black Sea and

Sevastopol Bay. These river valleys form natural moats. It was not so much the rivers themselves that blocked the approaches to Sevastopol – they were narrow and often dry in the summer months – rather it was the hills through which the valleys passed. In earlier times these three valleys were known for fruit that grew there abundantly, mostly pears and apples. Empress Catherine II, on her way to Sevastopol, crossed over the dry beds of the Kacha and Belbek Rivers from the direction of the city of Bakhchisaray, through the vineyards and rich orchards of the Souryenn (Suresnes) Valley.[8]

Beginning in the north, about 25km north of Sevastopol Bay, at the very extremity of the 1941 fortress perimeter is the Kacha River Valley. Between the Kacha and the Belbek River Valley is the *Kara-Tau* (Black Mountain) plateau, a massif about 15km long and 6km wide, running east from the Kacha Valley to a series of low hills that end at the Black Sea. The southern slopes of the Kara-Tau form the northern rampart of the Belbek Valley, scene of heavy fighting. The Belbek Heights run approximately from Pyrohovka to Lyubimovka. Another series of hills runs along the southern edge of the valley and range in height from about 160m in the east to less than 100m along the coast. The main battle zone began at the Kamyshly Ravine and ran along this series of hills to the coast.

The Mekenzievy Mountains comprise another plateau northeast of Sevastopol that run from Frontove on the Belbek River south to Cherkez-Kerman, west to Inkerman and north to Fruktove (formerly Belbek Village). The Mekenzievy landscape is rugged and densely wooded. *Cherkez-Kerman* or *Tcherkess-Kerman* – Circassian Fortress, in the southeast corner of the plateau, was an impregnable position in ancient times. It was a narrow gorge in the valley of Tcherkess-Kerman with steep cliffs rising 90m above an ancient Tatar village. Crypts were dug into the rock and filled with bones. The Turks built a tower on the eastern cliff called *Eski-Kerman* – Old Fort. The village looked out on the highest mountains in the Mekenzievy system including Mount Yaila-Bash (Yayla means Mountain; Bash means stream) and Mount Kaya-Bash. The Kara-Koba (Black Cave) Valley runs along the southern slopes of the Mekenzievy Mountains below Cherkez-Kerman, then heads southwest where it intersects the Black River Valley.

The Heights of Inkerman (*In* = cave, *Kerman* = castle) along the western edge of the Mekenzievy Mountains, consist of a group of hills beginning with Mount Kara-Koba, which runs along the western edge of the valley of the same name, Sugar Head and Gaytani. Inkerman East Lighthouse and the ancient Kalamita Fortress sit atop the heights and look out over Sevastopol Bay. The hill upon which Kalamita sits is pierced with prehistoric crypts converted in the first century AD to Christian places of worship.

A series of ravines drop down from these heights to the northern coast of the bay. Beginning at Inkerman and running north to west is Gypsy Ravine, Martynov,

German aerial photograph looking west towards the Black Sea. (Provided by John Calvin of www.wwii-photos-maps.com, altered by the author)

Grafskaya or Count (after Count and later Prince Woronzoff), Lighthouse, Kleopinyh (named for a nineteenth-century farm), Sukharnaya, Holland and Panayotova (named after a former Black Sea Fleet Captain). West of Panayotova, rising above Fort Constantine is Radio Hill, named for the location of a radio transmitter in the early twentieth century. Radio Hill continues to the Black Sea at Cape Tolstoy where the coastline continues north to the Belbek Valley.

East of the Mekenzievy Plateau is the Valley of Kareless, a natural pathway behind the plateau leading to Shuli and the Kara-Koba Valley. The towns of *Orto* (Middle) *Karaless* and *Youkáry* (Upper) *Karaless* are located along the valley. At the former village of *Kodja-Salá* (m. Khodzha Sala) is the *Tabana-derè* ravine that leads up to the former palace of *Mangoup-Kale*. The hill overlooks the village of Shuli. It consisted of dense undergrowth of dogberry, barberry, juniper and wild vines and is representative of the nature of the vegetation on the surrounding hills.[9] *Mangoup-Kale* – 'top of the glen' – perched on Mount Baba, was an ancient fortress ruin with walls 4m thick. Small dwellings and ancient crypts are carved into the rock. It lies in advance of the Chorgun Strongpoint and was not defended during the Second Defence.

Hills and ravines also run along the southern coast of the bay. Beginning at the mouth of the *Tchórnaya-retchka* or *Byouk-Ouzyn* – Black River, the first ravine, called Devil's, is at the northern extremity of a line of continuous heights called the *Sapounn-garà* – Sapun Ridge. Continuing north and west is the Stone Pit Ravine, later called the Soviet, followed by Bullock (also called Cowhide and Ox),

28　The Defence of Sevastopol 1941–1942

Sushilnaya (no information on origin), St. George, Trinity (through which the Trinity Tunnel passes), Killen, Ushakov and Korabelnaya Ravines. The Laboratory Ravine, known as Careenage during the Crimean War, runs into the South Bay. Southwest of Laboratory is the Delagardova Ravine, named for the Garde Farm. The Sarandinakinu Ravine, named for the former village of Sarandinaki, runs into the South Bay and includes smaller offshoots of Chomutov and the Delaragdova. It is also referred to on Crimean War-era maps as the English Ravine. West of Cape Alexander and running into the bay of the same name is Quarantine Ravine. Streletskaya or Musketeers' Ravine runs into the bay of the same name. Finally, the very lengthy Yuharinaya Ravine runs parallel to the southern Black Sea Coast and continues to Kamyshovaya Bay, just north of Cossack Bay and Cape Chersonese.

It is about 12km from Cape Chersonese to Cape Fiolent. There are no extraordinary features along the coast except for the high, rocky cliffs; hardly the perfect venue for an amphibious assault. From Fiolent it is 9km to Balaklava Bay, which was controlled by the Soviets during the entire defence. Ancient and modern fortifications were built on the hills overlooking Balaklava Bay. Balaklava began as a fifth-century BC Greek port. It was called *Symbolemportus* (Signal Harbour). The earliest forts overlooking the bay and sea that included the Genoese Towers were called Cembalo Fortress. The former inhabitants were pirates who lit huge bonfires on the shore to attract ships so they could be robbed. The fortifications guarded both the bay and the Yalta Highway, earlier known as the Woronzoff Road, where it left the mountains in the direction of Sapun Ridge and on to Sevastopol. The Balaklava North Fort on Hill 212.1 (referred to in most accounts as 'North Fort', overlooked the bay and the Balaklava 'South Fort' was built about 2,500m to the east.

The Yalta Highway passed between Mount Gasfort[10] and Canrobert[11] Hill.

Vintage map showing Killen (Careenage) Bay and the Killen Ravine. From Sebastopol and its Environs showing the Russian Defences and the Approaches and Other Works of Attack of the Allied Armies. *From the Report of General Niel, Chief of the French Eng.* (Author's collection)

A series of fortifications from the nineteenth century called the Turkish Redoubts were built along a series of low hills, the Semyukhiny Heights, also called 'The Causeway' during the Crimean War, that stretched from Canrobert Hill to the Sapun Ridge. Telegraph Hill,[12] Hill 90.5 and the villages of Lower and Upper Chorgun were located north of Mount Gasfort. Another series of hills, bordered on the north and west by the Kara-Koba Valley rose up to the west of Upper Chorgun; the main feature being Hill 154.7, called North Nose by the Germans and Hill 269.0, Mount Chirish-Tepe. The Fedyukhiny Heights, consisting of two main hills, 125.7 and 135.7, are across the Black River Valley, opposite Hill 90.5. The Fedyukhiny was a natural ravelin in front of Sapun Ridge.

The Sapun Ridge was the next challenge for an attacker. It was a continuation of the line of hills that ran from Inkerman to the Karan Valley south of the junction of the Yalta and Balaklava roads at the base of the Karagach Heights. The Karan Valley ran towards the plateau above the Black Sea coast. The Soviet defensive line ended at the monastery of St. George[13] which sat on the cliff tops 180m above the sea. The land above the Sapun Ridge was dotted with rolling hills broken by the ravines mentioned above, that dropped down to the Black Sea and Sevastopol Bay. The most prominent of these was the Suzdal Heights between Sevastopol Bay and Killen Ravine. Fortifications had been built on several of the smaller hills during the Crimean War, such as the English Victoria Redoubt and the English Cemetery, called Cathcart's Hill.[14] These were modified and used during the Second Defence. Sevastopol was a formidable fortress, even without any permanent fortifications.

After the death of Catherine II, Tsar Paul I allowed the defences to deteriorate. In 1801 Paul was deposed by Alexander I who set out to strengthen the defences. The commander of the Black Sea Fleet, the Marquis de Traverse, began work on the fortifications at a time when relations with Turkey had deteriorated into war. From 1805 to 1812, Traverse built ten batteries, numbered 1 to 10. He also built land fortifications north and south of Sevastopol Bay. In the north a system of earthworks extended from Panayotova Ravine to Cape Tolstoy, fronted by a moat 4m wide and walls 3.5m high. A citadel called the North Fort was built in the centre of the line. Several batteries in the south were protected by earthworks and could technically be called 'forts'. Battery 10 had its own defences protecting its rear, referred to as the Quarantine Fort. The perimeter defences of the south side were never completed; a combination of the lack of funding and the end of the war and avoidance of doing anything to aggravate tensions with Turkey.

The batteries guarding the entrance to the bay at Cape Alexander and Cape Paul were well placed and well-armed. They consisted of two-tiered structures defended along the front by a barbet, the upper tier 11m above sea level, the lower 5.5m (its purpose was to fire into the hulls of attacking ships). The design had some drawbacks, however. When the guns of the upper tier fired the lower tier was affected by the blast. Also, the open batteries were protected from direct fire but mortar shells could reach the gunners on top. The idea of placing guns in casemates was abandoned for financial reasons.

The North Fort was the main structure on the north side (never referred to by any other name). It was built from 1807 to 1811. The fort was initially an earthwork with a surrounding ditch and wall, octagonal in shape, the sides 170–210m in length. Small bastions for flank defence were built into four corners, with underground casemates for small guns to defend the ditch. The fort had three gates – Simferopol, Sevastopol and Inkerman – each surrounded by a ditch with a drawbridge. The North Fort was modified in 1834. The ditch was deepened to 5m and lined with limestone. A barracks, powder magazine and armoury were built within the walls. The fort housed an infantry regiment (no guns) that defended batteries 1 (Constantine), 2 (Nakhimovsky) and 3 (St. Michael). During the Crimean War the garrison consisted of about 3,900 men. The commander of the fort was Captain Bartenev.[15] It was armed with forty-seven guns, twenty-three of them small calibre. After the war the fort was used as a military warehouse and in 1900 a new barracks was built for an engineering company. The north side defences were also strengthened by the addition of a chain of infantry forts that ran towards the east called the Nagornykh Redoubts. These were a line of redoubts that guarded the entrances to the ravines on the north side.

From 1812 to 1829 the fortifications were improved. The walls of the coastal batteries received a limestone façade quarried at the Killen Ravine. During this period no improvements were made to the land defences except for the construction of barracks buildings. In 1831 a plan was drawn up to build a chain of landward fortifications connected by a defensive wall. The chain started at Battery 10 and continued to the top of South Bay. The defences were strengthened by large stone bastions

The city of Sebastopol in 1854–55. From Sebastopol and its Environs showing the Russian Defences and the Approaches and Other Works of Attack of the Allied Armies. From the Report of General Niel, Chief of the French Eng. (Author's collection)

connected by a curtain wall. On 1 August 1834, excavation began on the Third and Fourth Bastions and a new battery on the Fourth Bastion.

Construction was accelerated due to the deterioration of relations with Turkey. Tsar Nicholas I allocated one million roubles to improve the defences. The Lazarev Barracks were built on top of Artillery Bay, and other stone barracks were built near the shore batteries and forts. Additional magazines were built at Forts Constantine, St. Michael, Nicholas and Alexander. Construction of a small underground magazine at Battery 4 was unfinished when the Crimean War began.

During the Crimean War the Russians continued work to connect the bastions to form a continuous curtain wall to defend against an attack by land. Walls were built near the First Bastion and between the Fifth, Sixth and Seventh Bastions. The walls contained loopholes for infantry and were approximately 800m long and about 1m thick. The civilian inhabitants of Sevastopol built two unusual structures, the Malakhov Tower and the Martello Tower[16] (called the Volohova Tower). The Malakhov was built on the south side and the Volohova Tower on the north, located above the sea at Cape Tolstoy. The Malakhov Tower provided an outstanding view of the entire area, from the mountains to ships approaching the harbour. From the sea, Sevastopol was an impregnable fortress. But on the landward side, only a quarter of the planned seven miles of fortifications were completed.

Improvements to the defences of the south side continued, in particular along the Killen Ravine to Bastion 7. Battery Sviatoslav was built on the shore of Killen Bay by the sailors of the ship of the same name. The battery had seventeen guns. Battery Panayotova was built on the north side between Rusks and Holland Bay. A new battery, the Kartashevski, was built at Fort Constantine. The defence of Sevastopol was left to General Kornilov and Colonel Todleben the chief engineer.

The city was surrounded by Allied siege works that included numerous artillery batteries designed to pound down the walls and capture the city in short order. The Russian coastal batteries inflicted heavy damage on British and French ships. Both the siege works and defences continued to be improved during the long siege. The Turks built the Turkish Redoubts. Two other lines

Batteries 12 and 13 at Sevastopol; present day. (Nemenko Collection)

consisting of ditches with earthen ramparts and redoubts were built, one from the southern coast near Cape Fiolent to Musketeers' Bay and a second from Reed Bay to the coast and were used by Soviet troops in the defence of 1941 to 1942. The Sardinian redoubts built on Mount Gasfort also played a major role. The British Victoria Redoubt was used by Soviet troops as a command post for the 177th Coastal Defence Artillery Battalion.

After the war ended the victorious Allies took 867 captured Russian guns with them when they left. Some of them were used by the British to arm the fortress of Gibraltar. The defences of Sevastopol were left in bad condition but they were not destroyed.

Post-war Renaissance – 1876 to 1890

> Sevastopol, the former chief military port of the Black Sea Fleet is located on the southwestern coast of Crimea. Sevastopol … All value lies in its historical past; it is now only famous for its historical ruins … There is almost no population and [from] many houses gape broken windows and broken walls … The whole city is littered with graves; wherever you go, you will stumble on them everywhere … Sevastopol is now a dead town; a city of the dead.
> (Crimean Guidebook of 1876)

The city lay in ruins for over twenty years. In 1876 a new crisis with Turkey prompted Russia to rebuild its armed forces and its defences on the Black Sea. During the intervening years, a new generation of guns with rifled steel barrels was manufactured. Russia received a large supply of the new guns thanks to her new-found friendship with Germany and in particular with the Krupp[17] armaments works.

By 1877 the fortress had a total of sixty-two guns. The Russians repaired some of the Crimean War defensive lines including the Kamyshovaya (Kamezh) line built by the French to protect their base at Kamyshovaya Bay. This line began at a redoubt overlooking Musketeers' Bay and ended at the south coast. The line consisted of a ditch 7m wide with a stone rampart along the escarp that reached a height of 5m and was 6m thick, built of rubble and earth.

The Russo-Turkish War, in part instigated by Britain to draw attention from her interests in Central Asia, began in 1877 and Turkey suffered a crushing defeat. In 1885 relations between Britain and Russia worsened, prompting Russia to make additional improvements to coastal defences and artillery, including the delivery of 11in Krupp guns from Germany.

In the 1880s concrete was introduced and modifications were made to the coastal batteries. The new gun batteries were now built entirely of concrete. They varied in length, depending on the number of guns to be mounted in the battery.

The Fortress of Sevastopol 33

The guns were placed on open concrete platforms on top of the battery blocks. The gun crews were protected from the front by a concrete parapet. Concrete traverses for the storage of ammunition were built between the gun platforms. Traverse shelters on some of the batteries had two storage chambers, one for the gun on the right and one for the gun on the left. Using this design, each gun had two storage chambers at the gun level, one for shells and one for charges.

The main magazines were placed below and protected by the thickness of the gun platforms. An underground transverse gallery ran along the face of the battery below the parapet, connecting all of the underground facilities to entrances with steel doors on both ends of the battery. Shells were assembled in the underground chambers and moved by monorail along the ceiling of the casemate below the gun. Fuses and ammunition were delivered to the gun platform through an embrasure in the wall. Small-calibre ammunition was brought up by hand. The rangefinder, artillery command post, various offices and troop shelters were located on the flanks of the battery. The batteries were equipped with generators to power searchlights, ventilation and interior lighting.

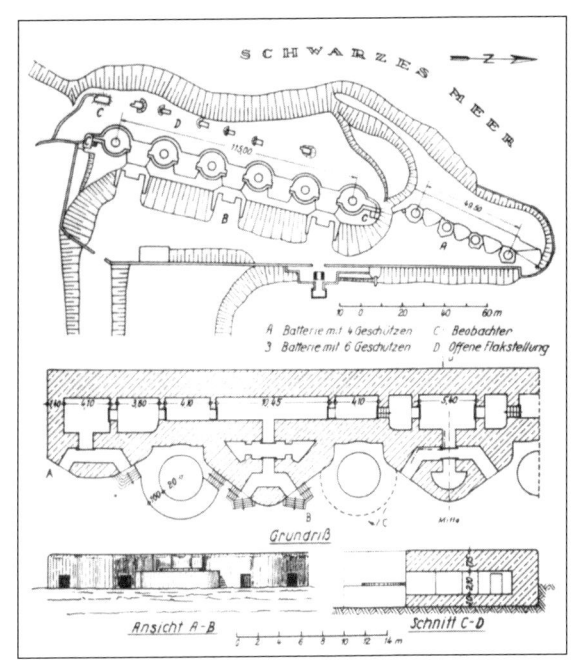

Battery 9 at Cape Alexander. (Nachtrag)

In 1895 a series of deep magazines were built on both the north and the south side. Two magazines for shells and one for powder storage were built in the north. These were called the Nakhimovsky Cellars,[18] located in a ravine above Matyushenko Bay. A large powder magazine was built into the cliffs near Sukharno Ravine. On the south side a storage cellar was placed near Battery 10. Later on, during the construction of Batteries 12 and 13, a cellar was built into the hillside below Battery 13.

The 1898 engineering plan included the replacement of the Nagornykh line and the strengthening of the outer line of forts in the south with new, detached concrete forts. Forts on the north side were given the letter designation 'B' while those on the south side were referred to as 'A'. Only two of these forts were built because, after the Russian experience at Port Arthur, the forts were considered obsolete. A single Fort B was built in the north and Fort A in the south. Fort B was called Fort Cheka by the Germans. These forts played no part in the Second Defence.

Transitional Batteries – 1904 to 1917

This period of construction can be broken down into three distinct phases. The first was the result of the lessons learned during the Russo-Japanese War; the second was the plan of 1910; and the third is associated with a modified plan in 1913. Specifically, the changes during the period of 1904 to 1917 included a significant increase in distance between the guns; a revised layout for magazines and in the manner in which ammunition was delivered to the guns; changes in the layout of the traverses; and the configuration of underground tunnels below the battery front. These developments coincided with ongoing changes in fortress technology and the introduction of new types of weapons.

During the first period (1904) Batteries 2, 4 and 14 were built and armed with 6in (15cm) Kane guns, named for the French artillery engineer. Batteries 15, 16 and 17 were planned for 10in (25cm) guns. Battery 15, located at Victory Park and Battery 16, near the Belbek Valley, blocked the approach to Sevastopol harbour. Battery 15 was operational in 1910. It had four 10in guns. Battery 16 was completed in 1912. Batteries 2, 4 and 14 were closer to the entrance to the bay and equipped with short-range 6in Kane guns.

Battery 15 was built from 1905 to 1910 at the head of Musketeers' Bay. Battery 15 was part of a plan for the construction of three batteries – Battery 15 on Cape Streletskaya,[19] Battery 17 at Cape Chersonese and Battery 16 at the mouth of the Belbek. These were built for 10in guns with a range of 20km to keep enemy ships out of the range of the mouth of the harbour. Because the batteries were located outside the perimeter of the fortress they were provided with their own defences against enemy landings or infantry attacks, in the form of a ditch and escarp wall and an iron fence. The ramparts had positions for field guns and machine guns to defend against an infantry attack.

Battery 15 was completed in 1910. It consisted of two separate sections, identified as 15A and 15B. The original plan called for four guns but was later amended to be armed with eight 10in guns after the second part of the battery was built. This part was added because the plans to build Battery 17 were scrapped and the guns were instead assigned to Battery 15. It was to be the most powerful battery at Sevastopol.

The fire-control position was located on the left flank of 15A. The rangefinder and a second fire-control position were located on the right flank of 15B. Personnel shelters and four machine-gun coffers were located on both flanks (two each). The Russians chose the wheeled Maxim machine gun for close defence. These were kept in the protective shelters and rolled out into position when needed. The primary naval guns were mounted in open positions and were protected by shields. Shells were brought by monorail from the magazines and lifted up to the gun level

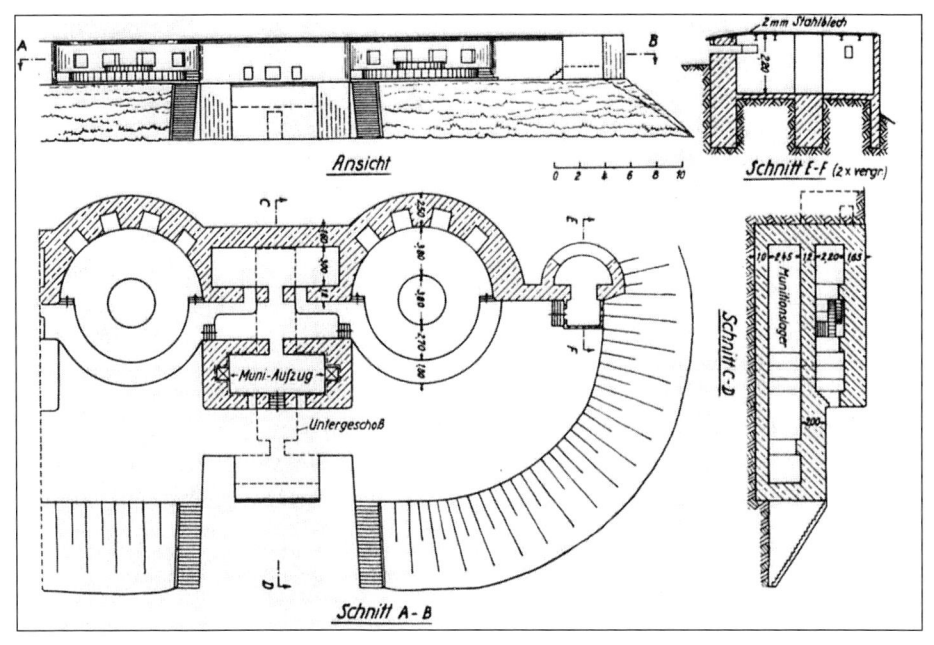

Concrete gun platforms at Battery 9. (Nachtrag)

through openings in the front of the battery. These were covered by protective steel plates. Each sub-battery (15A and 15B) had a gallery running along its front. The two sections were not connected to each other and there was an entrance through an armoured door at each end. The battery was equipped with diesel motors for electricity and to power the searchlights. The battery was armed until 1935 when Batteries 30 and 35 took over long-range coastal defence.

Battery 2 was the first coastal battery armed with 100mm B-24 guns that could fire on both sea and air targets. The guns had a high rate of fire. They were installed in the courtyards of the former Royal Battery 6. The Soviet plan was to install three 100mm batteries (one with three guns and two with four) in the former Royal Batteries 12, 13 and 14. The plan was later amended to include Batteries 18 and 19. Battery 2 was located on a hill above Fort Constantine. It was initially a two-gun battery. In December 1941 a third gun was added and placed on the right wing of the former Royal Battery 3. A fourth gun was added in May from a damaged minesweeper. The battery was re-designated as Battery 2 and Battery 2bis. Two guns were in the upper location and two were placed at Fort Constantine. These guns were later dismantled and transferred to the south side.

Battery 14 was completed after 1912. It was located between Musketeers' Bay and Sandy Bay. It was a standard battery for four 6in guns placed in triangular emplacements. The gun barrel extended over the parapet. Shells were lifted up by hand-operated hoists from the ammunition magazines to the gun platform. The guns were placed in a single row with a single connecting gallery similar to Batteries 2 and 4. A casemate was located on the right flank to shelter the gun crew. A power station was also located on the right flank. The entrance to the transverse gallery was located on the left flank. The battery had a ditch with a rampart topped by an iron fence. It was armed with four 6in Kane guns from scrapped ships, mounted behind shields built into the gun carriage. These guns were removed in 1935 and sent to the School of Coastal Defence. In 1940 four 45mm guns were installed in front of the battery to provide air defence. In August 1941 both the 45mm and 152mm guns were removed and installed in bunkers along the perimeter. In October the battery received four 130mm guns that defended the right flank of Sevastopol.

The arms race in the years leading up to the First World War led to a renewed emphasis on making improvements to Sevastopol. The range of battleship guns of the major powers increased to 20km and new destroyers with increased speed and armament potentially rendered the guns of Sevastopol obsolete. The engineers introduced the 120mm Vickers gun to the Sevastopol inventory. Battery 9 received Vickers guns in 1912. Two new batteries – 23 and 24 – were built next to Batteries 15 and 16 and equipped with 120mm guns. Their purpose was to combat enemy destroyers and repel landing forces in the vicinity of the batteries.

Battery 23 was armed with 120mm Vickers guns. It was built to cover the flanks of Battery 15 from both enemy ships and the landing of troops near the battery. The entrance was located in the parapet, with steps that led down to the transverse gallery that connected the magazines. The guns were 23m apart and separated by a triangular-shaped traverse. The shells were delivered to the guns from below by hand. There was no monorail system. A power station and retractable searchlight were located on the left flank, as well as casemates for Maxim machine guns. The guns were removed during the Russian Civil War. After that the battery was used as a power station and a coastal searchlight battery. During the Second Defence it was used by the Armoured Searchlight Company and provided illumination for the AA battery located at nearby Battery 15.

In 1913 a new programme was launched that included the construction of batteries along the southwest coast between Cape Chersonese and Balaklava. This also led to an expansion of the landward defences to cover the flanks of the expanded front. One of these batteries was the powerful Fort Maxim Gorki II, Battery 35. Two 12in batteries, 25 and 26, were planned to cover the northern and southern flanks of the fortress from enemy dreadnoughts. Battery 25 (later designated as Battery 30) was located below the Belbek Valley; Battery 26 (Battery 35) southeast of Cape Chersonese. Additional batteries were built far from the main base. They were given additional protection from attack because of their remoteness and could technically be considered detached 'forts'. They were equipped with field guns and machine guns, a ditch, wall and iron fence. The new batteries were also equipped with generators to power the ventilation, lighting and spotlights. Construction of Batteries 18, 19, 20, 21 and 22 began during this phase.

Between 1914 and 1917, many of Sevastopol's guns were removed, including the 10in guns, 9in mortars, 6in Kane guns and 57mm Nordenfelts. As of 1917, the inventory included: four 11in Model 1887 for training; six 10in Model 1895 (three each at Batteries 15 and 16); ten 6in Kane guns at Batteries 1, 2 and 14; twelve 120mm guns at Batteries 23, 24 and 9; sixteen 11in mortars at Batteries 3 and 12; plus four 9in mortars at Battery 7.

The Russian Civil War of 1920 was not kind to Sevastopol. The peninsula was controlled by the White Army. When they left they gutted the fortress, taking everything of value with them, including construction equipment, railway track and most of the guns. The new Soviet Red Army addressed the post-Civil War problems of coastal defence and placed them into three classifications: the first included batteries armed with modern artillery – 305mm, 203mm, 152mm, 75mm Kane and 120mm; the second group consisted of batteries with outdated guns that could be used if necessary or quickly placed into combat readiness in the event of war; the third group included batteries that no longer had any military significance and could be completely disarmed.

In 1925 a commission inspected the coastal batteries of the Black Sea and determined that Sevastopol was in no condition to successfully repel an enemy bombardment from the sea. The coastal batteries were only capable of defending the harbour and guarding against the approach of warships armed with similar short-range artillery. The Commission noted the inefficiencies and shortfalls of the construction of the gun batteries in regard to supplying ammunition to

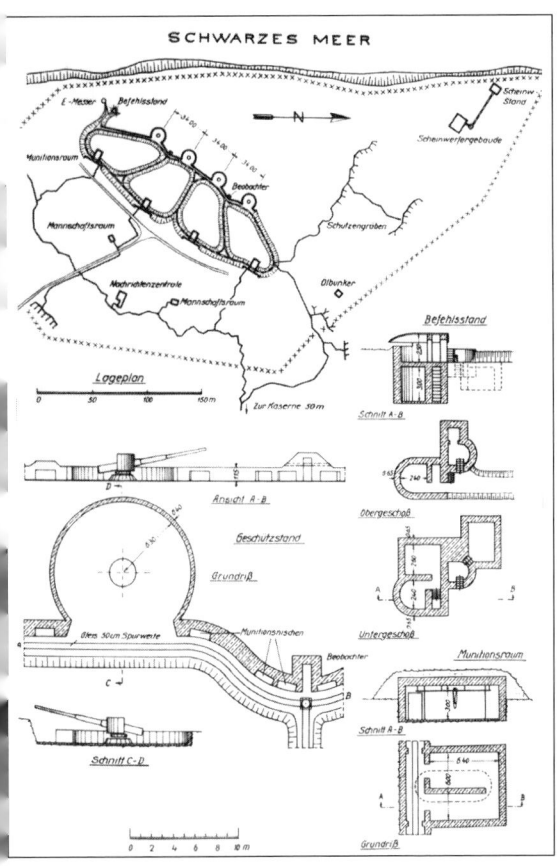

Battery 10, south of Kacha. (Nachtrag)

the guns, command and control, lack of shelter for the gunners and absence of camouflage. Air defence was completely absent. The only means of communication between the batteries and command centres was via land lines which could easily be cut. The Black Sea Fleet was incapable of contributing to the fight against modern European naval forces and of ensuring the safety of the coast from attack. Urgent measures needed to be taken to fix the problem.

In 1927 the first Soviet-era battery, Number 10, was built near the mouth of the Kacha River. It included the improvements identified by the commission, including a higher parapet around the guns and a narrow-gauge railway system to supply shells from the magazines. Battery 10 was equipped with four 203mm guns retrieved from the obsolete battleship *Evstafi*. The former Royal Battery 1 was equipped with 120mm guns to attack high-speed enemy vessels approaching the bay. Battery 6 was equipped with the quick-firing 100mm B-24 submarine gun. In 1931 work began on the completion of gun batteries for 305mm turret guns – 30 and 35 (formerly 25 and 26).

In the years prior to the Second World War, the city of Sevastopol expanded and was filled with the modern conveniences found in a typical Russian city. Bakeries, wineries, lime and marble quarries, macaroni and knitwear factories, fish-processing plants and dozens of other industries sprang up. In 1937 a power plant was built on the south side of the bay and provided electricity not only to Sevastopol, but also to Bakhchisaray, Yalta, Simferopol and Eupatoria. In 1941, the population of Sevastopol was about 114,000. The city had several Institutes of Science including the USSR Academy of Sciences, which enjoyed worldwide renown, three colleges, twenty-eight schools for children, thirteen public libraries, a theatre, three cinemas, two museums and an art gallery. Three large factory farms were located in the suburbs: the Sophia Perovskoy farm was a winery; Farm Number 14 was a horticultural farm; and Farm Number 10 was used for raising livestock. Thus, on the eve of the Second World War Sevastopol was considered a leading industrial and cultural centre and remained the main base of the Black Sea Fleet.

Sevastopol was home to the staff and management of the fleet Military Council and all of their sub-departments. The commander of the Black Sea Fleet was Vice-Admiral Filipp Sergeyevich Oktyabrsky.[20] The commander of Coastal Defence was Major-General Petr Alekseevich Morgunov.[21] Oktyabrsky also served as the main base commander and Morgunov commanded the garrison of Sevastopol.

The base had a number of large underground bomb-proof warehouses in which ammunition for all types of weapons, naval fuel, technical equipment and weapons, were stored. The 'Underground' was also home to repair factories, workshops and laboratories.

As war approached, an argument arose regarding how to best defend naval bases from a land attack. The question remained unsolved both practically and theoretically until after the war broke out. The defence of naval bases from the land was not considered a task of the navy. The Charter of Naval Forces of the Red Army in 1937 read that defence of the land front should include the use of coastal artillery batteries and ships. It did not address the command organisation of naval forces to be used to defend the base from land attacks. In other words, Sevastopol was not prepared to defend itself from an attack by land, only by sea. It could use the coastal batteries and ship's artillery to fire on land targets but it had no significant landward defences except for the remnants of the earlier lines. In the late 1930s there was little concern about an enemy attack from across the vast steppes of Ukraine. No one anticipated any major threat to Sevastopol and if it was attacked it would most likely be by sea. Therefore landward fortifications were not considered.

Defence against an airborne or amphibious attack on Sevastopol was bolstered after Germany's use of airborne troops in Belgium, Holland, Bessarabia and Rumania, showing they were capable of capturing territory and bases by air. German amphibious and airborne forces could be dropped anywhere. This sent a loud message to the naval command and resulted in plans for an upgrade to coastal defence equipment and the reorganisation of naval defence forces. In late summer 1940, coastal defence battalions were organised to include Marine Infantry regiments.[22]

On 16 December 1940 Admiral Nikolay Kuznetsov, People's Commissar of the Navy ordered an inspection of the main line of defence and the organisation of anti-aircraft and anti-amphibious landing defences. General Morgunov was in charge of the project. In the period from 21 February to 5 April 1941 a general line of seaward and landward defences was surveyed and planned. Construction was accelerated in May 1941 when the Germans launched a large-scale invasion of Crete.

The plan to update the defences included the construction of a new defensive line 20km out from the city, consisting of concrete bunkers armed with machine guns and anti-tank guns to guard the main roads leading to the city. The project did not provide for a continuous line of fortifications. Instead, strongpoints were built along the main roads and rail lines leading towards the city. Barbed wire, field works such as trenches and redoubts and minefields were to be placed between the strongpoints. Barracks for the troops were built nearby.

Morgunov was not happy with the final plans. He believed another line should be built closer to the city. He was concerned that a defensive line 20km out would not provide sufficient protection of the base should an amphibious assault take place somewhere between the base and the forward line. Furthermore, if the harbour was protected from airborne landings by a line at least 5km out, it would be out of the range of the types of artillery an airborne force could bring with them, such as the 75mm gun with a range of 3.5km. Kuznetsov agreed with Morgunov. The initial plan was amended with Morgunov's changes on 27 May 1941. Work on the outer line was suspended and the construction of the rear line began.

The construction of the rear line was in full swing by early August 1941. Work was initiated on a line of anti-tank bunkers for 45mm guns from the Belbek estuary to Mekenzievy Station, then through Inkerman, Suzdal, Killen Bay, to the English Cemetery to Balaklava Road, then along the Balaklava road through Maximova Farm to Musketeers' Bay.

In September 1941, attention was temporarily shifted to the defences of Perekop and Chongar. Thirty-four coastal guns were transferred from Sevastopol's warehouses and batteries to new batteries in the north. In addition to providing artillery support for Fifty-first Army, the Black Sea Fleet was also charged with defending the coast from Bakal Spit to Sevastopol and additional batteries were built up along the coast. More guns were transferred for placement on a group of armoured trains that served as heavy mobile batteries. The removal of guns to the north decimated the effectiveness of Sevastopol's coastal batteries.

The possibility of a German advance on Sevastopol following a breakthrough at Perekop caused another change to the construction plans. Work on the outer line had stopped in order to work on the rear line closer to the city. The Germans now had field artillery pieces capable of hitting the harbour from outside the second line. Therefore, work on the original, outer line of defence needed to be resumed immediately.

The updated plan called for the construction of additional bunkers and an anti-tank ditch around the city. The ditch stretched from the Belbek Valley to Inkerman and then across the Suzdal Heights to Musketeers' Bay. The outer line was comprised of long-range guns, barbed wire, anti-tank obstacles, minefields and a line of concrete bunkers. The line ran as follows: Kamary–Chorgun–Shuli–Cherkez-Kerman–Duvankoi–Mount Azis-Oba–Aranci and to the coast about 1.5km north of the mouth of the Kacha River. It passed through four main strongpoints: Chorgun, Cherkez-Kerman, Duvankoi and Aranci.

By 10 October the construction of fortifications at Duvankoi and Aranci came to an end and work started on the fortifications between the strongpoints. At this point the rear lines of defence were about 70 per cent complete. On 16 October all work was again put on hold. It was determined during a visit by Major-General A. F. Hrenov, Deputy Commander of Engineering, that the forward line was still too close to the city. He recommended that the line of defence be moved out to the Alma River. On 20 October, all the forces engaged in construction were put to work on the new outer line. The forward and rear lines remained unfinished. The new forward line was planned to receive seven bunkers and several machine-gun bunkers but none were built.

The Fortress of Sevastopol 41

Extraordinary measures had to be taken to find enough guns to equip the bunkers of Sevastopol. Guns were taken from training schools and recovered from sunken ships. According to Soviet literature and records, on 30 October, as the Germans descended on Sevastopol, the defences consisted of three lines with eighty-two bunkers equipped with various long-range and anti-tank guns and 214 machine-gun bunkers, ten coastal batteries and numerous anti-aircraft batteries.

According to General Morgunov, by 1 November, the defences were as follows: The rear line ran 3–6km from the city and was completed on 15 September. It was 19km in length, with a depth of 300–600m^2. It included twenty-eight concrete artillery bunkers for naval guns of a calibre of 45mm to 100mm, seventy-one machine-gun bunkers, ninety-one infantry trenches, an anti-tank ditch and 70km of barbed wire in two lines, five command posts, communication trenches and dugouts for two to three persons.

The main line of defence was 8–12km from the city. Its length was 35km with a depth of 300m. It included twenty-five artillery bunkers, eight located at Balaklava, fifty-seven machine-gun bunkers, sixty-six infantry trenches, three command posts and 13km of barbed wire. It was completed on 3 September.

The outer line was 15–17km from the city. Its length was 46km and it included twenty-nine artillery bunkers, ninety-two machine-gun bunkers, 232 infantry trenches, forty-eight dugouts, 8km of barbed wire, a 1.7km anti-tank ditch and over 9,000 anti-tank and anti-personnel mines. The ravines and gorges in the

Captured 130mm Soviet coastal gun. (Nemenko Collection)

outer line were equipped with 'fire curtains', metal troughs filled with flammable liquid ignited by a flamethrower. The fuel was stored nearby in cylindrical tanks. Altogether there were seventeen fire curtains placed across the main roads in the strongpoints.

The coastal defence batteries fell under command of the 1st Separate Artillery Battalion. It included Batteries 30 and 35 with 30.5cm guns (two twin turrets each), Battery 10 (203mm) and Battery 54[23] (102mm). The 2nd Separate Artillery Battalion commanded Batteries 2, 8, 12 and 14 with guns of a calibre of 102mm to 152mm. 3rd Separate Artillery Battalion commanded Batteries 18, 29 (152mm) and mobile batteries 724 and 725 (152mm guns) and seven groups of artillery bunker battalions with eighty-two naval guns ranging from 45mm to 130mm, plus 100 machine-gun pillboxes and bunkers. Finally the armoured train *Zhelezniakov*, with three 76mm guns, operated along the railway lines of Sevastopol.

There are some discrepancies from one account to another regarding the number of machine-gun bunkers built. General Morgunov was correct about the number of artillery bunkers – about eighty-two. He gave a total figure of 220 machine-gun pillboxes and bunkers. In other accounts this number is 100. Recent surveys[24] indicate the number is closer to about eighty-two artillery bunkers and about fifty pre-cast concrete bunkers for machine guns. There were many more earth-timber machine-gun emplacements and no figure is given for this.[25]

In conclusion, a solid, continuous defence simply did not exist. This can be attributed to a constant change of plan, movement of forces from one theatre to another and no single concept or agreement on a defensive approach (land defence vs. anti-amphibious/airborne assault). On 30 October 1941, none of the lines of defence were ready to firmly repel the attacker who was swiftly descending on Sevastopol.

Chapter 3

The First Assault – October to November 1941

Senior Lieutenant Greiser jotted down in his diary which our men found near Sevastopol: 'Near Bakhchisarai is a valley which the local inhabitants call "The Valley of Death." Now it has justified its name. A considerable portion of the population of Erfurt, Jena and my own Eisenach lie buried there... '[1]

Prisoner of war Kneidler: 'We did not expect such resistance. Here, every rock shoots. How I managed to get through this inferno is simply a miracle ...' Klein, another POW, admits: 'At first we felt pretty cocky. Now our men are terribly on edge. Many of them are doubtful whether we'll ever take the blasted city...'[2]

Coastal Battery 54 was located at Mykolaivka on the Black Sea coast, about 40km north of Sevastopol. On 30 October Lieutenant-Commander Ivan Zaika, the battery commander, was watching a column of Rumanian

120mm coastal guns of Battery 54 at Mykolaivka. (Nemenko Collection)

troops near Ivanivka Teplovka. The 132nd Infantry Division was 30km behind the Rumanians, approaching from Ak-Metchet. The battery was a small field work with a garrison of 150. Its 120mm guns had a range of 14km. It fell under the command of the 1st Separate Artillery Regiment at Sevastopol.[3] Lieutenant-Commander Zaika gave the order to load the battery's No. 1 gun and to fire three ranging shots. The Rumanians, the 6th Cavalry Brigade's Reconnaissance Battalion, part of the Ziegler Brigade, came to a halt. The battery then opened fire on the column with all of its guns, causing serious losses. The Rumanians backtracked to Chebotarka on the Saki-Simferopol road. Another Rumanian column advanced toward Kolodiazne and came under fire from the battery and the column set off in another direction. From then on advancing units looked for another road to take that was out of the range of the battery. The following day, German reconnaissance units from 132nd Division came under fire from the battery at the edge of Lake Kyzyl Yar, apparently not having been warned by the Rumanians.

October 30th was a day of advance and retreat. Soviet units from the north of Crimea were pouring back from the north as quickly as possible on any road they could find. The 7th Marine Brigade was ordered to move to the north to plug the gap in the defences between the Djankoi railway line and the Black Sea coast below Eupatoria.

The first defenders of Sevastopol were sailors and marines. The army came later. The term 'Marine' connotes an elite unit, designed for amphibious landings. However, in the early years of the war, it had a different meaning. Marines came from naval units and were used for coastal defence. They were mostly poorly trained volunteers. Only Marines of the Danube Flotilla and men of the 7th Marine Brigade received good military training. They were well equipped with small arms and ammunition but did not possess heavy artillery since their missions rarely required its use. From the beginning, Marine units were formed for defence against amphibious landings.

The 7th Marine Brigade, formed at Sevastopol, was commanded by Colonel Yevgeny Ivanovich Zhidilov, former Assistant Chief of Staff of the Black Sea Fleet. Three battalions of the 7th were formed by 24 August and were involved in training and building fortifications. The 4th and 5th Battalions, plus an artillery battalion, were formed later. By 24 September the 7th Marine Brigade was fully formed. It had 4,860 men of which 3,484 were drawn from the Black Sea Fleet. 7th Marine Brigade was a conventional infantry brigade, the heaviest unit at Sevastopol, with a full complement of heavy weapons including regimental 120mm mortars, 76mm guns and semi-automatic weapons. The brigade was well-trained and well-equipped, drawn from men of the highest moral character. The main mission of the 7th Marine Brigade was to defend Sevastopol.

The First Assault – October to November 1941   45

On 29 October the brigade began moving to the north. Part of the brigade arrived from Sevastopol by train at Kermen-Kemelchi and another part at Bink-Onlar (m. Oktyabrskoe), two railway stations along the Djankoi–Simferopol–Sevastopol line. Upon arrival, Zhidilov received a message from Simferopol stating that the enemy was already moving along the coast towards Saki and that the brigade should move to the line Tyumen (m. Komsomoske)–Stare Karagut (disappeared)–Temesh (m. Shelkovychnaya), villages near the coast below Saki. The distance from their current location was about 40km, an eight-hour march in a constant drizzle of rain on mud-covered roads. However, by the time the order came in the 7th Brigade was at their originally-assigned positions only to discover the Germans had passed through and they were now behind enemy lines. Zhidilov received orders from the commander of 51st Army and also from General Petrov, then 51st Army again. When General Petrov found out that the Germans were already past the appointed rally line, he issued orders to 7th Brigade because they were the only force guarding the right flank of the Coastal Army's retreat towards Simferopol. The manner in which the first orders were given is a very interesting story.

7th Brigade's headquarters was set up near the railway at Temesh. Around 1500 hours on 30 October, Zhidilov and his staff were standing on the rail platform when someone spotted a German column heading towards them from the north. Zhidilov describes the encounter:[4]

> I see in the back of the first truck sitting in rows, soldiers in German uniforms and grey helmets. In their hands, machine guns. The Nazis stare at us. Our green uniforms were covered with dirt and perhaps the Germans thought we were their officers; but suddenly realised we were Russians. We decided to demand their surrender and we did not shoot at them. The Germans opened fire on us and we fled Temesh.

After the withdrawal from Temesh, Zhidilov was approached by a General; tall, thin, with glasses. He describes the conversation:

'You – Colonel Zhidilov?'
   Yes, I answered, wondering how he knows me.
   'What's with you?' Asks the General, seeing that I am stained with blood and covered in dust. I told him about the meeting with the Germans.
   'Do you have a map?'
   We obtain a map from the bags. The General offers a detailed report on the situation. After listening to me, he writes an order on the map:
   'Commander, 7th Brigade, Colonel Zhidilov. Entrusted to you on the morning of 31 October to take a milestone: Knyazhevich, Stare Lezy

(m. Skortsov), intercepting the road leading from Saki. 510th and 565th Artillery Regiment will go to Sofievka'. [Signed] Major-General Petrov'.

The 7th Brigade was being ordered to intercept the advance forces of the German 50th Division. The brigade moved to its new position and stopped several attempts by German and Rumanian motorised units to pass, in particular the 121st Infantry Regiment and the 150th Reconnaissance Battalion.

There was a serious command-and-control problem during the retreat. The army did not want to obey the navy and vice-versa. Oktyabrsky only commanded the fleet. Defence of the borders was the responsibility of the Red Army and there was no Army authority at Sevastopol. The commander of troops in Crimea (Red Army and Red Navy) was Admiral C. Levchenko, who was based in Alushta and had no communication with army troops or with the fleet. Responsibility for the defence of the city fell to the Deputy Commander of the Defence of the Main Base of the Black Sea Fleet, Admiral Zhukov. His headquarters was on the fleet's flagship in the harbour. The Admiralty HQ was later set up in an underground facility near Kamennaya Quay (under the modern Black Sea Fleet Museum). The training detachments and several other small units obeyed his orders. The command of the defence of the city was relegated to the Commandant of Coastal Defence, P. A. Morgunov. He was responsible for the coastal batteries, coastal defences and air defences. His command post was in Royal Battery 11. Arriving units were placed under General Morgunov's and Admiral Zhukov's command, including their subsequent deployment.

Nevertheless, a joint decision was made by the commanders that Sevastopol was not going to be defended and orders went out to prepare for the evacuation of personnel and equipment. This included the dismantling and preparation for evacuation of anti-aircraft batteries, ammunition, factory equipment and hospitals. The coastal batteries were mined for destruction. General Oktyabrsky convinced Admiral Levchenko that Sevastopol needed to hold out for five to seven days to evacuate everything of value. The abandonment of the city seemed a foregone conclusion.

Throughout the day the Coastal Army continued to move along the road to Simferopol. The 80th Separate Reconnaissance Battalion scouted in the direction of Bakhchisarai and found out that the road to Sevastopol was closed. There were ways around this and the road blockade was weak but General Petrov decided to move to the left into the mountains. At 2200 hours Zhidilov received a telegram from Petrov ordering the brigade to concentrate in the area of Stare Lezy and move towards Sevastopol south of Simferopol via Bulganak (m. Kolchuhyne on the Bulganak River) and Hanyshkoy (m. Vidradne on the Alma). Another telegram arrived stating that the brigade should prepare to encounter German forces

The First Assault – October to November 1941   47

occupying the area of Bulganak. The 7th Brigade ran into the reconnaissance units of the 50th Division and the 123rd Regiment at the Village of Sably (m. Partyzanske). There was a battle and both sides lost about 100 dead but the Germans captured about 500 Soviet prisoners.

During these chaotic days, 7th Brigade lost about two and one-half battalions fighting rearguard actions. 1st, 2nd, 4th and 5th Battalions moved independently of each other. The 2nd Battalion suffered heavy losses when they moved away from Simferopol and past Bulganak Bodrak (m. Pozharskoe) to the village of Ahzek, where they were attacked by a large force from 132nd Infantry Division. Eighty soldiers of the battalion were captured and 172 killed, including the battalion commander, Colonel Illarionov. 1st Battalion was also involved in this battle. 5th Battalion fought with the 121st Regiment of 50th Division and was reduced to about fifty men. The battalion had thirty-eight men left when they finally reached Sevastopol. Of 5,000 men sent north on 29 October, only about 1,500 men of the 7th Brigade returned. Zhidilov and his staff followed the Coastal Army into the mountains and did not reach Sevastopol until 8 November.

On 28 October the 15th Marine Battalion (N. A. Stalberg), the 16th Marine Battalion (G. T. Lvovksy) and the 17th Battalion (Unchur) were evacuated from Yalta, Ak-Metchet and the Bakal Spit. The 18th (Horvich) and 19th (Captain Chernousov) Marine Battalions were also sent to Sevastopol. On 29 October the 2nd Perekop Regiment, commanded by Colonel N. N. Taran, was brought to Sevastopol on the cruiser *Chervona Ukraina* ('Red Ukraine') from the Tendra Spit. On 30 October other Black Sea Fleet ships delivered the Marine Battalion of the Danube Flotilla (commanded by Peter Anton Gerashimov). In the evening the 774th and 724th Motorised Coast Defence Batteries arrived, each with four 120mm ML-20 howitzers. On 2 November Sevastopol had thirty-two battalions totalling 23,623 men, of which about one-fifth were actually prepared for combat.

While the main Soviet forces moved south, General Morgunov moved whatever forces were available in Sevastopol at the time to the front. The greatest threat was from enemy forces moving along the coast towards Kacha and from the direction of Simferopol. Morgunov's initial deployment placed Soviet units along the Kacha River, across the Kara-Tau Plateau to Duvankoi, then on to Cherkez-Kerman. On 28 October the decision was made to deploy the 8th Marine Brigade to Sevastopol from Novorossiysk.

One of the rarely-discussed infantry units at Sevastopol, one that played a prominent role throughout the Second Defence, was the Regional (Guards) Infantry Regiment 1 of the Black Sea Fleet, commanded by Lieutenant-Colonel Baranov. After the Civil War, during the 1920s and 1930s, the protection of the Soviet coastline was assigned to regional infantry regiments, sometimes called

'Guards Regiments'. They were organised into separate guard battalions and companies and their task was the protection of naval bases and in some instances coastal defence. The men were well trained and well equipped with small arms, heavy machine guns and sub-machine guns, but had few mortars or artillery pieces. The regiment was composed of three battalions with a total of about 2,500 men. The 2nd and 3rd Battalions were placed in forward positions, next to 8th Marine Brigade. 2nd Battalion was at a barracks at Mamashai and the 3rd Battalion in the village of Mamashai.

The 8th Marine Brigade, commanded by Colonel V. L. Vilshansky, was formed on 10 September 1941 by order of the commander of the Black Sea Fleet. The brigade consisted of four battalions, plus a mortar and artillery battalion and a sapper platoon, totalling 4,300 men. The brigade was created to repel amphibious assaults and for the protection of the Novorossiysk naval base. It was deployed to Sevastopol in late October to early November.

On the evening of 29 October, a reconnaissance platoon and the 1st Rifle Company of 1st Battalion of 8th Marine Brigade arrived west of Aranci. The recon platoon sabotaged fuel tanks at the Kacha airfield while the rifle company built outposts at the Kacha River Bridge. The main forces of 1st Battalion moved out from the barracks at the Mekenzievy Mountain Station on 30 October. The 4th Battalion moved from the station at 2000 hours on 31 October and the 2nd Battalion at 0300 hours on 1 November. There is no information on the movement of 3rd Battalion. The order was sent out at 1600 hours on 1 November for the brigade to defend the Kara-Tau Plateau and Aranci strongpoint along a line stretching from Duvankoi–Azis-Oba–Efendikoy–Hill 36.5–Aranci village. The delay in deployment allowed the Germans to move in and capture positions near Azis-Oba and Koba-Djilga from the Guards Regiment. On the night of 1/2 November all four of 8th Brigade's battalions reached their advanced positions. The outposts of 3rd Battalion were on Hill 158.7 and Mount Azis-Oba. 2nd Battalion was unable to reach its advance position on Hill 103.4. They were engaged in a firefight with the Germans and entrenched at the Spring of Altyn-Bair and the slopes of Hill 165.4, north of the Kacha Valley.

Due to the delayed arrival of the 8th Brigade on the western outskirts of Duvankoi, the 19th Marine Battalion and an Air Force battalion, made up of airfield security troops, were deployed instead to Hill 103.4. The 8th Brigade was ordered to make contact with 19th Battalion. By the end of 2 November the forces near Duvankoi were reinforced by a battalion of the Joint Training School Detachment with three infantry companies and a machine-gun platoon.

The command situation was chaotic, as can be expected, especially on 30 and 31 October, but it soon began to straighten itself out. Some units had already started moving out to their assigned positions on 29 October, before the order was signed. That evening, the Cadets, having been ordered to 'fight the enemy to the last drop of blood', began the 35km trek to the front lines. Still, there was confusion. Morgunov's orders for the Guards Regiment, the Cadets, the 15th, 16th, 17th, 18th and 19th Battalions and the Danube Flotilla, were to move to Kacha–Kara-Tau–Duvankoi–Cherkez-Kerman. Zhukov, following Oktyabrsky's orders, deployed some troops to the Alma River. The Alma line ran from Alma-Tamak, along the river to Hanyshkoi (m. Otradnoye), then southeast in an arc to Mount Kazan-Tash to the location of 16th Battalion north of Bakhchisarai. Two battalions of the Electromechanical School and a battalion of the Joint School Training Detachment deployed along the Alma. By the morning of 31 October some of the defences were set up, however, the deployment was disorganised and some battalions were already fighting the Germans, some were surrounded and connections between units broken. The Alma defences quickly caved in.

On 31 October the Soviets were deployed as follows:

- 2nd Marine Regiment – Kamary–Chorgun–Shuli.
- 3rd Marine Regiment – Cherkez-Kerman–Zalankoi–Kefeli–Hill 142.4 (5km in front of Mount Azis-Oba).
- Guards Regiment with two battalions – Mount Azis-Oba–Aranci–Hill 42.7–Lighthouse mound southeast of Kacha. One battalion deployed in the Aranci Strongpoint and one battalion deployed in forward outposts. One company was placed at the mouth of the Alma River.
- Black Sea Fleet Training Detachment – two battalions and a company of the Guards Regiment – Cherkez-Eli–Tarhenlar–Burliuk–Alma Tamak.
- Cadets of the Military – Naval School of Coastal Defence (*Voenno-Morskoye Uchilische beregovoy oborony* – VMUBO) – one battalion with a 76mm battery to defend Towle–Mount Azis-Oba–Aranci.
- VMUBO Cadets – One battalion (commanded by Kostyshin) ordered to defend from Aranka to Towle.[5]

A battalion of the Naval College was ordered to move to the bank of the Alma near the railway station north of Bakhchisarai. They are shown in that position on Soviet situation maps, but in fact they never made it north of Bakhchisarai and instead dug in on the Kacha River to guard the railway and road crossings between Towle (m. Dachnoe) and Zaliznychne. It was an excellent position. 1st Company with four platoons, commanded by Captain Kompaniysta, was placed on twin hills on the right bank of the river between the railway and highway. The cadet battery with three 107mm mortars was located on the reverse slope of the hill. 3rd Company's four platoons, commanded by Major Demyanova, set up on the right bank of the river to the left of the railway. 2nd Company, with four platoons,

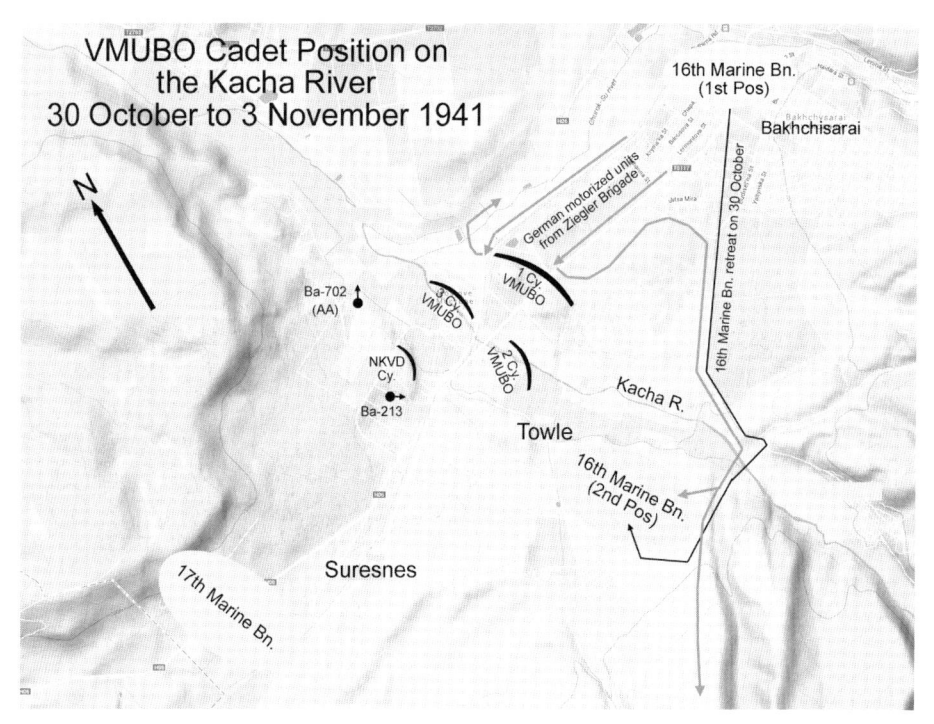

The defensive position of the Sevastopol Black Sea Fleet cadets (VMUBO). (© OpenStreetMap contributors, Author's collection)

commanded by Lieutenant-Colonel Kornychuka, was in the second line on the left bank behind 1st Company. The deployment left the road heading northwest to the Kacha Valley uncovered except for the 76mm guns of 217th AA Battery located above Aranka, but unfortunately the guns were located out of sight of the road and the Germans could slip past into the Kacha Valley.

On the morning of 31 October soldiers of the Ziegler Brigade, consisting of between 7,500 and 10,000 troops, plus StuG III assault guns and Rumanian R-1 tanks, were moving in three columns. The German plan was to avoid the main roads; to move with great speed on the right, closer to the Black Sea, stay out of the villages, get ahead of retreating Soviet forces and cut the roads and railways. They wanted to intercept and destroy the Coastal Army and Fifty-first Army between Simferopol and Bakhchisarai. The roads here were sandwiched between two mountain ranges. The narrow mountain roads were almost impassable for vehicles and equipment. The width of the planned intercept zone was about 7km wide and the Germans only needed 7,000 to 8,000 troops to do so.

The Rumanian 10th Rosioru Regiment moved at about 35–40kph and reached the vicinity of Battery 54 ahead of the 132nd Division Reconnaissance Battalion. This was on 30 October. They moved out of range of the battery along the road

The armoured train Ordzhonikidzevets *prior to its destruction and abandonment in October 1942.* (Nemenko Collection)

1.5km north of the Alma. This action blocked the Soviets from moving to Sevastopol via the Simferopol Highway. The 10th Rosioru took up defensive positions along the river Bodrak near Novopavlivka (m. Skalyste) and set up two 15cm batteries to block the road. Because of this, the Coastal Army units abandoned their advance towards Sevastopol and headed into the mountains. The Rumanian 6th Rosioru Regiment tried to move along the road that passed between the Alma and Kacha Rivers but met the Cadets of the training detachment guarding the bridge. In a brief battle the Rumanians captured the Alma River crossing near Burliuk (m. Vilino) and Hanyshkoy (m. Otradnoe) and held it until the arrival of the German 132nd Infantry Division.

The third column, made up mostly of German troops, moved along the Simferopol Highway. The column included 3rd Company of 46th Pioneer Battalion, the 190th Assault Gun Battalion, 6th Company of the 800th Brandenburg, a platoon of machine gunners of the 170th Infantry Division and the 22nd Motorised Reconnaissance Regiment. The column ran into the 16th Marine Battalion 4km before Bakhchisarai. The 16th Marines were dug in north of Bakhchisarai where they were joined by crews of two destroyed armoured trains, *Ordzhonikidzevets* and *Voykovets*.

Armoured Train *Zhelezniakov*

Three armoured trains were built by the workers of the Sevastopol Marine Plant – the *Sevastopolets*, *Ordzhonikidzevets* and *Zhelezniakov*.[6] *Zhelezniakov* was named for Anatoly Zhelezniakov, commander of armoured trains during the October Revolution and the Civil War. The history of the first two trains identified above is rather short and they were destroyed in the initial fighting for Crimea. The *Zhelezniakov* was completed on 4 November 1941. The train consisted of a powerful steam locomotive plus four wagons. It was assembled by the Marine Plant workers who most likely received the assistance of the crews of the destroyed armoured trains who had made their way to Sevastopol. The gun platforms were built using steel sheets strengthened by reinforced concrete. Three 76mm 34K guns and a 76mm Lender model AA gun were mounted on the armoured platform. The train was equipped with fifteen machine guns and eight mortars. It was a powerful cruiser that moved on land. Captain Sahakyan commanded the crew.

The first mission of the *Zhelezniakov* was to engage enemy infantry and artillery at Duvankoi on 7 November 1941 from the Kamyshly Ravine Bridge. The train survived only thanks to its speed and stealth capabilities. It moved fast, changed position often and remained hidden from German observers using tunnels and narrow ravines or cuttings through which the railway lines passed. It could move forward and in reverse. The Germans made numerous attempts to find the train, including the assignment of a dedicated spotter plane to keep a lookout and bombardment of the tracks by heavy artillery. The train was hit on several occasions but received only minor damage. The Germans gave it the nickname 'Green Ghost' because of its camouflage scheme. The *Zhelezniakov* continually changed its appearance. The sailors painted the wagons and locomotives with stripes and camouflage so that the train was indistinguishable from the terrain. In December Captain Sahakyan was seriously injured and replaced by Lieutenant Tchaikovsky, who had served on the *Ordzhonikidzevets*. Later it was commanded by an engineer, Captain M. F. Kharchenko.

The *Ordzhonikidzevets* and *Voykovet*s were retreating from Ishun. As they approached Kurman Kemelchi station (m. Krasnohvardiis'ke, 25km s. of Dzhankoi) they were attacked by German Ju 87 dive bombers and Rumanian troops from Ziegler Brigade and the *Ordzhonikidzevets* was heavily damaged. The crew removed the machine guns and 76mm ammunition, sabotaged the train and headed to Sarabuz (m. Ostriakovo) station. At Sarabuz they discovered the *Voykovets*, climbed aboard and headed to Alma Station, but the tracks leading to the station had been damaged. Both crews left the *Voykovets* and headed to the positions north of Bakhchisarai where they were later joined by the 16th Battalion. They expected the arrival of 15th and 17th Battalions but the battle with the Germans began before they arrived. The Germans attacked the Soviets with assault guns and aircraft and there were heavy losses on both sides. Around 1200 hours the marines broke and retreated in two groups. One group headed south with the train crews towards Sevastopol. The two right-flank companies moved into the mountains where they met up with the Coastal Army (they returned to Sevastopol eight days later).

The Germans now moved south through Bakhchisarai. Around 1730 hours the German 22nd Reconnaissance Battalion opened fire with artillery and mortars on the 1st Company of Cadets dug in along the Kacha River. Ten assault guns of the 190th Assault Gun Battalion appeared from the direction of Bakhchisarai and hit the cadet's trenches from 300–500m. The Cadets put up a strong defence on the two hills north of the river and the Germans were unable to capture them. The Germans tried to move northwest of the heights but came under fire from the 3rd Company of Cadets. The position was well supported by Soviet artillery – three 76mm guns, a mortar battery and Battery 701 at Duvankoi. The Cadets' refusal to budge from their position was the key factor in blocking the main road across the Kacha. The Germans were unable to move ahead; instead they moved down the undefended road to Kalymtay in the Kacha Valley. 17th Marine Battalion arrived in the area of the Cadets later in the day and 18th and 19th Battalions were now positioned behind the Cadets at Duvankoi.

Aranci Strongpoint – Kacha River

Construction began on Bunkers 1 and 2 in June 1941. Work was suspended when the troops were sent to work on the coastal defences. It resumed in August. Much of the work was done by men of the 7th Marine Brigade. Emphasis was placed on

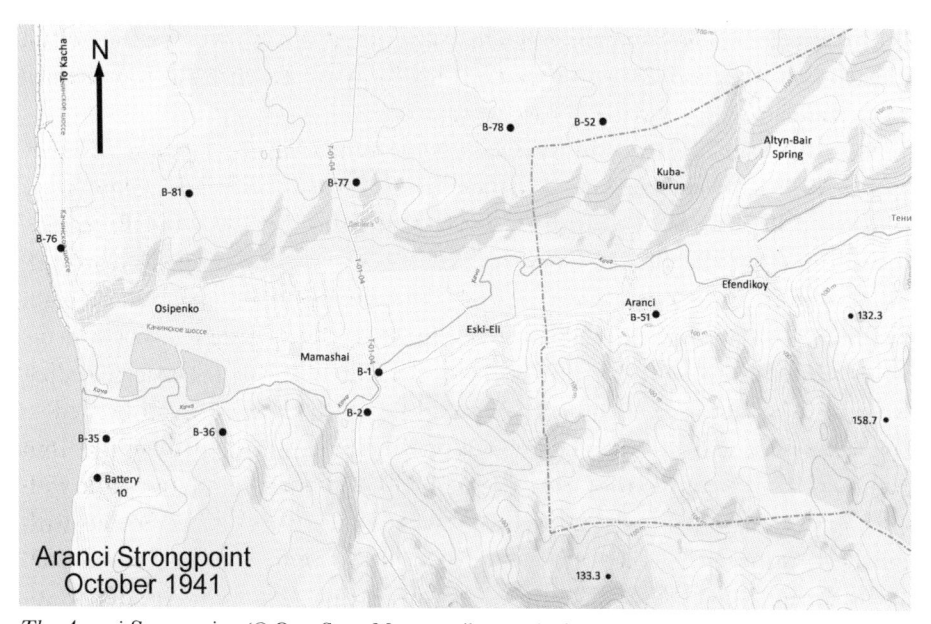

The Aranci Strongpoint. (© OpenStreetMap contributors, Author's collection)

control of the dominant heights overlooking the roads from Simferopol and Kacha to Sevastopol. Materials for forms and finishing pieces came from warehouses in Sevastopol. Concrete was mixed and poured at the construction locations. In mid-September the work crews were called to the Duvankoi and Cherkez-Kerman strongpoints and work at Aranci was suspended once again. By this time, Bunkers 1, 2, 35 and 36 were about 50 per cent complete. Work picked up again in October 1941. Bunkers 1, 2 and 36 received 45mm 21K guns. Bunkers 35 and 37 received 100mm B-24 submarine guns. Bunkers 51 and 52 blocked the Kacha River Valley. They received 45mm and 76mm guns from the VMUBO. After a visit by General Hrenov on 14 October, a new group of bunkers was built along the right bank of the Kacha River to bolster the defences on the heights of the left bank. Construction began on Bunkers 76, 77 and 78, which were armed with 130mm and 100mm guns.

The Aranci defences ran from the coast at a point about 700m in front of Bunker 76 (the line was later moved forward to Solnechny and Kara-Oba hill, Hill 76.4). A second line of defence was built at a later date by the men of the Guards Regiment and the 90th Regiment of 95th Rifle Division. It followed a line from Kara-Oba to the height of Kuba-Burun and the spring of Altyn Bair (1km northwest of Kuba-Burun). The line of defence consisted of outposts near Solnechny and Kara-Oba. Bunkers built by the 90th Rifle Regiment were located 500–800m behind the outpost line. The Aranci Strongpoint was not a continuous line, but small entrenched outposts located on hills and manned by platoon-sized units.

When the Germans attacked, Bunkers 1, 2, 37, 51, 52, 76, 77 and 78 were completed and armed, while Bunker 36 was unfinished and Bunker 35 had not yet received its gun. Work continued between the First and Second Assaults (20 November to 1 December) on Bunkers 76 and 77. A 130mm gun was recovered from the damaged destroyer *Besposhchadny* and mounted in a new Bunker 81. Most of the later construction work was done at night by crews of thirty to forty men from the 2nd Battalion of 7th Brigade.

Bunkers 77, 78 and 81 – it may be incorrect to call these 'bunkers' – were built for large-calibre 130mm naval guns and consisted of circular concrete platforms on which the guns were bolted down. They could fire in a 360-degree arc. Ammunition was stored in underground shelters below the platforms. There was no roof overhead. Bunker 76, located along the road in Kacha village about 300m from the sea, housed a 100mm B-24 gun, forming the left-most position of the Sevastopol line. The bunker's arc of fire was about 120 degrees and covered the Kacha Road. It was protected by two machine-gun emplacements 150–200m away and closer to the sea. Bunker 35 was completed in December 1941 and was built for the 100mm B-24 gun. It was 350m from the sea about 1.5km behind Bunker 76. It covered the Kacha River valley and blocked the approaches to Battery 10. The gun fired in an arc of 115 degrees. Bunker 36 also covered the approaches to

Bunker 1 for a 45mm anti-tank gun. (Nemenko Collection)

Battery 10. It was located on a hill overlooking the road to Belbek airfield and the bridge over the Kacha River. It was built for a 45mm 21K gun. Bunker 37 was similar to Bunkers 77 and 78: a flat concrete platform built for the 100mm B-24 gun.

The 45mm guns of Bunker 1 covered the Sevastopol–Eupatoria Road. It was located near the bridge over the Kacha River. It also covered the road running along the Kacha Valley through Eski-Eli in case of an enemy breakthrough past Bunker 52 at Aranci. Its arc of fire was 120 degrees and covered the direction of Mamashai, Kacha and Eski-Eli. The bunker was flat on the sides and curved along the front above the embrasure. It was smaller than other bunkers, measuring 4.5m x 3.5m. It was built in June and July 1941 and was damaged by the Germans during the First Assault, repaired then blown up after the Second Assault retreat.

Bunker 2 was located along the Sevastopol–Eupatoria Road, around the corner from Bunker 1 and looked out on the Kacha River Bridge. It provided coverage in case of a breakthrough along the road past Bunker 1. It covered the road from Kacha to Mamashai. It was originally planned as an anti-tank bunker for a 45mm gun. During the First Assault the bunker was hit by German artillery fire that passed through the embrasure and detonated ammunition inside. Between the First and Second Assaults it was repaired and used for a 75mm guns. The bunker played a major role in repelling the Second Assault in December. It was sabotaged by the Soviets when they withdrew from the position.

During the night of 1 November the German 437th Regiment continued to move down the Kacha Valley and up to the plateau of Kara-Tau. The 132nd Division and the motorised units of the Ziegler Brigade attacked so as to drive a wedge between the Guards Regiment and 8th Marine Brigade in the Kacha Valley and on the Kara-Tau plateau. Participating in the attack was a reconnaissance battalion of 50th Division, an anti-tank battalion of 22nd Division and three squadrons of Rumanian cavalry. During the night the 8th Marine Brigade and the Guards Regiment restored communications. The battalion of the Training School Detachment moved back from the Alma to the Kacha Valley and fell under command of the 8th Brigade. The battalion of the Combined Arms School was included in this group and was designated as 5th Battalion of 8th Brigade. The 8th Brigade now held the Duvankoi position but the left flank of the position was void of Soviet troops who had withdrawn to the Belbek Valley. The defenders remaining on the Kacha River were the Cadets, 16th and 17th Battalions and 8th Marine Brigade.

Kara-Tau Plateau

The plateau of Kara-Tau was 15km long and about 7km wide, located between the Kacha and Belbek River Valleys. The Kacha Road (from Kacha to Sevastopol) rose up below Orlivka near Bunker 2 and crossed over the western end of the plateau. Several unpaved roads ran up to the plateau from the small villages in the valley. There were no major fortifications on the forward edge of the plateau. The 7th Brigade started construction in August 1941 but it was abandoned when the brigade was redeployed. Five bunkers were built near Semirenko and ran across the plateau along the Zelinske Ravine, in a northwest to southeast direction. All of the fortifications on the plateau were field fortifications. Seven earth-timber[7] machine-gun nests ran across the flat plateau. A total of ten of these emplacements were built, plus a command post and mortar position near the village of Tenistoye. The defensive line of the 8th Brigade ran from Aranci along the heights of the village of Efendikoy (m. Aivove) where it turned southwest across the plateau to the opposite slope above the Belbek. The second line of defence ran along the Zelinske Ravine to Mount Azis-Oba. The defences continued along a line of small hills that were fought over in the coming weeks – Hills 165.4, 158.7 and 132.3.

The battle for the Kara-Tau plateau began at 0700 hours on 2 November. German troops proceeded along the road up to the plateau from the village of Golumbey (m. Nekrasovka). They quickly subdued two Soviet machine-gun emplacements and attacked the positions of 8th Marine Brigade. The Germans captured the height of the plateau above Duvankoi. A second force attacked along the Kacha River Valley. The 132nd Infantry Division attacked the area of

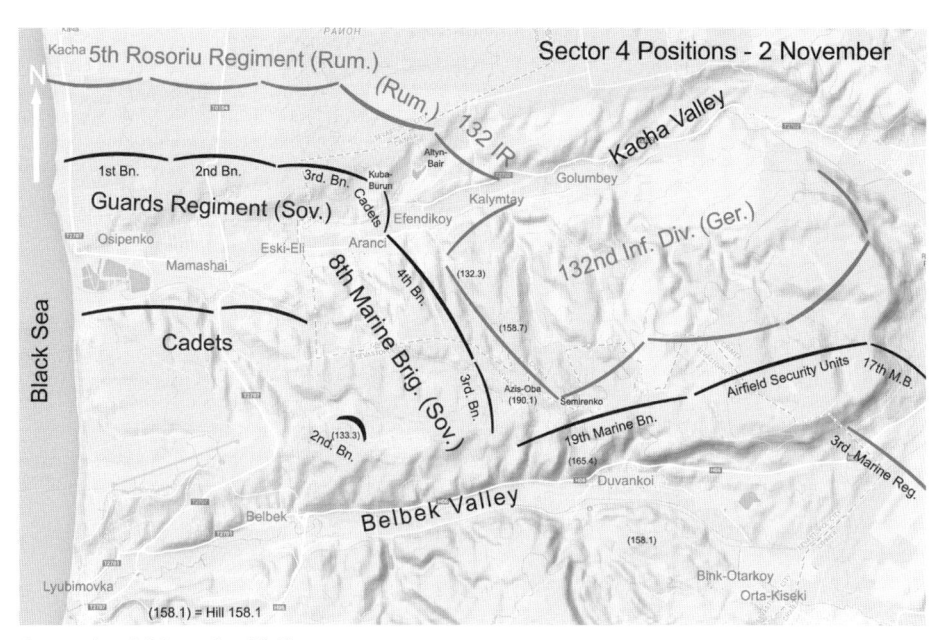

Sector 4 on 2 November 1941. (© OpenStreetMap contributors, Author's collection)

the Aranci strongpoint occupied by the Guards Regiment. Artillery support to Soviet troops was provided by the 203mm guns of Battery 10, mobile AA Battery 724 and Bunkers 51 and 52.[8] Support was provided by AA batteries 218, 227 and 453. In the evening the German attacks were stopped but they had set up artillery and mortar batteries on the Kara-Tau plateau to fire on the Duvankoi strongpoint.

Further to the north, the 54th Coastal Battery was still holding out against attacks by the 438th Infantry Regiment. The battery continued to be a danger to the German flank. It was well defended; an earthwork with guns placed in stone pits, with underground ammunition and personnel shelters, surrounded by a double row of barbed wire and several earth-timber bunkers. A dummy battery was set up nearby to draw enemy fire and it was shelled by three German field batteries and attacked from the air. The 438th Infantry Regiment attacked from the west and southwest. Squads of assault troops attacked the false position defended by a platoon of gunners and two platoons of the 321st Rifle Division armed with three heavy machine guns. The battle for the dummy battery lasted for two hours, but on the third assault the position was captured. Immediately realising their mistake, the attackers launched a heavy artillery bombardment and at 1600 hours attacked the actual battery. The fighting was brutal and the Soviets held the trenches surrounding the battery. They were finally driven out as darkness approached and managed to escape to the coast where some survivors were picked up by a Soviet

Bunker 52 for 45mm and 76mm guns. (Nemenko Collection)

minesweeper. Lieutenant Zaika escaped to a nearby village and later joined the partisans.

On Monday, 3 November Vice-Admiral Levchenko, Commander of the Crimean Front, Lieutenant-General Batov, commander of the Fifty-first Army, along with the commander of the Coastal Army Major-General Petrov and his staff arrived in Balaklava harbour. Army Headquarters was set up in the Chersoneses barracks near the 12th and 13th Royal Batteries. Vice-Admiral Oktyabrsky persuaded Admiral Levchenko to appoint General Petrov to command the defences of the city. General Morgunov and Zhukov commanded the coastal and base defences.

Boris Voyetkhov, a writer and journalist, spent the final month of the Second Defence in Sevastopol. He wrote a book about his experiences, *The Last Days of Sevastopol*, set in June 1942. The following is a description of The Admiralty Headquarters. It is easy to imagine the HQ as the same frenzied place in November 1941:[9]

> HQ was located on the south shore in a tunnel. The entrance opened on to the face of a cliff and was camouflaged with a projecting concrete barricade. Inside was the nerve centre of the defence. The narrow reception room for General Petrov was clean and orderly. A table was crowded with telephones; and adjutants, impeccably dressed, relayed messages. The room was filled with high-ranking officers, some bandaged from wounds suffered at the front. Each commander was accompanied by a political commissar who followed them every step of the way. These men were calm and reflective. The place was full of

tension and excitement. Men who were present at the Sevastopol headquarters say it reminded them of the Smolny [taken over by the Petrograd Soviet in 1917 as HQ of the Bolshevik Revolution. From there Lenin directed the uprising.] in Petrograd in 1918, during the October revolution. Narrow corridors with arched ceilings led deep into the rock. Dim, battery-supplied electric lamps provided the only light. The men slept in three-tiered bunks. Telephone conversations, radios, the rattle of typewriters, voices of switchboard operators and the screams of the wounded could be heard. The largest chamber had its own telephone system, radio stations, diesel engines, a well and a drainage system, restaurant, barber shop and other services.

The Coastal Army was not far behind General Petrov. In the morning the 95th Rifle Division passed by Biya-Salah (m. Verkhorichchya) on the Kacha River about 10km southeast of Bakhchisarai. They were followed by the 25th Chapaevsky Division.[10] The 25th covered the retreat of 388th Regiment of 172nd Division. The 51st Rifle Regiment of the 172nd Rifle Division, commanded by Lieutenant-Colonel Ustinov, the 2nd Perekop Regiment, commanded by Major Kulagin, the 80th Reconnaissance Battalion commanded by Captain Antipolv and a number of smaller units also arrived.

Meanwhile, on the forward line, the Cadets and the 16th and 17th Battalions continued to hold out along the Kacha. Later in the day the Germans were on the verge of surrounding them and they pulled back to Suresnes (m. Tankove) and then into the Belbek Valley towards Duvankoi.

German artillery and mortar fire pounded the Duvankoi strongpoint. This was followed up by German attempts to break through to the Belbek Valley. They were stopped by the 130mm gun of Bunker 60, anti-aircraft battery fire and three machine-gun bunkers on the outskirts of the villages of Bink-Otarkoy (m. Frontove) and Orta-Kiseki (a few hundred metres southeast of Bink-Otarkoy). The 217th Battery of 62nd AA Regiment held a dominant position overlooking the Simferopol-Sevastopol road at present-day Frontove. A German StuG III appeared on the road and the battery opened fire. Infantry arrived and the Germans counter-attacked with artillery and mortar support. The Germans were stopped from advancing down the road for the remainder of the night. The battery covered the retreat of the 3rd Marine Regiment from the Duvankoi Strongpoint.

Duvankoi Strongpoint

The Duvankoi strongpoint was the largest of the strongpoints built around Sevastopol and played an important role in holding up the Germans during the First Assault. It was built to cover the approaches to the Belbek Valley and

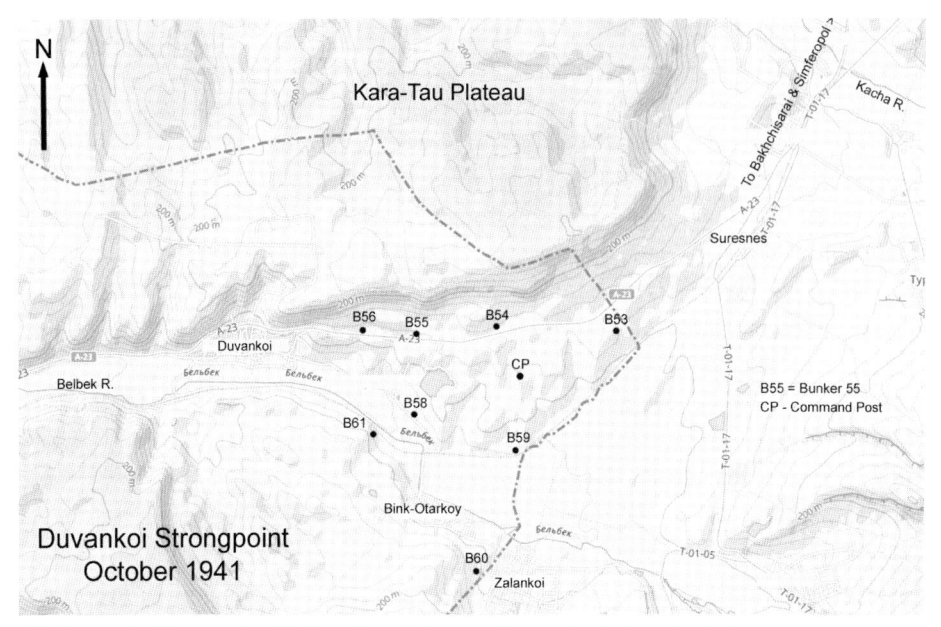

The Duvankoi Strongpoint. (© OpenStreetMap contributors, Author's collection)

positioned in advance of the village of Duvankoi (m. Verkhnesadovoye). It included nine artillery bunkers equipped with guns from the coastal defence schools. Two of the 130mm bunkers were open platforms, two for 100mm B24 guns, four 45mm and one 45mm gun in an open platform. The position did not have any anti-aircraft protection nor did it have a sufficient number of machine-gun or infantry emplacements. The bunkers were placed primarily along the Duvankoi–Zalankoy Road in the south and along the Simferopol – Sevastopol road below the Kara-Tau plateau in the north.

The bunkers in the Duvankoi strongpoint were built in the same manner as the artillery bunkers at Aranci, using a steel framework. The concrete floor was poured and a steel mesh embedded. Forms were placed around the mesh and the concrete walls were poured. Finally the roof was poured on top. Only six machine-gun emplacements covered the entire position. Two anti-tank ditches were built across the two main roads and were interspersed with anti-tank obstacles and fire curtains. Infantry trenches were shallow and located mostly to the rear of the main defences.

On the evening of 3 November the German 50th Infantry Division was moving towards the Belbek Valley; 132nd Division was moving on the Kara-Tau plateau attempting to break into the valley from above. The Duvankoi strongpoint's defences were starting to collapse but the Germans were unable to complete the breakthrough. During the night of 3 to 4 November the 16th and 17th Battalions and the Cadet battalions were withdrawn and ordered to support 3rd Regiment at Bink-Otarkoy and Cherkez-Kerman. All attacks on the Aranci strongpoint by parts of the 132nd Division and the Ziegler Brigade were repulsed.

The Germans were looking for other weaknesses in the defences and attacked the villages of Kacha and Aji-Bulat (Uhlove) in the direction of Mamashai. This area was held by the Guards Regiment and the Cadet Training Detachment under Colonel Kasilova. The Germans, supported by Rumanian armoured vehicles, attacked the 4th Battalion of 8th Marine Brigade. The attack was focused on the junction between the Guards Regiment and left flank of 8th Marine Brigade. Coastal Battery 10 and AA Batteries 724 and 227 continued a relentless fire and the German attack halted. The Germans shifted their attack to the 3rd Battalion in the centre which was holding a position on Hill 158.7, 1.5km southeast of Efendikoy. Colonel Vilshansky, 8th Marine Brigade commander, attempted to restore the position and organised a counter-attack by 8th and 11th Machine Gun Companies of 3rd Battalion and 2nd Company of 5th Battalion. After a 15-minute artillery barrage the Marines launched the attack and reached the southwest slopes of Hill 158.7. In the evening, two German columns supported by armoured vehicles launched another attack on the position but they were again driven back. In the process Bunker 52 was attacked, killing most of the occupants and damaging the 37mm gun. The gun was repaired during the night and resumed firing.

On 4 November the Sevastopol Defence Area[11] was established by order of Vice-Admiral Levchenko. It was to be defended by the Coastal Army, coastal defence forces of the Black Sea Fleet base and all sea and land units of the Black Sea Fleet. All actions of the ground troops and the defence of Sevastopol were delegated to the Commander of the Coastal Army, Major-General I. E. Petrov. The Deputy Commander of the Black Sea Fleet, Rear-Admiral G. Zhukov, was ordered to take command of the main base of Sevastopol. On the morning of 4 November Generals Petrov and Morgunov toured the defence sectors, familiarising themselves with the positions and composition of the defending units, as well as the status of communications between the infantry units and the coastal batteries and air and artillery support. They also reviewed the terrain and defensive preparations.

Around 1430 hours the Germans attempted to break through the Duvankoi strongpoint at the position held by 3rd Marine Regiment, the right flank regiments of 8th Marine Brigade and a small unit of Air Force defence troops. 17th Marine Battalion moved into the Duvankoi area and was ordered to counter-attack with 3rd Marine Regiment. The forward bunkers in the Duvankoi strongpoint continued to fire but had no infantry support and it was impossible to resupply them with ammunition. The Germans moved past the bunker and down the railway line into the Belbek Valley. The Duvankoi bunkers continued to fight but they could not hold out without infantry support and the strongpoint was near collapse. The

3rd Marine Regiment retreated to the line of Orta-Kiseki–Bink–Otarkoy (m. Frontove). The 19th Marine Battalion also fell back.

Bunker 53 covered the ground between the Simferopol to Sevastopol road and the railway, southwest of Suresnes. The bunker, actually an open platform for a shielded gun, was located 1.5km from Suresnes rail station on the Simferopol line. Originally it was to be equipped with a 45mm anti-tank gun but ended up with a 102mm B-2. The bunker was built on a hill between the railway and the road, but it was too far forward to receive mutual protection from the other bunkers at Duvankoi. Otherwise it was in a prime location and covered the roads and railway leading into the Belbek Valley. It covered the Suresnes railway station and the bridge over the Kacha River further to the north. Several pre-cast concrete bunkers were located nearby. Bunker 53 was built in the shape of an isosceles triangle with rounded corners to deflect shots.

Bunker 54 was located about 2km behind Bunker 53 on a hillside about 30m north of the Simferopol-Sevastopol Highway. It was built for a 45mm anti-tank gun to defend against tanks approaching along the highway. A machine-gun bunker was located nearby. The front of the bunker was built at a 45-degree angle to the road. It had an arc of fire of 100 degrees, allowing it to cover the valley and the adjacent machine-gun position. It was 4.5m x 4.5m and rails were used to support the concrete roof. The bunker was heavily damaged during the assault.

Bunker 55 was located 1.5km behind Bunker 54, also on the north side of the road. It was equipped with a 100mm B-24 gun, therefore it was a circular gun platform without a roof. A hill rose up behind the bunker so, even though it could revolve 360 degrees, its actual arc of fire was about 270 degrees. The gun's two magazines were built underneath the gun platform, while ready-use niches in the side of the parapet could hold approximately sixty shells. 50m from the bunker was an anti-tank ditch and a pre-cast concrete machine-gun bunker was across the road. This bunker was manned by the 80th Reconnaissance Battalion. On 7 November 1941 the pre-cast bunker was hit and destroyed by a German 75mm gun.

Bunker 56 was also an open platform for a 100mm B-24 gun. It was located on the north side of the highway. Its angle of fire was 110 degrees and it covered the highway and the valley. Bunkers 57 and 58 were built behind Bunker 56 and covered the road from Zalankoy (m. Holmovka) and the road and rail bridge over the Belbek River. Bunker 57 was built for a 100mm B-24, Bunker 58 housed a 45mm gun and Bunker 59 was built for a 130mm gun. It had an open platform with a diameter of 8.4m and two magazines which had exits leading to a trench surrounding the bunker. Bunker 60 was a 130mm bunker located between the villages of Bink-Otarkoy and Zalankoy. The gun, combined with the 130mm gun of Bunker 59, covered the Belbek River Valley, the Zalankoy road and the Belbek bridges. The position was also protected by three pre-cast concrete bunkers.

Bunker 61 was a 45mm 21K bunker of the same design as Bunkers 54 and 58. It was located on a hillside above the railway line with an excellent vantage point over the valley and the Zalankoy Road and bridges.

The Duvankoi Command Post was a round machine-gun bunker with six embrasures. It was built of stone with cement mortar. Only the roof was entirely of concrete. It was located to the left of and on a hill overlooking Bunker 59. Field-gun pits were located in front of the bunker. Five machine-gun emplacements were in the vicinity but infantry protection was very weak.

All in all, the Duvankoi Strongpoint was equipped with powerful guns that provided a significant coverage of the roads and bridges along the Belbek Valley. As such it should have been a powerful obstacle to advancing German forces but the bunkers were too far apart and isolated to provide mutual support. This allowed the Germans to bypass the bunkers, cut them off and surround the crews, one by one, until they ran out of ammunition.

In the Kacha Valley the Germans attacked the village of Mamashai and the Aranci position. Batteries 10, 30 and 724 provided artillery support throughout the day and the attacks were repulsed. Towards the end of the day, however, superior German attacks were taking a heavy toll on the defenders. Soviet counter-attacks, a determined and stubborn defence and relentless Soviet artillery fire was also taking its toll on German and Rumanian troops.

On the morning of 5 November the Germans attacked Duvankoi with two regiments supported by twelve armoured vehicles. 1st and 3rd Battalions of 3rd Marine Regiment suffered heavy losses and withdrew to a line south of Duvankoi. About fifty men from the regiment dug in near Bunker 58. 18th Marine Battalion was positioned around Bunkers 55, 56 and 57 and prevented the Germans from crossing the anti-tank ditch. The machine-gun bunker covered the ditch. Bunker 55's gun ran out of ammunition but the gunners replaced it with a machine gun from a nearby bunker. Bunker 54 hit an armoured vehicle and three motorcycles and the Germans withdrew. Bunker 59's 130mm gun also continued to fire and damaged an armoured vehicle. The position was well defended with rifle trenches and dugouts. Bunker 59 was occupied by a crew of twelve gunners and four wounded marines. Two of the wounded were sent to get reinforcements but at that moment the Germans attacked the bunker, capturing the commander. A platoon of 3rd Marine Regiment then counter-attacked and the Germans scattered. During the battle for Duvankoi, Bunkers 53, 54, 60 and 61 were captured by the Germans. The garrison of Bunker 58 withdrew to Bunker 67.

Around 1530 hours 17th Battalion was ordered to move to Duvankoi and join up with 3rd Marine Regiment for a counter-attack. Major Zatylkina, commander of 3rd Marine Regiment, led the attack. Two flamethrower tanks, two armoured cars and 76mm guns towed by tractors were sent to support the counter-attack

64   The Defence of Sevastopol 1941–1942

which was successful and the German offensive against Duvankoi was temporarily stopped. After dismantling the guns of Bunkers 55, 56 and 57, 18th Marine Battalion dug in along the road south of Duvankoi to block the Belbek Valley.

On 6 November fighting continued on the outskirts of Duvankoi. Realising that the attempt to capture Sevastopol in a surprise attack had failed, the German command disbanded the Ziegler Brigade. The two Rumanian motorised regiments continued to act against the Aranci strongpoint. Only a small part of the Duvankoi Strongpoint remained in Soviet hands. By the end of the day the strongpoint was lost. Fighting had started the previous night at the Cherkez-Kerman Strongpoint when the Germans attempted to bypass the Duvankoi position.

Cherkez-Kerman (Circassian Fortress) Strongpoint

At one time the main road to Sevastopol (the Roman Road) passed through this area, past the medieval tower of *Kiz-Kul* (Maiden Tower) near the ancient town of *Eski-Kerman* (Old Fortress). A second route passed through Shuli (Ternivka) and the Valley of Kara-Koba. The Cherkez-Kerman strongpoint covered these roads with seven artillery and seven machine-gun bunkers. The main bunkers – 64, 65, 66, 67 and 68 – were located near the village of Shuli. Two bunkers, 62 and 63, were built to cover the road from Cherkez-Kerman village to Mackenzie Farm. Bunker 62 was equipped with a 45mm gun and Bunker 63 was an open position for a larger naval gun. These were completed in late October 1941.

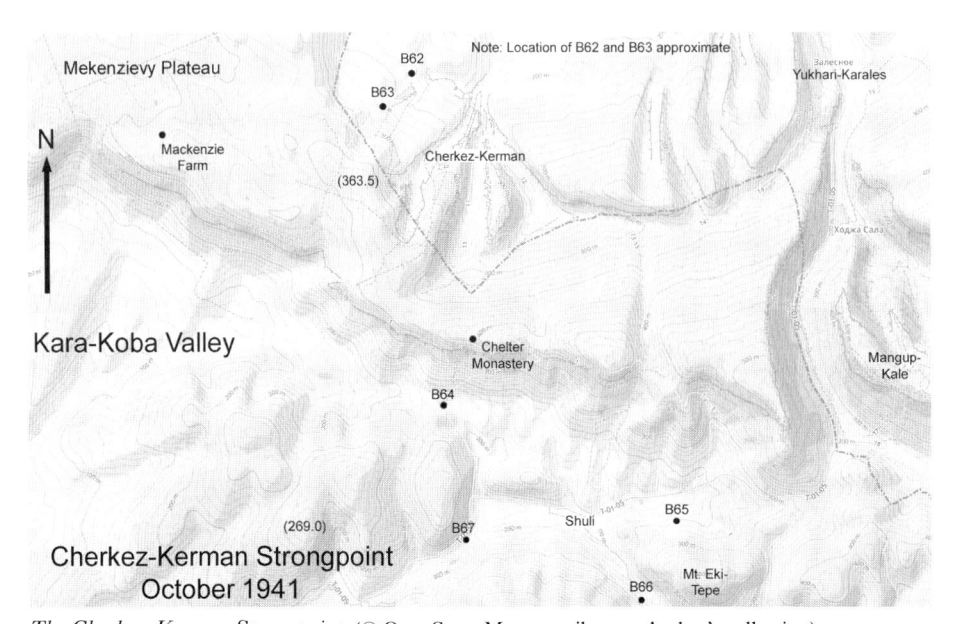

The Cherkez-Kerman Strongpoint. (© OpenStreetMap contributors, Author's collection)

The approach to Shuli on the modern road to Sevastopol came around a bend in the hill and the rapid-fire guns of the bunkers defending the road were waiting. The ancient road and the new road intersected at Shuli and the old road was covered on the east side of the village by Bunker 66. Here the road heads south towards Chorgun (Upper and Lower) and west towards the Kara-Koba and Inkerman Valleys. Bunker 64 blocked the road to Sevastopol through the Kara-Koba Valley. It was supported by two machine-gun positions. Bunker 67, with a 45mm gun, covered the road leading to Chorgun. It could fire along the valley towards Shuli and on troops heading into the Kara-Koba Valley. Its neighbour, Bunker 68, was further south to guard the road to Upper Chorgun. It was equipped with a 100mm B-24 gun. The guns that covered the Kara-Koba valley also covered anti-tank obstacles in the valley. Unfortunately there was not enough time set them up and most of them were just piled in the fields.

Bunker 65 was equipped with a 75mm gun. This bunker covered the road to Yukhari-Karaless (m. Zalisne) in the valley east of Cherkez-Kerman. It did not have any infantry protection nearby, such as machine-gun emplacements or trenches. Bunker 66's 45mm gun covered the road to the village Uppal, west of Shuli. Several infantry machine-gun positions surrounded the bunker.[12] Bunker 63 was designed for a 100mm B-24 gun. The gun platform was built into the hillside.

The German 50th Infantry Division now pushed on towards the village of Cherkez-Kerman, held by 2nd Battalion of 3rd Marine Regiment. The battalion

Bunker 65, built for a 75mm gun. (Nemenko Collection)

was forced to pull out of the village. In the afternoon 3rd Marine Regiment, having moved from the Duvankoi position, counter-attacked and captured Hill 363.5, 500m southwest of Cherkez-Kerman (near Eski-Kerman). 2nd Perekop Regiment, recently arrived from Ishun, Cadets from the Battalion Officer's School and 19th Marine Battalion all quickly rushed towards Cherkez-Kerman to block the threat of a German advance to Inkerman.

During the day the 31st Rifle Regiment and 25th Chapaevsky Division of the Coastal Army approached Sevastopol and concentrated in the vicinity of Hill 154.7, northwest of Upper Chorgun at the crossroads in the upper Kara-Koba valley. The 134th Howitzer Artillery Regiment was sent towards the Mackenzie Mountains.

At the same time the Germans appeared in the rear of 2nd Marine Regiment in the Karaless valley near the village of Yukhari-Karaless and moved on towards Shuli. The Germans had taken an old road from Suresnes to Kuchka. German motorcycle troops rushed past Mangoup Kale to Shuli but were stopped by gunfire from Bunker 64. The Germans bypassed the hill at the foot of Bunker 65, hoping to break into Shuli from the other side of the hill. There they ran into more gunfire from Bunker 66, armed with an old 57mm gun which proved to be very effective against the motorcyclists. Crews from the two bunkers prevented the Germans from breaking through to the villages of Uppal through Kuchka, 1.5km south of modern Ridne and reaching the highway through the Black River Valley.

The 50th Infantry Division, now with a three- to fourfold advantage in manpower, continued to batter their way through Cherkez-Kerman and the Mackenzie Plateau. The Germans had over 3,000 troops and ninety-two guns against about 1,000 Soviet troops with four field guns and the crews in Bunkers 62 and 63. The Germans attacked 2nd Battalion of 3rd Marine Regiment with 450 men and broke through on the old road to seize Mackenzie Farm.[13] Passing by the farm, a German battalion moved along a forest road that hugged the edge of the cliff and led into the Kara-Koba Valley. Three companies attempted to advance into the valley towards the Black River and ran into three platoons of the 54th NKVD Battalion troops from Novo Shuli, supported by 2nd Marine Regiment and 31st Rifle Regiment, which stopped the German attack.

By 1900 hours Coastal Army troops arrived at Tashlyk (Hill 363.5) and the Germans were driven back. 3rd Marine Regiment troops were unable to push the Germans away from Mackenzie Farm. The farm was a strategic location. A Soviet battery was located there to cover the road and there was a second road leading from the farm to the Martynov Ravine which led to Inkerman and the bay. The Germans had to be stopped before they reached the farm.

The First Assault – October to November 1941

Bunker 67, originally built for a 45mm anti-tank gun. Its armament appears to have been replaced with a German gun. (Nemenko Collection)

Later in the evening Bunker 66 was left without infantry cover. German pioneers moved towards it and threw grenades into the embrasure. The ammunition stored inside exploded, destroying the bunker and killing the occupants. Bunker 65 was hit by German heavy guns that fired point-blank into the rear entrance, again setting off the ammunition inside and destroying the bunker. The Germans got past Bunker 65 and now expected to have an open path to Shuli, but as they approached the village they were hit by fire from Bunkers 67 and 68 and forced to retreat. However, the destruction of Bunker 66 opened the road to the village of Upper Chorgun and the Chorgun Strongpoint. Due to the withdrawal of Soviet troops into the Kara-Koba Valley, the Germans advanced to the southeast of Shuli and concentrated for an advance to Uppal, Uzenbash and Ai-Todor. The Germans entrenched for the night in a field near Shuli. The temperature dropped and it started to rain. During the night Soviet engineers brought tools up to Bunker 67 and widened the embrasure to allow the gun to cover the entire valley.

The 1330th Rifle Regiment of 421st Infantry Division, the 7th Marine Brigade and a battalion of the 172nd Infantry Division reached Yalta. General Petrov ordered the Mortar Regiment of the 7th Marine Brigade to be brought immediately to Sevastopol by truck. The rest of the brigade would be transferred by sea. The destroyers *Boykiy* ('Courageous') and *Bezuprechnyy* ('Flawless') were ready at the Yalta docks.

On 6 November the medical staff of eleven Black Sea Fleet hospitals, mostly nurses, was evacuated from Sevastopol. Their ship, the transport *Armenia*, left Sevastopol on 6 November at 0025 hours, headed towards Yalta. It was a five-hour trip at 10 knots. It would take three hours to load supplies at Yalta before heading to the Caucasus. Those supplies included personal belongings of the Black Sea Fleet staff. The *Armenia* had to wait at anchor for the loading of the two destroyers. It took until 0518 hours for the destroyers to load up and move out, leaving space for the *Armenia* to dock. She was loaded up by 0800 hours. The destroyers had taken the guns from 17th Anti-aircraft Regiment. These were all of the AA guns that protected Yalta harbour, now defenceless against air attack. Petrov states that he ordered the ship to wait until it was safe to sail, but waiting at the port was suicidal so the captain was forced to set sail. German troops were already on the outskirts of Yalta so time was of the essence. But when the ship was out at sea she was bombed and sunk, all but eight of the 5,000 people on board being drowned.

This was of course a tragedy, but it was made worse by Stalin's directive of 7 November, reversing the order to evacuate Sevastopol and instead ordering its defence. The directive read as follows, although only points 1 and 2 are relevant:

DIRECTIVE Stavka number 004433 Commander of the Crimea, the Black Sea Fleet on measures to strengthen the defence of the Crimea, November 7, 1941 02 h 00 min

In order to tie down the enemy forces in the Crimea and the Caucasus and to prevent him from moving through the Taman Peninsula GHQ orders:

1. BSF to conduct an active defence of Sevastopol and Kerch Peninsula.
2. Sevastopol to be defended at all costs.

Thus, the stage was now set for the all-out defence of Sevastopol – The Second Defence.

In the morning of 7 November, after a brief artillery barrage by coastal Batteries 10 and 724 and a battery of the 265th Artillery Regiment, the 8th Marine Brigade counter-attacked to capture Hills 165.4 (on the slopes above Duvankoi), 158.1 and 132.3. These three hills were located to the rear of the Duvankoi strongpoint, the first two north of the Belbek River, 132.3 about 3km to the northeast of the village of Duvankoi. This offensive was successful in improving the brigade's position due to the capture of the commanding heights. The armoured train *Zhelezniakov* supported the counter-attack. The train suppressed German artillery fire and 8th Brigade's 4th Battalion attacked Hill 158.1, quickly capturing the trenches on the western slope. 3rd Battalion captured the trenches on the southwest slope. By 1000 hours the hill was cleared of Germans. 2nd Battalion attacked Hill 165.4 and the Germans fled. A platoon from 2nd Battalion captured Hill 132.3, but a German counter-attack recaptured Hill 165.4. The Germans suffered heavy casualties and the Soviets captured three guns, ten mortars and twenty machine guns, plus rifles and ammunition.

Battery 10 played a dual role in the Second Defence. First of all as a powerful Soviet offensive weapon in the early days of the battle that continually harassed German troops in the vicinity of Kacha and later as a German battery that became a thorn in the side of the Soviets. The battery was unique among the Sevastopol coastal batteries, being one of the first batteries built under the Soviet regime but used components of the pre-revolutionary batteries. Construction began in 1925 and completed in 1927. It was equipped with four 203mm naval guns removed from the battleship *Evstafi*. The rangefinder was also taken from the battleship. The guns were installed in four emplacements and each gun had its own magazine. The shells were moved from the cellars to the guns along a 50cm railway track. The battery had a rangefinder position and a two-story command and observation post.

In 1939, anti-aircraft Battery 80 was built near Battery 10 and was armed with four 76.2mm guns. The battery was part of the 1st Coastal Defence Artillery Battalion and played a role in the First and Second Assaults. After the Second Assault the 80th AA Battery was moved to the south and Battery 10 was covered only by the 218th Anti-Aircraft Battery. This gave the Germans the opportunity to launch air raids on Battery 10, which, on 17 December, destroyed three of the battery's guns. The battery fought on with the last gun until 22 December. On that date it was decided to withdraw to a new line of defence. This meant the end of Battery 10. All of the guns were blown up and the crews moved to Sevastopol.

It was raining on the morning of 8 November. The roads were covered with mud and some had washed away from the rains. The Soviets attempted to recapture Mackenzie Farm. In the early morning Generals Petrov and Morgunov rode up to the Mekenzievy Mountains where the right column of 7th Marine Brigade was arriving from Yalta. At 0930 hours General Petrov ordered the brigade to attack Mackenzie Farm with two battalions and restore the former position of 3rd Marine Regiment and to seize Hill 200.3, Cherkez-Kerman village and the heights 1km north of the village – a very tall order. The counter-attack was preceded by an artillery barrage. The 4th Battalion of 3rd Marine Regiment moved up to the front line and stopped at a fork in the road near Hill 248, between the head of the Kamyshly and Martynov Ravines. 3rd Battalion was 800m behind the 4th and continued up to Hill 137.5 west of Mackenzie Farm. The Germans had positioned a machine-gun battery on the hill. At 1200 hours the 7th Brigade led the attack on the hill. The artillery preparation was weak due to lack of ammunition and the two battalions were met with heavy artillery and mortar fire and had to wait for more Soviet troops and mortars. At 1500 hours a second attack was made, this time supported by Batteries 30 and 35, the 264th Artillery Regiment and the guns of the *Chervona Ukraina* which was docked in Sevastopol harbour. The second attack succeeded in capturing Hill 137.5 which was given the name 'Machine Gun Hill'.

At 0200 hours on Sunday, 9 November, the order was given to streamline the command and control of the original defensive sectors of Sevastopol. It divided Sevastopol into four sectors, radiating out from the city.

- Sector 1 was commanded by Major-General Petr G. Novikov and the boundary line ran as follows: Right – Black Sea Coast. Left – on the southeastern tip of Sevastopol, through Sapun Ridge, then to the east of the Grace Farm (m. Blagodatnoye) through Hills 440.8 and 555.3 (Mount Tubac). The command post was located at the Maximova Farm near the English Cemetery (Cathcart's Hill).
- Sector 2 was commanded by Colonel Ivan Laskin, commander of the 172nd Infantry Division, and the boundary line ran as follows: Right – the dividing line with the first sector. Left – the southeastern extremity of the North Bay, through the heights above Gypsy ravine (119.9) to the southwest of Cherkez-Kerman. The command post was located in the Victoria Redoubt.
- Sector 3 was commanded by Major-General Trofim K. Kolomiets, commander of the 25th Chapaevsky Division. The boundary line ran as follows: Right – the dividing line with the second sector. Left – Mekenzievy Mountain Station to Qamishli and the Belbek Valley to Bink-Otarkoy. The command post was located 1.5km southeast of Mekenzievy Mountain Station.
- Sector 4 was commanded by Major-General V. F. Vorobiev and the boundaries ran as follows: Right – the dividing line with the third sector, Left – the Black Sea coast. The sector command post was located southeast of the village of Lyubimovka.

The command structure of Sevastopol was also reorganised. The Black Sea Fleet commander, Vice-Admiral Oktyabrsky, was given command of the overall defence. On the same day, Oktyabrsky published his own order regarding the defence and organisation of the city. Command of the army was delegated to Major-General Petrov.

On the morning of 9 November, units of 8th Brigade continued to fight for Hill 158.7 on the plateau of Kara-Tau. The battle lasted throughout the day. 7th Brigade fought on the other side of the Belbek Valley on Mekenzievy Plateau. During the night, 7th Brigade scouts sent a patrol to Cherkez-Kerman to observe the movement of German troops and to plot out the location of the German mortar and gun positions. Two battalions were chosen to attack at dawn to retake

Mackenzie Farm. The 7th Brigade waited for reinforcements to arrive as two of the battalions had suffered heavy losses. The 4th Battalion and divisional artillery brigade arrived and at 0640 hours the gunners opened fire on the Germans who returned fire with rocket artillery. Each side poured artillery and rifle fire into each other, forcing the soldiers to hug the ground, but the Germans held their position.

Further north the German 132nd Infantry Division attempted to break through between 8th Marine Brigade and 18th Battalion on the northern slopes of the Belbek Valley. The two Soviet units, with support from 227th AA Battery and 2nd Battalion of 265th Corps Artillery Regiment of the Coastal Army, repulsed the initial German attack. During the battle, 18th Battalion lost 30 per cent of its men and during a subsequent attack two German battalions broke through, pushing 18th Battalion back to the Belbek River. The Germans moved down into the valley towards Duvankoi where they were stopped at Bunker 4.

This 45mm anti-tank gun bunker was built in September 1941. It was located on the Sevastopol-Simferopol Highway about 2km from Belbek village. It was oriented thirty degrees with respect to the road to cover the road and the railway along the valley from Belbek to Kamyshly Ravine. It also covered the bridge over the river on a side road that led to the south side of the valley and into the ravine. It was originally equipped with a 45mm gun. Bunker 4 was blown up in November 1941 during the German breakthrough into the valley, but it was rebuilt and armed

Soviet 76.2mm Lender anti-aircraft gun. (Nemenko Collection)

with a 76.2mm Lender gun. It was pentagonal in shape with a curved embrasure and measured 7m x 8m. During the Second Assault Bunker 4 was badly damaged by artillery fire and blown up by retreating Soviet troops.

A platoon of reinforcements from 8th Marine Brigade was brought in by truck. A reserve artillery regiment was brought in by rail and was immediately attacked as the gunners disembarked. The fighting went on into the night but the German advance in the Belbek Valley was eventually stopped. The 18th Battalion lost nearly all of its men.

German attacks continued on all fronts, including Cherkez-Kerman. All of the defences at Cherkez-Kerman were captured, including Mackenzie Farm and Bunkers 62, 63, 64, 65 and 66. The Germans now approached the Chorgun Strongpoint which was much better prepared than the others. The Germans delayed the attack on Chorgun, which allowed improvements to the defences to be completed.

Chorgun Strongpoint

The Chorgun Strongpoint was centred on the villages of Upper and Lower Chorgun through which runs the Black River. The Black River Valley runs into Sevastopol Bay and the river flowed past and was guarded by Hills 90.5 and 154.7. The main purpose of the strongpoint was to guard the road from Shuli

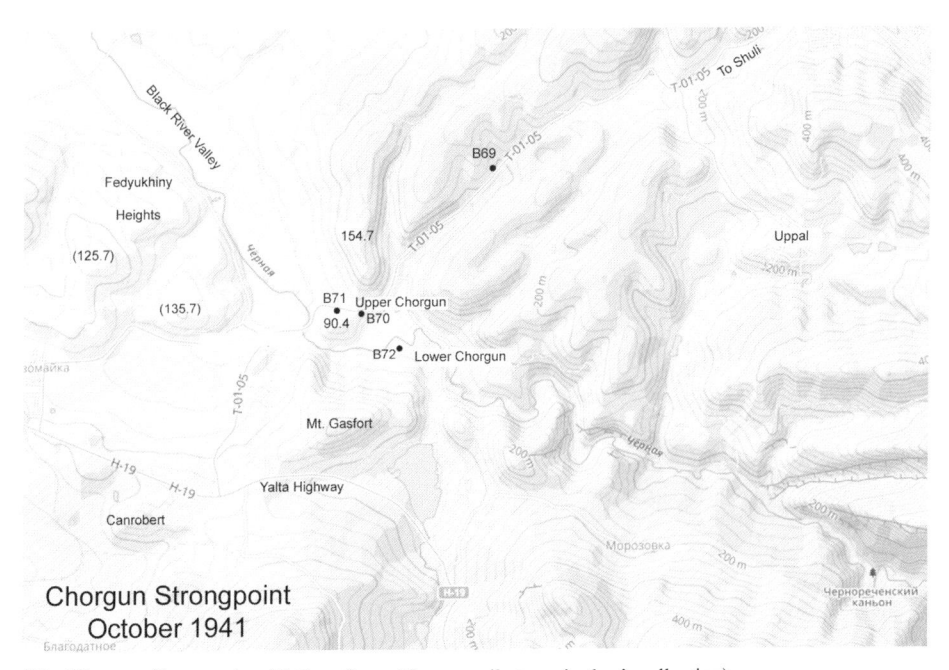

The Chorgun Strongpoint. (© OpenStreetMap contributors, Author's collection)

to Sevastopol and also block access to the Yalta Highway. The defences included six artillery bunkers – 69, 70, 71, 72, 73 and 74. Bunkers 69 and 72 were open platforms built for the 100mm B-24PL, 73 and 74 for the 100mm B-24M and the other bunkers for 45mm 21K anti-tank guns. Due to the lay of the land the coastal guns could not reach the Chorgun Strongpoint. Several machine-gun bunkers were built to defend against enemy infantry. The entrance to the Black River Valley below Mount Telegraph was blocked by dragon's teeth anti-tank obstacles.

Bunker 69 was located along the Shuli-Sevastopol road. It was armed with a 100mm B-24 gun from the submarine *S-37*. The bunker's embrasure was perpendicular to the road to reduce its vulnerability to enemy troops approaching from Shuli. It was originally intended to face to the east but the cost of cutting into the rock was too much so it was moved to the east side of the road to face west. To the rear of the bunker was a deep valley with a stream. Two machine-gun emplacements guarded against an attack from this valley. Another machine gun was placed on a hill above the road. Bunker 69 and other bunkers in the Chorgun Strongpoint were equipped with an additional ammunition niche, most likely to stock extra shells due to the distance from the storage warehouses. The concrete was reinforced with steel rails from the former Sevastopol-Balaklava railway. Its field of fire was about 150 degrees. The bunker had two steel and wood doors and the floor was made of wood. Camouflage nets were placed over top.

Just beyond the bunker was the village of Upper Chorgun where the road split towards Lower Chorgun, Alsou and the Baydar valley. Bunkers 70 and 71 covered this road. Both were armed with 45mm anti-tank guns. Bunker 70 had a 110-degree arc of fire, allowing it to guard the road from Shuli and Kuchki as well as the Black River valley. Bunkers 70, 71 and 72 were defended against infantry attack by two pre-cast concrete machine-gun bunkers, one on a hill above Bunkers 70 and 71, the other below Bunker 70. Bunker 72 was located on a hillside where the slopes of Mount Gasfort and the Black River Valley meet. The arc of fire was 120 degrees, allowing the gun to fire along the entire valley and all the roads that passed through it. The bunker was 9m x 8.5m, one of the largest. It was equipped with a 100mm B-24 gun. The bunker was constructed with different materials than other bunkers at Chorgun, indicating it was probably built during a different period.[14] It was supported by two earth-timber machine-gun bunkers.

Bunker 73 was located at the foot of Mount Gasfort at the exit to the dirt road that runs from the top of the mountain to Lower Chorgun. Bunker 74 covered the Yalta Road near Kamary and blocked the Black River Valley. These two bunkers were open platforms for 100mm B-24 naval guns. Three pre-cast machine-gun bunkers were built in this area.

The intention of the First Assault was to quickly break through the outer defences and capture Sevastopol before the Soviets retreating from the north had time to reach it. However, by 10 November, Soviet resistance, thrown together to block the advance at strategic points, succeeded in ending any hopes of achieving that goal and set the scene for the carnage that was to follow.

Only minor skirmishes took place on 10 November in the area of Shuli, Upper Chorgun, Cherkez-Kerman and the Mackenzie Farm. One reason for the pause in the action was the arrival of and consolidation of additional German and Rumanian forces. By the end of the day Eleventh Army was concentrating four divisions (the 22nd, 50th, 72nd and 132nd) as well as the Rumanian Motorised Brigade, fifteen artillery battalions, assault guns (StuG III) and close to 350 aircraft, to break the defences of Sevastopol.

The next phase of the plan was to strike in the south in the direction of Varnutka, a few kilometres from the southern Black Sea coast west of Yalta and then to move along the Yalta highway to Balaklava. This task was assigned to 72nd Infantry Division. A secondary attack by 50th Infantry Division and the 118th Motorised Detachment with twenty assault guns was planned to take place at the junction of Sector 2 and 3 between the Mackenzie Farm and the Kara-Koba Valley in the direction of Sevastopol Bay.

There was no armistice[15] at Sevastopol on the morning of 11 November 1941. The Germans returned to the offensive and attacked 40th Cavalry Division outposts along the Yalta Road on the outskirts of Kucuk-Muskomoya. The 149th Regiment of 40th Cavalry Division was on the other side of the village. The remaining units were in Kucuk-Muskomoya, between Yalta and Balaklava. The attack was a surprise and the battle at Varnutka lasted about two hours. The 154th Regiment of 40th Cavalry Division moved up towards the village to counter-attack but the Germans deployed additional troops and the Soviets were forced to pull back, leaving Varnutka and Kucuk-Muskomoya in German hands. The road to Balaklava was now open.

The Military Council of Sevastopol gave the order to organise the local production of military equipment. A factory was established in the underground galleries of the formal naval warehouses at Trinity Ravine and in the Inkerman champagne cellars. Civilian workers, citizens of Sevastopol, produced mortars, mines, hand grenades, anti-tank and other weapons, as well as clothes, shoes and uniforms. This became known as 'Underground Sevastopol'.

The city did not sleep. Daytime work gave way to work at night; work just as intense. All around Sevastopol picks and shovels rang against stones. Engirdled with fortifications, the city ate its way into the stone and every day dug itself deeper into the earth. Underground nurseries, kindergartens, schools, hospitals and even factories made their appearance. (*City Nights* – L. Solovyev and M. Kogut[16])

On 12 November fighting broke out in Sector 3 for Hill 137.5 and the Germans recaptured it. 7th Brigade counter-attacked with a battalion of Cadets. Twenty-seven Cadets were killed in the fighting and the Soviets were pushed back to their starting position. At 1100 hours twenty-three German aircraft struck the main naval base including the port, naval facilities and several gun batteries. Raids continued throughout the day. Dozens of buildings in the city were destroyed or damaged. The cruiser *Chervona Ukraina*, moored on the north side of the bay to fire at German troops, was also hit.

> Never forget the clear nights of November 1941. The stars gleamed high and clear over a city shrouded in darkness, while the buildings trembled with the alarming roar that seemed to come from under the very earth and in response to it the windowpanes rattled complainingly in their frames. It was the roar of war. In it merged the measured tread of infantry, the clatter of hooves, the clanking of caterpillar tracks, the thunder of the cast-iron wheels of carts and cannon, the rumbling of overloaded trucks.
>
> In the deepest hours of the night the scream of a siren suddenly cut through all the other sounds and two minutes later anti-aircraft guns and machine guns began their enraged barking. In a twinkling the clear southern skies became sullenly ominous, crisscrossed with the rays of searchlights and

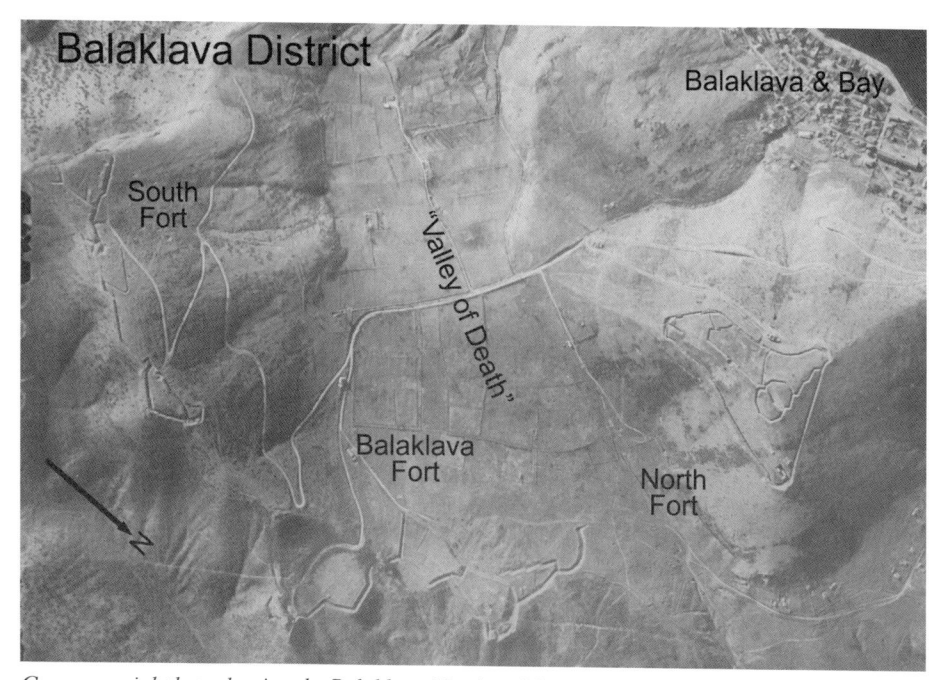

German aerial photo showing the Balaklava North and South Forts. (Author's collection)

red, yellow, green tracer bullets and shells. The drone of alien motors hung over the city. Our fighter planes took off to intercept the enemy. (*City Nights* – L. Solovyev and M. Kogut)[17]

On 13 November the German 72nd Division was still moving troops down the Baydar Valley from Simferopol to Yalta. The 301st Regiment of 72nd Division found a dirt road that ran along the Black River Valley from Baydar, through the village of Mordvinova and on to Blagodatnoye northeast of Balaklava. The road was left uncovered by Soviet troops and two battalions of the 301st moved towards the Yalta Highway, cutting off the 147th Regiment of 40th Division.

Balaklava North and South Forts

The Genoese Towers – Fort Cembalo – comprise the original fortifications of Balaklava. There is a second group of fortifications built at a much later date. They are the North Balaklava Fort (Hill 212.1) and the South Balaklava Fort (2,500m east of Hill 212.1) plus an unfinished annex about 500m northeast of the southern part of the fort. Technically they were supposed to be one fortress linked together across the valley that separates them.

North Balaklava overlooks Balaklava Bay. It was triangular in shape based on its conformance to the terrain. The entrance to the fort was located to the rear of the fort and was blocked by a steel gate. Outside the gate was a wooden sentry box. Near the gate, built into the rock, was a concrete barracks protected by a flanking casemate for infantry weapons to guard the ditch and entrance. The barracks housed bunkrooms for a platoon, latrines and an office. A second, unfinished barracks building was located next to the first, intended to house two platoons. The fort's ditch was surmounted by rifle positions and contained shelters for field guns. An underground barracks was located on the right flank of the fort to house a second platoon. A second exit from the fort and an additional ramp for field guns was located on the right flank. An NKVD battery with four 45mm guns was stationed at the fort at the beginning of the Second Defence.

The South Fort was located across a narrow valley from its neighbour. During the Second Defence this was referred to as 'The Valley of Death' (nothing to do with the Light Brigade). The road to the fort ran through this valley and up to the top of the hill. South Fort followed the elongated ridge that made up the two adjacent hills. The southern flank of the fort ended in an abrupt drop to the sea. There was an open gallery running along the edge with a machine-gun position on one side and an observation post 50m away from that. A casemate for field guns plus an ammunition store were located near the machine gun. A system of rifle trenches encircled the top of the hill. There were five different-sized barracks

The First Assault – October to November 1941

buildings to accommodate two to three companies. The unfinished section was 500m northeast of the fort.

Heavy fighting took place to capture the fort and it changed hands several times before finally falling into the possession of the Germans. On 13 November a platoon of Cadets from the NKVD school moved up to the South Fort to relieve the 3rd NKVD Battalion. The NKVD School at Balaklava was set up to train Junior Coast Guard Commanders. There were a small number of students at the school at the beginning of the Second Defence – about one battalion. The Cadets ran into the German 105th Infantry Regiment which approached the fort on a mountain road from the village of Varnutka and sneaked into the Soviet trenches in front of the fort. A battle took place with heavy German losses but the Soviets were trap inside two of the barracks building inside the fort. The Germans demanded their surrender and when the Soviets refused they began to blow up the buildings to drive them out. The Cadets counter-attacked several times and requested assistance from the 3rd NKVD Battalion but they were blocked from coming to their aid. At 1700 hours the short siege was over and the Cadet platoons were destroyed almost to the last man. A few escaped from the hilltop. The fort was badly damaged by German demolition charges.

The attack on the South Fort was one of many that took place across Sectors 1 and 2 on 13 November. 72nd Infantry Division launched its main attack in Sector 2 along the Yalta Highway. In the northeast part of the sector, 50th Division attacked the bunkers of the Chorgun Strongpoint. Bunker 72 recorded a large number of German kills. By the end of the day the Germans had captured both sections of the South Fort. Further north, German pioneers built a pontoon bridge across the Black River and the 301st German Regiment established contact with 50th Infantry Division in the village of Kuchki (which no longer exists).

The Soviets launched another attack to recapture Mackenzie Farm. 2nd Battalion of 31st Rifle Regiment moved 1km north of Hill 269 (Mount Chirish-Tepe), part of a group of hills below the Kara-Koba Valley and west of Shuli. Hill 269 followed the range of hills from 90.5 to 154.7. Simultaneously 1st and 2nd Battalions of 3rd Marine Regiment moved up towards the farm while 1st and 2nd Battalions of 7th Marine Brigade were 500m to the east. The 54th Rifle Regiment and 3rd Battalion of 2nd Perekop Regiment moved south of hill 319.6 (about 3km northwest of Cherkez-Kerman). The action was supported by Battery 35 and Battery 725. 3rd Marine Regiment, coming from the north, moved 1.5km west of Cherkez-Kerman. However, the Soviet attack was not coordinated. 7th Marine Brigade attacked too late, squandering an opportunity to surround the Germans at Mackenzie Farm. The brigade's attack was lacklustre and the opportunity disappeared. The Germans counter-attacked from Cherkez-Kerman and Mackenzie Farm, driving back the 3rd Marine Regiment to the south of the road that ran between the two locations, removing the threat to the German forces at the farm.

On the morning of 14 November the Soviet 383rd and 514th Rifle Regiments of the 172nd Rifle Division counter-attacked east of Balaklava. The first attack was between South Fort and Hill 386.6, which allowed the trapped 147th Regiment of 40th Cavalry Division to break out of encirclement. Coastal Battery 19 provided artillery support. The Germans fired artillery and mortars on the left flank of Battery 19 from the South Fort. The traverses did not protect the guns from shells coming from that direction and the explosions threatened to ignite ammunition in the storage bunkers, but the fires were brought under control and the battery kept firing.

Battery 19 is an example of the confusion of numbering that prevailed at Sevastopol. There were two Battery 19s. One was built near Cape Fiolent in 1912. It was an interesting structure, built in concrete with an underground transverse gallery, generator and retractable searchlight. Armoured observation posts were located on the flanks. The battery was surrounded by a ditch with a bridge running across, defended by machine guns and field guns. In 1935 the battery was used as a surveillance and communications centre. In 1941 it was a Coastal Defence headquarters. From 19 to 24 June 1942, ammunition was moved here from Sukharno Arsenal.

The former Battery 19 at Balaklava. The Soviet guns have been replaced by German field guns. (NARA)

The First Assault – October to November 1941   79

The 'other' Battery 19 began its history as Battery 22. It was built in 1913–14 for four 152mm guns on the heights northwest of and overlooking Balaklava Bay. In 1925 it was designated Battery 10 and late Battery 19. Its first commander was Captain G. Aleksander, future commander of Battery 30. During the war it was commanded by Captain Mark Semenovich Drapushko.

The guns were installed on concrete bases with a parapet running along the front to protect the gunners. They had a firing arc of 130 degrees and had a rate of fire of ten rounds per minute. The guns were not protected from the landward side, which proved to be a major disadvantage during the Second Defence. The guns continually fired on German troops approaching along the coast but their layout, in a straight line, made them a key target of enfilading German fire from guns on South Fort. Two of the guns were completely destroyed and the remainder were moved to near Maximova Farm. Despite the loss of the guns, the battery maintained its designation as No 19. In June 1942, more guns were installed on the battery but it is not known what they were, although one veteran of the 456th Rifle Regiment claims they were 75mm.

On the evening of 14 November, the Germans made a breach in the right flank of the Soviet defences and began to filter through to the heights around Balaklava. Every 6 to 7 minutes, Captain Mark Semenovich Drapushko's 19th battery sent salvoes into a village on the perimeter [of Sector 1] where large German forces were billeted. On the morning of 15 November the battery fired point-blank at the German trench mortar and machine-gun emplacements on the slopes of the opposite mountains and in the valleys. The guns became so hot with the incessant firing that the paint on them bubbled up. The gunners had no sleep for two days and nights but continued to fire on the approaching Germans.

The Germans concentrated the fire of two artillery and several trench mortar batteries on Drapushko's battery in an attempt to destroy it. Shells of 100 and 150mm burst near the gun emplacements, showering the position with shrapnel. The bursting shells destroyed communications with the [rangefinder.] The camouflage over the guns caught fire. The flames threatened to spread to the shells and munitions dumps. A bursting shell blinded gunner Shcherbakov at Gun #3. The gun emplacements were nearly buried under showers of stones, powdered cement and earth. The terrain was pitted with huge craters. All night long the men cleared the debris, replaced damaged parts on the guns and they were again ready to fire. (*The Brave Gunners* – Senior Political Officer B. Efremov)[18]

Vice-Admiral Oktyabrsky was well aware of the desperate situation of Sevastopol's defences. He notified Vice-Admiral Kuznetsov of the details of the offensive against Balaklava and that the entire coast from Kerch to Balaklava was now under German control. He reported that the Soviets had lost around 5,000 men in the last couple of days and, despite several requests, the base had not received any replacements of men or equipment. There were only enough artillery shells for three more days of fighting.

In the evening it began to rain and overnight turned to sleet. Early in the morning of 15 November the Germans continued to attack Sectors 1 and 2. 72nd Infantry Division attacked the position of the 383rd Rifle Regiment and by the end of the day pushed towards the Genoese Towers. The fighting continued into the night. By the end of the day the Germans were on the slopes of Balaklava North Fort, Hill 212.1, breaking through the first line of defence. General Petrov sent in the 1330th Rifle Regiment and the German advance was stopped.

On 16 November the German 50th Infantry Division launched a massive attack in Sector 2, striking from the area of Cherkez-Kerman, along the valley of Kara-Koba and from Shuli and Uppal towards Upper Chorgun. By the end of the day, two German battalions pushed the left flank of 31st Rifle Regiment from the Kara-Koba Valley and moved 1km from the base of Mount Kara-Koba. From Uppal village they drove into the lines of 2nd Perekop Regiment and took Hill 287.4, Mount Kara-Bair, about 1.5km northwest of Uppal.

On 17 November Sector 1 was the main target of attack. The Germans were stopped on the Yalta Highway by Soviet artillery but made some gains in the mountains, seizing the slopes of Hill 212.1 (Balaklava North Fort). The fighting continued into the night. At 2045 hours, 1st Battalion of the 1330th Rifle Regiment and dismounted troopers from 149th Regiment of 40th Cavalry Division attacked the Germans from the top of the hill and held off any further advance up the slope. German attacks in Sector 4 near Kalymtay and Efendikoy failed to achieve their goals.

For the next couple of days, there was inconclusive fighting in Sector 1 as both sides continued to shell each other's positions. By the night of 19 November the Soviets were running out of 152mm, 155mm, 76mm and 45mm ammunition.

General Petrov decided to relieve some of the units that had been at the front the longest time and sustained the heaviest losses. The 383rd Rifle Regiment was moved to the second line of defence. The Cadets on Hill 212.1 were replaced by an NKVD Border Regiment. The Cadets descended from the hill, their uniforms blackened, frozen after three days under enemy fire, clinging to the rocks. A witness, K. Malyavkina, described the condition of the Cadets: 'We got to meet the column of sailors, torn and dirty, wearily moving their feet. Something was wrong with this group of sailors, then I realised, almost all of them were in their forties; all with beards grown, thin and wild to look at. "Where were you, brother," I asked. Someone in the column said hoarsely: "There," and nodded at the Balaklava Heights.'

On 20 November attack and counter-attack continued throughout the day, at South Fort and on the junction of Sectors 1 and 2. The 72nd Infantry Division, reinforced by 17th, 22nd and 70th Sapper Battalions targeted the North Fort and Kamary Village. The 161st Rifle Regiment was unable to hold the village and pulled out. The Germans advanced but were stopped by a rapid-fire naval gun dug into the ground, pouring in a hail of fire from a range of less than a kilometre. The Germans rushed towards the gun and ran into a group of heavily-armed Soviet soldiers. Hand-to-hand combat resulted and some soldiers were hacked to death by sharpened shovels. It was a brutal battle and the Germans were forced to retreat.

The 50th Infantry division attacked the positions of the 2nd Marine Regiment and the 31st Rifle Regiment in the Chorgun Strongpoint. All attacks were repulsed by Soviet troops supported by Bunkers 70, 71 and 72. The Germans approached Bunker 69 with grenades. The defenders repelled the attack but the bunker's gun was destroyed. By 2100 hours on 21 November the 72nd and 50th German Divisions losses had mounted to the point where Manstein halted the attacks. This was the last attempt by the Germans to break into Sevastopol in November and the First Assault came to an end.

During the pause in the German offensive, General Petrov ordered counter-attacks to improve the Soviet position in Sectors 3 and 4, where the Germans held Mackenzie Farm and a portion of the Kara-Koba Valley. He ordered 54th Rifle Regiment, 2nd Perekop Regiment and 3rd Marine Regiment to attack Mackenzie Farm. 31st Rifle Regiment was ordered to attack the Germans from their defences in front of Mount Kara-Koba. At 0800 hours Soviet troops went on the offensive but met a stubborn resistance. 2nd Perekop

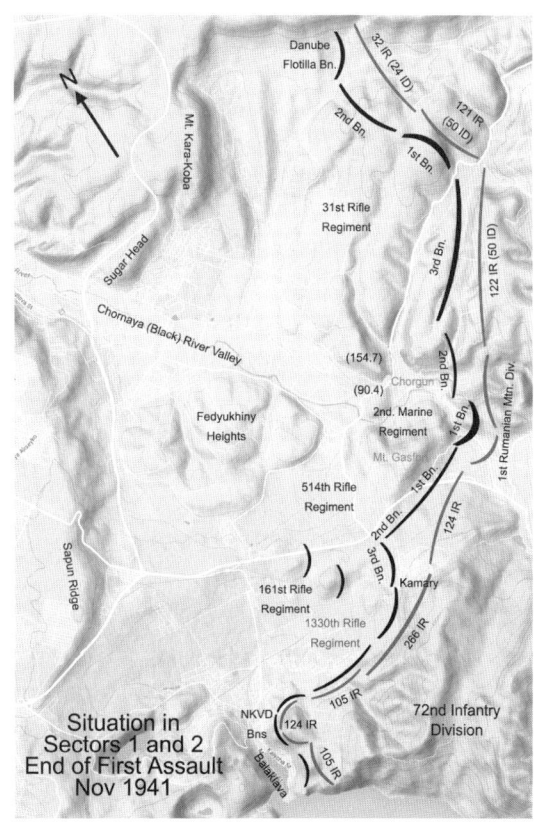

Sectors 1 and 2 in November 1941. (© OpenStreetMap contributors, Author's collection)

Regiment moved forward and blocked the road from Mackenzie Farm to Cherkez-Kerman but could advance no further. 31st Rifle Regiment's attempt to advance in Sector 2 failed.

There were no further German attacks on Sevastopol in November. The First Assault failed to achieve its overall objective, the surprise capture of Sevastopol. In reality the 'First Assault' consisted of two phases. The first phase was a 'surprise attack' to cut off retreating Soviet forces and seize the base before the Soviets could stabilise their defence. This phase included attacks with motorised units mainly in the north and northeast in an attempt to capture the Belbek Valley and move to the bay. Phase two was directed against the south with the arrival of the 72nd Division, attacking Balaklava, accompanied by attacks in the centre against Mackenzie Farm and the Kara-Koba Valley.

To call the First Assault a total failure would be unfair to the Germans and Rumanians. They had penetrated as far as the eastern Belbek Valley and the Duvankoi Strongpoint, parts of Aranci Strongpoint had fallen and the Cherkez-Kerman position was in German hands. They controlled the Mekenzievy Mountain plateau to the edge of Martynov Ravine and they had a strong foothold in the Kara-Koba Valley. They had less success in Sector 2, however, failing to take Mount Gasfort and they had yet to capture the Balaklava Heights and to move along the Yalta Highway.

The Soviets still held the major defensive positions around Sevastopol. They continued to hold most of the Aranci Strongpoint including the western part of the Kara-Tau plateau and the Belbek Valley west of Duvankoi. Shuli and the eastern Kara-Koba Valley were in German hands but the Soviets held the heights on either side of the Black River Valley that led to the bay and their line extended to the Fedyukhiny Heights and on to Mount Gasfort and Canrobert Hill. The Germans east of Balaklava were surrounded on three sides.

Most of the battles fought during the First Assault followed a pattern

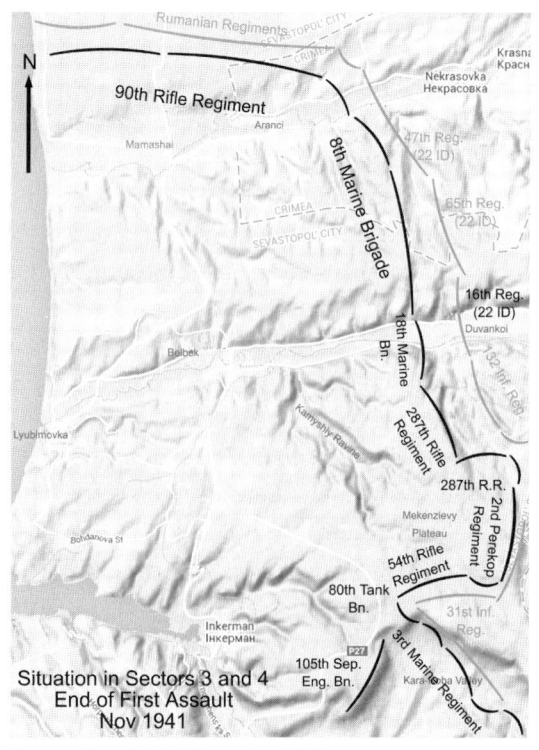

Sectors 3 and 4 in November 1941. (© OpenStreetMap contributors, Author's collection)

of artillery bombardment followed by infantry and tank attack, followed by counter-attack, followed by artillery shelling, followed by a return to the original position. This was also true of the upcoming Second and Third Assaults. German troops reached the slopes but not always the heights. And in most cases, from their vantage point on the hills surrounding the city, they could see their goal, Sevastopol Bay, close but not to be attained for another six bloody months. In twenty-five days of fighting the Germans lost about 15,000 killed and wounded and dozens of armoured vehicles and aircraft destroyed. The Soviets lost about 16,500, more than half of them wounded.

Credit must be given to the organisation of the defence. The army and navy commanders at Sevastopol skilfully plugged the gaps with whatever assets they could get their hands on. The Soviets took advantage of terrain, in particular the construction of permanent and field fortifications. The tactical interaction between army and naval units was remarkable. Soldier and marine fought closely together, often in mutual support, with the ability to request and receive artillery support from naval coastal defence batteries, anti-aircraft units, heavy mobile batteries, field guns and mortars and of course aircraft. Eleven surface ships fired over 2,000 shells from offshore or from within Sevastopol harbour. The AA units played an important role in breaking up the German offensive. Their guns were used not only against enemy aircraft but also for direct fire against enemy troops.

Naval support was excellent. Along with artillery support the warships provided a vital link between Sevastopol and the Caucasus ports. Warships escorted 114 of 178 transport missions. During November the ships delivered over 25,000 tons of supplies including 4 tons of ammunition; brought in 15,000 reinforcements and evacuated 5,700 wounded and civilians. Soviet ships docked at Kholodinik and Ugolnaya piers on the south side and Suharnaya quay on the north side near the arsenal.

Guerrilla units operated behind enemy lines. Soldiers who became cut off from Fifty-first Army and Coastal Army units unable to join their regular units during the retreat from the north joined partisan detachments. By mid-November, twenty-eight partisan detachments with 3,700 fighters were operating in Crimea. They were commanded by Colonel Alexei Mokrousova, leader of the movement in Crimea during the Civil War. The guerrillas mined roads, blew up bridges, derailed trains carrying troops and equipment and ambushed enemy columns. They tore down telegraph and telephone lines to cut enemy communications. As a result of their activities, the German command gave orders for their units not to operate in densely-wooded areas.

The pause after the First Assault lasted from 21 November to 16 December. During this time both sides prepared for the next round of fighting. The Sevastopol command took measures to improve land defences, including the repair and improvement of damaged bunkers and construction of additional artillery and machine-gun bunkers. In late November alone engineers built bunkers, command and observation posts, dugouts and trenches and placed over 20,000 mines and 28km of barbed wire. Acres of wood and brush were cleared to provide unobstructed fields of fire. Emphasis was placed on creating lines of defence in depth and in training troops in engineering and entrenching techniques.

The front lines were adjusted based on the results of the first attack. The forward line was 46km long. It started at the sea and ran through the Genoese Towers to Balaklava North Fort, the State Farm Grace, Kamary Village, Lower Chorgun, the western slopes of Hill 269 to the western edge of the Mekenzievy Plateau to Efendikoy along the Kacha River to Aranci, terminating at the Black Sea. The centre line was 38km long and ran from the southern coast at Cape Kaya-Bash to Kadykova, Fedyukhiny Height, Sugar Head, Kamyshly Ravine, across the Belbek Valley to Hill 103.9, north of Belbek and then to Mamashai along the Black Sea. The rear line was 30km long. It began at St. George's Monastery and ran along the Sapun Ridge to Inkerman, to Mackenzie Station to Hill 104.5, ending at Lyubimovka on the sea.

On 26 November the Fleet Military Council directed the following assets to be sent to Sevastopol: one rifle division, one tank battalion; about fifty 76mm guns, twelve howitzers and about 150 machine guns. The Sevastopol Defence Area was to be provided with four rifle companies and one machine gun company per week.

A German gunner from 24th Infantry Division in the Mekenzievy Mountains gave the following account of the conditions there:

> It was freezing during the second half of November. Fortunately in Crimea the winter is not harsh as in other parts of Russia and we were not exposed for long to sub-zero temperatures. The winter is similar to what happens in Germany, with frost and snow. On this 'Russian Riviera', the weather remains relatively mild. Nevertheless, we were forced to live in open trenches or behind stone walls; our only cover was light canvas capes used as tents. We were open to the elements which were worse with the onset of cold and rain.
>
> Soviet fighters and bombers attacked our positions relentlessly, hitting our batteries, field hospitals, supply convoys and command posts. Roads and trails became covered with holes and thick mud and turned into bottomless swamps, impassable to heavy trucks. Delivery of supplies to the front lines depended on the tireless Ukrainian donkeys hauling primitive carts.
>
> Roads built of clay soil became almost impassable for mechanised units as they tried to make their way in the squishy, rain-soaked earth. The very question of supply became a critical issue for the whole of the Eleventh Army.

The First Assault – October to November 1941

Before us loomed the prospect of the [renewed] assault on Sevastopol. Together with the 22nd Infantry Division we had to attack the northern flank of the enemy's defences and to overcome a complex system of fortifications, field works and steep slopes of the northern sector of the Sevastopol stronghold to make our way to the bay, knowing full well that the most powerful defences are concentrated in the northern sector. For this next attack the army brought in all available forces. Only one division was left at Kerch.

Supply problems plagued our preparations, especially our heavy artillery, with barely enough ammunition for an extended battle. We also desperately lacked armour and the few we had were faced with the enormous challenge of crossing difficult terrain and punching our way through a network of fortifications defended by steadfast warriors.

Chapter 4

The Second Assault – 17 December 1941 to 1 January 1942

As winter approached, Operation Barbarossa ground to a halt and German defeats began to mount as the Soviets counter-attacked along the Eastern Front. The Soviet command planned a major offensive in Crimea, one of Stalin's winter offensives; in this particular case an amphibious assault on the Kerch Peninsula. The plan included an offensive by Soviet troops at Sevastopol towards Simferopol to prevent the Germans from bringing in reserves to Kerch. The preparation for the Soviet landing operation took time and instead of an attack on the Germans, on 17 December the Germans attacked Sevastopol. The Military Council of the Black Sea Fleet was convinced the Germans did not have sufficient forces for a decisive attack on Sevastopol, so the December offensive – the Second Assault – took the Soviets by surprise.

Marshal Krylov wrote: 'Some of our comrades even began to doubt whether the Nazis [would once again attack] Sevastopol.'[1] The commander of the 25th Chapaevsky Division, Major-General Kolomiets, noted: 'The Germans launched an offensive earlier than we expected.'[2] He believed the initial attacks were purely for reconnaissance but it soon became clear that it was a major offensive. Political Commissar L. N. Efimenko of 8th Marine Brigade wrote: 'In the early morning hours of 17 December the Soviets did not know that the last hours of rest were about to expire.'[3] One of the reasons was poor intelligence. The Soviets had no idea the assault would begin when it did. General Petrov believed any new offensive would take place along the Yalta Highway because it was wider and more favourable for tanks. The left flank seemed less dangerous because the front at Mamashai and Aranci was far from the city. Even if the Germans succeeded they still had to confront the major obstacle of Sevastopol Bay. According to Petrov, 'The assumption that the Germans would attack from the same direction as in November was not justified.'[4]

Supplies and troops arrived in Sevastopol throughout December by sea and civilians and the wounded were evacuated on the outgoing ships. At 0622 hours on 5 December the *Kharkov* arrived in Sevastopol carrying 500 troops. On 7 December troops from 388th Rifle Division began to embark at Poti on transports and warships for Sevastopol. On 8 December the cruiser *Krasnyy Kavkaz* ('Red Caucasus') and the destroyer *Soobrazitelnyy* delivered 1,200 men of the 782nd

Regiment of 388th Division. They continued to arrive over the next few days. On 9 December 2,700 men from the 388th arrived and another 5,200 on 12 December. A total of 11,197 troops from 388th Division were brought in, along with twenty-one 76mm guns, five 122mm howitzers, 146 82mm and 50mm mortars. On 12 December the 388th was deployed as a reserve, along with 40th Cavalry Division and 7th Marine Brigade to Inkerman. On 15 December 1,800 more troops were delivered, plus 137 horses, fifty-one field kitchens and 250 tons of ammunition.

> And once again, the endless movement of troops along the road. In the port, transport after transport discharged its cargo and, without waiting for dawn, sailed off again into the inky, storm-tossed sea. Russian, Ukrainian, Kazakh, Georgian and Armenian could be heard on the streets. People from the Central Asian steppes, the Caucasian Mountains, the Russian plains, the Siberian taiga had all gathered here, on the streets of Sevastopol and all of them were Sevastopolites, sons of the city. (*City Nights* – L. Solovyev and M. Kogut)[5]

On 9 December Vice-Admiral Oktyabrsky left Sevastopol aboard the *Krasnyy Kavkaz*, bound for Novorossiysk, to prepare the Kerch-Feodosiya landing operation with the command of the Transcausasus Front.

Daily bombardments by air and sea continued against German positions. On 8 December the 8th Marine Brigade launched an attack against the Germans on Hill 164.5 near the spring of Altyn Bair and captured the western slopes. The next day the Germans brought in reserves and, supported by armour, launched a counter-attack and drove the Soviets from the hill. On 12 December the Germans launched a surprise attack against the left flank of the 1st Battalion of 8th Marine Brigade and the right flank of 3rd Battalion of the 90th Rifle Regiment in the vicinity of Altyn-Bair. The 9th Company of 3rd Battalion was forced to withdraw and the Germans seized their trenches. The Germans then attacked 8th Brigade's 1st Battalion in the vicinity of the village of Aranci but fire from the 57th Artillery Regiment halted German attempts to infiltrate the battalion's defences.

On Monday 15 December, German infantry patrols skirmished with Soviet defenders at several locations in the Belbek Valley. Their purpose was to scout the Soviet positions and, if possible, to capture certain high points, but they were unsuccessful. Around noon German artillery at Kacha fired on Battery 10, knocking out two of the 203mm guns and starting a large fire. The gunners rushed to extinguish the flames while under continuous shelling by the Germans. The Political Commissar Chernousov was killed and several gunners wounded, but the fire was extinguished before it could set off the shells in the magazine.

88   The Defence of Sevastopol 1941–1942

Führer Directive 39, dated 8 December 1941, stipulated: 'Sevastopol will be captured as soon as possible. The future employment of the bulk of 11th Army (with the exception of units required for coastal defence) will be decided at the end of the fighting there.' The capture of Sevastopol would of course make up for the German reverses in other sectors of the front and would raise the spirits of the German troops. Manstein's offensive included 22nd, 24th, 50th, 72nd, 132nd and 170th Infantry Divisions plus the 1st Rumanian Mountain Brigade. A portion of the 73rd Infantry Division, now positioned at Kerch, was moved to Sevastopol and placed 10km east of Duvankoi. German forces included the 190th and 197th Assault Gun Battalions and two heavy artillery battalions (with guns up to 356mm calibre). In total the Germans had 645 field guns and 252 anti-tank guns, 378 mortars, including six-barrelled rocket mortars, the *Nebelwerfer*, giving the Germans twenty-seven guns and mortars per kilometre of the defensive line. Eleventh Army was also supported by 200 aircraft from the Luftwaffe's IV Air Corps.

Sevastopol was defended by 25th, 95th, 172nd and 388th Rifle Divisions, 40th Cavalry Division, 7th and 8th Marine Brigades, 1st, 2nd and 3rd Marine and 2nd Perekop Regiments and the Guards Regiment. Artillery included 191 guns, 111 in coastal batteries, plus 120 mortars. The average density was 6.5 barrels per kilometre of front. The Soviets had only twenty-six T-26 and T-27 light tanks, one equipped as a flamethrower. A small force of ninety aircraft was available. Thus, the Germans had twice the number of troops, guns and aircraft, plus a vast superiority in armour.

The *Zhelezniakov* supported Soviet troops during the Second Assault. On 17 December 1941 the train acted in support of 8th Marine Brigade and the 95th Rifle Division firing its mortars and 76mm guns. The train was sent to the rear late in the year for replacement of worn-out gun barrels. Four of the 82mm mortars were replaced with 120mm models. On 22 December the train was sent to fire on German soldiers concentrating near the Mekenzievy

The armoured train Zhelezniakov's *76mm guns. The photo was taken as the train passed by the Inkerman marshes.* (Nemenko Collection)

Mountain Station. During the battle the locomotive was damaged and derailed and needed to be repaired. The engineers worked under heavy German fire to repair the locomotive and get it back on to the track. The repairs were made and the train moved to safety. On 28–29 December the train was hiding in a narrow cut near Inkerman when it was hit by a German air raid. Several of the crew were killed but the train managed to shoot down two German fighters. Repairs were made and the 'Green Ghost' slipped away again.

Manstein's plan for the December offensive was to launch a major attack by 22nd, 24th and 132nd Infantry Divisions at the junction of Sectors 3 and 4 at Mount Yaila-Bash in the Mekenzievy Mountains. The axis of attack was the Belbek Valley towards the Kamyshly Ravine then across the plateau west of the ravine to the Mekenzievy Railway Station, across Hill 60 and on to Sevastopol Bay. A secondary attack by 50th Infantry Division would be carried out at Upper Chorgun and along the Black River towards Inkerman. 72nd Infantry Division, 1st Rumanian Mountain Brigade and 170th Infantry Division would pin down Soviet troops south of the Black River. The goal was to draw enough Soviet troops south so as to weaken the defences in the north and allow the Germans to encircle and destroy troops in Sector 4, proceed to the bay and seize the port, then strike the Soviet flanks in Sector 3. Manstein expected to capture Sevastopol by 21 December – in five days.

At 0610 hours on 17 December 1941, after a short artillery bombardment, the Germans launched an offensive in all four sectors. The Luftwaffe bombed Soviet infantry and artillery positions. The initial attack was launched by 132nd and 22nd Infantry Divisions against the 287th Regiment of the 25th Chapaevsky Division and 2nd Marine Regiment in Sector 3 north and south of Mount Yaila-Bash. It then converged in the direction of the southern end of Kamyshly Ravine. Two battalions supported by ten StuG IIIs attacked the left flank while two battalions with seven guns attacked the right. The most violent attacks were against the 1st Battalion

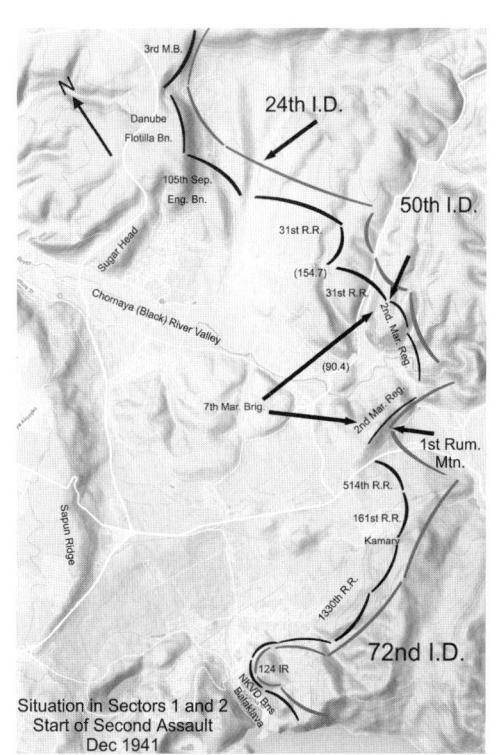

Sectors 1 and 2 in December 1941.
(© OpenStreetMap contributors, Author's collection)

of the 287th Regiment which was forced to retreat. 5th Company of 2nd Battalion resorted to hand-to-hand combat to hold their trenches, but at 1300 hours, facing increasingly strong attacks, the regiment retreated towards Kamyshly village and dug in along the hill 800m east of the village. By the end of the day the 287th was on the northeast slopes of Kamyshly Ravine and 2nd Marine Regiment on the western slopes.

Infantry and armoured attacks were carried out across the entire line of Sector 4. The 22nd Infantry Division attacked the 241st Regiment of 95th Division and 3rd Company of the 241st was pushed back but counter-attacked to retake their former position. 90th Regiment attacked the German left flank to break through the attack lines but was unsuccessful. 22nd Infantry Division attacked the junction of 2nd and 3rd Battalions of 8th Marine Brigade, still holding the western half of the Kara-Tau Plateau. 5th Battalion of 8th Marine Brigade counter-attacked to seal the gap and a bayonet charge broke up the German attack. A fresh attack in the afternoon pushed the three battalions back and the Germans captured Mount Azis-Oba.

In Sector 2, the German 50th Infantry Division attempted to capture the positions of 2nd Regiment of 7th Marine Brigade, 514th Rifle Regiment of 172nd Division and 31st Regiment of 25th Chapaevsky Division. They captured some of the infantry trenches of 2nd Marine Regiment and pushed back several units of 31st Regiment. The sector commander, Colonel Laskin, sent in reserves from 7th Marine Brigade and together with 1st Battalion, 2nd Regiment, drove the Germans from the heights of the Italian Cemetery on Mount Gasfort back to their original position. 2nd Battalion of 7th Marine Brigade attacked and pushed the Germans back. 4th Battalion of 7th Brigade, supported by 31st Rifle Regiment, halted the German advance towards Lower Chorgun.

> On the third day of the offensive the sun shone through the lowering clouds. A thick shroud of smoke hung over the field. The Italian Cemetery had changed hands several times that day. 'Surrender, Podchashensky!' shouted the Germans brazenly to the gallant commander of the 5th Battalion when he stormed the steep hill at the head of his men under rifle and machine gun fire. Podchashensky's men replied with a bayonet attack and the concentrated fire of a trench mortar battery. The Germans were unable to hold out and the hill was captured. The Germans halted their offensive, waiting for replacements. Taking advantage of the lull, the men of the 7th Brigade fortified the positions they had occupied, biting into the flinty rock of the hill. (*The Heroic Defence of Sevastopol* – 7th Marine Brigade)[6]

The Luftwaffe bombed the city and the airfield on Cape Chersonese. During this raid, bombs were dropped on Battery 35, badly damaging one of the turrets and wounding and killing several gunners. General Petrov sent in more troops to strengthen Sectors 3 and 4. The 40th Cavalry Division and 773rd Rifle Regiment of 388th Division were sent to Sector 4. Major-General Vorobiev, commander of Sector 4, was ordered to counter-attack with the newly arrived troops of the 388th plus the 8th Marine Brigade in the area of Mount Azis-Oba to restore the line and close the gap between Sectors 3 and 4.

The 778th Regiment of 388th Rifle Division was sent to reinforce Sector 3. 3rd Battalion, 7th Marine Brigade was also sent into the sector to retake hill 209 (Mount Kaya-Bash) and establish contact with the 241st Rifle Regiment in the Belbek Valley on the right flank of Sector 4.

Before dawn on 18 December, Soviet coastal batteries and field artillery in Sector 4 shelled German troops, after which Soviet infantry were to launch an attack. However, the Germans got the jump on them and went on the offensive first, attacking 40th Cavalry Division and 8th Marine Brigade. The Germans captured about 500m of Soviet territory near Mount Aziz-Oba. The commander of the 151st Cavalry Regiment of the 40th Cavalry Division was killed during the battle.

The 773rd Regiment of 388th Rifle Division was in an isolated position on the right flank of 8th Brigade and came under attack around 0900 hours, having been spotted by German reconnaissance aircraft. The regiment was hit by aircraft and artillery, followed by an infantry and armoured attack and was forced to retreat, losing contact with the 241st Rifle Regiment, which was also cut off from the Soviet troops on its right flank. General Vorobiev sent in the 149th Cavalry Regiment and a reconnaissance unit of the 90th Rifle Regiment to halt the advance but they were unable to close the gap on the right flank. The 241st Regiment was surrounded by the Germans.

Throughout the afternoon heavy pressure was placed on the 8th Marine Brigade, especially against the 4th Battalion. German armour broke through the brigade's lines and came in contact with the brigade's artillery regiment. A 76mm gun from 4th Battery, firing directly, opened fire and

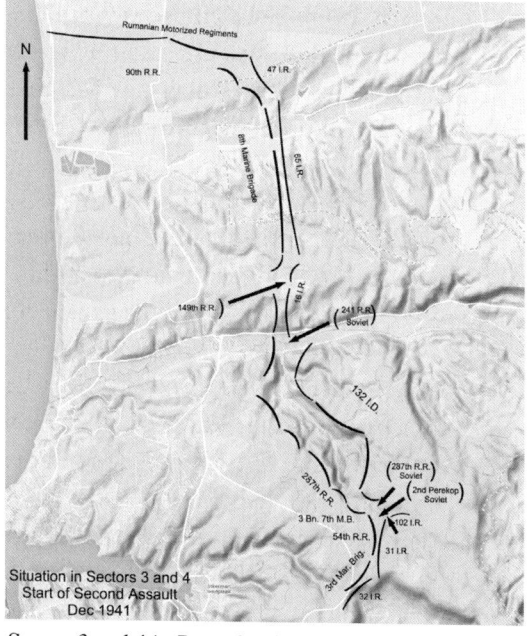

Sectors 3 and 4 in December 1941.
(© OpenStreetMap contributors, Author's collection)

destroyed two vehicles. A third vehicle turned back. By the end of the day the 8th Marine Brigade's command post was surrounded. Many of the men escaped, carrying the wounded to the rear.

In Sector 3, the 287th Regiment, the 2nd Perekop Regiment and 3rd Battalion of 7th Marine Brigade launched an attack to recapture Mount Kaya-Bash and to re-establish contact with the 241st Regiment in Sector 4. The attack was initially successful but the Germans responded with heavy artillery and mortar fire and a follow-up attack by infantry with armour and air support. By the end of the day the Germans had pushed the line back to the southeast spur of Kamyshly Ravine.

Defences of the Belbek Valley

The first line of defence of the Belbek Valley crossed the valley in the area of Duvankoi. A second line of defence was based around Bunkers 4 and 39. Bunker 39 was on the opposite side of the Belbek Valley from Bunker 4. It covered the road out of the Kamyshly Ravine. It was equipped with a 45mm gun and was part of a group of bunkers that also included Bunkers 13, 14 and 15.

Bunker 3 was located on top of the southern edge of the Kara-Tau plateau and covered the road descending from the plateau directly across from the entrance to the Kamyshly Ravine. Bunker 5, built for a 100mm gun was located at the fork of the Sevastopol-Simferopol Road and Eupatoria Road. It covered the bend where the Sevastopol-Simferopol Road turned and headed south across the Belbek and climbed up between Hills 104.5 and 124.5. The gun fired along this road and the Belbek Valley. It had a nine-man crew that took an active part in the December battle. The crew retreated on 22 December to the outskirts of the village of Belbek and continued to fight in the area. The bunker and surrounding defensive trenches were held by the 172nd Division during the Third Assault.

Bunkers 13, 14 and 15 were located in the Belbek Valley above the Kamyshly Ravine entrance. Bunker 15 was on the north side of the valley, Bunker 13 and 14 on the south.[7] In the early days of the Second Assault the Germans set up an anti-tank gun and opened fire on Bunker 15. One of the crewmembers, Grinko, threw an anti-tank grenade at the assault gun and it was silenced but Grinko was killed. In the evening a German tank approached and fired at point-blank range. The gun commander was killed, the gun was destroyed and the shells caught fire. Attacks on the bunker continued. Finally the Germans approached and threw grenades towards the bunker. The survivors jumped out through the embrasure and escaped.

Kamyshly Ravine

The Kamyshly Ravine runs from the Mekenzievy Mountain plateau through narrow ravines where it widens near the village of the same name. A couple of

The Second Assault – 17 December 1941 to 1 January 1942

roads run through the valley, the most important being the one that leads up on to the plateau behind Hill 126.5. There is access to the ravine from the Belbek Valley and also through some of the smaller ravines that open into the Kamyshly from the Mekenzievy plateau.

There were three lines of defence running along the steep slopes of the ravine, mostly earth-timber emplacements and trenches. The first line ran along the southwestern slope of the ravine from the Belbek Valley to Mackenzie Farm and consisted of a double line of trenches with dugouts and communication trenches leading to the rear. The trench floors were lined with concrete. Barbed wire was strung between the trees in the forested areas. There were ten pre-cast concrete bunkers arranged in a line about 800m apart. Most of these were destroyed by German artillery fire.

The second line ran 500m west of Mackenzie Farm. It was a strong position with deep trenches and shelters and was defended by the guns of several pre-cast bunkers built from August to September 1941, in December and still more from January to March 1942. Most of the bunkers were destroyed by German artillery fire during the second assault and were not restored. Some of the bunkers and emplacements built from January to March used pieces of the destroyed bunkers. The third line consisted of earth-timber emplacements and three pre-cast bunkers. It was not a continuous line and was scattered throughout the forest and along the upper slopes of the Martynov Ravine.

The machine-gun companies in Bunkers 11, 12, 13 and 14 were engaged in the December battle and came under heavy fire. Bunker 11 was located on the slope of Hill 192, 200m west of Kamyshly Village. It was manned by students of the Black Sea Fleet Electromechanical School. Early in the morning of 18 December the Germans opened fire on the bunker. Incoming artillery shells detonated mines around the perimeter. Shrapnel flew through the embrasure but no one was hurt. German pioneers attacked the bunker and the crew opened fire with rifles and machine guns. The commander was wounded in the head but continued to fight. At 1500 hours another mine exploded, again sending shrapnel into the bunker and this time he was mortally wounded. Only two of the ten defenders of the bunker were left. The fight went on into the evening and at nightfall the Germans withdrew, leaving a large number of casualties at the foot of the bunker.

In Sector 2, the Germans attacked the positions of 2nd Marine Regiment, 7th Marine Brigade and 31st Rifle Regiment. By 1300 hours 1st Battalion of 7th Marine Brigade and 1st Battalion of 2nd Marine Regiment were pushed out of the Italian Cemetery and the Germans seized the eastern slopes of Mount Gasfort. The reserve company of the Communications School Training Detachment counter-attacked and the lines were restored. 2nd and 3rd Battalions of 2nd Perekop Regiment were pushed back from the heights 1km south of Lower Chorgun.

The Soviet artillery batteries were running out of ammunition. Rear-Admiral Zhukov, now acting commander at Sevastopol, sent an urgent request to Vice-Admiral Oktyabrsky for delivery of ammunition. If it wasn't delivered soon the batteries would run out of ammo. He also reported 3,500 killed and wounded in the fighting on 17 and 18 December and requested replacements. 8th Marine Brigade had suffered the greatest losses, about 1,700 men. Soviet reserve capabilities were reaching a critical point. The intense fighting of the past two days in Sectors 3 and 4 had forced the Soviets to withdraw deeper into the Kamyshly Ravine. The danger of a breakthrough in the Belbek Valley was now much greater. General Petrov's orders stipulated counter-attacks only in exceptional cases.

At dawn on 19 December the German offensive resumed. It was particularly strong in Sector 3 against the 2nd Perekop Regiment, 54th and 287th Rifle Regiment of the 25th Chapaevsky Division and 778th Regiment of the 388th Division in Kamyshly Ravine. Attacks were made against 8th Marine Brigade, 40th Cavalry Division and 90th Regiment of 95th Rifle Division in Sector 4. In the afternoon the Germans broke through at the junction of 2nd Battalion, 8th Brigade and 40th Cavalry Division. Reserves from 90th Rifle Regiment delayed the advance but heavy pressure was placed against the left flank of the brigade and a breakthrough was imminent. 8th Brigade and 40th Cavalry Division pulled back 1.5km to the east of Hill 133.3. Other units in Sectors 3 and 4 pulled back to maintain a solid line. The 241st Rifle Regiment broke out of its encirclement and joined up with other units in the sector.

The 50th Infantry Division, supported by armour and aircraft, attempted to break through in Sector 2 in the villages of Lower and Upper Chorgun. By the end of the day, after several attacks, 2nd Marine Regiment and 7th Marine Brigade were driven back and the Germans captured the eastern edge of Lower Chorgun. The feint by German forces in Sector 1 continued to prevent the Soviets from transferring troops to other sectors.

Rear-Admiral Zhukov was informed by the Black Sea Fleet command that transport ships were needed to support the Kerch-Feodisiya landings. Nevertheless, Sevastopol received as much support as possible. Kerch and Sevastopol – attack and defence – were interconnected. The transport *Abkhazia* arrived on 20 December with 1,500 men of 9th Marine Brigade and badly-needed supplies of ammunition. The *Chapaev* arrived on the 20th also carrying a large supply of ammunition. General Petrov and Rear-Admiral Zhukov reported that Sevastopol could hold for approximately three more days with the reinforcement of at least one rifle division, plus replacement of depleted companies, aircraft and ammunition. This report from Sevastopol brought immediate results. The General Staff of the Red

The Second Assault – 17 December 1941 to 1 January 1942

Army ordered one rifle division and two rifle brigades shipped to Sevastopol, plus additional aircraft and the desperately-needed ammunition for 107mm, 120mm and 80mm mortars, which had completely run out.

On 20 December fighting continued along the same fronts as on the previous days. Infantry and armour from 50th Division attempted to exploit their successes in Sector 2 by pushing through the Black Valley towards Inkerman. Fighting for the Italian Cemetery continued throughout the day. With the arrival of 1330th Rifle Regiment the Soviets attacked and recaptured the cemetery. In Sector 4 the Germans broke through at several points defended by 40th Cavalry Division and 773rd Regiment. General Petrov urged the commanders to hold out for the arrival of fresh troops on 21 December. 8th Marine Brigade and 90th and 241st Regiments held. The German 436th Infantry Regiment captured Kamyshly village and the 438th Regiment captured Hill 251.0. Both the 132nd and 22nd Divisions penetrated deep into the Soviet defences in the mountains. At the end of the day General Petrov assigned 778th and 782nd Regiments of 388th Rifle Division to Sector 4 to bolster the 773rd Regiment which had been at the front since the beginning of December.

Elements of the 9th Marine Brigade, the 345th Rifle Division and 79th Marine Brigade were scheduled to arrive in the next couple of days. They were loaded on transports at Tuapse and Novorossiysk. Ten infantry companies departed from Poti. 81st Tank Battalion from the 400th Rifle Division was loaded at Novorossiysk. Additional ammunition was also dispatched.

German attacks on 21 December were intended to complete the rout of Soviet forces and capture Sevastopol but that did not happen. Fighting was concentrated in Sectors 3 and 4 and was more violent than on the previous day. The Germans attacked the junction of 3rd Marine Regiment and 54th Rifle Regiments. The flanks caved in and the units were surrounded, but they counter-attacked and stabilised the line. In the vicinity of the 778th and 782nd Regiments, hill 192, later called *Trapez* by the Germans, changed hands several times. The hill overlooked Kamyshly Ravine. The Soviets lost 40 per cent of their men during this battle. The Germans had to bring in fresh troops and armour to recapture and finally hold the hill, the two Soviet regiments pulling back 1.5km southwest of Kamyshly. The 241st Regiment held the junction of the Kamyshly Ravine and the Belbek Valley across to the northern slopes of the valley at the foot of Kara-Tau. 8th Marine Brigade and 90th Rifle Regiment held off three attacks at Aranci. The village was captured but retaken.

Since 17 December the Soviets had suffered 2,000 killed and 6,000 wounded. In the morning of 21 December transports brought in the 79th Marine Brigade with 4,000 troops from Novorossiysk. The transport *Kharkov* brought in the 9th Marine Brigade from Tuapse. 79th Marine Brigade was sent to the Mekenzievy

Mountains to prepare to attack the following day. The good news was that the 345th Rifle Division and 81st Tank Battalion were also on their way to Sevastopol. General Petrov and Rear-Admiral Zhukov were informed that the 386th Rifle Division was also being sent to Sevastopol, scheduled to arrive on 26 December. Despite this great news for the Soviets, the Germans had advanced in the northern sectors and threatened the rear of the Soviet line. German losses were also heavy, however, and Eleventh Army was forced to reduce the intensity of its attacks.

On 22 December the Germans planned an advance through the defences north of Lyubimovka to attack towards Battery 30 and to continue attacks along the front of Sectors 3 and 4. 22nd, 24th and 132nd Infantry Divisions attacked along a 9km front. They drove a wedge between the 388th Rifle Division on the right flank of Sector 4 and the newly-arrived 79th Marine Brigade. A Soviet counter-attack was launched towards Kamyshly and the gap was closed. 40th Cavalry Division and 773rd Rifle Regiment maintained their positions north of the Belbek despite heavy German attacks.

The Soviet lines north of the Belbek were thinly held. If the Germans turned this line and reached the sea they could move along the coast south of Lyubimovka, flank Soviet positions on the Belbek and advance to the bay. Consequently, the troops defending Sector 4 were pulled back to shorter lines, decreasing the number of defenders necessary to hold the line. The withdrawal in Sector 4 forced the evacuation of and abandonment of Coastal Battery 10. The 388th Rifle Division was moved towards Inkerman to bolster the defences in the Black River Valley. 8th Marine Brigade pulled back to Hill 104.5. The hill overlooked the Simferopol highway and the road to Lyubimovka. On 23 December the Soviets counter-attacked from Sector 3 with the newly-arrived 79th Brigade and 287th Regiment in the direction of Kamyshly and were successful in keeping the Germans from advancing.

The German offensive resumed on Christmas Eve 1941, but was concentrated mainly in the north. The 24th, 132nd, 50th and part of the 22nd Infantry Divisions were on a 6km front supported by 300 guns. 22nd Infantry Division attacked in the Mekenzievy Mountains, towards the south, supported by assault guns. 1165th Rifle Regiment of 345th Rifle Division counter-attacked. The 1165th was commanded by Lieutenant-Colonel N. O. Guz, a veteran of the First World War. The counter-attack, supported by the 365th Anti-Aircraft Battery, called Fort Stalin by the Germans, drove the 22nd Division back to their original positions. Soviet aircraft attacked German infantry in the valley of Kara-Koba and in the Belbek Valley and Mekenzievy Mountains, and destroyers fired over 500 rounds on German targets. The Soviet artillery situation was critical. Ammunition warehouses only had 1,400 82mm and 120mm mortar shells remaining and the defenders lacked small-arms ammunition. Supplies were beginning to arrive but

The Second Assault – 17 December 1941 to 1 January 1942

they couldn't come in fast enough. The transport of the 345th Division's 10,000 soldiers was completed and the division moved up to the Mekenzievy Mountains and the forest north of Inkerman.

On 25 December German activity in Sectors 3 and 4 was minimal with the exception of a fight for hill 192 in Sector 4 and an attack on 241st Regiment and 40th Cavalry Division in Sector 3. The newly-arrived 1163rd Rifle Regiment was sent in to stabilise the lines. In late afternoon 8th Marine Brigade, together with 81st Tank Battalion and 1165th Rifle Regiment, launched a counter-attack. They were supported by the 905th and 397th Artillery Regiments and the armoured train *Zhelezniakov*, as well as three destroyers in the Black Sea. The Germans were pushed back from their trenches but countered with intense artillery and mortar fire and the Soviets were pushed back from the German lines. Back and forth, back and forth it went, but no major breakthroughs occurred.

The Kerch Peninsula landing operation began at dawn on 26 December, but the German offensive at Sevastopol continued, at least for the time being. In the morning the Germans attacked the junction of 79th Brigade and 287th Rifle Regiment and broke through to the defensive trenches of 1st Battalion of 69th Artillery Regiment. The gunners joined in the defence and depressed their guns to fire directly at German troops. Once again the Germans were pushed back. At 0900 the 8th Marine Brigade was attacked. The brigade received the support of Battery 57, Coastal Batteries 2, 12 and 14 and Anti-aircraft Batteries 75 and 365. The Soviet destroyer *Tashkent* also shelled the advancing Germans, halting the attack.

German troops at Sevastopol felt the immediate effects of the Soviet landings on the Kerch Peninsula. The attacks continued at Sevastopol but on a much smaller scale. The Germans continued to probe for weak points in the defence, still looking for the magic door key. At 1145 hours on 27 December 50th Infantry Division attacked Upper Chorgun, held by 7th Marine Brigade. Troops from 1st and 2nd Battalion repelled the attack. 79th Marine Brigade's position was also attacked but it too failed to gain any ground. On 27 December 8th Marine Brigade was replaced by two battalions of the 1165th Rifle Regiment. The remaining troops were withdrawn to the barracks of the Guards Regiment on the south side.

The 22nd Infantry Division attacked the 345th Rifle Division near the Mekenzievy Railway Station and met with mixed success. 1165th Rifle Regiment was pushed back but received support from its mortar battalion. The Germans were temporarily held back but broke through at the junction of the 1165th and 1163rd Regiments. This attack was stopped by Soviet artillery and mortar fire. The Germans then used rocket artillery and penetrated to the third line of defence, putting pressure on the 345th Division. After heavy fighting, the rail station was captured.

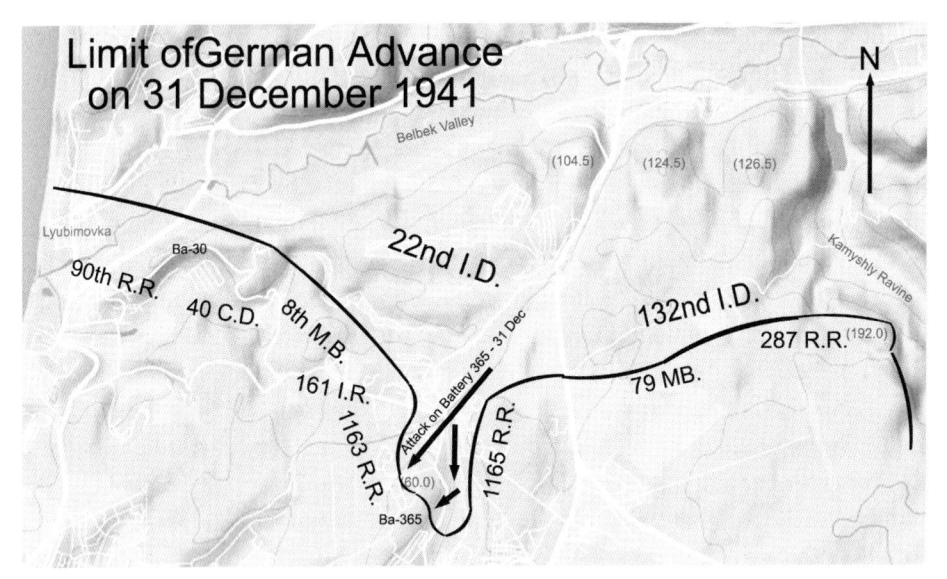

German line of advance in December 1941. (© OpenStreetMap contributors, Author's collection)

In Sector 3, despite the arrival of reserves, the 2nd Perekop Regiment was forced to retreat. 3rd Battalion of 7th Marine Brigade moved into the 2nd Perekop Regiment's position. General Petrov moved 4th Battalion of 161st Rifle Regiment to a position 1km south of the Mekenzievy Mountains. The loss of the Mekenzievy Mountain Station position was critical for troops in Sectors 3 and 4. The Germans were in striking distance of Inkerman and Sevastopol Bay. Naval gunfire support continued throughout the day and the battleship *Parizhskaya Kommuna* (Paris Commune) approached Sevastopol. Soviet aircraft bombed German troop concentrations while the Luftwaffe attacked the Chersonese airfield near the lighthouse, and 165 bombs were also dropped on the city. In the evening of 28 December Soviet radio operators intercepted a transmission directing German artillery and air to concentrate their fire on Battery 365, which the Germans called Fort Stalin.

At 0540 on the morning of 29 December the cruiser *Molotov* arrived, carrying 1,200 men of the 769th Regiment of 386th Rifle Division. This was the first contingent of the division to arrive in Sevastopol. At dawn, heavy artillery and mortar fire fell on Battery 30 and the Germans resumed their offensive in Sector 4. The Soviets countered with field and coastal artillery. 79th Brigade and 345th Division attacked the Mekenzievy Station. The *Parizhskaya Kommuna* fired 179 305mm and 265 120mm shells, and *Molotov* fired 205 180mm and 170 100mm shells. Destroyers and minesweepers fired about 200 shells. These caused heavy losses to German vehicles and personnel. The Soviet infantry attack met with initial success but by evening the Germans were once again in control of the station.

Further west, the Germans broke through the junction between 90th Rifle Regiment and 8th Marine Brigade, which had moved up from the south after a brief rest and captured the peacetime barracks that housed the troops of Battery 30. They began to move towards the command post of the battery in the eastern portion of the fort, which they referred to as 'The Bastion'. Two companies from 8th Brigade fought on the surface of the battery but didn't have enough men to hold off the attack. In response, General Petrov called in air strikes and concentrated coastal battery fire in the vicinity of the barracks adjacent to the command post. The bombardment began at 1330 hours, followed by strikes by Il-2 and Pe-2 bombers. Units from 90th Rifle Regiment and 8th Marine Brigade counter-attacked, clearing the barracks area.

In Sector 3 the Germans were determined to press their earlier success at Mekenzievy Station and proceeded to Hill 60, the location of Battery 365. They also attacked the junction of 287th Regiment and 79th Marine Brigade southeast of Hill 192. 80th Tank Battalion moved in to support the defenders and drove the Germans back. A Soviet counter-attack northeast of the station failed. General Petrov sent 2nd Battalion of 161st Rifle Regiment from Sector 2 to the vicinity of Mekenzievy Station. 2nd Battalion of 1330th Rifle Regiment was sent to shore up the defences of 7th Marine Brigade at the Italian Cemetery. Late that night the armoured train *Zhelezniakov* left its tunnel shelter several times to fire on Mekenzievy Station, then moved to Inkerman for maintenance. While there, it came under German fire. The train's sleeping compartment was hit and several crewmembers were killed. The train was immediately moved back into the shelter.

The fighting on 30 December was intense. In Sector 4 it was concentrated around Mekenzievy Station, which changed hands twice during the day. In the afternoon the Germans attacked 1165th Regiment of 345th Division, gaining 400m of territory south of the station. By the end of the day the attacks against Sector 4 stopped. The Soviets held Hill 192 across to Lyubimovka where an earlier German attempt to break through to Battery 30 had failed. Sectors 1 and 2 were quiet.

On Wednesday 31 December the Sevastopol command received a directive from the Military Council of the Caucasus Front to go on the offensive at Sevastopol to pin down German forces and expand the defensive zone. This task was impossible. Artillery stocks were almost gone. Many of the fighting units had suffered 50 per cent losses. The 241st Rifle Regiment had about 100 men left and 8th Marine Brigade and 40th Cavalry Divisions had even fewer. 79th Marine Brigade had 1,200 men remaining and 345th Rifle Division about 2,000. Oktyabrsky informed the council of the current situation and requested that the remaining elements of 386th Rifle Division and replacement companies be sent to Sevastopol post-haste.

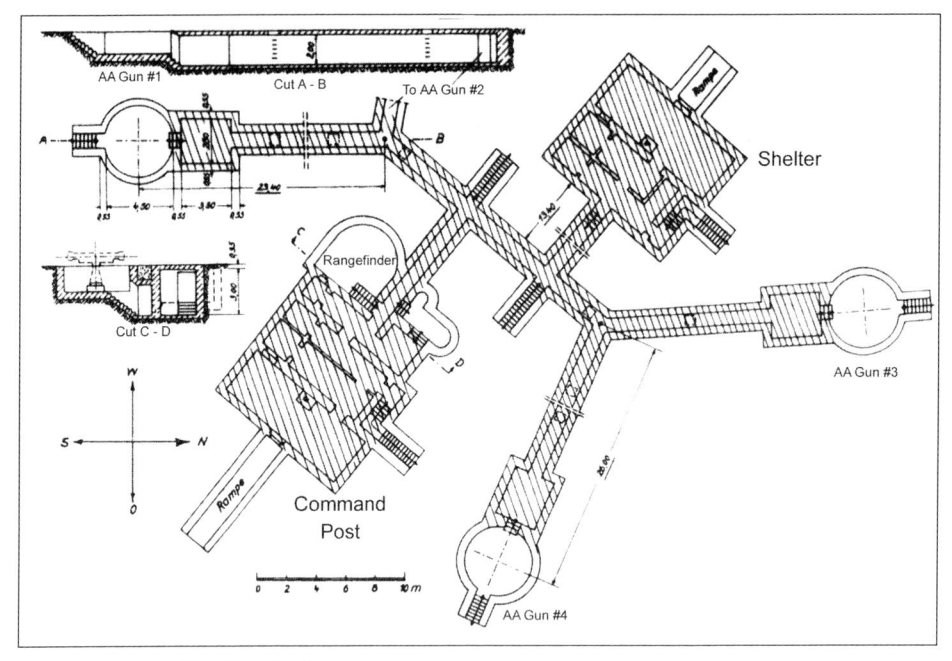

Plan of Battery 365 – Fort Stalin. (Nachtrag)

Oktyabrsky was also concerned with the situation of Anti-Aircraft Battery 365. The battery covered the approaches to the north side of the bay and it was currently threatened from three sides by German units. German attacks the previous day had focussed on the battery and it was clear they intended to capture it. The battery commander, Lieutenant Vorobyov, was ordered not to surrender the position under any circumstances.

December 31st was not only the last day of the year, but also the last day of Eleventh Army's Second Assault on Sevastopol. At dawn the Soviets took the initiative, unleashing a powerful artillery bombardment along a 3km front around Mekenzievy Station where the Germans were preparing for a final push to take Battery 365. The bombardment forced the German attack to be postponed for two hours. At 1000 hours two battalions from 22nd Infantry Division with six assault guns attacked the centre and right flank of 345th Rifle Division along the highway running from the station. Units of 8th Marine Brigade and 90th Rifle Regiment were also attacked. The initial attack was repulsed. At 1235 hours two fresh German battalions were brought in to attack the 345th while a second battalion attacked the left flank of 79th Infantry Brigade. The 1165th Regiment held its ground while 79th Brigade's left flank was pressured.

The 2nd Battalion of 7th Marine Brigade attacked from Upper Chorgun to the Italian Cemetery. 31st Rifle Regiment attacked Hill 154.7. The attack on the

Italian Cemetery by 2nd Battalion failed. Fighting at Upper Chorgun was initially successful but the Germans countered there as well. 31st Regiment held off the counter-attack and the fighting continued into the night.

At 1800 hours the 8th Marine Brigade and 90th and 161st Regiments of 95th Rifle Division, now having integrated 40th Cavalry Division's assets, launched an offensive in the Belbek Valley to relieve pressure on the 345th Division above Mekenzievy Station. The advance of 90th Regiment was met with heavy machine gun fire and grenades. The Regiment advanced about 300m.

Anti-Aircraft Battery 365 was hard pressed. After a massive bombardment, German infantry, supported by tanks, moved forward. Two of the battery's four guns were damaged and the two remaining guns opened fire on the tanks and infantry. Thirty German soldiers approached the battery but were pushed back by machine-gun fire. An hour later the offensive resumed but the Germans were unable to get through the barbed wire defences surrounding the battery. Only one of the battery's guns was in working condition. The attack continued from several different directions and the gun fired shrapnel rounds into the ranks of the advancing Germans. By nightfall the attack on Battery 365 ended and with it the Second Assault. Eight of Battery 365's gunners were killed and thirteen wounded but the battery held.

On New Year's Eve, German hopes were fading while Sevastopol's were looking up. At 1050 hours the 772nd Regiment of 386th Rifle Division and 3rd Guards Division of 8th Guards Reserve Command arrived by sea and moved to Dergacheva on the Suzdal Heights. Sevastopol command also received word that additional troops from 386th Division were on the way from Poti plus four companies of replacements totalling 1,000 men. German losses during the offensive were heavy and, due to the Kerch offensive, Manstein was forced to send two divisions there from Sevastopol. They would not return until late May 1942.

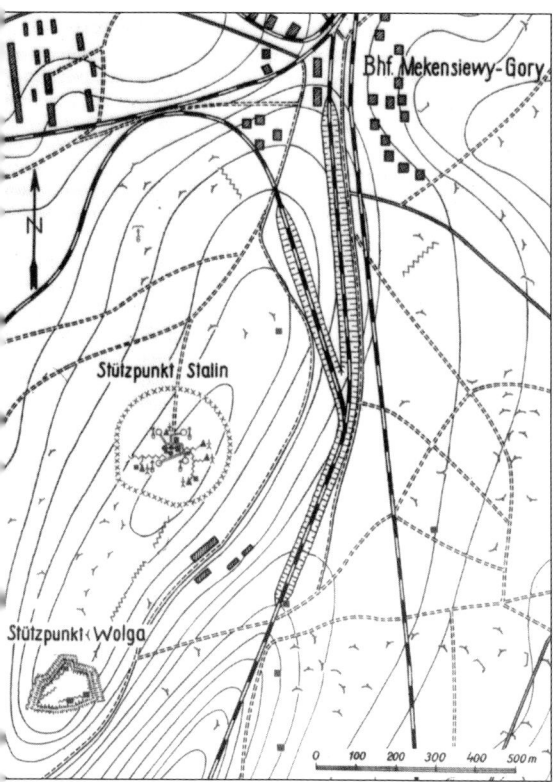

Hill 60 south of the Mekenzievy Mountain Station.
(Nachtrag)

On 31 December German troops learned they would be pulling back from their forward positions. At night the gunners dragged their guns along the road leading away from the Mekenzievy Station towards Kamyshly and a few hours later they arrived near Bakhchisarai. Over the last two days the assault division had penetrated deep into the Soviet positions and the men could hear the foghorns in Sevastopol harbour. However, these deep infiltrations left the German flanks vulnerable to a Soviet counter-attack and the Soviets were continually receiving reinforcements by sea. Therefore the front line was straightened to avoid the possibility of being cut off from the main force.

The Germans ended the Second Assault on Sevastopol, but they still had a significant force. Soviet attacks had failed to dislodge the Germans and so far the Kerch offensive had also failed to force them to withdraw more forces from Sevastopol. Vice-Admiral Oktyabrsky was ordered to continue to launch attacks in conjunction with the Kerch offensive to keep German troops pinned down at Sevastopol.

The objective of the Second Assault was to force Soviet troops into isolated pockets where they could be destroyed piecemeal and the city captured. To achieve this objective the Germans concentrated a greater force on a narrow front, unlike the First Assault which was launched on a broad front. However, German units were introduced into the battle piecemeal. Manstein planned to take Sevastopol in five days. Instead his forces lost thousands of men and achieved only minor tactical successes. The Soviets reacted swiftly and effectively in the threatened areas. Manstein did not expect the high state of morale of the defenders and the huge advantage the Soviets enjoyed through open lines of communication and the continuing capability of bringing in additional troops and supplies by sea.

As a result, the Germans made advances only in the Mekenzievy Mountains and north of the Belbek Valley, some of that due to the Soviet tactical withdrawal. They nearly succeeded in breaking through below Mekenzievy Mountain Station but the stubborn defence of Battery 365 wore them down. There the fate of the Second Assault was determined. A breakthrough put the Germans on the road to the ravines leading to the bay and encirclement of Soviet troops north of the bay. But with the grit and determination exhibited throughout the Second Defence and despite being vastly outnumbered and outgunned, the Soviets held on to the battery and slammed shut the door to the bay.

Soviet forces launched dozens of counter-attacks to retake ground they had lost. Most of the counter-attacks failed, as they had so far throughout the campaign and the battle ground into a stalemate. Determination came at a great cost; 23,000 Soviet casualties. Of this, more than half were wounded and many taken prisoner. But the Germans also suffered heavily, with 8,600 casualties between 17 and 31 December.

The Second Assault – 17 December 1941 to 1 January 1942

Replacements and reinforcements had continued to pour in to Sevastopol. In December the 79th Marine Brigade, 345th Rifle Division and 81st Tank Battalion arrived and played a critical role in stopping the offensive in Sector 4. Transports delivered 33,500 troops, 4,700 tons of ammunitions, 346 guns and mortars, twenty-six tanks, 178 other vehicles, 4,100 tons of fuel and 5,500 tons of miscellaneous cargo. They also evacuated 10,000 wounded and 2,200 civilians. Soviet pilots flew over 1,000 sorties in December. Seventeen different Soviet warships, on more than 200 missions, fired nearly 6,000 heavy shells at German troops.

1941 ended and with it the German First and Second Assaults. The main focus shifted to the Soviet offensives at Feodosia and Kerch. The heaviest fighting in Crimea took place there but it was anything but quiet on the Sevastopol front.

Chapter 5

January to June 1942

It has been quite common for historians – German, Soviet and others – to overlook or to provide very few details about the fighting that took place at Sevastopol during the period from January to late May 1942, instead shifting focus, rightly so, to the battles on the Kerch Peninsula. However, a closer examination of German and Soviet activities shows that significant events took place that are worthy of mention. In fact, Soviet casualties from January to March were quite high but this fact is left out of most accounts. It is also absent from both official German and Soviet records.

Four major attacks took place at Sevastopol on 6 and 16 January, 27 February and 11 March, to keep the pressure on German forces which might otherwise be transferred to Kerch. The Sevastopol offensives were poorly organised and not much is written about them officially because there wasn't much to boast about. Nevertheless, both sides launched attacks in the first few days of January. The Germans did so to consolidate their new defensive positions and to make the Soviets believe they had more troops than they actually did. The Soviet attacks were likewise aimed at improving their positions by taking ground abandoned by the Germans and by capturing lost ground from which to have greater chances of success in future attacks.

Mekenzievy Cordon Number 1 was a former barracks and guard house surrounded by a stone wall, used as a checkpoint along the Simferopol-Sevastopol Road. Prior to the Revolution it was used by paramilitary forest guards, so it was known as *Forsthaus* – Forest House – by the Germans. Cordon Number 2 was located near Mackenzie Farm. Cordon Number 3 was located along a road that led from the Martynov Ravine to Inkerman. At 0200 hours on 1 January about 200 men of the German 132nd Infantry Division, with three assault guns, attacked the Simferopol Highway at Mekenzievy Cordon Number 1, in the direction of the Grafkskaya (Count's) Ravine. The attacking company was formerly the 1st Battalion, 438th Regiment but the casualties had been extreme, one platoon having only eight men left. The three assault guns were all that then remained of the 190th Assault Gun Battalion. Another company of the 437th Infantry Regiment with four assault guns attacked the 1163rd and 1167th Regiments of the 345th Rifle Division in the vicinity of Mekenzievy Mountain Station. The aim of the attack was to mask the loss of units sent to Kerch. The Germans also wished to pull back to more natural defensive positions along the Kamyshly Ravine. The attack was a failure and this was the last attempt by the Germans to break through the Soviet line for several months.

In Sector 1, the 1330th Rifle Regiment, supported by artillery fire from 51st Artillery Regiment attacked North Fort (Hill 212.1) above Balaklava. As was the typical result, the Germans responded with heavy artillery and mortar fire and pushed the Soviets back to their starting position. In Sector 2 the 31st Rifle Regiment and the 7th Marine Brigade fought to regain previously lost positions and improving their position by eliminating a Rumanian salient between Hill 154.7 – the North Nose – and Mount Gasfort. They were party successful. A counter-attack by the Rumanian 1st Brigade was repulsed by the 5th Battalion of 7th Brigade and the battalion seized Hill 90.5 – Telegraph Hill. The Rumanians retreated.

Heavy fighting broke out in the area of the Italian cemetery and Upper Chorgun. However, in the second half of the day in all areas of the second sector, Soviet troops were forced to retreat. 31st Rifle Regiment also attacked and moved ahead 300m in the Kara-Koba valley and on to the reverse slopes of Mount Chirish-Tepe (Hill 269.0).

In Sector 3 the 79th Marine Brigade and the left-flank units of the 287th Rifle Regiment of the 25th Chapaevsky Division fought for possession of Hill 192.0. They advanced 300m and by the end of the day had dug in 800m southeast of the height and 500m north of Cordon Number 1. The Regiment's 2nd Battalion moved up 1km and took over the road running along Kamyshly Ravine. In Sector 4 the 345th and 95th Rifle Divisions, supported by field artillery, coastal and anti-aircraft artillery and the armoured train *Zhelezniakov*, fought to recapture Mekenzievy Mountain Station but the attack failed. The cruiser *Molotov* and destroyer *Soobrazitelnyy*, at anchor in Sevastopol Bay, opened fire against enemy troop concentrations. The *Molotov* fired ninety-four shells and the *Soobrazitelnyy* fired fifty-six. On 1 January the Local Infantry Regiment took over the positions of 8th Marine Brigade. On 14 January the brigade was disbanded by order of Admiral Oktyabrsky. In a strange twist, the 1st Marine Regiment of Sevastopol was renamed the 8th Marine Brigade.

In Sector 4 there was a battle for Hill 90.2 1km northwest of Mekenzievy Station, near the barracks of Battery 30. Two companies of 22nd Infantry Division were guarding the station which had been fortified to prevent its capture. The Germans kept up the pressure on the Soviets until the morning of 2 January. They then moved back to new positions and on 4 January moved to the division collection point near Bakhchisarai. In the afternoon 345th and 95th Rifle Divisions and 8th Marine Brigade, supported by coastal and anti-aircraft artillery and the *Zhelezniakov*, fought for the station but were unsuccessful in capturing it. The Germans claim there was no fighting, perhaps only clashes with the rearguard of retreating German troops. Soviet accounts claim that they moved forward cautiously to find the fortifications abandoned. They tossed grenades into the dugouts and bunkers and ran into small groups of Germans who quickly retreated. The Soviet advance that day was significant, averaging 1.5km. However, these gains appear to be more the result of German tactical retreats than victories in battle.

The 772nd Rifle Regiment of 386th Rifle Division arrived in Sevastopol without any of their heavy weapons or equipment, except for small arms. The completion of the arrival of the division was a big boost to the Soviets. They were placed opposite the Rumanian 1st Mountain Brigade.

The Kerch offensive reduced the number of German troops at Sevastopol. By 1 January most of the 170th Infantry Division was gone. As of 2 January the 132nd, 72nd and 50th Divisions remained in their positions. The 105th Infantry Regiment of 72nd Division and most of the 132nd Division were preparing to move to Kerch. After the recapture of Feodosia by the Germans most of the 132nd Division returned to Sevastopol. Eleventh Army had sufficient strength to maintain their land blockade of Sevastopol and to counter Soviet landings at Kerch, but it did not have enough to mount a major attack.

The Soviets created a strong offensive force in Sector 4 that included the redeployed 172nd Division, with 514th and 31st Regiments. This newly-formed strike group planned an offensive for 6 January with the goal of retaking the heights above Mamashai at the mouth of the Kacha River.

On 6 January the Soviets attacked, but the German positions were still strongly defended. The 95th Rifle Division attacked the 161st Infantry Regiment, which had fallen back to defences at the former Belbek airfield. The attack was stopped and two Soviet T-26 tanks were hit by artillery. The move towards the coastal road to Kacha failed.

The 172nd Division crossed the Belbek Valley and attacked along the road leading up towards Hill 133.3. They reached the Belbek River, then headed towards the German 31st Regiment's position but were stopped by German artillery. The 514th Regiment attacked the village of Belbek and crossed the river, capturing the outskirts of the village. They ran into trouble trying to take artillery Bunker 5. Despite the weakness of the attack, 172nd Division moved up about 750m to the northwestern outskirts of Belbek at the junction of the road leading to what is identified as the 'Tomato Plant'. The Germans then retreated to the heights above the Simferopol Highway. Soviet attacks were carried out with minimal air or artillery support. Batteries 30 and 35 were out of commission for repairs. Battery 116 at Maximova Farm fired on the area of Battery 10, now occupied by German gunners and was hit by German artillery, knocking out a 130mm gun. It was quickly repaired and the battery soon returned to action.

On 7 January the 95th and 172nd Rifle Divisions continued the offensive but were hit by German shelling from 22nd Artillery Regiment's guns. The 95th reached the barbed wire perimeter of Belbek airfield but, after close combat with German troops, they were forced to withdraw and the offensive came to an end.

On 10 January German heavy mortars continued to shell the front. The heavy batteries were set up near Battery 10 and counter-battery fire from Soviet Coastal Batteries 114 and 113 stopped the German shelling. The Germans withdrew several batteries to Kerch but left the 857th Artillery Regiment with four batteries of 210mm mortars (two guns each), the 815th Heavy Division with four batteries of two 305mm Skoda mortars and the 737th Heavy Howitzer Battalion with Czech 150mm howitzers.

On 16 January the Soviets launched a second attack at Sevastopol, in conjunction with an attack at Feodosia. This one was more successful. The main attack was focused in Sector 4 in the direction of the Belbek airfield. 7th Marine Brigade conducted diversionary attacks in the Kara-Koba Valley and at Mount Gasfort. The Germans were pushed back at Kara-Koba and about 800m from the Martynov Ravine. The Soviets captured the heights above the ravine. The 514th Rifle Regiment, sent from Sector 4, came close to victory near Mount Gasfort but was unable to dislodge the Rumanian defenders. German positions on Telegraph Hill and the bend of the Black River were captured by 5th Battalion of 7th Marine Brigade.

Soviet forces at Feodosia were defeated on 17 January, which allowed the Germans to release the infantry regiments of the 132nd Division to return to Sevastopol. The offensive at Sevastopol continued but without any further shift in the lines. Batteries 116, 111 and 19 shelled German positions on the eastern slopes of the Italian Cemetery and Soviet aircraft launched several attacks. In the evening the Soviets, certainly not helped by the news from Feodosia, ran out of steam. Soviet troops lost about 2,500 wounded and 1,000 dead in just two days. Rumanian losses totalled 280 dead and 500 wounded. Total German losses are not known, except that 22nd Division records show 327 wounded and 185 dead.

On 19 January a small-scale amphibious landing was carried out at the mouth of the Kacha River near Mamashai by a company of 126 marines, former members of 8th Brigade. While the Germans were distracted by this force, another party landed further north and blew up the remains of Battery 10.

Repair work was completed on the damaged turret of Battery 35. Further repairs to put the battery back into working condition would take another month. The replacement barrels were stored in a warehouse in Cossack Bay and were brought up by cranes. The repairs were carried out by specialists from the Bolshevik (former Obukhov) plant. The team then moved on to make repairs at Battery 30 when they were finished at Battery 35. On 26 January teams began to change out

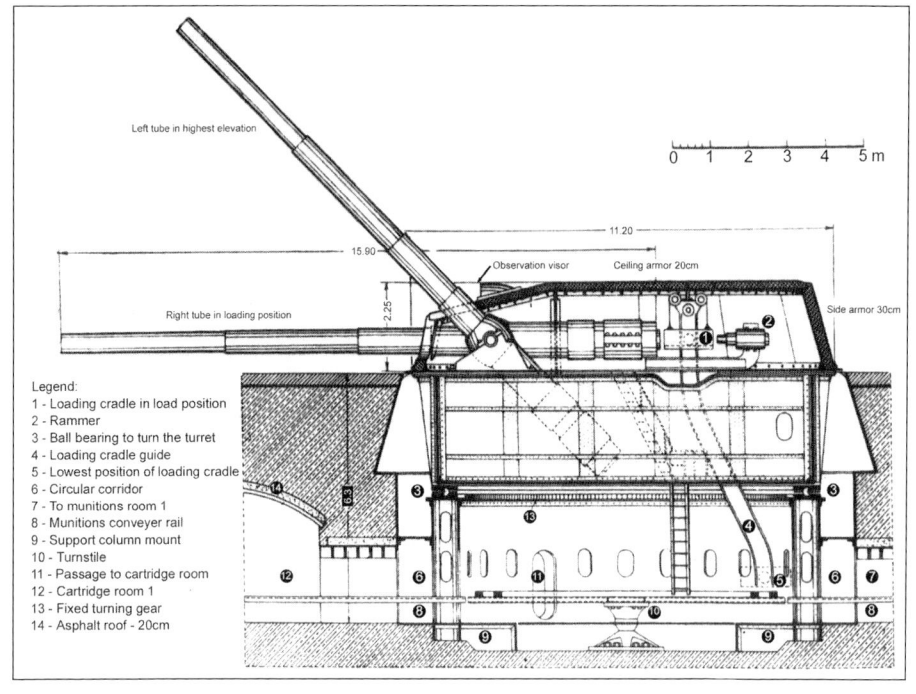

Schematic of one of the 305mm gun turrets of Battery 30 – Fort Maxim Gorki I. (Nachtrag)

the barrels of the guns at Battery 30. The dismantling of the damaged barrels took one week and sixteen days later the battery was back in operation.

Most of the coastal battery guns were beginning to wear out. Batteries 113, 115 and 116 each only had one gun remaining. One major problem was that the Bolshevik production plant where the naval guns were produced was in Leningrad, currently under siege by the German army. An attempt was made by divers to raise the casemate guns from the cruiser *Chervona Ukraina* at the request of General Morgunov, as they were less worn than the coastal battery guns. The request was initially denied because the removal of the guns would damage the deck of the ship, which could possibly be raised and repaired. The guns were later removed by the divers, however.

On 2 February the exchange of barrels in Coastal Batteries 114 and 112 was completed. The replacement guns were recovered from sunken ships by divers from the Naval Diver's School (EPRON). Battery 2's guns, worn to about 30 per cent, were replaced and the old barrels moved to the former Royal Battery 4 on the north side of the bay and the former Battery 5 on Matyushenko Bay. The numerical designation of coastal batteries was changed. For example, Battery 111 was designated 701, 112 became 702bis, 113 became 702, etc.

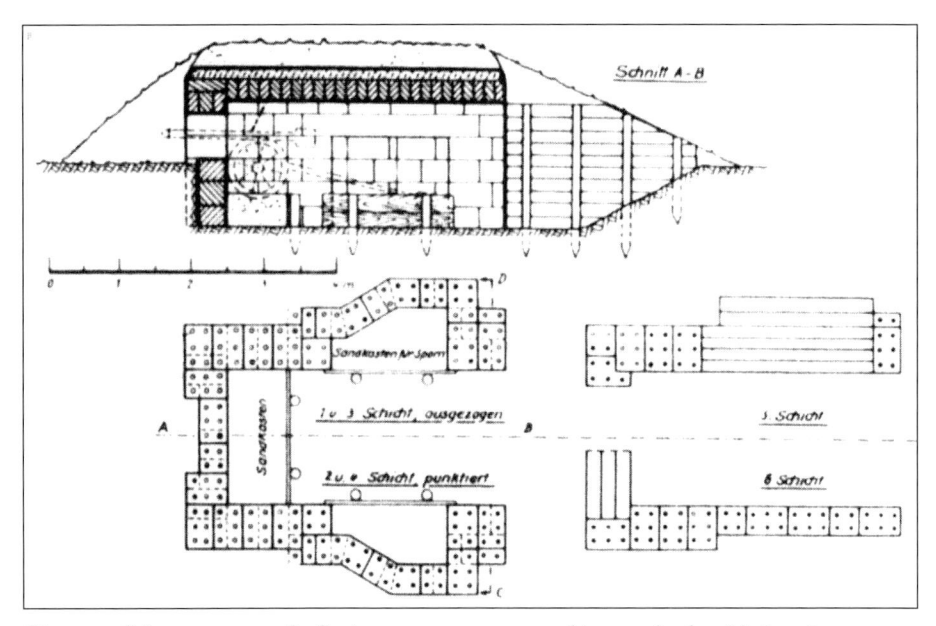

Diagram of the components of a Soviet pre-cast concrete machine-gun bunker. (Nachtrag)

On 28 January the transport *Bialystok* arrived in Sevastopol, carrying 528 replacement troops and ammunition. At the same time the 952nd Artillery Regiment with 122mm guns arrived aboard the transport *Krasnyy Kuban* ('Red Kuban') along with artillery units of the 386th Rifle Division.

Soviet soldiers continued to improve the defences in preparation for the next attack that was sure to come. Despite the cold, they worked in round-the-clock shifts, following the directions of the engineering and construction battalions. A soldier from the 287th Regiment wrote: 'Infantrymen walked around with bloody blisters on their hands; but every soldier continued to bite into the folds of the Mekenzievy Mountains.'[1]

Construction of bunkers was mostly done at night and the work was carefully camouflaged. Pre-cast concrete bunkers were installed along the rear lines of defence. These were cast in the assembly plant and brought to the front where they were connected together with steel bars. German engineers who examined the pre-cast bunkers gave their assessment:

> The individual blocks were rather negligently manufactured. They were missing a gravel compound, had bent rods and cement was not used to anchor the rods in place. When fired on by 88mm anti-tank guns from a distance of 800m such structures were completely destroyed after being hit by three shells. The blocks themselves were damaged only slightly. This is

A Soviet pre-cast concrete machine-gun bunker in the Laboratory Ravine. (Nemenko Collection)

explained, first, by a poor manufacturing process and secondly, hasty and careless construction operations.[2]

The Germans also strengthened their positions and sent out patrols to keep watch on the enemy and to pinpoint targets for their artillery batteries. Day after day German artillery and mortars struck the Soviet positions, perhaps to send a reminder that they were still there. The Germans began to use code names to refer to their positions among Sevastopol's geographical features. The ridge running from Hill 104.5, which they called *Ölberg*, to Battery 30 was renamed *Haccius* Ridge. Hill 192.0 was called *Trapez* and Gasfort Mountain was renamed *Kappelenberg* (Chapel Hill). Many other heights and landmarks were renamed, including the most heavily fortified flak batteries and to these were given the nomenclature 'Fort'. Battery 365 was renamed Fort Stalin. The upland redoubts, which had no Soviet names given to them, were designated as Fort Donets, Ural, Molotov, GPU and Siberia. Fort B was renamed Fort Cheka. Battery 366 adjacent to North Fort was called Fort Lenin. Battery 30 became Fort Maxim Gorki I; Battery 35 Fort Maxim Gorki II.

Supplies, including ammunition, winter clothing and food continued to arrive aboard ships of the Black Sea Fleet. Each delivery was followed by the loading of wounded and civilians and spent artillery shell casing.[3] The underground factories continued to produce replacement weapons for Soviet units. During December Sevastopol's underground factories manufactured and sent to the front ninety-three mortars, 8,000 grenades, 4,439 mortar bombs and 9,650 anti-tank mines, plus miscellaneous property and equipment. Production continued into the spring.

Boris Voyetkhov describes his visit to one of the underground factories:

> The biggest underground store was on Matushenko Hill in the quarry and in the tunnel of the northern hydroelectric station. Another place was located at Inkerman Quarry. The entrance to underground Sevastopol was through a long dark tunnel. This huge cellar was divided by heavy metal screens into cubicles where hundreds of lathes produced mines. The motor of a tractor roared, generating electricity. When the motor stopped the lights went out. When that happened every worker lit a cigarette. They had agreed to only smoke when the lights went out. Workers of other shifts slept on three tiers of bunks connected to the tunnel walls. The machines turned 24 hours a day. The air smelled of cooking, gas, cigarette smoke and stale air. The entire front relied on the factory for mines.[4]

S. Klebanov also wrote about one of the underground factories:

> The enemy storms, bombs, shells, attempting to break up the military rhythm of the life of our city and in Sevastopol a second city arises – under the ground. The factory shops and hospital wards, the schools and laboratories of underground Sevastopol – these are the dugouts of the city stronghold. And the front receives an uninterrupted supply of shells and trench mortars, bombs and grenades.
>
> At first one scarcely believes that somewhere in the bowels of these cliffs is an industrial giant. The corridor is in no way different from the corridors in many factories, long and spacious, with a narrow gauge line running down the middle of it. Moving down it one gradually forgets that one is underground. I walked together with Telichev, foreman of the machine shop, along the central aisle, past the noisy machine tools. The huge halls were almost indistinguishable from the ordinary factory shop. The foreman stopped near a stack of bombs and grenades. 'These are Sevastopol made,' he said. 'The people working here think a lot of this and are proud of it.' We came out of the aisle and entered a hall as large as a subway station. There were beds here; many of them. This was a dormitory.
>
> It was necessary to ensure constant ventilation, to maintain a normal temperature. The first few days, after three to four hours of hard work people

112   The Defence of Sevastopol 1941–1942

Soviet workers in one of the underground factories at Sevastopol, 1941 or 1942. (LOC)

breathed heavily and the imprint of fatigue was stamped on their faces. Another ventilator was obtained somehow, a suction fan was installed and fresh sea air came in.[5]

M. Turovsky described living conditions underground:

In the spacious galleries where new champagne used to be stored for years, the sound of shoemakers' hammers and the whirring of sewing machines can now be heard. It is here that the big shops of a clothing and boot factory which supplies the front with footwear, uniforms and underwear are located.

The dormitories are located in the adjoining gallery. There are several of them here, dormitories for men, dormitories for women, rooms for families, separated from one another by plywood walls. 'I live on Trade Union Street'. 'And I live on International Boulevard', is what the workers say to one another jokingly about the narrow lanes within the great gallery. It is pleasant to enter a family 'apartment'. The beds are neatly made and in the centre of the room is a small table. Many people have brought carpets here from their city apartments. The walls are decorated with portraits and photographs. Only the heavy stone arch overhead reminds one that this is not an apartment but an underground gallery. There is a kitchen factory in the underground city, a Red Cross station, nurseries, a kindergarten, a school, a cinema, a library, a reading room and a playroom.[6]

The workers in the underground factories were very adept at developing or improvising weapons. For example, 'Sevastopol grenades' were 50mm-diameter pipes 20cm long, packed with explosives. Flamethrowers were modified for use on tanks. The underground factories that lined the shore of Sevastopol Bay produced homemade mines, mortars and a variety of other weapons and tools. Beginning on 1 February, worn-out 76mm gun barrels were converted to 82mm mortars and delivered to the front lines.

On 8 February the Germans shelled troops in Sector 4 and hit the turrets of Battery 30. A total of 700 projectiles ranging from 105mm to 305mm calibre were fired at the battery. Despite the number of shells fired, Battery 30 returned fire on 57th and 256th Corps Artillery Regiments. Later, Batteries 2 and 702 and the destroyer *Kharkov* opened fire.

The bombardment of Battery 30 is described by P. I. Musyakov:

The Germans began firing on the battery in the early morning. Their guns were zeroed in and the shells fell precisely on the battery's firing position. The camouflaged masking used to conceal the work being done on the barrels caught fire, filling the hilltop with yellow smoke. Sailors rushed to the surface to deal with the fires and shells continued to explode, throwing debris and mud mixed with sleet on the workers. Other batteries came to the rescue and soon silenced the German guns. Orderlies carried wounded and dead on stretchers.[7]

Soviet shipping was hit hard during the Kerch offensive. Luftwaffe raids damaged and sunk several transport ships. As a result, the shipment of material to Sevastopol was reduced. In December forty-one ships delivered supplies to the base, but this fell to twenty-eight in January and twenty-four in February. Despite the drop in ammunition deliveries the Soviets kept up harassing strikes on German positions. The armoured train *Zhelezniakov* recorded seventy raids from 7 January to 1 March in which fifteen German bunkers, thirteen machine-gun nests, one heavy battery and several aircraft and vehicles were destroyed.

On 27 February the third Soviet offensive at Sevastopol began. The 172nd and 345th Rifle Divisions bore the brunt of the fighting. The main attack was delivered in Sectors 3 and 4. At 0730 hours, after a thirty-minute artillery barrage, 172nd Rifle Division and 25th Chapaevsky Division moved out. 345th Rifle Division headed to the Martynov Ravine. 40th Cavalry Division attacked Mekenzievy Mountain Station and moved up the slopes from Sukharno Ravine to a hill near the railway track about 60m from the Sukharno railway tunnel.

161st Rifle Regiment attacked the front line of German defences in the vicinity of Belbek airfield that had been improved by the Germans over the last few weeks.

They advanced 400m but were stopped by heavy artillery fire. An attack took place on Hill 103.9 at the junction of the German 65th and 47th Regiments. The 33rd Rumanian Regiment, a reserve unit, moved in to plug the gap. Soviet tanks broke through to the Kacha highway but were repelled by the 560th Anti-Tank Battalion.

An attack by the 514th and 31st Rifle Regiments of 172nd Rifle Division against 16th Infantry Regiment was repulsed, but the 287th and 2nd Perekop Regiments were more successful. They attacked the slopes of Kamyshly Ravine and reached the top, advancing almost 2km. The fighting was brutal but short and the Germans were pushed out of their trenches. 50th Infantry Division was not prepared for the attack. Part of the division was being sent to Kerch, and also they didn't believe the Soviets were capable of an offensive. 2nd Perekop Regiment battled the 24th Infantry Division and advanced about 3km to Mackenzie Farm but could not capture it. Fighting in the Mekenzievy Mountain forests was difficult, especially communication between units and the ability to respond to enemy action in a timely manner. The 345th Rifle Division attacked on the right flank of the 1st Battalion of 79th Brigade, in order to align the front with that of the 287th Regiment.

At 0730 hours on 27 February the Soviets attacked in Sector 2, beginning with an artillery bombardment supporting an attack by the 1330th Regiment. The Germans returned fire and for an hour or so the exploding shells and mines enveloped the entire front in smoke. The hardest fighting was in the area of 4th Battalion of the 1330th. 13th Company of 4th Battalion moved to the German flank and opened fire on the trenches, clearing out the enemy. The Soviets then dug into the new position. 14th Company advanced 50m and captured a German machine-gun outpost. New trenches were dug overnight and new mines were laid along the front. The advance had taken the Soviets to the area of Bunker 72.

On 28 February the Soviets consolidated their gains on the Mekenzievy plateau, capturing hill 100 behind Mackenzie Farm which was held by the 24th Infantry Division. 2nd Perekop Regiment and 54th Rifle Regiment headed in the direction of the farm but failed to capture it.

The Soviet offensive ended on 1 March. The German 50th and 24th Infantry Divisions had been pushed back from their previously-held positions. The 1165th Rifle Regiment reached Zalankoi (m. Holmovka) and the 1163rd took Bink-Otarkoy (m. Frontove). The Soviets crept closer to the German positions on Mounts Kaya-Bash and Yaila-Bash and at Cherkez-Kerman. On Monday, 2 March the Germans counter-attacked from the north to the southeast near Mackenzie Farm and the Kamyshly Ravine. They slipped into a gap between 1163rd Regiment of 345th Division and 79th Marine Brigade. The gap was caused when 287th Regiment lagged behind to capture Hill 115.7 and to await further orders. As a result the Germans broke through to the rear of 1163rd Regiment. Some troops stayed behind to fight but the situation was very dangerous for the entire division. 2nd

Perekop Regiment also found itself behind the German lines and was forced to retreat. Some companies were isolated and had to make their way through the wooded maze of the Mekenzievy Mountains. Others broke through the deep gorges into the German defences but many were lost and their fates unknown.

On 3 March the Germans pressed their attack. Units of the 132nd and 50th Divisions recaptured hill 115.7, ejecting the 287th Regiment troops. By evening the 79th Brigade was forced to leave Hill 100. The 149th and 151st Regiments of 40th Cavalry Division were sent into the battle but stopped from advancing by German artillery. The 40th Division attempted to recapture Hill 115.7 but failed and part of the division was trapped, although men from the two cavalry regiments escaped on horseback into the mountains. They were forced to dismount in the thick forest but eventually made their way back to their barracks.

The 345th and 40th Divisions suffered serious losses during the two-day battle. LIV Corps documents[8] report the capture of 3,872 Soviets. The 1167th Rifle Regiment of 345th Division was disbanded and the 40th Cavalry Division folded into 2nd Perekop Regiment. The 80th Reconnaissance Battalion of the 25th Chapaevsky Division was destroyed. Of those not captured, about 3,500 were wounded and killed. The Sevastopol garrison went back on the defensive.

Eleven new artillery bunkers were completed by 10 March. Bunker 7 was repaired and a precast concrete roof added. It was equipped with a 76mm gun. Bunker 8 was repaired with concrete blocks. The front was stabilised along a line 2km north of and 2.5km northeast of Lyubimovka and the Belbek Valley to Kamyshly Ravine west of Mackenzie Farm. It followed the line: Mount Kara-Koba–Hill 154.7–Hill 90.5–Mount Gasfort–Yalta Highway–Kamary–Genoese Tower. On 12 March 7th Brigade attacked between Hill 154.7 and Hill 90.5 to improve its defensive position. They moved as far as the forward German trenches but could move no further forward. Other demonstration attacks were unsuccessful.

The sea remained Sevastopol's lifeline. In February 10,823 men were transported to Sevastopol raising the total number of troops to about 79,000. In March about 4,500 troops were transported and the total, with losses and wounded, remained around 80,000. In April 8,327 arrived, raising the garrison to 87,000. In May, 14,973 were brought in, raising the total to 101,000. In June about 3,500 troops arrived. The total reached a peak of 104,000 before 6 June after which losses outweighed gains.

April picked up where March left off with shelling, sniping and the construction of fortifications. Luftwaffe attacks on ships increased and cargo transport was greatly reduced. Other significant events in April are as follows:

- April 6th 1942 – deployment of 436th, 437th and 438th German Infantry Regiments to Kerch.

- April 22th 1942 – Headquarters of VIII Air Corps, commanded by Baron Wolfram von Richthofen, arrived in Crimea.
- April 27th 1942 – according to German documents, the number of German and Rumanian troops reached a low of 73,800. The Soviets, by comparison, had 82,887, of which 73,103 were combat troops.
- April 28th 1942 – Vice-Admiral Oktyabrsky returned to Sevastopol.

On 29 April a new German Air Group, III/JG52, arrived in Crimea. In early May the German VIII Air Corps began to arrive in Crimea in greater numbers, composed of I/KG76 with twenty-eight Ju 88A-4s, I/JG3 (twenty-six Bf 109F-4s) and I/JG77 (thirty-seven Bf 109F-4s). The number of bombers doubled and fighters increased five-fold. For the time being, however, the number of sorties against Sevastopol was minimal, the attacks concentrating on Soviet transports at Kerch, Tuapse and Novorossiysk.

On 6 May the city was attacked by air from several different directions. About 100 high explosive and incendiary bombs fell. The Luftwaffe flew non-stop sorties from 6 to 8 May. Soviet accounts claim the reason was to divert attention from the Kerch front but in reality the increased activity was also to conceal the arrival by train of the 781st Heavy Artillery Regiment from Simferopol. The trains were delivering Dora, the largest artillery gun in the world, which was set up on a triple railway track in a cutting in Kazan-Tash hill, north of Bakhchisarai. The gun's range was 30km and from its location it was 25km to Battery 30, its primary target.

On 7 May the German offensive to recapture the Kerch Peninsula began and six days later the Kerch front collapsed. Transport ships were used to evacuate what was left of Soviet forces from the Kerch Peninsula. Vice-Admiral Oktyabrsky protested against the removal of troops from Kerch as it would mean the only troops left in Crimea were at Sevastopol and returning German troops would give them a greater advantage in numbers. Otherwise it was a quiet day in Sevastopol but the storm was coming.

The period of January to May was used by the Soviets to make significant improvements to their defences. Here is a description of Sectors 1 and 2.

Sector 2 followed a twisting line 17.5km long. Troops assigned to the sector during the Third Assault were: 386th Rifle Division (769th, 775th, 772nd Rifle Regiments and 952nd Artillery Regiment), 7th Marine Brigade (five battalions) and 8th Marine Brigade (four battalions). The sector was supported by Battery 702 and Battery 703. Each battery had two 130mm B-7 guns taken from the sunken cruiser *Chervona Ukraina*. Battery 18bis, a 152mm battery, was located near the village of Dergacheva. One other stationary battery was located near Novo Shuli.

Sector 2 had three lines of defence consisting of twenty battalion strongpoints. The forward line passed through the top of the heights and along the reverse

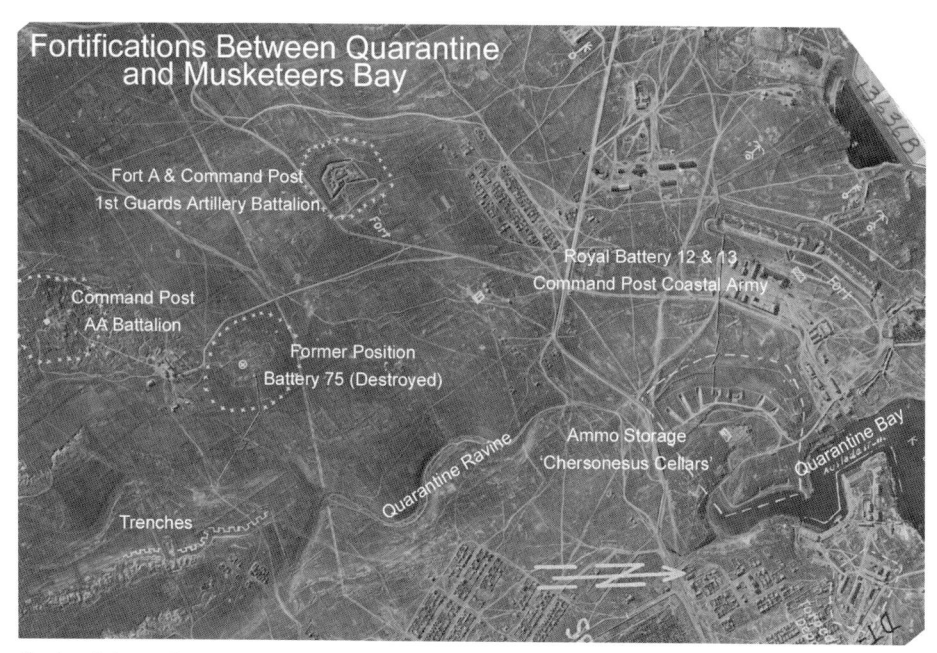

Soviet defences between Quarantine and Musketeers' Bays. (Aerial photograph provided by John Calvin of www.wwii-photos-maps.com, altered by the author)

slopes of Mount Gasfort, Telegraph Hill and the heights above the Chorguns to Shuli. The main line was sub-divided into several defensive areas:

- The rear line along the slopes of Sapun Ridge.
- Mount Gasfort.
- Fedyukhiny Heights and the Black River.
- The forward line of heights along the road from Chorgun to Shuli.
- Strongpoints in the Kara-Koba Valley.
- The foot of the heights of Sugar Head and Mount Kara-Koba.

The second line began 300m south of the Yalta Highway and ran to the rear slopes of Mount Gasfort, a key position in the defence of the highway and the valley between Balaklava and the Fedyukhiny Heights. The Soviet troops defending this position were placed on the reverse slopes for their protection but most of the actual fighting had taken place on top of the mountain around the former Italian (Sardinian) Cemetery and the chapel ruins that account for its German name – Chapel Hill. The crest of the hill was dotted with observation posts. The 7th Marine Brigade was posted on and around Mount Gasfort, the 1st Battalion on the right, the 2nd Battalion in the centre and 5th Battalion on the left. The 4th Battalion was in the rear. The command post of 7th Brigade was located on the

Fedyukhiny Heights. 5th Battalion defended the hollow between Mount Gasfort and Telegraph Hill near the Chorgun aqueduct and 2nd Battalion was in the valley between the Fedyukhiny Heights and the Yalta Highway.

The Italian Cemetery was located on top of Mount Gasfort. The cemetery's chapel was built of stone and the walls of the cellar were 1.2m thick. It was situated in a defile. The cemetery was surrounded by a high stone wall. A series of trenches with dugouts were located all along the heights. 2nd Battalion's position was located on difficult, rocky ground. It was impossible to dig shelters in the hard ground and the battalion had to use boulders and remnants of the stone wall for protection.

The road to Shuli passed between the positions of 7th Brigade on Telegraph Hill and 386th Division on Hill 154.7 and was covered by Bunkers 70 and 71. The guns from these bunkers were removed during the spring and replaced with machine guns. The lines of the 386th Division consisted mostly of trenches and a few pre-cast bunkers. The lines of 8th Brigade were a continuation of the lines of the 386th Division. They ran from the top of Mount Chirish-Tepe (Hill 269.0) and along the road that ran from the Kara-Koba Valley to the Mekenzievy Mountains. The defences in the area of 8th Brigade were the same as the 386th Division – trenches with dugouts and bunkers.

This zone had a defensive ditch with a rampart running parallel to the cliffs and overlapped two roads that descended from the Mekenzievy Plateau. The ditch and rampart ran along the foot of the mountain. The left flank of the line joined up with the defensive line of Sector 3. The entire line was blocked by barbed wire and mines. Two strongpoints equipped with bunkers and field fortifications were located on top of several heights in the valley. These belonged to 386th Division and were represented by three lines of defence along the slopes of Mounts Kara-Koba and Sugar Head. The first line was a ditch with a rampart about 3.5km long. The second line was along the road to the Kara-Koba Farm on the Black River. Several bunkers and anti-tank obstacles were located along this line, including a pre-cast concrete bunker with a 45mm gun. At the foot of Mount Kara-Koba, along the road to Sugar Head were several pre-cast concrete bunkers on the mountain side of the road. All of them were destroyed by heavy artillery fire. The last line of defence was located on top of Mount Kara-Koba and consisted of trenches cut into the rock and several bunkers.

The Inkerman Valley was well defended. Cadets from the VMUBO built one line of defences at the foot of the Fedyukhiny Heights along the Black River. The line ran along the former Balaklava-Inkerman road that passed through the Fedyukhiny Heights. All gun and machine-gun positions were made of earth-timber except for one reinforced concrete bunker on the outskirts of Novo Shuli.

Evidence[9] shows that construction of bunkers in Sector 2 was not of the same quality as in other sectors. The thickness of the concrete was 20–25cm versus

80cm in the coastal defence bunkers built in 1941. In some bunkers the thickness of the steel reinforcement was only 6cm, inadequate to withstand heavy artillery shells.[10] The reason is unknown. There was no naval blockade of Sevastopol from January to May 1942. Perhaps the command believed the thinner-walled bunkers were sufficient to withstand shelling from German 75mm and perhaps even 88mm shells, but they were not prepared for 210mm shells.

Mount Kara-Koba

In November German troops had broken through beyond Shuli into the valley of Kara-Koba. The advance was stopped but the Germans captured a large portion of the valley. The Soviets held the slopes to the north and west of the valley from Inkerman Heights to Telegraph Hill. Mount Kara-Koba was a major strongpoint of the defence of the valley. In December the defences consisted of a single line of trenches with bunkers running along the edge of the mountain and continuing along the heights to Mackenzie Farm. Pre-cast reinforced concrete bunkers were added from January to March 1942. The first line of defence began in the narrower part of the valley east of Shuli. This consisted of a line of trenches running across the valley below the Chelter Cave Monastery complex west of Mount Chelter-

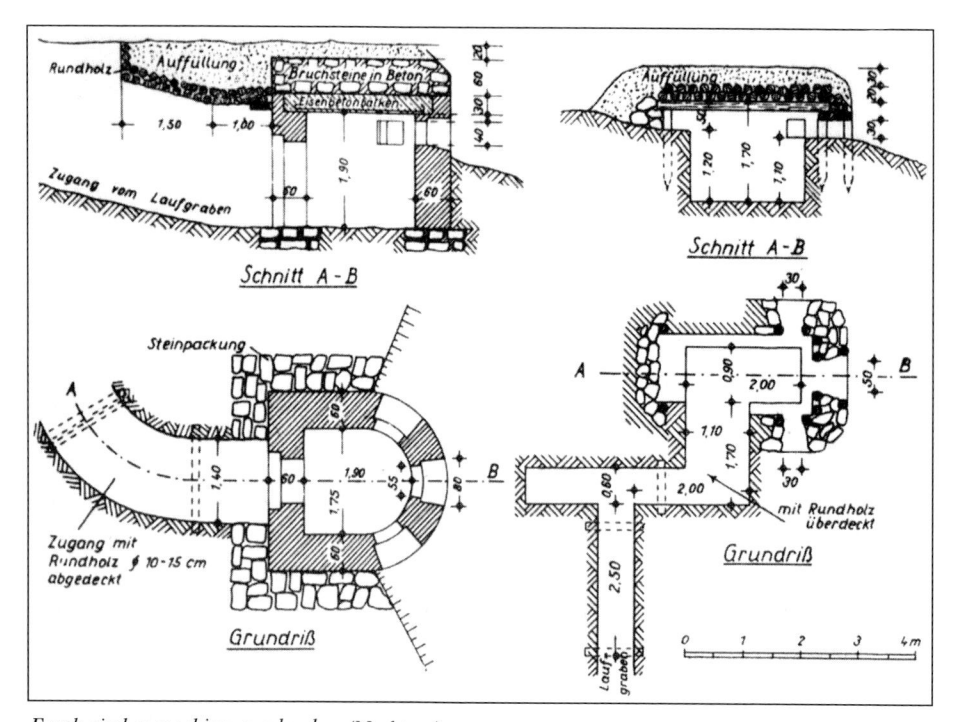

Earth-timber machine-gun bunker. (Nachtrag)

Kai. This part of the valley was intended to have a belt of dragon's teeth, concrete pillars 2.5m high with a 30cm x 30cm base, to block the valley, but there was not enough time to put the obstacles in place. There was also a concrete pyramid model 60cm high, that belonged to a later period.

The strongpoint on top of Mount Kara-Koba was protected by a ditch and a rampart with two wooden bridges running across it. The fortifications were earthworks and bunkers carved into the rock. The 105th Separate Engineering Battalion occupied the position and were housed in pre-revolutionary barracks inside the perimeter. The Battalion Command Post was defended by earth-timber emplacements. Five pre-cast concrete emplacements were located at the top of the plateau. The approach to the position was on the reverse side of the hill and was covered by two machine-gun emplacements plus a ditch with a rampart. The flank of the position in the direction of Sugar Head was defended by five bunkers. A battalion command post was located at the top of Sugar Head, carved into the soft rock with several rooms connected by communication trenches. Shelters on top of Sugar Head were also carved out of the rock. A tall tower that carried power lines was located on top of the mountain and used during the war as an observation post to monitor the valley.

Bunker 40 was located at the foot of Sugar Head, in the Inkerman Valley. It was a standard 45mm bunker with an underground ammunition shelter behind it. The bunker covered the Inkerman Road and the Kara-Koba Valley. It was blown up by troops of 386th Rifle Division during the retreat in June 1942. Additional bunkers were stretched along the base of Mount Kara-Koba and along the road leading up to Mackenzie Farm and plateau and continuing to Cordon Number 2. Eighteen pre-cast concrete machine-gun bunkers and a bunker for a 76mm mountain gun were placed between Sugar Head and Mackenzie Farm.

Fedyukhiny Heights

The defences of the Fedyukhiny Heights were subjected to intense bombardment during the Third Assault and most traces were removed after the war. All that remains are circular gun platforms and anchor bolts for 130mm guns. During the Second Assault the guns were located on the slopes above Novo Shuli and m. Pervomaika. Between the Second and Third Assaults the guns were moved 100m apart and shared a common magazine. A machine-gun bunker was built at the foot of the hill outside Pervomaika, along the railway. The gun above Pervomaika could sweep the Yalta Highway and part of the Balaklava Valley to the North Fort. The gun platform was 8.4m in diameter and the concrete base 1.2m thick. The second gun could fire on the Kara-Koba Valley. A command bunker was located above the second gun platform. Prior to the Second Assault only one bunker, No. 44, was identified on the Soviet maps. This bunker number was also assigned to another bunker near Lyubimovka, therefore this was most likely Bunker 46, part of a group with Bunkers 27 and 29, located at the foot of Sapun Ridge.

Hill 135.7 had eight machine-gun and four artillery bunkers. A line of trenches was dug on the edge of the slope. The pre-cast bunkers were joined by communication trenches 3–4m deep. The French were positioned on this hill during the Crimean War.

The artillery battalion of 7th Brigade, with two 76mm guns, was located in a ravine between Hill 135.7 and 125.7 (the main hills that make up the Fedyukhiny Heights). This was the location of the former Inkerman – Balaklava Road. A mortar battalion and the command post of 1st Battalion of 7th Brigade were also located in the ravine. The 7th Brigade command post was located further west near the serpentine road on Sapun Ridge. The Inkerman Road was covered by two artillery bunkers. Ten pre-cast bunkers were built at this same location. Four machine-gun bunkers and a 76mm bunker faced the Black River Valley. Five bunkers were located on the south side of the heights facing the Yalta Highway. The bunkers also covered a deep ditch that ran along the slope of the heights. Another three machine-gun bunkers linked the heights to the Third Turkish Redoubt (Hill 33.1).

Sapun Ridge

Bunker 41, built for a 100mm gun, was located on Sapun Ridge and completed in February 1942. The bunker covered the bridge over the Black River. Bunker 44 was built over the Sevastopol-Simferopol Road. It was damaged by Rumanian artillery. Bunker 42 was built using Inkerman stone and therefore it was of a later date. It was at the base of the ridge northeast of the Balaklava Highway, 10m from the railway track. A line of pre-cast bunkers continued along the ridge towards Dergacheva. The 386th Division command post was located above the modern substation, overlooking Dergacheva, on a redoubt from the Crimean War. Many of the fortifications of Sapun Ridge were dug into the rock. Communication trenches and dugouts were often dug to a depth of 3 to 5m.

Dergacheva or Dergachy has a very interesting history that begins in the late eighteenth century. Land was allotted to naval officers to build farms and gardens. This particular parcel went to Captain 2nd Rank Ilya Ivanovich Oznobishin. The farm was built in 1806. A few years later it came into the possession of retired Major-General Vasily Dergacheva. During the Crimean War a French compound and the British Victoria Redoubt were built near the Dergacheva Farm, including a camp used by the British. In January 1855 the Farm came into the possession of the French when their allies moved to a new position. The French built a theatre at Dergacheva Farm named the Théatre de Moulin for vaudeville shows. Actors

122   The Defence of Sevastopol 1941–1942

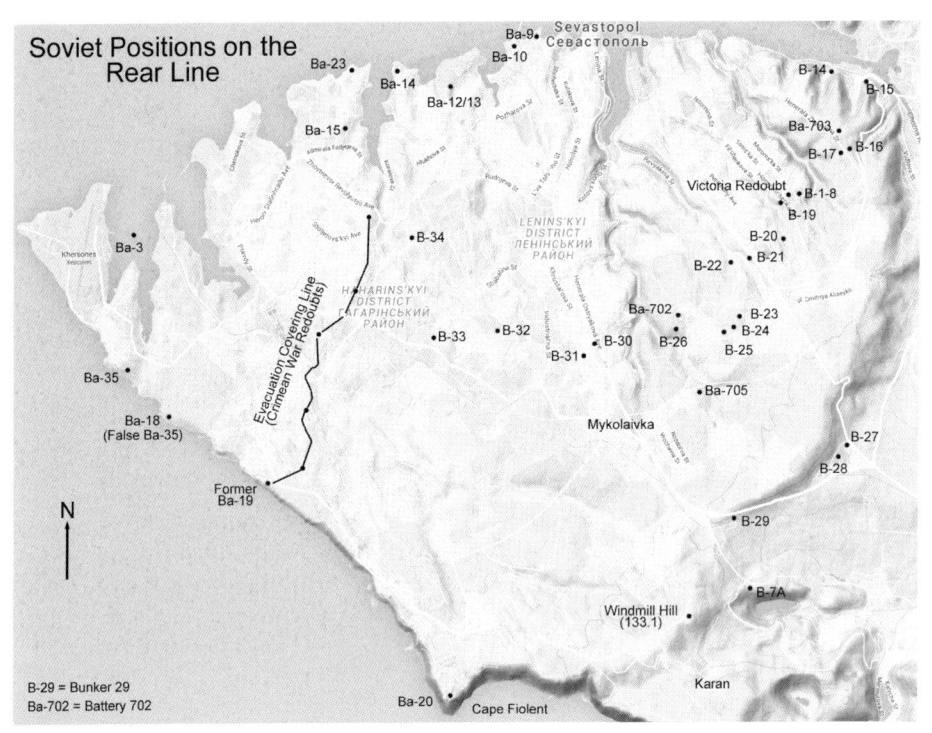

The rear line of the Soviet defences. (© OpenStreetMap contributors, Author's collection)

came from within the ranks. In addition to the theatre the French built a stone mill. A farmhouse was located on the property and a nearby spring provided plenty of water. During the Second Defence the anti-tank ditch passed through Dergacheva. It was 8m wide and 6m deep and was part of the rear line of defence. Three field hospitals were located nearby.

Bunkers 27, 28 and 29 were located on the southwestern slopes of Sapun Ridge. Bunkers 27 and 28 were at the base of the ridge where the highway began its ascent to the hairpin turn at the top of the ridge. Bunker 27 housed a 75mm gun during the assault. Bunker 28, located 100m from Bunker 27, also housed a long-barrelled 75mm naval gun. It was secured to the floor of the bunker with a ring of eighteen anchor bolts. It was built during the winter of 1941 to 1942.

Bunker 29 was armed with a 102mm gun taken from the destroyer *Shkval* in December 1941. The gun was placed in a circular concrete pit and covered the slopes of Sapun Ridge to the Karan position and the Yalta Highway to Balaklava. It was located along the road that passed through the Karagach height on the right flank of Sapun Ridge and also covered the pass through Karagach. Bunker 7A, a large gun pad, was located nearby. The area was defended by three machine-gun emplacements.

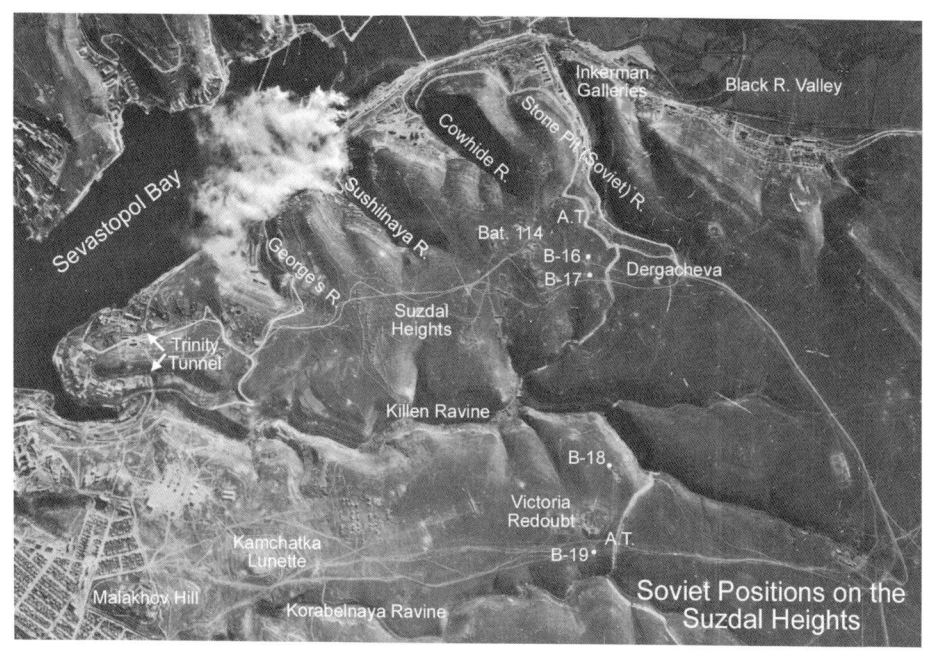

Defences on Suzdal Heights. (Aerial photograph provided by John Calvin of www.wwii-photos-maps.com, altered by the author)

Bunker 25 was originally designated number 23 before the addition of Bunkers 18 and 20 in February 1942. The bunker housed a 102mm Vickers gun from the *Shkval*. The bunker was originally the location of Battery 702 but that was later moved to the vicinity of the English Redoubt of the Crimean War when the bunker was built. It was an open gun platform that covered the Sarandinakinu Ravine and provided mutual support for Bunkers 22, 23 and 24, located at the English Cemetery, also called Cathcart's Hill during the Crimean War, plus Bunkers 30 and 31 along the Balaklava Highway. The crew consisted of nine men commanded by Lieutenant S. V. Terekhov. It was blown up by retreating troops on 30 June 1942.

Bunker 26 was 350m from Bunker 25. It was on top of the hill above the Maximova Dacha (used as a field hospital during the assault). It was pentagonal in shape, 7m x 7m, equipped with a 76.2mm gun. It had a crew of seven commanded by Sergeant-Major J. F. Kurumov and was destroyed by the crew during the retreat.

Bunkers 23 and 24 were on a hill at the location of the English Cemetery. They were about 350m apart and housed 45mm 21K guns. Their sector of fire was 110 degrees and they covered the upper slopes of the Sapun Ridge and the Yalta Highway. Several underground shelters made of timber for troops and ammunition

Bunker 24 near the English Cemetery. (Nemenko Collection)

were located nearby. Bunker 22 covered the Laboratory (Vorontsov) Highway and Ravine. It was built for a 45mm gun. Bunker 21 was located 300m from Bunker 22 and also covered the ravine and highway with its 45mm anti-tank gun. An earth-timber dugout for troops was located on the slope behind the bunker. The bunker covered the retreat of troops along the Laboratory Highway.

Bunker 20 was built for a 76.2mm 8K gun. Its sector of fire covered the Sapun road to Dergacheva. The bunker was blown up by the retreating crew, who moved on to Battery 2bis, 300m from the bunker, then on to Victoria Redoubt and finally Malakhov Hill. Bunker 19 was located opposite the Victoria Redoubt. Its 45mm gun covered the road running below the hill. Bunker 18 was 100m away from Victoria Redoubt near Killen Ravine. It was built for a 76mm gun. These two bunkers covered the retreat of Soviet troops to Victoria Redoubt and Malakhov Hill. There were also several pre-cast concrete bunkers running along the Killen Ravine, built around November 1941.

Bunkers 14, 15, 16 and 17 were the last bunkers located on the south side of the bay and ran across the Suzdal Heights towards the electrical power plant, above which Bunker 14 was located near the railway tracks. Battery 703 (114) was also located on Suzdal Heights near Bunker 16's 45mm gun. These bunkers did not participate in the defence of the heights because the Germans, after crossing the bay on 29 June, penetrated through the Ox Ravine behind the Suzdal position and they were cut off. The former bridge over the Black River was covered by Bunkers 14 and 15. In March 1942 the crew of Bunker 15 was transferred to a position next to Battery 703.

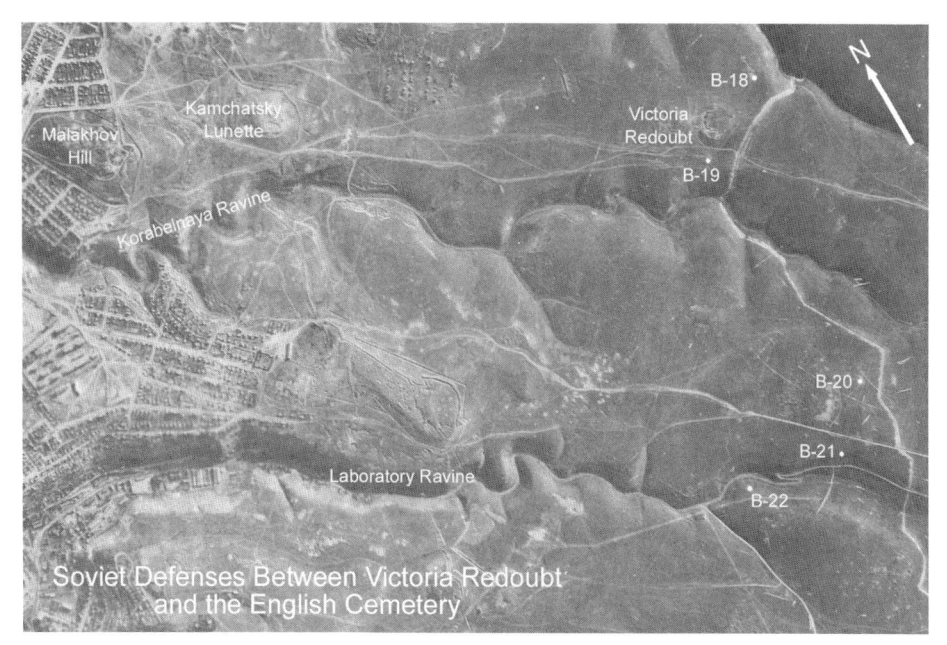

Soviet defences between Victoria Redoubt and the English Cemetery. (Aerial photograph provided by John Calvin of www.wwii-photos-maps.com, altered by the author)

Sector 1's defences included the Turkish Redoubts and fortifications along the Yalta Highway, a line of defence along the Balaklava Highway, the Karan Valley, the rear line and the evacuation covering line. The first sector defensive line ran from the Genoese Towers above Balaklava to the Yalta Highway near Mount Gasfort. Seven kilometres long, it ran from the upper slopes of Hill 212.1 to the village of Kamary and from there to the Yalta Highway at the foot of Mount Gasfort.

The Yalta Highway formed the border with Sector 2. The sector included narrow communication trenches, machine-gun nests, concrete bunkers with machine guns and artillery, plus minefields and searchlights. Soldiers on the front lines were housed in dugouts in the trenches. The trenches were further protected by minefields and barbed wire. The first sector was divided into a number of battalion strongpoints and consisted of three lines of defence. Eight strongpoints were in the first line at the foot of the Balaklava Heights. Another eight were in the second line in the valley of Balaklava. Four more were located to the rear. It was not possible to build permanent fortifications on the front line due to constant German fire. Farms were also used as strongpoints. Kamary Village was a strongpoint. The front line near the Yalta Highway was defended by an anti-tank ditch, which ran from Kamary to Canrobert hill 169.4.

The Soviets built several pre-cast bunkers around Hill 212.1 to cover the road to the Genoese Towers. The right flank of the second line hugged the shore and ran through the Turkish Redoubts to the base of Sapun Ridge. Five bunkers for 45mm, 100mm and 76mm guns were located on a line from Cape Kaya-Bash to Sapun Ridge. This included Bunkers 34 to 30 plus an anti-tank ditch and minefields.

Turkish Redoubts

The First Turkish Redoubt was located on Canrobert Hill (169.4). A platform for a 100mm gun was built on the side of the hill plus several communications trenches cut into the rock to a depth of 3–4m. The floors of the trenches were lined with wood. The command post for 1st Battalion, 782nd Regiment of 388th Division was located on top of the hill inside the old redoubt. The First Turkish Redoubt was built on two levels, the bottom for infantry and the top for guns. The foot of Canrobert Hill was defended by a complex of trenches that linked up with Mount Gasfort. Several pre-cast bunkers were located in the defensive zone. The hill was struck by heavy German artillery including 203mm shells. Below Hill 169.4 was the Second Turkish Redoubt. This was a powerful defensive point surrounded by a ditch and rampart. There were three firing positions, two on the front. The Third Redoubt was equipped with three machine-gun and one artillery position. The Fourth Redoubt had only timber fortifications.

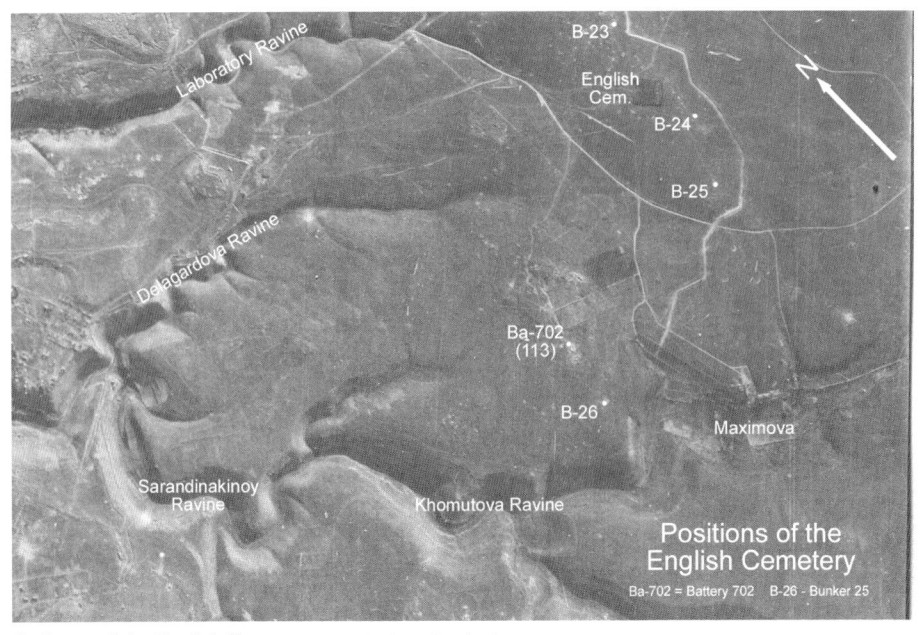

Defences of the English Cemetery. (Author's collection)

Balaklava Highway

The line of bunkers along the Balaklava Highway was built from May to June 1942 by 373rd Rifle Regiment of 388th Division and the 9th Marine Brigade. The line began at the junction of the Balaklava and Yalta Highway and followed the Balaklava Road. The defences consisted of pre-cast bunkers defended by the 256th Anti-tank Battalion with ten 45mm guns.

Karan Valley

This position ran along the heights above the Karan Valley, which extended from the Balaklava Road near the Karagach Heights and continued to the Karan Plateau along the Black Sea. It included several French and Turkish Crimean War redoubts. Most of the fortifications were destroyed during the assault. Some trenches and redoubts remained. The former village of Karani (m. Flotske) was at the end of the valley.

There were twelve major defensive emplacements located along the Karan Valley, mostly trenches with dugouts and pre-cast bunkers. The high point was Windmill Hill (133.1), named for the pre-war wind turbine that stood atop a metal tower. The buildings of the turbine facility were used as the command post for Sector 1. The tower was used as an observation post. Some of the rooms for the command post were carved into the rock. The vantage point on top of Windmill Hill was excellent, providing a view over the Balaklava District. In the front was a deep ditch cut into the rock with shelters for vehicles. The position was surrounded by three pre-cast concrete bunkers. The command post was blown up during the retreat on 29 to 30 June 1942. The command post for the 456th Regiment (NKVD) was located in the village of Karan. Soldiers from the regiment are buried in a nearby cemetery. Between the valley and the sea are a number of emplacements, including thirteen machine-gun and one artillery bunker. The plateau also contains Crimean War redoubts. Most of the emplacements, built in June 1942 are earth-timber.

Bunker 34 was located about 1.5km from the mouth of Musketeer's Bay, positioned along the Kamezh line and covering the roads leading to the bays and towards the Black Sea to the southwest – the line of retreat. The bunker's arc of fire was 120 degrees and it was armed with a 45mm gun. From 28 to 30 June 1942 this bunker, along with Bunkers 32 and 33 covered the retreat of Soviet forces behind the Kamezh Line to the Chersonese Peninsula. Bunker 32 and 33 were located south of Bunker 34 and covered the roads and railway line that led towards the coast. Bunker 32 was built for a 45mm gun and Bunker 33 for a 75mm gun. The crews of both bunkers offered stubborn resistance to the German advance and most likely died during the fighting. Bunker 31 for a 45mm gun covered the

Bunker 14, located along the railway east of the electrical power plant. Taken after the beginning of the German occupation. (Nemenko Collection)

Balaklava Road and the road from Mykolaivka to Reed Bay. The arc of fire was 100 degrees. Bunker 30 was very near to Bunker 31. It housed a 76.2mm anti-aircraft gun. Its field of fire was 110 degrees and it covered the same area as its neighbour. This part of the line was placed in areas where the threat of enemy tank infiltration was the greatest. The crew fought until 30 June and then retreated. Their fate is unknown. Five pre-cast concrete bunkers were built along the line of Bunkers 34 to 30.

Such was the state of defences in late May 1942. The Germans began to return from victory at Kerch and prepared for the third and final assault on Sevastopol.

Chapter 6

The Third Assault (1) – The Bombardment of 2 to 6 June 1942

It was German practice to begin their attacks with air and artillery strikes to soften up Soviet positions. Hitler denied Manstein nothing for the Third Assault, in his desire to see Sevastopol fall quickly this time. The number and destructive force of the German guns brought to Sevastopol was unprecedented in war and included a large number of heavy siege guns. There was a battery equipped with a Czech 420mm gun (Model 17), two battalions of 305mm guns (Model 16), a group of 355mm mortars, German and Czech 210mm mortars and French 194mm self-propelled guns, plus a Krupp 420mm Gamma howitzer of First World War vintage.

Soviet intelligence failed to notice several key German construction sites, including heavy artillery batteries and the 600mm Karl mortars. These huge

A German pioneer climbing into a hole at Fort Molotov. The damage was caused by an 800mm shell from the German heavy gun Dora. (NARA)

guns required the excavation of 5,000 cubic metres of rock to create their firing positions. They also failed to notice the arrival of Dora, the largest artillery piece ever made. It was an 800mm railway gun the size of a large apartment building. Dora's carriage moved on three sets of tracks, built in a curve at the firing position so that the gun could be moved back and forth to change the direction of fire. The Germans had a total of 208 batteries (not counting anti-aircraft guns) over a 35km front, giving them around eight batteries per kilometre. Since they were concentrated in the attack sectors, the actual concentration was even greater.

On 15 May Soviet reconnaissance aircraft spotted the arrival of eight trains at Djankoi and seven at Kurman-Kemelchi Station, unloading German troops and equipment. On 21 May a column of German infantry was spotted on the highway near Kacha. The convoy was hit by Soviet anti-aircraft guns, which fired on the head of the column, causing a large number of casualties. Artillery duels increased in the final days of May, as did German reconnaissance flights.

One of the major factors that contributed to the collapse of the defence of Sevastopol was the dominance of the Luftwaffe. On paper, Sevastopol seemed to have a sufficient number of guns to create an effective umbrella over the battlefield, but by June the air shield was gone.

In May 1942 the following anti-aircraft assets were in place:

Northern Air Defence Zone – 61st Anti-Aircraft Artillery Regiment (Colonel Gorsky):
- 2nd Battalion: Battery 75, 229, 370, 851 (three 85mm and ten 76.2mm guns).
- 3rd Battalion: Battery 54, 926, 927 (three 85mm and eight 76.2mm guns).
- 4th Battalion: Battery 459, 357 (eight 37mm guns).

Southern Air Defence Zone – 110th Anti-Aircraft Artillery Regiment (Colonel Matveev):
- 1st Battalion (formerly 61st Regiment): Battery 78, 79, 80 (four 85mm and eight 76.2mm guns).
- 114th Battalion: Battery 219, 365, 366 (ten 76.2mm guns).
- 55th Battalion: Battery 551, 552, 553 (twelve 45mm guns).

Chersonese Air Defence Zone:
- 92nd Separate Anti-Aircraft Artillery Battalion: Battery 227, 364, 928 (three 85mm and six 76.2mm guns).
- Floating Battery 3 (four 76.2mm and three 37mm guns).
- Three Anti-Aircraft Machine Gun Companies (twelve M-4 guns).
- Three searchlight companies with radar equipment.

The Third Assault (1) – The Bombardment of 2 to 6 June 1942

The air defences also included assets from the Coastal Army, including:
- 880th Anti-Aircraft Artillery Regiment (Colonel Kuharenko) with seven batteries[1] (twenty 85mm guns).
- 26th Separate Anti-Aircraft Artillery Battalion with three batteries (nine 76.2mm guns).

Divisional artillery included:
- 25th Chapaevsky Division: Battery 193 (three 76.2mm guns).
- 95th Rifle Division: Battery 194 (four 76.2mm guns).
- The anti-aircraft guns destined for the 345th, 386th and 388th Rifle Divisions were lost at sea in the spring of 1942.

There seemed to be a sufficient number of batteries to mount a formidable air defence, but the Luftwaffe had complete freedom of the skies during the Third Assault.

On 20 May the Luftwaffe tested the air defences by attacking four anti-aircraft batteries. Battery 227, at Cape Chersonese, was attacked by German bombers. Long-range artillery from the vicinity of Kacha shelled the airfield and lighthouse. The Soviets were unable to suppress the German guns or mount any air defence and Battery 227 was a total loss. During the day Battery 229 and 79 were also attacked. Battery 79 was attacked over a three-day period. On 23 May the battery was attacked by a squadron of nine Ju 87s. They approached the battery which threw up a curtain of flak, forcing the Stukas to turn back out to sea. The dive bombers changed direction and attacked the battery again, this time dropping their bombs on target. They then turned to Battery 78 in wave after wave. The battery commander, Alyushin, was wounded and the battery was wrecked. On 25 May Battery 926 was likewise attacked and destroyed. One by one the German pilots picked off the Soviet air defences.

In May, the 61st Regiment alone fired 3,266 85mm, 10,219 76mm, 1,869 45mm and 4,885 37mm shells. The results were pathetic. Out of all of the shells fired only seven German aircraft were shot down. Efficiency was terrible – 3,000–4,000 shells to bring down one aircraft. The Germans were flying missions in order to exhaust the air defences and it worked. They lured the gunners into firing thousands of shells which would be greatly missed during the upcoming assault. The expenditure of shells as the days went by were as follows: 22 May – 628; 23 May – 1,098; 24 May – 1,111; 25 May – 1,384; 26 May – 1,625; 27 May – 2,980; 28 May – 3,000; 1 and 2 June – 11,265. This does not include Army artillery. By 11 June ammunition was seriously depleted; only 3,000 85mm shells remained.

Furthermore, the load placed on the AA batteries increased when they were ordered to use their guns for anti-tank defence, because the 95th and 172nd Rifle Divisions did not have anti-tank battalions. Battery 79 and 80 were given an anti-tank role and they suffered heavily in early June. The dual use of the guns reduced their effectiveness even further and used up large quantities of shells.

In late May there was a dramatic escalation in the intensity of attacks on Soviet targets. At night, the enemy fired on the old Turkish redoubts on the Semyukhiny causeway along the Yalta highway. Rumanian artillery bombarded positions of the 8th Brigade at Mount Kara-Koba. 7th Brigade troops on Mount Gasfort and troops in the Mekenzievy Mountains were also targeted. On the night of 23 May the Germans shelled Canrobert Hill, location of the First Turkish Redoubt, a strongpoint of the 782nd Regiment of 388th Rifle Division.

The German Army directive for 24 May outlined the preparation of the assault on Sevastopol. General Petrov expected an attack against all four sectors, preceded by a heavy artillery and air barrage. In relation to forces, Petrov wrote, 'The Germans may have an advantage in tanks and aircraft. Manpower is equal. Artillery strength was on the Soviet side in the amount of guns and in fire organisation.' Petrov was correct about tanks and aircraft in terms of numbers, but the Germans had superior technology. His comment about artillery was not close to reality. His intelligence units had completely missed the massive concentration of heavy guns of an overwhelming number and calibre.

According to Manstein, it was impossible to launch a massive, simultaneous attack on both the northern and southern sectors due to a shortage of infantry and supporting air power; nevertheless, attacks were to be carried out in both the north and the south (Petrov was correct). This had the purpose of preventing the Russians from shifting their reserves from one area to another and concentrating their heavy artillery. The attack was initially focused in the north, the objective being the northern shore of the bay and the capture of the high ground behind Gaytani, southeast of Inkerman and the Black River Valley. From Gaytani attacks could be launched across the valley against the Sapun Heights.

The Rumanian Mountain Corps (18th Infantry Division and 1st Mountain Division) was tasked with tying down Soviet forces in the centre and covering the southern flank of the LIV Corps. LIV Corps was to move forward to capture the western edge of the Mekenzievy Mountains and ravines above the eastern end of Sevastopol Bay where the Black River flows into the bay and to protect the flanks of adjacent forces. General Erik Hansen, commander of LIV Corps, ordered every division to 'carry out its attack without regard for its neighbour and not to stop as long as it could still move forward'.[2]

The specific plan for each unit was outlined as follows:

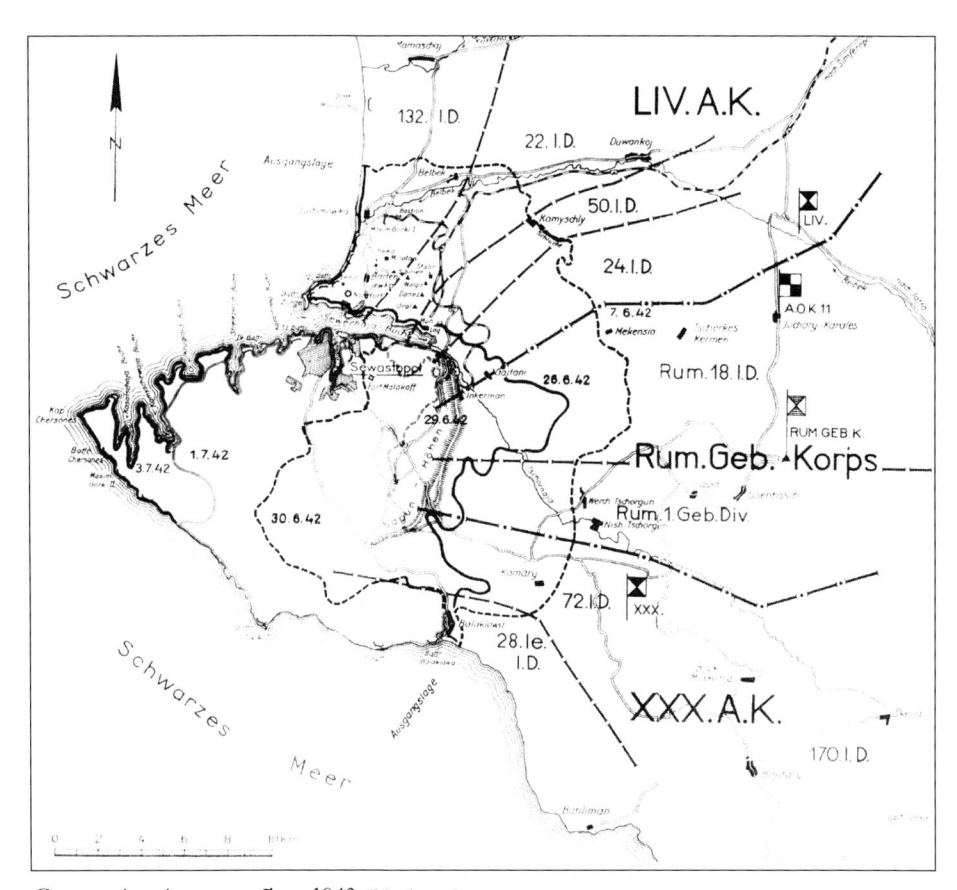

The Third Assault (1) – The Bombardment of 2 to 6 June 1942   133

German situation map – June 1942. (Nachtrag)

- The attack on the northern front would be carried out by LIV Corps, consisting of 22nd Infantry Division (General Ludwig Wolff), 24th Infantry Division (General Hans von Tettau), 50th Infantry Division (Lieutenant-General August Schmidt) and 132nd Infantry Division (General Fritz Lindemann) plus the reinforced 213th Infantry Regiment. General Erik Hansen's LIV Corps was to concentrate so as to attack the high ground north of the bay. Any terrain bypassed during the attack was to be kept pinned down and taken at a later time. The main tactic was to move quickly and keep moving towards the bay. The left wing of LIV Corps was to take the heights of Gaytani and the terrain to the southeast of the heights to cover the advance of the Rumanian Mountain Corps further to the south.
- The attack on the southern front was to be carried out by XXX Corps, commanded by General Maximilian Fretter-Pico, including 72nd Infantry Division (Lieutenant-General Philipp Müller-Gebhard), 170th Infantry Division (Lieutenant-General Irwin Sander) and 28th Light Division, commanded by

Lieutenant-General Johann Sinnhuber. The initial task of XXX Corps was to proceed so as to develop a forward line from which to advance at a later time to the Sapun Heights. This required the capture of the Soviet strongpoints called North Nose, Chapel Hill, Ruin Hill, Kamary and south of Kamary to remove the threat of flanking fire coming from Balaklava. In order to do this the 72nd Infantry Division was directed to advance north and south of the Yalta Highway, while the 28th Light Division captured the northern summits of the mountains east of Balaklava Bay. 170th Division remained in reserve.
- The Rumanian Corps' task was to pin down the Soviets and keep them from moving troops and equipment to the northern or southern fronts. 18th Rumanian Division was to protect the left wing of LIV Corps through local attacks and artillery bombardment. The 1st Rumanian Mountain Division would perform the same task to cover the right flank of XXX Corps. They would accomplish this by capturing the Sugar Head position.

The attack would begin with an intensive air and artillery bombardment. The artillery would be directed on pinpoint targets such as supply lines and troop concentrations. Soviet artillery was to be reduced and defensive positions were to be softened up prior to the infantry assault. This decision was made due to the difficult terrain into which the Soviet defences were embedded. It would take too many shells to destroy every one of these, if they could all be located, which they could not. The bombardment would start five days before the assault, on 2 June. At the same time VIII Air Corps would continue to attack the remaining military installations in the city of Sevastopol, such as the harbours, supply warehouses, barracks and airfields.

The attack divisions moved to their assigned locations on 31 May. Additional artillery reinforcements began to arrive on 22 May. There was no time to train the troops on the nature of the terrain but the commanders of the various units were flown over the battlefield to become familiar with their own lines and terrain. It was evident that the assault in June would be far more challenging for German-Rumanian troops than in December as the Soviets had five months to improve their defences and to bring their forces up to strength. Sevastopol's main strength was the difficulty of the terrain and the manner in which it was prepared.

The Battlefield (as described by General von Manstein)

The Northern Front constituted the ground between the Belbek Valley along the northern edge, North Bay on the southern and the top of the Kamyshly Ravine to the east. The Belbek Valley and the southern slopes were enfiladed

The Third Assault (1) – The Bombardment of 2 to 6 June 1942   135

by the 305mm guns of Battery 30. The slopes of the valley were covered by a thick network of field works, some in concrete, one mile in depth. Behind the valley was a line of strongpoints containing anti-aircraft and machine-gun batteries. These were called Forts Stalin, Volga, Siberia, Molotov, GPU and Cheka, and were linked together by trenches. Forts Donets and Lenin were positioned on the heights above North Bay. The Bartenyevka strongpoint and the bastioned North Fort guarded the coastal strip. The final obstacle was the Battery Headland on which sat Fort Constantine.

The Eastern Front ran perpendicular to the northern front boundary of the Belbek River along the Kamyshly Ravine. At the northern end of the ravine the terrain was covered with dense undergrowth in which the Soviets had constructed strongpoints in holes blown in the rock. These pockets were very difficult to hit with artillery. The ravine was wooded and ended in a series of steep cliffs south and southeast of Gaytani, at the southern end of the ravine. The woods ended further to the south but the terrain to the coast was difficult and rocky.

Access to the southern part of the fortress was blocked by a series of steep, dome-shaped summits that had been converted to strongpoints. They were named Sugarloaf, North Nose, Chapel Hill and Ruin Hill. Beyond that were the defended village of Kamary and then the rocky massif of Balaklava Bay. Each successive hill flanked the next one.

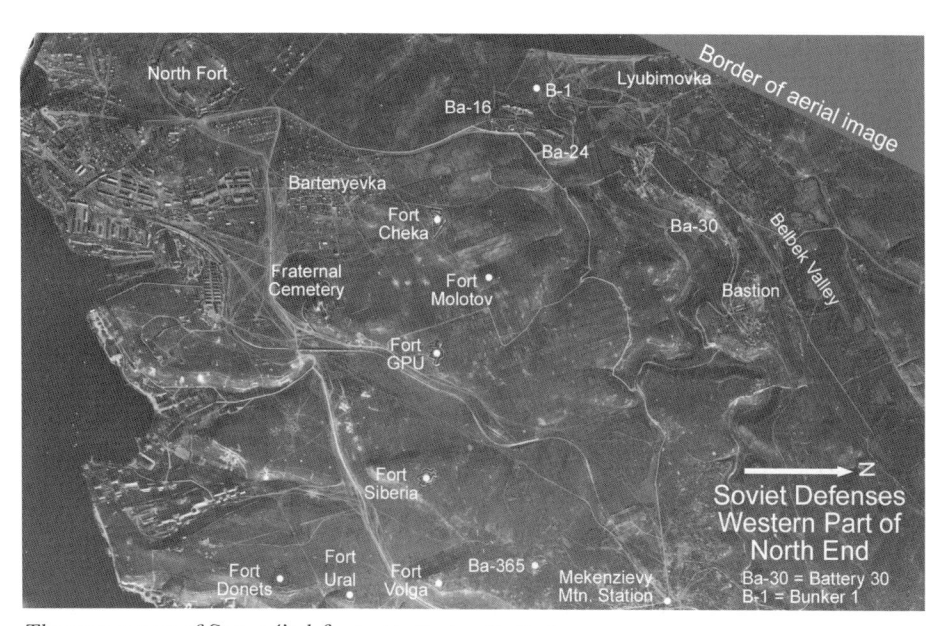

The western part of Sector 4's defences. (Author's collection)

Behind the forward defences in the south, north of the road from Sevastopol to the coast, was the massif of the Fedyukhiny Heights. This was linked to the coast by additional strongpoints – Eagle's Perch (nest) and the fortified village of Kadykova. These defences formed a front to the more formidable Sapun Heights, a natural defence consisting of a range of hills with steep slopes to the east, beginning with the cliffs of Inkerman and following the Chornaya valley to the south of Gaytani, where they turn southwest to block the Sevastopol Road and run to the sea through Windmill Hill, which was the western spur of the coastal range. The Sapun Heights were extremely difficult for infantry attack due to steep slopes protected by mutually flanking fire positions. Artillery observers on the Sapun command the entire battlefield.

To make matters worse, the defences didn't end at the top of the heights. The city's defences continued from Inkerman along the southern perimeter of the city to the coast at Streletskaya (Musketeer) Bay. The defences were composed of an extensive anti-tank ditch, barbed wire and a nest of bunkers. The British cemetery had been converted to a strongpoint. There was also a line of fortifications covering the Chersonese Peninsula at the southernmost point of the fortress.

Not only were the Soviets skilled at creating camouflaged field defences but they also had excellent terrain to work with that afforded the opportunity for flanking fire. The rocky terrain made it possible to have cover for guns so narrow that they could only be destroyed by a direct hit. And finally the battlefield, both in front of and behind the defences, was dotted with minefields.

Manstein's description of the battlefield is excellent and quite accurate, but it seems to be full of foreboding. Rightly so.

The German artillery barrage began as planned on 2 June 1942. Approximately 6,000 shells fell each day of the five-day bombardment (about 250 tons). The Luftwaffe flew an average of 500 sorties per day. The bombardment, starting from the first day, had the effect of cutting off communications between units in the field as well as with the Black Sea Fleet staff in their command headquarters under the streets of Sevastopol.

At 0226 hours the *Tashkent* and destroyer *Bezuprechnyy* arrived from Novorossiysk bringing 1,015 replacement troops and 130 tons of ammunition. They took on board 130 wounded and 722 civilians. At 0346 hours the transport *Abkhazia*, escorted by two minesweepers and three patrol boats, arrived from Novorossiysk with 1,770 troops and 225 tons of ammunition, plus a large amount of food. On 3 June at 0230 the cruiser *Krasnyy Krim*, escorted by two destroyers, arrived from Novorossiysk. The ship delivered 1,759 troops, 180

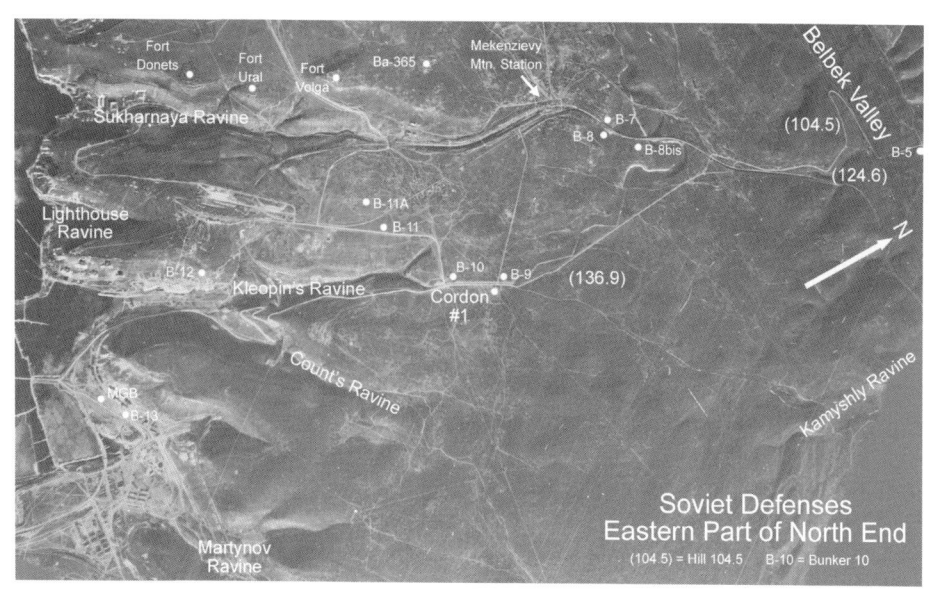

The Third Assault (1) – The Bombardment of 2 to 6 June 1942 137

The defences of the eastern part of Sector 3 and 4. (Author's collection)

tons of ammunition, eight 45mm guns, seventy-six anti-tank rifles, 225 machine guns, fourteen 82mm and five 50mm mortars, 2000 rifles and two tons of medical supplies. The submarine *S-32* brought in ten tons of ammunition and nine tons of food.

On 3 June the scale of enemy air attacks was the same, about 500 sorties. There was likewise no reduction in the heavy shelling. During the day Battery 30 was hit heavily by 305mm and 420mm mortars, but causing only minor damage to the concrete. During the night German pioneers began to find paths through minefields and obstacles in preparation for infantry attacks. On 4 June the shelling was concentrated against the 79th Marine Brigade and 172nd Rifle Division. About 3,500 artillery and 1,500 mortar rounds were fired, although air sorties were down about 50 per cent from the previous days.

G. I. Vaneev[3] wrote the following in his memoirs: 'Despite the massive air strikes and artillery fire, the losses of troops and military equipment were insignificant.' According to the former chief of staff of the Coastal Army, Nicolai I. Krylov, 'On this day the medical battalion took in 178 wounded mainly from the rear areas.'[4] Vaneev's opinion may not be accurate. If the shelling was as intense as described, it is conceivable that many of the men were buried in trenches or shelters and it would have been difficult to locate and move them to the hospital. Therefore, most likely many more were killed and wounded than was reported or admitted to.

Ignatieff's account[5] backs up this idea:

The Nazis fired large calibre guns. The prefabricated bunkers were falling apart, as if they were not composed of concrete blocks but rather, cubes of cardboard. The entrances to many shelters were buried. We were forced to dig out our comrades under enemy fire. Many could not be saved and they have remained permanently underground. After jumping out of the concrete casemates, I did not recognise the area: it was ploughed by artillery fire. German shells exploding in the stony ground of Sevastopol carved from it a cloud of small and microscopic stones, which ended up in the wounds.

Zoe Smirnova-Medvedeva[6] (287th Rifle Regiment) also remembered:

Preliminary bombardment was very cruel. We did not hear specific explosions just a solid, deafening noise. Our bunker swayed from side to side. Twice, large-calibre shells were exploding so close that the gun fell to the floor. The land itself seemed to be in anguish. The bunker became unbearable; we were suffocating from heat, dust, powder, burning.

The German shelling continued on 5 June. Only about 2,000 shells were fired this day, but the Luftwaffe made up for it by flying 1,250 sorties. All communications with the city were damaged as well as the main water tower. The hospital took in 265 wounded.

Boris Voyetkhov wrote about a visit to the Panorama Museum in Sevastopol:

During one air raid the Panorama, one of the main tourist sights of Sevastopol, was badly damaged. It contained a huge circular panorama representing the storming of Sevastopol by the British and French on 6 June 1855. As much as could possibly be saved of the painting was stored in the basement of the Panorama building. The painting was created by Franz Roubaud. It was 495 feet long and 49 feet high. The curator pointed to pieces of the painting that were not burned. 'Here is Malakhov Kurgan. Today it is called Kornilov Kurgan. On the other side of Quarantine Bay is Chersonese-Tauricus, celebrated long ago for its wealth, trade and possessions. It was founded in 600 years BC.' He pointed towards Balaklava. 'Long ago Balaklava was a pirates' harbour. Do you see the Chersonese Lighthouse? It was called the Cape of the Virgin. There lay the virgin forest of Diana and on the cape were the sacrificial altars of the gods.' The man's eyes teared up. He threw all that remained of the painting into the cellar.[7]

Battery 30 was hit by a very heavy shell, mostly likely from a 600mm Karl mortar, and one of the turrets was put out of action. One shot from Dora's 800mm barrel landed at the barracks of Mekenzievy Mountain Station. Eight shots were fired at Batteries 16 and 24, which were adjacent to Battery 30. Battery 365 was also shelled and the battery commander Lieutenant Vorobyov was wounded. He was replaced by Lieutenant Matveev.

On 6 June German aircraft flew several hundred sorties, hitting mostly the forward edge of the defences. The two Karl mortars, Odin and Thor, each fired on Battery 30. Despite the damage to its gun, Battery 30 was quickly back in action, but only one gun was firing and its rate of fire was significantly reduced. Dora fired on Battery 110 and the command post of the 1st Anti-Aircraft Artillery Regiment at Fort Molotov, destroying the battery's magazine.

Boris Voyetkhov described the city during this bombardment:

A daylight journey into the city; the ruins of the houses appeared through the smokescreens in the harbour. Birds chased the wave tops in search of fish but they had all left the bay for the open sea. A sea of flame enveloped the city. Half-submerged ships rose above the water, their holds still full of cargoes of the dead, the bay their graveyard. A large ship was capsized, barnacles showing on the bottom. Another ship was full of jagged holes where birds took refuge. Naval ships, barges, small ships, floating derricks showed their masts above the water level. A tanker was cut in two.[8]

Chapter 7

The Third Assault (2) – 7 to 16 June 1942

'Sevastopol is still holding out – it was a question of three days, a week at the outside. The Germans boasted: "On the fifteenth of June we'll be drinking champagne on the Grafsky." They overlooked one thing: Sevastopol is no ordinary city. Sevastopol is the glory of Russia, the pride of the Soviet Union.'[1] Kurt Kunsewitz wrote from Braunschweig to his brother Otto, a corporal: 'I hope to hear that you're in Sevastopol soon; once you're there don't hesitate. If you see anybody suspicious, stand him up against the wall!' On 11 June, Otto Kunsewitz was killed on the approaches to Sevastopol.[2]

Eleventh Army attacked Sevastopol for the third and what would be the final, time early on the morning of 7 June (sunrise at this time of year was about 0500 hours; sunset around 2130 hours). Despite unleashing on the Soviets the heaviest pounding by air and artillery ever delivered to an enemy, the bombardment had not produced the desired effect, that is, a demoralised, cowering remnant, hiding under rocks, anxious to raise the white flag at the sight of the first grey helmet to appear over the parapet. The 50th Division report for 7 June states:

> Hour after hour the artillery has been raining shells on the enemy positions and the Luftwaffe appears to bomb newly designated targets in the foreground, but the enemy stubbornly holds on to its positions. Thousands of mines buried in the ground have been blown up by the shells. Enemy airplanes attack with phosphorous and other bombs and with great determination. Step by step the attack was carried forward.[3]

At 0250 hours Soviet artillery and aircraft carried out a pre-emptive strike, having been informed of H-Hour by German deserters. This action temporarily disrupted the German attack but it lasted only twenty minutes and did not have any long-term effects. The Germans replied with their own, powerful artillery and air attack.

The German offensive, identified by Manstein as *Unternehmen Störfang* (Operation Sturgeon Catch) and to the Soviets as the Third Assault, began at 0700 hours Soviet time.[4] The attacks were carried out from several different directions but the initial offensive was conducted by the 22nd and 132nd Infantry Divisions. The 437th Infantry Regiment of the 132nd Infantry Division advanced to Hill 103.9, above the Simferopol highway near Belbek. The village of Belbek was

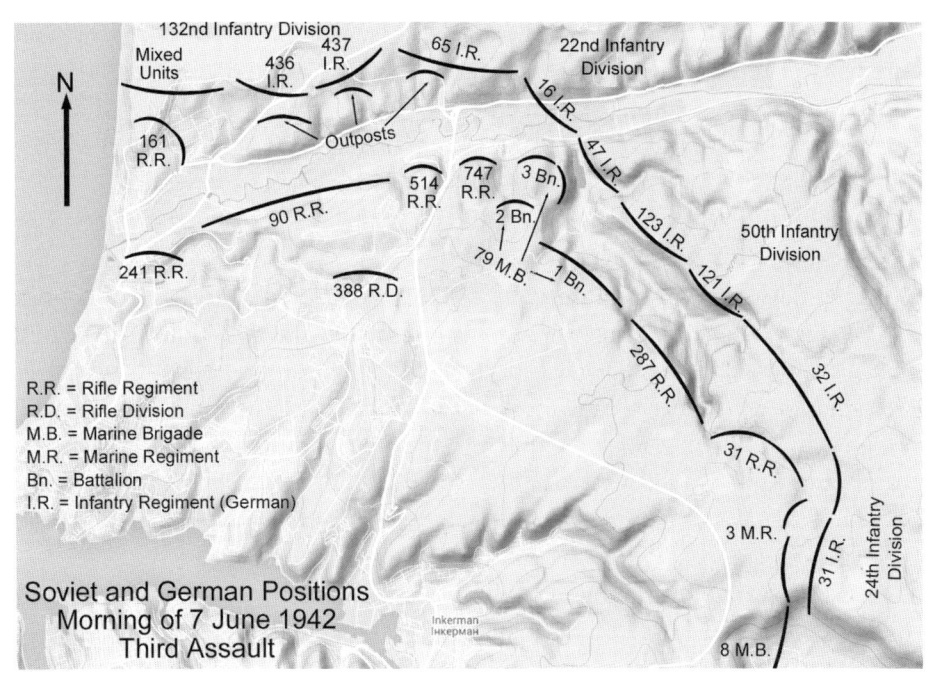

Soviet and German position in Sectors 3 and 4 on 7 June 1942. (© OpenStreetMap contributors, Author's collection)

attacked by 2nd Battalion, 16th Infantry Regiment of the 22nd Infantry Division. The 3rd Battalion of the 16th moved south from Hill 133.3 on the Kara-Tau plateau towards the Belbek Valley. 1st Battalion of the 47th Regiment of 22nd Infantry Division moved along the Belbek Valley and 3rd Battalion moved out of the long, deep ravine near the mouth of the Kamyshly Ravine.

The 79th Marine Brigade was located on Hill 126.5, what the Germans called the *Stellenberg*, which looked down on the mouth of the Kamyshly Ravine where it intersected the Belbek Valley. The 79th Brigade's sector of defence ran along the slopes of the *Stellenberg* to the junction with the 747th Regiment of 172nd Division posted on the adjacent Hill 124.5, called the *Bunkerberg*. The 1st Battalion of the 79th was adjacent to 3rd Battalion on the heights above Kamyshly ravine, while 2nd Battalion was in the trenches of the second line, to the rear of the 1st and 3rd Battalions.

The troops of the 172nd Infantry Division, on the left of 79th Marine Brigade, were more densely packed than the 79th. The 1st Battalion of the 747th Rifle Regiment, located on the left flank of 79th Brigade, guarded the *Bunkerberg*, while 1st Battalion of the 514th Regiment, on the left of 747th, held Hill 104.5, the *Ölberg*. The 4th Company, 2nd Battalion of 747th Regiment of 172nd Rifle Division and 6th Company, 2nd Battalion of the 514th Rifle Regiment manned forward outposts north of the Belbek Valley. The 3rd Company (1st Battalion), 4th Company (2nd Battalion) of 747th Rifle Regiment, and 4th and 5th Companies of the 514th Regiment manned four strongpoints on the floor of the Belbek Valley. The 3rd Battalion, 514th Regiment and 3rd Battalion, 747th Rifle Regiment occupied the third line, behind the *Ölberg*. The 383rd Rifle Regiment was in reserve.

The 90th Rifle Regiment of 95th Rifle Division was positioned to the left of the 747th, on the heights south of the Belbek Valley called *Haccius* Ridge by the Germans. The regiment's position ran along the ridge to the barracks of Battery 30. The 161st Regiment of 95th Rifle Division was positioned diagonally across the valley and north of the small village of Lyubimovka. The 241st Regiment of 95th Division was in reserve.

Everything was in place for a quick breakthrough to the bay and that sip of champagne at the Count's Quay, if there was anything left of it. Colonel Laskin, commander of 172nd Division, observed:

> The German command, undoubtedly, has done everything to ensure that its troops would quickly break through the Soviet defences. Furthermore, they were quite sure that the lengthy and powerful artillery and air bombardment would by now have completely suppressed the Soviet troops who would no longer be able to offer any serious resistance. Therefore the Germans advanced in unusually dense formations. The Soviets then focused their artillery fire on the advancing infantry. As the Soviet shells rained down, they began to lie down and find concealment; in a sense disappearing for a time. But after a few minutes they rose up and rushed forward. Again the Soviet shells forced them to go to ground.[5]

The outposts of the 79th Marine Brigade and the 172nd Rifle Division on the outskirts of Kamyshly and in the Belbek Valley were the first targets. Hundreds of German infantrymen rushed the trenches held by 2nd Company of 514th Regiment, firing on the run. The Soviets tossed grenades at the approaching Germans and, after about five minutes, broke up the attack. German troops from the 47th Infantry Regiment, along with pioneers of the 22nd Pioneer Battalion, attacked the junction of the 1st and 3rd Battalions of the 79th Brigade, but were fired on from heavy machine-gun bunkers and forced to retreat after suffering serious losses. German infantry losses mounted as the day wore on

After the first unsuccessful attacks, the Germans reopened their artillery barrage and air strikes. Laskin describes this renewed bombardment.

> The earth shook. All our positions were caught up in a fiery whirlwind. Dust and smoke from the bombs and shells turned the sky dull. German

aircraft flew over in wave after wave and bombs rained down on us almost continuously. Huge chunks of earth and trees flew into the air. The 172nd Division and the left flank of the 79th Brigade were hit especially hard. The target area was a narrow front of four to five kilometres and it was struck by thousands of shells from the guns and mortars and bombed by an uncounted number of aircraft. Huge clouds of dark grey smoke and dust rose up and blocked out the sun. A bright day became gloomy as during an eclipse.[6]

Soon after the second bombardment the Germans moved ahead but this time they were supported by StuG IIIs. 3rd Battalion of 47th Infantry Regiment moved along the Belbek Valley, supported by two batteries of assault guns from the 190th Assault Gun Battalion. 16th Infantry Regiment was supported by two more batteries of the 197th Assault Gun Battalion. Soviet scouts reported seeing about three dozen vehicles moving down the valley under cover of an artillery barrage, the infantry following closely behind. All available Soviet artillery was thrown against the advancing assault vehicles. Despite the intensity of this fire, the Germans continued to creep forward towards the Soviet outposts, followed by the infantry.

After the initial attacks were repulsed, the troops manning the 514th Regiment's outposts were nevertheless forced to fall back to the main lines, but the 6th Company of 2nd Battalion, 514th Regiment remained in its position on the left

German infantry sit atop a StuG III, somewhere near Sevastopol in June 1942. (NARA)

of the 79th Brigade. The brigade commander spotted the German 65th Infantry Regiment moving towards the Soviet outpost and wanted to order an artillery strike but the Germans were too close to the Soviet lines and the gunners risked hitting their own men. The Germans approached even closer and tossed grenades into the Soviet trenches. The battle lasted about two hours. Reconnaissance reports indicated that the Germans attacked the position from two sides and made it into the trenches where they engaged in hand-to-hand combat. The 6th Company retreated into the Belbek Valley.[7]

Breaking through the outposts of the 172nd Rifle Division proved to be more difficult and the Germans suffered heavy losses in the minefields of the Belbek Valley. Before reaching the outposts, the StuG IIIs encountered anti-tank obstacles[8] plus the waters of the Belbek River. The valley was difficult to navigate. The river, where it meets the Kamyshly Ravine, made several large loops that formed small oxbow lakes. The German 197th Assault Gun Battalion's vehicles were moving down from the plateau of Kara-Tau to the Simferopol highway and became trapped at the river. The Soviet 2nd Battalion of the 134th Artillery Regiment, positioned behind the *Stellenberg*, opened fire on the tanks in the Belbek Valley and the batteries of the 1st Battalion targeted the assault guns emerging from the Kamyshly ravine. They were also hit by the guns of Battery 30, which enfiladed the valley. Despite the efforts of the German pioneers, not all of the vehicles got across the river. Three vehicles were hit by Soviet guns and six more were stuck in the river. Those that could do so retreated.

Both battalions of the 16th Infantry Regiment suffered heavy losses trying to break through the minefields and obstacles in the Belbek Valley. The commander of 6th Company, Captain Nagel and 5th Company, Lieutenant Stefan, were killed in the minefields. 3rd Battalion of the 16th Regiment also suffered heavy losses. 11th Company's commander, Captain Loges and 9th Company's Lieutenant Heger were also killed.

Vaneev writes:

A difficult situation has developed in the area of the 79th Marine Brigade and 172nd Rifle Division. A group of StuG IIIs of the 190th Assault Gun Battalion tried to break through between the two Soviet units while another group in the Kamyshly ravine attacked the centre of 79th Brigade. That Brigade's anti-tank guns opened fire and the first volleys stopped two enemy guns. The assault guns approached the left of the position and were hit with Molotov cocktails and grenades. They closed in on the position of the 5th Company of the 2nd Battalion, 79th Brigade. They were unable to reach the top of the hill, but the company was eventually surrounded and their strength was reduced to a single platoon. A handful of men escaped.[9]

The Germans attacked to the north of the village of Kamyshly with seven assault guns and one armoured car. A dense formation of German infantry followed the StuG IIIs. Soviet artillery opened fire, one assault gun caught fire and the formation pulled back. About ten minutes later the same group appeared in the ravine without any infantry trailing behind and headed towards Kamyshly village. For the next several hours the Germans advanced to the plateau above the ravine, cutting off the 5th Company, 2nd Battalion of 79th Brigade.

German machine-gunners reached the observation posts of the 3rd Battalion of the 79th Brigade and the 134th Howitzer Artillery Regiment's 9th Battery. German shells exploded near the battery command post. Infantrymen of the 3rd Battalion took up positions at the trench parapets and hurled grenades at the advancing Germans, who nonetheless pressed on and overran the position. The few Soviet survivors pulled back to the rear. German assault guns moved up the hill and the 1st Battalion position fell. 3rd Battalion now had to fight on two fronts. It was hit in the flank by 1st Battalion of the 47th Regiment, supported by assault guns and in the rear by the 3rd Battalion of the 47th Regiment.

Meanwhile, 5th Company of the 514th Rifle Regiment found a strongpoint among some of the concrete bunkers on the south side of the valley and around the 'Tomato Plant', a former processing plant for the collective farms. The plant was located between a bend in the Belbek River where the Simferopol Highway crossed the valley from north to south before it climbed up to the plateau between the *Ölberg* and the *Bunkerberg*. 5th Company was reinforced by the 174th Anti-tank Battalion, a machine gun platoon and a battery of 76mm guns. The buildings and cellars of the plant were fortified and it became a powerful position.

Colonel Laskin stated:

Four supporting strongpoints were created in our defences. One of them was in the centre section of the 747th Regiment. Its armament included regimental guns, mortars, anti-tank guns and machine guns. The commander of the strongpoint was Senior Lieutenant Kaplan. When the avalanche of [tanks] and infantry approached the trenches and enemy artillery fire began to strike our position, Kaplan loudly commanded: – 'Fire! Fire! With all guns!' Shots rang out. The 76mm battery, commanded by Senior Lieutenant Bondarenko, fired point blank on the assault guns and a few of them were enveloped in smoke. The German infantry dropped to the ground but most of the guns continued to move forward, establishing a foothold on the *Bunkerberg*.[10]

They were immediately hit by a barrage of artillery and mortar fire. Many of the Soviet defenders were wounded but held their position. 172nd Division held on to the position but Germans were spotted to the right, on the height held by 79th Brigade. The right flank of the division quickly deteriorated.

The Germans brought in the 1st Battalion of the 16th Regiment to take advantage of the difficult situation in the area of the 79th Marine Brigade, which could not retreat to the rear. The battalion struck the junction between the 172nd Rifle Division and the 79th Brigade between the *Bunkerberg* and the *Stellenberg*. The Germans reached the railway line in the ravine. Soldiers of the 747th Rifle Regiment quickly took up defensive positions across the railway embankment.

172nd Rifle Division was tasked with maintaining liaison with 79th Marine Brigade. The 1st Battalion of the 747th Regiment tried but was unable to restore the connection. The Germans broke through between the two units. By 1500 hours, two German units, the 3rd Battalion of the 47th and 1st Battalion of 16th Regiment linked up behind the *Stellenberg* 700m east of Hill 64.4, completing the encirclement of the companies of the Soviet 79th Brigade. The Germans were in control of about one square kilometre of Soviet defences. At the end of the day several companies of the 2nd Battalion, 79th Brigade and three forward outposts were taken. The telephone line from the forward positions was cut, requiring the commanders to make visual observations. It took three hours for news of the breakthrough at the junction of the 747th and 79th to reach the command post.

General Petrov was ordered by Vice-Admiral Oktyabrsky to stop the German breakthrough at Hill 64.4 at all costs. Petrov ordered Colonel Potapov, commander of 79th Brigade to have 2nd Battalion stop the Germans and push them back. 2nd and 3rd Battalions then went on the offensive and according to Vaneev 'restored the situation'.[11] But this was not entirely the case. The Soviet battalions were greatly weakened and unprepared for an assault on a superior opponent. Nevertheless, the 2nd and 3rd Battalions of 79th Brigade managed to stop the further advance of the 16th Regiment and restored the connection with 747th Rifle Regiment, but they were unable to push the Germans off of their foothold on the lower slopes of the *Stellenberg*.

Around 1500 hours the battle on the left flank of 172nd Rifle Division, at the junction between the division and the 90th Rifle Regiment of 95th Rifle Division, escalated. The German 65th Regiment of 22nd Division, in reserve up to this point, supported the attack of the two regiments of the 132nd Division. Of the four strongholds north of and in the Belbek Valley, only the Tomato Plant continued to resist, but the defenders suffered heavy losses, including the commander of the 1st Battalion of 514th Regiment, who was killed. The commander of 5th Company, Lieutenant Kaplan, was seriously wounded. However, the Tomato Plant and the *Ölberg* defences continued to hold. Around 2000 hours the 22nd Infantry Division offensive came to a halt. The 2nd Battalion, 16th Infantry Regiment had suffered very heavy losses and was greatly weakened. The commanders of the 3rd and

4th Companies had been killed but the regiment reached its objective. The 47th Infantry Regiment lost both of its battalion commanders.

The 50th Division's 123rd and 121st Regiments were located on the plateau at the southern end of the Kamyshly Ravine. Around 1600 the 123rd Regiment began to probe the right flank of 79th Marine Brigade, now engaged with the 47th Regiment. Two companies of the 123rd moved towards the junction between 1st Battalion of 79th Marine Brigade and the 287th Regiment. 1st Battalion was positioned along the top of Hill 192.0, which the Germans called '*Trapez*'. The Germans moved along a road that led up the Gyubernovskoy Ravine on the northwestern slope of *Trapez*. Artillery Commander Orishko sent a rifle and machine-gun platoon to stop the Germans. The two groups met and battled in the dense undergrowth on the slopes of *Trapez*. Forty men from 79th Brigade were killed, including the machine-gun platoon commander.

Laskin wrote:

For the Soviets, the positions had been hit so hard it was nearly impossible to identify which men were with which units. The terrain was completely altered and it was impossible to recognise landmarks such as trenches and trails that had been there in the morning. The faces of the soldiers were black from the smoke. Each man's nerves were at the breaking point after eighteen hours of hell. On 7 June thousands of bombs and shells fell on the men of the 79th Marine Brigade and 172nd Rifle Division. Many were seriously wounded and unable to get out of the trenches. When they looked up and spotted another man they were happy to find out he was Soviet and that they had not fallen into enemy hands.[12]

In the south, the German 28th Light Division attacked the 381st Rifle Regiment at the 'Gracious'[13] Farm (m. Blagodatnoye, a suburb of Balaklava), but the 381st held on. At the same time, the Germans attacked Canrobert Hill northeast of Kamary, location of the 782nd Regiment of 388th Rifle Division. The 602nd Rifle Regiment was attacked by the 83rd German Regiment. The Luftwaffe destroyed four of the seven pre-cast bunkers located on the hill near the Second Turkish Redoubt. Two kilometres to the northeast the Italian Cemetery was also attacked. The Germans moved out of their forward trenches but were quickly struck by Soviet artillery and forced back. Further north, 1st Rumanian Guards Division attacked the left flank of the 7th Marine Brigade and the 772nd Regiment of 386th Rifle Division in the vicinity of the village of Upper Chorgun. 404th Artillery Regiment's 152mm guns and the Soviet coastal batteries within range of the position stopped the German attacks.

Despite heavy losses the Germans managed to gain a foothold in the Soviet defences. The Soviet defenders, for the most part, held their original positions except for 3rd Battalion of the 79th Brigade which lost a part of the northern edge of the *Stellenberg*, allowing the Germans to move up on the plateau. A small group of men from the 79th Brigade used the cover of darkness to break out of the German encirclement. This included a machine gun company and mortar company. The Germans failed to capture the *Ölberg*, but they managed to seize control of most of the Belbek Valley. The Soviets held on to the Tomato Plant south of Belbek village and its strategic location meant the Soviets could still cover the Simferopol Highway. Soviet losses amounted to 1,785 killed, wounded and missing.

At 0150 hours on 8 June, the transport *Georgia* and its destroyer escort arrived at Sevastopol harbour with 750 replacement soldiers, 233 tons of ammunition and 227 tons of food. Then 850 wounded and 630 civilian evacuees were taken on board and the ships left at 0600 hours. Among the wounded was Nikolai Vorobiev, commander of Battery 365 – Fort Stalin. During his absence Lieutenant Matveev took command of the battery, but the following morning Matveev was himself wounded and sent to the hospital. Overnight the Germans fired artillery and mortars at Battery 365 and in the morning the Luftwaffe attacked the battery, causing heavy casualties among the gunners.

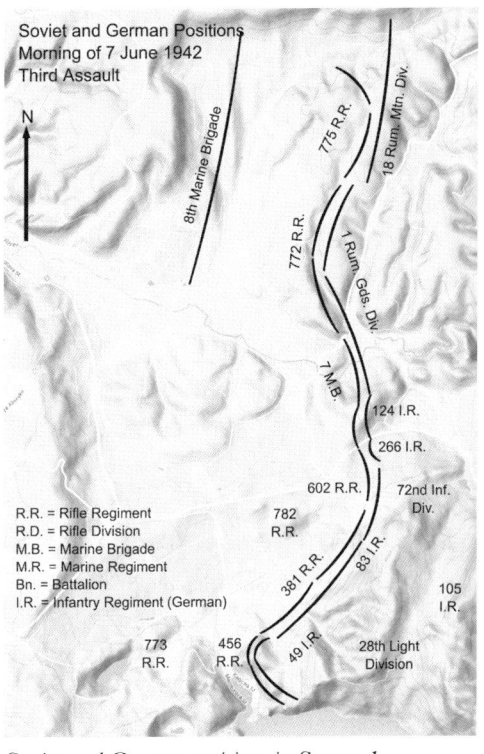

Soviet and German positions in Sectors 1 and 2 on 7 June 1942. (© OpenStreetMap contributors, Author's collection)

On the morning of 8 June the 79th Marine Brigade and 172nd Rifle Division were in trouble. The Germans gained a perch on top of the *Stellenberg* and surrounded 3rd Battalion of the 79th. Now they needed to whittle away at the defences running along the southwest edge of Kamyshly Ravine in order to sweep across the flatter ground towards Mekenzievy Station.

Due south of Kamyshly Village was a grouping of three hills. The first two were called by the Germans *Schanzhöhe* on the left and *Sandhöhe* on the right. To the rear of these was *Trapez*. A forest road passed below *Sandhöhe* and swung around to the northeast between *Schanzhöhe* and *Trapez*. The road was defended by dozens of machine-gun nests and trenches. The strongpoint was defended by 1st Battalion of the 287th Rifle Regiment, plus two mortar batteries with 82mm and 120mm mortars. There was also an anti-tank bunker on the *Schanzhöhe* with a 45mm gun pointed down the road. Further back was the second line defended by 2nd Battalion of the 287th supported by anti-tank guns and machine guns. The machine guns were set up in the ruins of an old barracks building located in the centre of the plateau on Hill 136.9, below the road that led up from a ravine in which the Mekenzievy Cordon 1 Forest House was located. The road then turned 90 degrees towards the southeast behind the positions of the 747th Rifle Regiment on the *Bunkerberg*.

The 747th was positioned along the top of the *Bunkerberg*. On their right was the former location of the 79th Marine Brigade on the

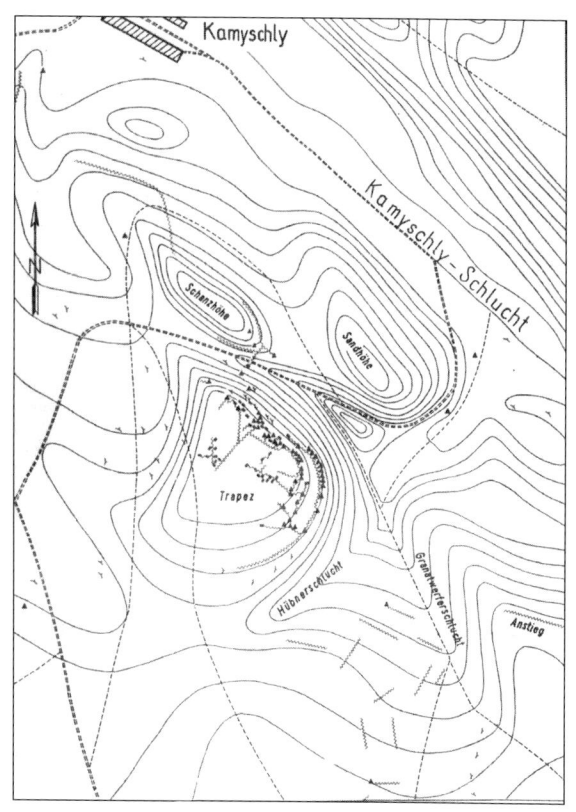

Trapez *(Hill 192.0) southwest of the Kamyshly Ravine.* (Nachtrag)

Stellenberg but the ravine between the *Stellenberg* and *Bunkerberg* was now occupied by troops of the German 16th Infantry Regiment. They had penetrated along the narrow valley and were moving eastward behind the 747th towards the railway. The 747th's position ran along the railway tracks. It was at the location between the *Bunkerberg* and *Ölberg* where the railway line and the Simferopol Highway curved to the southeast in the direction of the Mekenzievy Mountain station. To the left of the 747th was the 514th Rifle Regiment on the *Ölberg*. Overnight the Germans located the minefields below the *Ölberg* and *Bunkerberg* by interrogating a Soviet prisoner from the 172nd Division. In the hours of darkness the 47th Infantry Regiment moved up to the plateau from the Kamyshly Ravine while the 65th Infantry Regiment moved below the railway.

General Petrov ordered a counter-attack by 2nd Battalion of 79th Brigade, 2nd Perekop Regiment and 2nd Company of the 125th Tank Battalion in the area of the 79th Brigade. The attack would be carried out on 8 June. It pitted two battalions plus a company against three regiments. The odds were about 1:7 against the Soviets.

At 0600 hours the Soviet 134th Howitzer Regiment, 18th Guards Artillery Regiment and Battery 724 opened fire on the Kamyshly Ravine and the eastern Belbek Valley. Soon after, 2nd Battalion of 79th Marine Brigade led the poorly-coordinated counter-attack. The battalion was stretched out over a line 2.5km long. 2nd Perekop Regiment, 2nd Battalion of the 79th and the tank company moved up to their starting line when 2nd Battalion launched the attack too early. At 0730 hours the German 65th Regiment, waiting to launch their own attack, opened an artillery barrage and began to advance to attack the flanks of 2nd Battalion of the 79th above the railway line at the *Bunkerberg*, after which the battalion was forced to retreat. At 0900 hours the 2nd Battalion of 2nd Perekop Regiment arrived in their attack position but by then it was too late as the attack had already been launched. 2nd Battalion of 79th Brigade lost 126 men killed and wounded and fifty-eight missing.

The 2nd Perekop Regiment and the tank company, despite their late arrival, waded into the battle. They reached the German trenches and engaged in hand-to-hand combat with the bayonet. The Germans sent in fresh troops and the Soviets were forced to withdraw. The obsolete Soviet T-26 tanks failed to provide any support and were withdrawn from action due to German artillery fire. 3rd Battalion of 47th Infantry Regiment, supported by StuG IIIs, broke through the line of defence along the slopes and advanced to the rear of 747th Rifle Regiment on the *Bunkerberg*.

There was a brief pause before the German shells started to fall again. Groups of StuG IIIs advanced across the Belbek Valley followed by infantry, in the same manner as the previous day. The Luftwaffe attacked the Soviet front lines in groups of six to twelve aircraft. The 3rd Company of the 747th Regiment was reduced to twenty men; the company commander badly wounded and the political officer killed. The company was being attacked by armour and infantry from two sides. The Soviets tossed grenades at the tanks, killing and wounding a large number of Germans but the defenders' numbers continued to dwindle.

The junction between the 747th and 514th Regiments was threatened by the 65th Infantry Regiment and communication between the command post and the front lines was cut. The command post of the 747th Regiment was located near the top of the *Stellenberg*. A machine-gun company was ordered to move up to support 2nd Battalion of 747th Regiment troops but the Germans broke through to the 2nd Battalion headquarters and the remnants of the battalion were surrounded. Some of the men, including the headquarters staff, attempted to break out but ran into a German machine-gun company. Oddly, the Germans were now the ones being attacked from two sides, by the escaping Soviets and additional Soviet forces to the rear. But the German attack was too strong and they got into the Soviet defences, including the main observation post of the 514th and 747th Regiments

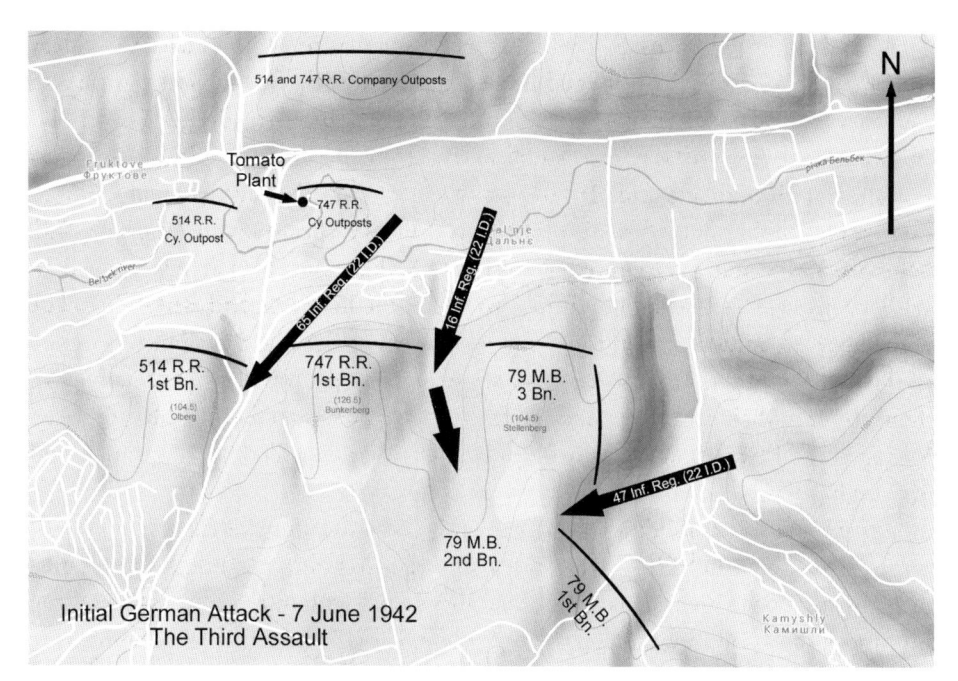

The initial German attack of 7 June 1942. (© OpenStreetMap contributors, Author's collection)

where most of the regimental, artillery and reconnaissance commanders were gathered. Sometime later, a machine gun company of the 514th Regiment and a group of signallers from 747th Regiment reached the observation post but the battle was over. About 150 Soviets had been captured: the remaining defenders and about sixty Germans lay dead. The 747th Rifle Regiment ceased to exist at that point except for a few stragglers who escaped to the third line of defence further to the south.

At the bottom of the hill in the Belbek Valley the battle for the Tomato Plant continued. The 2nd Battalion of 514th Regiment, defending the plant, was surrounded. The two-day battle cost the Germans heavily, but the 2nd Battalion lost the entire 2nd and 5th Companies along with their commanders. Some men escaped to the rear later that evening.

The Germans now moved across the ridge line towards the third line of defence defended by 3rd Battalion of 514th Regiment. An unidentified Soviet machine-gunner from one of the platoons described the fighting:

> Everywhere was heavy fighting. On 7 June the enemy efforts were directed to the right flank of the division against the 747th Rifle Regiment and 79th Marine Brigade and on the next day he fell with full force on the 514th Regiment. The Germans slowly but steadily gnawed into our defences. They

crawled towards our trench in which there were about 15 men and began pelting them with grenades, shouting 'Rus Kaput.' Lt Sergey Biryukov, the platoon commander, shouted for the men to attack and with grenades in hand we rushed forward screaming, 'Kaput.' The Germans moved back but another group approached the flank. We were down to ten men. Biryukov was killed. The intensity of the battle increased but in the evening only three men were left.

The 388th Rifle Division and 5th Anti-Tank Battery, plus the 674th Regiment, stopped the Germans from making a complete breakthrough at the third defensive line. The Germans captured the *Stellenberg* and approached the position of the batteries of the 134th Howitzer Regiment which had not received the order to pull back. 1st Battery positioned three 122mm howitzers for direct fire against the approaching troops of 47th Regiment, who were accompanied by eight assault guns. The Soviet guns engaged the German armour and after about thirty minutes they pulled back, leaving three damaged vehicles behind. Additional artillery support came from Battery 724 at the junction between 79th Brigade and the 287th Regiment at *Trapez*.

1st and 2nd Battalions of the 122nd Infantry Regiment of the German 50th Infantry Division were tasked with the attack on *Trapez*. They attacked through the Gyubernovskoy Ravine against its northeast slope. On their left the 31st and 32nd Infantry Regiments of the 24th Division joined in the attack, the 31st along with the 122nd in the ravine, the 32nd further to the southeast to cut off the small spur the Germans called the *Anstieg*. The plan first called for the capture of the hills adjacent to *Trapez*, then the main target while suppressing any Soviet response with artillery fire. The 1st Battalion of the 122nd Infantry Regiment moved to its position and was immediately hit by artillery and mortar fire.

Visibility was very poor in the dense undergrowth of the hillsides. German artillery succeeded in suppressing flanking fire from the top of *Trapez*. Around noon the commander of the 1st Battalion of the 122nd was wounded and a company commander from 3rd Battalion took over. The battalion was tasked with maintaining communication with the 31st Regiment but the troops lost contact in the thick brush. 2nd Battalion was now in a position to attack the northwest slope of *Trapez* and took advantage of German shelling on top of the slopes to move up through the ravine. Three companies of 2nd Battalion, following the 71st Engineer Battalion which had breached some of the defences, cleared the forward Soviet trenches and gun emplacements and took control of the top of *Trapez*. A defensive position was set up to face the southwest and to guard the flanks from the adjacent hilltops. The Germans had successfully established a deep wedge between the 287th Regiment and the 1st Battalion of 79th Brigade. The 287th attempted to re-establish contact with the 79th but could not. By 1700 hours German armour appeared on the road leading up to the top of the plateau. The 287th was flanked on both sides and several units of the 122nd and 31st Infantry Regiments and the 71st Pioneer Battalion, broke through between the 287th and 1st Battalion of the 79th Marine Brigade. By the end of the day the 287th Rifle Regiment was surrounded by the 122nd Infantry Regiment on one side and 31st Infantry Regiment on the other.

The Luftwaffe flew 1,724 sorties during the day. German bombers attacked Coastal Battery 14, dropping 300 bombs. Several flak batteries were hit, including Battery 80. A gunner wrote about the state of the battery:

> I looked around and did not recognise the position, until now well-groomed and green. One of the cannons was blown up and landed in the gun pit. All around lay the dead; the wounded moaning. The gunner, cut in two, still tightly gripped in his right hand the wheel of the training mechanism. Lieutenant Pyanzin, the commander, stood near the destroyed command post, clutching the sleeve of his closest friend Zakamenelov, whose lips were blue and tightly clenched, eyes staring. I reached out and shook Pyanzin awake. He knelt on the ground and wept like a child for his friend. I told him that nothing could be done. A shell whistled overhead and Pyanzin abruptly stood up and dusted himself off and once again, in front of me stood the former battery commander, screaming orders as the shells came in.[14]

In the evening Battery 80's guns were destroyed but the men continued to fight among the ruins. The crew cut down telephone poles and installed them in the pits on the broken gun cradles and barrels. In the morning the regimental headquarters realised the battery was no longer defensible and the men were ordered to pull back and form a rifle company from the survivors.[15] Heavy damage was inflicted on Batteries 366, 227, 219 and 79. Battery 365 had only two operational guns remaining. Thus, at the point of the main enemy attack there were almost no anti-aircraft guns left and German aircraft could operate in the north with impunity.

The Soviets in Sector 4 were in desperate need of reinforcements. Colonel Laskin wrote that his troops were stretched so thin they were beginning to merge with the artillery batteries. 134th Howitzer Regiment was mixed in with the 747th Rifle Regiment. The 2nd Battalion was down to five guns. Behind the 172nd Division was nothing – no manpower or firepower. Overnight, stragglers from surrounding units were thrown together to form a rear defensive line. The defenders included elements of the newly arriving 345th Rifle Division.

The next German attack began at dawn on 9 June. 132nd Division moved along the Kacha road towards the Belbek Valley. 22nd Division was below the *Ölberg*, supported by two battalions of assault guns and a tank company. 50th Infantry Division was in the upper Kamyshly Ravine and on *Trapez*. 24th Division was in the Mekenzievy forest surrounding the Soviet 287th Regiment.

Major-General Kolomiec, commander of Sector 3, discusses 9 June in his memoirs:

> On the morning of the ninth of June, on the third day of the assault, the enemy again held a five-hour artillery preparation and bombing. Against us and our neighbours were thrown into the battle the 50th and 132nd Infantry Divisions with replenished manpower and equipment. The attack was supported by numerous tanks, the Germans obviously having in mind that one more effort and the front will be broken and the path to North Bay opened. But the enemy overestimated his chances. The tanks were moving ahead of the infantry – so many that it was difficult to count. We desperately needed artillery fire. The artillery commander, Colonel Grossman, telephoned the local battery commander to open fire on the approaching infantrymen and tanks. A minute later there was a roar of artillery from the coastal batteries and field artillery. The phone rang. It was a forward observer announcing with disbelief that the ground where the Germans were approaching was covered with burning tanks and littered with corpses.[16]

Near the headwaters of the Kamyshly Ravine the 287th Rifle Regiment was now completely surrounded. More than 500 men of the regiment had been wounded and when the ambulances did not show up to pick them up they realised they were surrounded. The 1st Battalion of 79th Brigade was also surrounded. The 287th held out for another two days. They attempted to break out but could not and had no choice but to surrender. 1st Battalion fought until 12 June then surrendered.

Another critical situation was developing to the west. The 172nd Rifle Division had been on the retreat the past couple of days but it was a fighting retreat and they continued to block the defensive line. On the morning of 9 June the 213th Infantry Regiment, sent over from the 73rd Infantry Division, appeared in front of the 90th Rifle Regiment, at the junction between the 95th and 172nd Divisions. The arrival of the regiment gave the 22nd Infantry Division more freedom of movement in their advance against the Soviet 514th Regiment. The German assault guns moved quickly through the defences and surrounded the regiment's command post. They reached the observation post where Colonel Laskin and his staff, along with the 172nd and 514th commanders, were located. The telephone wires between headquarters and the forward positions were cut, repaired, then cut again and the commanders could communicate only by radio. Everyone was firing a weapon of some kind and the Soviets escaped, but only after taking heavy losses. Laskin was wounded and out of action and command of the division passed to Colonel Rupasov. Colonel Ustinov, the 514th Regiment commander, was killed. The regiment was reduced to 150 men and the observation post was lost. The commander of the 747th Rifle Regiment, Colonel Shashlo was also killed. On 9 June the Soviets lost 444 killed, 1,407 wounded and 820 missing. The 172nd Division had ceased to exist as a viable unit; only certain groups were left with a mix of troops. The Germans moved through the 172nd Division to the rear lines where there were no infantry troops, just the 4th Bunker Battalion troops manning the concrete bunkers.

Battery 365 was highly effective against German armour and infantry and was therefore a prime target, German bombers turning their attention to it after the destruction of Battery 80. On 8 June the battery commander, Nikolai Vorobiev, was wounded and was replaced by the platoon commander, Lieutenant Matveev. On 9 June two German squadrons dropped bombs on the battery. Late in the evening German artillery unleashed a barrage of shells on the battery and, as was common practice, as soon as the shelling ended the Soviet gunners moved out of the dugouts and took their place at the guns. Lieutenant Matveev was wounded in the arm but refused to go to the infirmary. Matveev left the confines of the battery to get a closer look and was hit by shrapnel. He was carried to the infirmary

Identified as the entrance to a Soviet AA battery at Sevastopol. Possibly Battery 365 (Fort Stalin). (NARA)

for treatment and later taken to the hospital and replaced by Lieutenant Pyanzin, former commander of Battery 80. While much of the attention on Hill 60 is given to Battery 365, it is also worth noting that several divisional batteries and Battery 227 also fought and sacrificed themselves to hold back the German attack.

The 345th Rifle Division arrived at the front with the 1163rd and 1167th Rifle Regiments. They were positioned behind the anti-tank ditch. 1167th Rifle Regiment was near Fort Stalin. 250 men that remained of the 172nd Rifle Division were placed among the regiments of the 345th and the 95th Rifle Divisions.

Boris Voyetkhov describes the activities taking place in the harbour:

Sevastopol was engulfed in flame and smoke. Searchlights cut through the night sky, searching for German bombers. Within the beams, dogfights took place between Russians and Germans. A German plane, caught in the beam, tried to escape the light but it could not and was shot down, crashing in Korabelnaya Harbour with a loud explosion. The beams of light followed the plane to its final resting point then, satisfied that it no longer posed a threat, the searchlight beams arced back towards the sky, looking for the next target.

The sky above Sevastopol flashed with explosions of bombs, flares and tracer. Incendiary bombs lit up the entire harbour like daylight. Barracks, warehouses and other buildings next to the harbour were ablaze.

A destroyer approached the dock, the gangway was put up and the unloading began. It had to be done quickly. The docks were chaos; voices raised in command; arguments; shouting; screams. Hundreds of civilians jostled to reach the docks to evacuate the city with their children. Barges pulled up to the quay loaded with wounded Marines and Army soldiers from the battlefield. They were to be loaded on the destroyer and taken back to Novorossiysk. The wounded were taken off the barges and laid on top of baggage and equipment destined for loading on the destroyer. Fresh soldiers pushed their way off the ship and formed up in line on the dock. They would be sent straight to the front lines. The crew of the ship unloaded it themselves. This shipment included aircraft engines, boxes of artillery shells, aircraft bombs, machine guns, artillery pieces, liquids like oil and lubricants, spare parts for tanks, plus sacks of flour and salt and foodstuffs. The destroyer had to be unloaded and loaded quickly in order to leave one hour before dawn. The ability to do this under these terrible conditions was miraculous

After the ship was unloaded the crew took on the evacuees with thousands of pieces of luggage. There was no restriction on what they could bring with them. This policy made it easier for them to leave their homes as they did not have to leave prized possessions behind. People brought things that reminded them of their lives in Sevastopol. The city was abandoned, houses dark and empty. The evacuees crowded the deck of the destroyer, looking back at their burned, bombed homes.

The German artillery zeroed in on a burning building above the wharf. Debris showered down on to the docks and the crews rush to put out the blaze before it could spread to the priceless munitions waiting to be moved to the front. The destroyer untied, gangplanks were pulled up and the ship moved slowly away from the docks, headed for Battery Constantine at the entrance to the harbour, then out of sight into the Black Sea.[17]

Early in the morning of 10 June the transport *Abkhazia* arrived in Sevastopol, all the while being harassed by German aircraft. The bombers dropped twenty-four torpedoes but none of them hit the transport. *Abkhazia* delivered 287 troops, 561 tons of ammunition, aircraft engines, food, cement, machine guns and automatic rifles. What Sevastopol needed most, besides soldiers, was ammunition. In the past ten days the Soviets had used up 70,000 shells. The warehouses still held 3.2 tons but most of that was 45mm shells and naval ammunition. It was 122mm and 107mm shells that were in short supply, as were 85mm mortar bombs and 76mm anti-aircraft shells.

The *Abkhazia* was scheduled to unload during the hours of darkness and leave before daylight but for unknown reasons the unloading of the ship at the Sukharno dock was delayed. The ship was sent there because the primary unloading pier was blocked by another sunken ship. The transport was unloading when an air raid began. A smokescreen was set up to conceal the operation but it stopped for unknown reasons and the ship came into full view of the German pilots. At 0920 hours several bombs hit *Abkhazia*, starting a fire. A few minutes later, Ju 87s attacked, scoring direct hits on the ship and it began to list to starboard. The crew and the men unloading the ship ran to the docks and took shelter in one of the tunnels of the Sukharno Arsenal. The ship continued to burn and sank later in the day, but the ammunition aboard did not explode. *Abkhazia* was the last ship unloaded at Sukharno.

German infantry, supported by artillery, aircraft and armour, continued attacks against Sector 3 and 4, mainly in the Mekenzievy Mountains in the direction of the railway station. The 190th and 197th Assault Gun Battalions had about sixteen StuG IIIs remaining. The 22nd Infantry Division also had a number of captured tanks available to them.

Two regiments of the 345th Rifle Division stood in the path of the 22nd Infantry Division's advance. The 1163rd Regiment was located behind Mekenzievy Mountain Station; the 1165th at the junction with the remnant of the 79th Marine Brigade. After a heavy pounding the German 438th Infantry Regiment of 132nd Infantry Division attacked the anti-tank ditch and swiftly crossed over, overwhelming the defenders from 1163rd Rifle Regiment. They proceeded down the Simferopol-Sevastopol Road. Meanwhile, 16th Infantry Regiment followed up the attack, crossed the ditch and captured the Mekenzievy Mountain Station and the nearby barracks. The 47th Infantry Regiment, to the left of the 16th, captured the Forest House – Mekenzievy Cordon Number 1.

The commander of 345th Division, Colonel Guz, ordered 1165th Regiment to dislodge the Germans from the station. The commander of the 1165th Regiment was Lieutenant-Colonel V. V. Babkov, who distinguished himself as the former commander of the 361st Regiment of 106th Division and 383rd Regiment of 172nd Division at Perekop and Ishun. In the morning of 10 June the 1165th counter-attacked, but by the end of the day the station was firmly in German hands.

On the left flank the remnants of the 172nd Division were defeated. The Germans captured 120 prisoners from the 1163rd Regiment and other regiments also lost prisoners, dead and wounded. But, during the day the Germans gained only 200 to 300m along the front and the 22nd Division ran out of steam. The front defended by 79th Brigade and 345th Division remained relatively unchanged. The lines also held in other sectors. German air raids increased, 600 aircraft dropping about 2,000 bombs. Soviet air capabilities, both aircraft and anti-aircraft guns, were seriously diminished.

In the first ten days of the month the Soviets lost about 9,000 men. The *Abkhazia*'s sinking left a large number of wounded to be evacuated. The defenders of Sectors 3 and 4 were exhausted and badly in need of reinforcements. In the evening, however, the garrison got the welcome news that the 138th Rifle Brigade was on the way to Sevastopol, scheduled to arrive on 12 June on the cruiser *Molotov*.

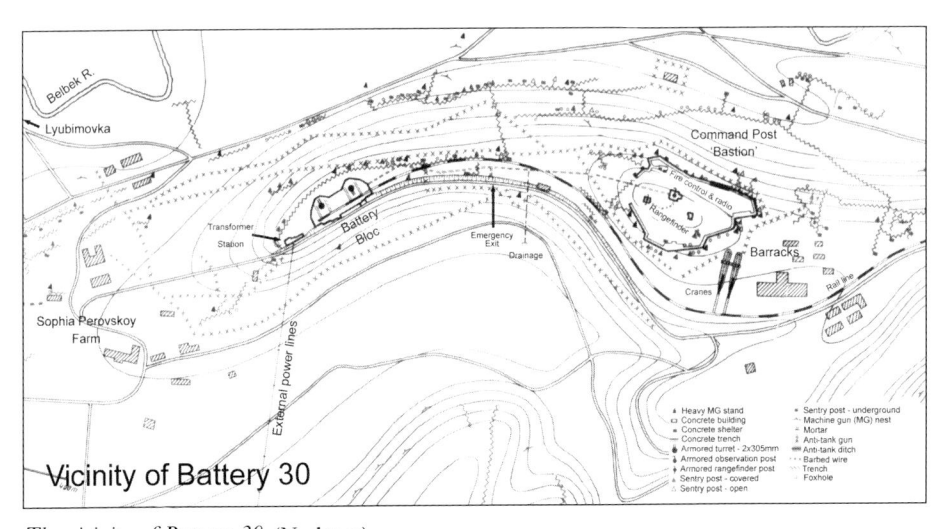

The vicinity of Battery 30. (Nachtrag)

The general staff at fleet headquarters discussed how to eliminate the wedge forming in the Soviet lines around the railway station. They planned a counter-attack for the following day, but the chances of success of such an attack were almost nil. Troops would have to be sent from other sectors of the battlefield. The 9th Marine Brigade, 778th Regiment, 81st Tank Battalion and a number of smaller units were combat-ready. The north shore was nearing the end of the road while relatively little action had taken place in the south. However, Oktyabrsky still feared an amphibious landing and did not want to relocate 9th Brigade. Overnight, troops of 2nd and 3rd Battalions of 7th Marine Brigade assembled at the former Tsarist pier in the South Bay and were transported by barge to the north side. From there they moved up to the Sophia Perovskoya State Farm at Lyubimovka.

At 0800 hours on 11 June an artillery barrage preceded the Soviet counter-attack. The 7th Marine Brigade moved out to the Alkadar Ravine that ran behind Battery 30 and along the anti-tank ditch that intersected the Simferopol Highway. Their objective was to recapture the positions recently taken by the Germans. The fighting was intense, the sides barely 50m apart, but the Germans had twice the number of men. The Germans counter-attacked from Hill 107.2. The Soviets requested artillery support on the hill and mortar shells starting falling. The fighting raged back and forth. The 22nd Infantry Division also suffered significant losses, but 3rd Battalion of 7th Marine Brigade lost one-third of its men.

A simultaneous Soviet counter-attack was launched in Sector 3. The battle lasted for 2½ hours. The Soviets advanced about 1.5km but their tanks were unable to break through the German lines. The main failure was caused by the Soviets' inability to follow up their tank penetrations with infantry support, the Soviet units simply not having enough men to do so. The Germans launched an unrelated offensive against the 345th Division but the German attack failed.

Around 1000 hours on 12 June the Germans dealt a major blow in the vicinity of the railway station. The Germans used captured KV heavy tanks and the Soviets broke and ran. The Germans moved as far as the head of the Grafskaya and Sukharno Ravines, about 1km south of Mekenzievy Station, and the Soviets now had lost the eastern flank of the ridge running towards Battery 365. Soviet troops, consisting of the remnants of 79th Marine Brigade, 345th Rifle Division and 25th Chapaevsky Division, supported by eight coastal defence batteries and field artillery, established a new line of defence and stopped the German advance. Battery 704 was surrounded.

Battery 115 (704) was established on 12 December 1941. It was equipped with guns from the *Chervona Ukraina*[18] and initially commanded by First Lieutenant V. I. Durikov. In late December the Germans broke through in Sector 4 and came to within 500m of the battery. The anti-aircraft guns of Battery 365 protected Battery 115 from German air attack. The battery came in very close contact with

130mm gun of Battery 14. St. Vladimir's Cathedral is in the background, across Sandy Bay. (Nemenko Collection)

the Germans during the Second Assault and the crew often had to defend the position with machine guns and rifles. At the end of December soldiers from the 345th Rifle Division took refuge at the battery and fought with the Germans in close combat.

In February 1942 the battery was re-designated Battery 704. It was shifted to a new position and provided with a railway spur to supply ammunition. A dummy battery was set up in its former location. The battery's 130mm guns were placed on concrete platforms. Ammunition was stored in concrete shelters about 40m from the guns, accessible through covered trenches. It was protected by the anti-tank ditch and several earth-timber machine-gun emplacements. Bunkers 11 and 11A also protected the battery.

During the Third Assault the battery was under constant air attack and artillery fire. Despite this it continued to fire on German tanks and infantry. On 10 June the battery was stormed by German infantry, supported by assault guns and attacked continually by the Luftwaffe. The attacks were repulsed by the gunners but one of the guns was disabled. A German tank broke through the defences and knocked out the second gun. The gunners, supported by the 100mm guns of Bunker 11, managed to hold on to the battery. The battery commander, V. G. Pavlov, was mortally wounded and died on the way to the hospital. He was replaced by Senior Lieutenant I. K. Khanin. Second in command was Petty Officer First Class N. P.

Aleynikov. The fighting ended at nightfall. The battery had lost about thirty men but the Germans four times that number plus a number of their assault guns. The survivors – about twenty men – prepared to continue fighting the next day. On 12 June the Germans brought up reserves and continued their attack. At the end of the day the Germans advanced towards the battery which was now out of ammunition. The battery was surrounded and almost all of the defenders were killed, including men from 95th and 25th Divisions and 79th Marine Brigade.[19]

Battery 365 was pounded by artillery and air strikes and the Germans, supported by tanks, mounted an infantry attack. The defences on Hill 60 behind the railway station simply didn't exist as they had back in November when the German offensive was stopped. The battery's defenders fought back and the Germans were driven off from the battery's perimeter trenches. Lieutenant Pyanzin, the newly-appointed battery commander, sent a message to the artillery command post around midnight on 11 June that there were twenty-five wounded and no food, water or fuzes for grenades. An hour later six sailors arrived at the battery with water, bread, biscuit and fuzes. The Germans moved closer and the battle for each trench and gun pit continued. Nearly all of the anti-tank gunners were killed. Lieutenant Pyanzin radioed the command post and requested that the artillery fire shrapnel shells directly on top of the battery. The coastal defence command fulfilled his request but it only delayed the inevitable for a few hours.

The 90th Rifle Regiment defended the terrain around Battery 30. Both sides suffered heavy losses but the Germans kept coming. Machine gunners pushed the Soviets farther and farther south and the Germans moved around the flanks of the battery. The defenders on the east side of the battery were almost completely wiped out.

There were new developments at the junction of Sectors 1 and 2. The Germans knew that 7th Brigade units had moved up to the north. They started a powerful artillery barrage followed up by an infantry attack. Soviet artillery strikes brought an end to the attack. Colonel Zhidilov, who had moved to the north with his troops, was now called back by General Petrov to take control of the defence of the Fedyukhiny Heights.[20] The brigade was placed under command of General Kapitohin, commander of Sector 4 and took over the defence of Batteries 16 and 24.

At 2330 hours the destroyer *Bditel'nyy* ('Vigilant') and the cruiser *Molotov* arrived from Novorossiysk with 3,000 men of the 138th Brigade. They were sent to the vicinity of the Suzdal heights southeast of Sevastopol above the Killen Ravine, from where they were to be deployed to the north side. The ship also delivered an artillery brigade with sixteen 76mm guns, twelve 45mm anti-tank guns and eight 120mm mortars, plus about 200 tons of ammunition. During the first six days of fighting about 5,000 reinforcements arrived in Sevastopol by sea.

June 13th was a pivotal day for the defence of Sevastopol. One of the single most critical events took place – the fall of Battery 365 – Fort Stalin. Its capture gave the Germans a huge advantage by removing one of strongest positions in the north and providing a place for German artillery to directly observe and fire on the bay. The area surrounding the battery had gentle slopes to the north, south and west and the Sukharno (Wolf's) Ravine to the east. The hill top was covered with low shrubs and was an excellent observation vantage point to the north and east.

During the siege the battery's 76mm anti-aircraft guns were repositioned and used as field guns. Twenty machine-gun and sniper nests and four machine-gun bunkers were built for additional protection of the battery. It was also surrounded by barbed wire. The 16th Infantry Regiment, commanded by Colonel von Choltitz and 744th Pioneer Battalion were tasked with the capture of the battery. Despite the tons of bombs and shells dropped, the perimeter defences and the guns had not been eliminated.

Early in the morning of 13 June the 16th Infantry Regiment attacked Battery 365. The garrison was waiting for reinforcements but none were coming. The two remaining guns had run out of shells. The Germans planned a surprise attack in the dark without any preliminary bombardment. At 0350 hours the attack began, the Germans rushing the perimeter from three sides. The Soviets had nowhere to go and the Germans fought their way inside. Paul Karel, in his account of Sevastopol, described the battle for Fort Stalin: 'A direct hit on the pillbox embrasure killed thirty men. Ten of the survivors fought like devils. They dragged the bodies of dead comrades to the broken battlements, piling them up like sandbags.'[21] The battle surged back and forth, pioneers using flamethrowers and grenades to finish off what was left of the defenders. Finally in the afternoon it was over. A few Soviets crawled out from under the rubble and surrendered. Some made a break for it, carrying their wounded with them and headed for Battery 366, Fort Lenin.

The capture of Fort Stalin was very costly for the Germans. In the fight for the battery, two battalions of the 16th Infantry Regiment suffered heavy losses. Not a single officer remained. In the 1st and 3rd Battalions of the 16th Regiment nearly all of the officers were killed, among them three recipients of the Knight's Cross. The survivors of the two battalions were merged into one. The pioneers from 744th Battalion also suffered serious losses, many being killed during the Soviet artillery barrage. The capture of the battery was considered by Manstein to be a great achievement and he was correct, but more significant and worthy of the same accolade was the battery's fighting to the last man.

The battles in Sector 4 lasted throughout the day. The Germans continued to throw new forces into the attack and pounded the forward battle area with tanks and massive air strikes. The Soviets fought hard and by the end of the day the Germans had achieved only a slight forward advance. Vice-Admiral Oktyabrsky reported that the 79th Brigade had re-established links with 2nd Perekop Regiment, which was also in communication with 1165th Rifle Regiment. However, at this point the 2nd Perekop Regiment was down to seventy-two men. The Soviet line was far from secure and 2nd Perekop lost contact with 79th Brigade. The sector commander ordered the regimental commander, Colonel Taran, to re-establish contact with the remnants of the 79th Brigade. Taran sent out scouts to locate them, and they were found in the upper Martynov Ravine in a heavily-wooded area the Germans did not yet want to venture into. The 79th Brigade was reduced to 112 men with four 82mm mortars and several machine guns. Colonel Potapov, commander of the brigade, informed Oktyabrsky that the link with 2nd Perekop Regiment and 25th Chapaevsky Division had been re-established. The sector commander reported that a solid defence and junction with 345th Rifle Division was restored, but this was not true. Having captured Battery 365, the Germans pushed the Soviets towards the bay. However, formidable defences still remained.

North End Defences

The rear defence line began near Batteries 16 and 24, overlooking the Kacha Road. Bunker 6 was located northwest of the two batteries and was equipped with a 45mm gun. It was built in August 1941. The bunker covered Lyubimovka village, the Kacha Highway to the Perovskoy Farm, plus the road that ran behind Battery 30 to Mekenzievy and Sevastopol. Batteries 16 and 24 were surrounded by six machine-gun emplacements, two adjacent to the battery walls, and four pre-cast bunkers, plus a position for a 76mm mountain gun.

The next line covered the road to Mekenzievy Station and consisted of pre-cast bunkers. Several of these were damaged during the Second Assault then repaired in the interim. There were seven pre-cast bunkers behind Battery 30 guarding the anti-tank ditch, which passed behind the battery and wound towards the rail station. Several fortifications were built in advance of the Mekenzievy Station, overlooking the road leading to the station. Artillery Bunker 7 was original built for a 45mm gun but was armed with a 75mm gun. The bunker was heavily damaged during the Second Assault and was rebuilt afterwards. It changed hands several times during the fighting. A trench covered with logs led to the bunker entrance. Bunker 8 was located on the opposite side of the railway. It was also built for a 45mm gun but a 75mm gun was installed. It was positioned to guard the railway line as it approached the city. It was badly damaged during the assault. Several pre-cast machine-gun bunkers were located nearby.

Bunker 9, built for a 45mm gun, was located about 225m from Bunker 10 along the Simferopol-Sevastopol Highway, 15m from the road. Bunker 10 was located

Machine-gun bunker near Battery 30. (Nemenko Collection)

at the intersection of the Simferopol-Sevastopol Highway and the road leading to the Mekenzievy cemetery. It was also a 45mm bunker and was heavily damaged (it still bears the traces of explosions inside). 300m away was Bunker 11 and its neighbour designated 11A, both armed with 100mm B-24 guns. They were open gun platforms each with two magazines under the platform.[22] The gun platform from Battery 704 (115) was located near Bunker 11. An underground personnel shelter was also located near Batteries 11 and 704.

Bunker 12 was located on the slope of the lighthouse ravine overlooking the Sevastopol-Simferopol Road as it approached Inkerman. Bunker 13, with a 45mm gun, covered the road leading from the Martynov Ravine to the Simferopol Highway, and 50m away from it was a large machine-gun bunker built as part of the fourth line of Sector 4 in August 1941 as part of the plan to strengthen the anti-tank defences. The fourth line passed along the tops of the ridges and included machine-gun bunkers and the earthworks of the Crimean War. The bunkers resembled the pre-cast type but were solid concrete. Similar bunkers were built near the fuel tank farm, in the upper slopes of the Sukharno Ravine, in the area of the Holland Ridge and in the area of St. Michael's cemetery.

The upland redoubts guarded the tops of the ravines leading down to Sevastopol Bay. They included:

Bunker 13 near the Martynov Ravine. (Nemenko Collection)

- Fort Lenin – anti-aircraft battery adjacent to North Fort.
- North Fort.
- Fort Cheka (Fort B).
- Fort Molotov – anti-aircraft battalion command post and AA battery.
- Fort Stalin – Battery 365 – fixed AA battery (captured 13 June).
- Fort GPU – earthen redoubt with four bunkers on each corner.
- Fort Siberia – earthen fort with two pre-cast bunkers and concrete shelters.
- Fort Volga – earthen fort with two pre-cast bunkers and two regular bunkers.
- Fort Ural – earthwork with gun emplacements at each corner and earth-timber personnel shelters.
- Fort Donets – earthwork with gun emplacements at the corners and earth-timber personnel shelters.[23]

The Fraternal Cemetery was turned into a defensive position. The command post of Sector 4 was located here. The cemetery was surrounded by trenches and firing positions. The command post was underground and covered with three layers of steel rails. It was about 200 metres square. The entrance was located 100m from a large pyramid-shaped Crimean War monument.

In Sector 4 the battle shifted to the outskirts of the Fraternal Cemetery. Forts Volga, Siberia and GPU were located close by and blocked access to the cemetery. Siberia was 850m northwest of Volga and GPU 650m northwest of Siberia. Fort Molotov was 750m northwest of GPU. Fort Volga covered the Sukharno Ravine that led to the munitions arsenal along the bay. Forts Siberia and GPU covered the road leading to the bay just east of the North Fort.

After the fall of Battery 365 the main point of resistance was Fort Volga, 750m to the south. The surface was heavily bombed and badly damaged, including the bunkers. Around 1800 hours the Germans captured a small section of the fort and consolidated their position in preparation for Soviet counter-attacks which were unsuccessful in dislodging the Germans. The fighting in Sector 3 was very heavy but the Soviets, supported by the coastal batteries, kept the Germans from advancing towards Inkerman and this led to a relative standoff in the fighting in the north for the next few days. The Germans now shifted their focus to the southern battlefield; in particular the junction of Sectors 1 and 2 on the Yalta Highway.

In Sector 1 the German 72nd Infantry Regiment launched a surprise attack on the 602nd Rifle Regiment and advanced 2km along the Yalta Highway. They were stopped by 782nd Regiment of 388th Rifle Division, deployed near the Turkish Redoubt on Canrobert Hill. Soviet fighters attempting to interdict German troops on the Yalta Highway were driven off by German air cover. The situation in Sector 1 was on the brink of disaster in terms of the number of defenders and quantities of ammunition. The 76mm guns were down to fifteen rounds each as the heavy, brutal fighting continued. An urgent telegram was sent by Oktyabrsky requesting additional replacement troops and ammunition.

June 13th was also a difficult day for Soviet shipping. Two destroyers bringing in large shipments of ammunition and food were sunk by German aircraft. Divers attempted to recover some of the ammunition. Their diving barges were continually harassed from the air, but they did manage to raise thirty-eight tons of materiel. The Soviet Naval Command considered ending transport runs to Sevastopol but changed their mind when informed of the situation in Sector 1.

On 14 June the fighting on the northern flank consisted of an artillery duel. Any German movement was immediately stopped by Soviet shelling from field artillery and coastal batteries. German return fire was minimal: they were also running out of ammunition and conserving as much as they could until more came in for a final push. The Soviets also had difficulties with ammunition supplies on the north side. One reason was that the Germans could now fire on the warehouses located along the cliffs overlooking the bay. Tons of ammunition was stored in the underground bunkers but it was difficult to move it out of them and transport it to where it was needed. Furthermore, communications with the batteries in the north had been cut so there was no way of knowing where the ammunition was needed. German aircraft kept a close watch on the movement of supplies out of the bunkers, and by this time most of the anti-aircraft guns had been disabled or destroyed, only one anti-aircraft machine-gun battery and one 76mm battery remaining. On 14 June alone the Luftwaffe made 900 sorties and dropped several thousand bombs, hundreds falling on Battery 30.

Fighting ebbed in the north but intensified in the south. The 2nd Battalion, 602nd Rifle Regiment and the men of the 2nd Battalion, 782nd Regiment of 388th Rifle Division, defended Canrobert Hill. The hill was hit hard by German air and artillery strikes. June 14th was the third day of these relentless attacks. Overnight, two regiments of the 72nd Infantry Division dug in below the front slope of Canrobert Hill, out of the sight of Soviet troops on top of the hill. German artillery and tanks shelled machine-gun and anti-tank gun bunkers scattered across the slopes. Most of the Soviet troops were in shelters on the reverse slope of the hill. The 1st Battalion of the 782nd Regiment repelled the initial German attempt to capture the hill. Several tanks from 3rd Battery, 249th Assault Gun Battalion with StuG IIIs suddenly appeared on the Yalta Highway heading towards the hill. The Soviets only had one 45mm gun remaining but it scored a hit on one of the tanks. However, they kept moving towards the Soviet strongpoint and rolled right over several gun emplacements. The Germans captured the trenches on the eastern slope of the hill, but the advance was stopped by machine-gun fire from two concrete bunkers at the foot of the hill on which the Second Turkish Redoubt was perched. The Germans pinned down the bunker crews with suppressive fire. Pioneers moved ahead and tossed grenades into the Soviet shelters and dugouts and the infantry captured the hill. Shelling from the coastal guns stopped the Germans from moving any further. They had now driven a wedge 700m deep and 3km wide into the Soviet line in Sector 1.

The 72nd Infantry Division captured two more key positions at the entrance to the valley leading to Balaklava. The Germans captured the Third Turkish Redoubt, called the *Gabelberg* by the Germans. This was made easier by the lack of strong defences between the highway and Canrobert Hill, in particular concrete artillery bunkers. The 109th Rifle Regiment was forced to retreat to the Fourth Turkish Redoubt 800m to the northwest – the Germans called it Rose Hill. It was strengthened by a ditch and a scattering of prefabricated bunkers. Two of these bunkers located on the slopes of the hill were quickly destroyed. The Germans drove a wedge centred on the Yalta Highway that cut into the first and second lines of defence. Kamary was abandoned and the left flank of the 109th Rifle Regiment was turned to the north toward the Fedyukhiny Heights. The breakthrough came at a heavy cost to the German 72nd Division and it could not move forward the following day. In Sector 2 the battle now shifted to the forward slopes of the Fedyukhiny Heights.

On 15 June the Germans held their positions across the entire front. Manstein moved up his reserves; 24th Infantry Division into Sector 4 and 170th Infantry Division to Sector 1. The General was now preparing for the final, decisive

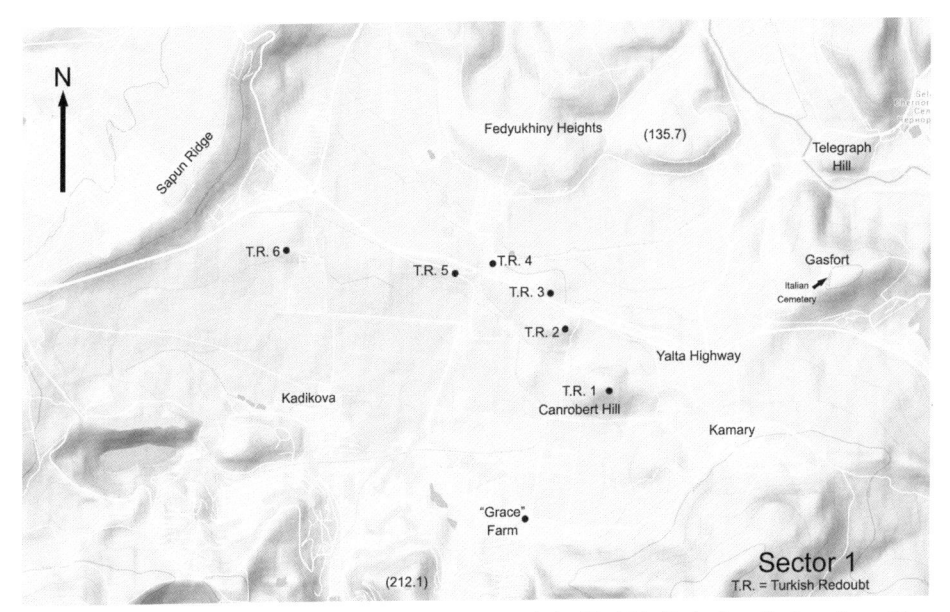

The valley north of Balaklava showing the location of the Turkish Redoubts. (© OpenStreetMap contributors, Author's collection)

offensive. Skirmishes continued throughout the day. At dawn, the Germans opened fire on the Soviet positions along Sapun Ridge, the Fedyukhiny Heights and the Yalta Highway. Tanks from the 72nd Division attacked the Fifth Turkish Redoubt but were pushed back by flanking fire from Soviet guns on the Fedyukhiny Heights.

On 14 and 15 June several Soviet convoys delivered supplies, including 30 tons of gasoline which was badly needed for vehicles and aircraft. The most welcome delivery of the day came from the cruiser *Molotov*: the second contingent of the 138th Rifle Brigade, consisting of 2,325 troops and twenty-four 82mm mortars. She also delivered 1,075 other replacement troops, 442 tons of ammunition and fifty anti-tank guns. The total strength of the 138th Brigade was about 5,000 men with anti-tank, mortar and artillery battalions, but the brigade lacked heavy- and medium-calibre guns.

In Sector 4, the 50th Division, supported by armour from the 197th Assault Gun Battalion, attempted to complete the envelopment of Coastal Battery 30. The Germans closed in on Fort Cheka and Fort Molotov, the command post of the 110th Anti-Aircraft Battalion. There were not many defenders left in Sector 4. The 345th Division had about 900 men remaining. The 79th Brigade received 300 reinforcements from the reserves. The 95th Division and 7th Brigade had about 2,000 troops left.

The Luftwaffe attacked the Soviet defences at Lyubimovka and the Grafskaya and Sukharno Ravines. On 16 June the Luftwaffe continued air strikes across the entire forward line of battle, mostly on Soviet artillery positions, Battery 705 (formerly 116) in particular. Ninety bombs and 300 shells were fired at the battery during the day. The battery's guns were damaged and concrete shelters and gun parapets were badly damaged. Shells gouged out large craters that reached the tunnels below the main structure. Most of the gunners were killed or wounded. Battery 19 at Balaklava was also heavily hit. One large bomb created a crater 10m wide and 6m deep but somehow the battery continued to function.

The German offensive in Sector 1 continued. Despite numerous attacks by 28th Light Infantry Division, the 456th Rifle Regiment maintained its position. The 1330th Regiment fell back about 900m. The 602nd and 782nd Regiment of the 388th Division also retreated.

Oktyabrsky reported that a German force of three regiments, supported by tanks and strong air and artillery, broke through the front at the junction of Sectors 1 and 2 and captured Hill 33.1 and a major battle had taken place at Hill 56.0 which was captured by the Germans. Enemy pressure was especially heavy against Hills 74.0, 57.5 and 113.2 (Windmill Hill), located on the Yalta Highway near Sapun Ridge. Oktyabrsky mentions the fighting in Sector 1 but he does not mention any activity in Sector 3. General Kolomiets, commander of 79th Marine Brigade, wrote in his memoirs[24] that he was ordered to take his remaining troops toward Inkerman heights and to create a line of defence along the southern slope of the Martynov Ravine. He disagreed with the order because it endangered troops in Sector 4 and opened up the possibility of an enemy breakthrough out of the ravine. There were bunkers but no other field works on the south side of the ravine plus it required him to pull his troops away from 2nd Perekop Regiment and 25th Chapaevsky Division. According to Kolomiets, Oktyabrsky agreed with his analysis and the line remained north of the ravine. However, a couple of questions arose concerning his account; in particular that the 79th Brigade remained on the northern slope of the ravine. A monument to the 79th Brigade is located where the railway embankment crossed the lower part of the ravine, well below the northern slope. It indicates this as the location of the last fighting by the brigade's mortar company, all that was left of the 79th Marine Brigade.

The records of the German 50th Infantry Division[25] clear things up. At 1500 hours on 16 June the 122nd Infantry Regiment, with support from five StuG IIIs, broke through the junction of 79th Brigade and 2nd Perekop Regiment. They followed a dirt road that ran along one of the branches of the Martynov Ravine to the railway embankment. The Germans moved down the ravine to the embankment. They attempted to rush forward to trap Soviet troops in the Grafskaya Ravine but were hit by machine guns from two bunkers at the head of the ravine. They pulled back to the railway embankment where they fought near the forest house (Cordon Number 2) with the mortar battalion of 79th Brigade which was supported by an artillery bunker at the fork of the two ravines. This delay allowed the Soviets to move from the cliffs towards Inkerman Lighthouse. It also shows that 79th Brigade had withdrawn from the northern slope of the ravine, leaving an opening for the Germans to squeeze through.

In the evening of 16 June, Oktyabrsky ordered his forces to hold Lyubimovka, believing the Germans would be afraid to move past the village if their flank was threatened. This played into the hands of Manstein whose initial directive ordered his troops to move past and isolate stubborn Soviet pockets. The Germans advanced to the fortified Sophia Perovskoy farm east of Lyubimovka and were closing in on Battery 30 which was about 500m west of the farm. The Soviets continued to hold on to Battery 30, which, by this time was unfit for action. It could only fire one gun out of four but the turret mechanisms were damaged so they could no longer turn. The command post of the battery, identified by the Germans as 'Bastion 1', was useless for self-defence. The viewing ports were too narrow and directed towards the sea, so German troops could approach the fort from the east without fear of being spotted. The order to hold Lyubimovka and Battery 30 was a serious mistake and allowed the Germans to surround Soviet forces in the north, not that this small number of troops would have made much of a difference in the days to come.

The entrance to a surface block at Battery 30 (Fort Maxim Gorki I); possibly the radio or transformer station. (NARA)

The Germans bypassed Fort Cheka as it posed little threat and headed for the coast, cutting the road to Lyubimovka and Battery 30. The Soviet 52nd Artillery regiment temporarily held up the German advance but their 155mm guns ran out of ammunition. When the Germans eventually reached the coast it was impossible for the trapped Soviet forces to escape from the north side. The 161st Rifle Regiment remained to fight in the area of Lyubimovka and the 90th Regiment fought in the area of Battery 30. The old Tsarist Batteries 16 and 24 (Fort Shishkova) became the main point of defence in the coastal pocket. The main aim was to hold on to Battery 30 but this ended up being a complete waste of time and manpower. German troops had already moved past the battery and there was no tactical reason to continue to defend it. But that was not the Soviet way of thinking.

In the afternoon of 16 June the Germans stormed the Fraternal Cemetery, defended by the 95th Rifle Division, whose headquarters were located in a shelter between the graves and the chapel. The headquarters was threatened with encirclement and capture. In order to escape it was necessary for Soviet artillery to open fire on the cemetery. Battery 366 opened fire from its position next to the North Fort. Several dozen shells scattered the Germans and gave the 95th Division troops time to move south to the engineering pier on the bay. The rest of the defences of the Fraternal Cemetery held.

Despite many setbacks and failures the resistance of the Soviets completely drained German forces. As of 16 June the 132nd, 22nd and 50th Divisions were just a fraction of their original strength. Losses in just these three divisions alone were huge. Manstein describes these days on the North Side:

> In spite of these hard-won successes, the fate of the offensive seemed to hang in the balance. Yet there was no sign of weakening of the enemy's will to resist and the strength of our forces significantly decreased. LIV Corps was forced to withdraw temporarily from the front the 132nd Division, whose infantry regiments suffered heavy losses and replace them with troops from 46th Division now located on the Kerch Peninsula.[26]

On 16 June the German command sent to Crimea battalions originally intended for the Seventeenth Army.

Chapter 8

The Third Assault (3) – 17 to 23 June 1942 – Fall of the North

The wife of Staff Sergeant Ludwig Reihert wrote to her husband: 'I dreamt I was looking for you near Sevastopol and couldn't find you – everywhere were graves, graves, graves. What a nightmare!'[1]

The Germans occupied a Soviet trench. The men began to fall back. Political Officer Gakokhidze, armed with a rifle and hand grenades, hurled himself at the Germans. Three men dashed after him. Gakokhidze burst into the trench, let fly two hand grenades, bayoneted a German officer and three soldiers and then, seizing their submachine gun, began to mow down the Germans at short range. The four heroes destroyed seventy Germans. The lost trench was recaptured.[2]

On 17 June the Germans resumed the northern offensive. At 0330 hours artillery from 22nd and 24th Infantry Divisions opened fire on the former Crimean War redoubts. Infantry attacks were carried out against Forts Volga, Ural, Donets, Siberia, GPU, Molotov and Cheka. The attacking force included the 31st and 102nd Regiments of 24th Division. The 42nd Regiment of 46th Division from Kerch and the 103rd Regiment were in the second line, while 22nd Division carried out a secondary attack. Twelve StuG III assault guns and ten captured tanks were included in the force and a dozen armoured vehicles broke through the line and reached the head of the Sukharno Ravine. Further north, the Germans shelled Batteries 16 and 24 to dislodge Soviet troops holding out there.

The construction of Battery 16 had begun in 1905 but proceeded slowly. By 1910 only earthworks had been completed. Concrete was not added until 1912. During construction the decision was made to build a flanking battery for 120mm guns, designated Battery 24. Battery 16's concrete gun platforms were separated by triangular concrete traverses and each of those had an entrance to the lower level of the battery. The reinforced concrete of the outer wall was 1.5m thick and 2.4m between the surface and the magazines. Armoured observation posts were placed on top. A searchlight casemate, a generator and two rangefinder positions were added to the flank of the battery. A monorail system was built into the ceiling of the underground passage that ran along the front of the battery and connected

The Third Assault (3) – 17 to 23 June 1942 – Fall of the North   173

Fort Shishkova and the Sophia Perovskoy Farm west of Battery 30. (Author's collection)

the magazines. Shells were moved along the monorail and hoisted up to the guns; charges were delivered separately by hand. The gun platforms were wider than in previous construction because each gun had two, rather than one, magazines on the flank of each traverse on the left and right, a traditional practice for the transition batteries. This enabled the crews to store more shells and move them more quickly to the guns.

The battery was armed with four 10in (254mm) guns, each with a range of 20km. They were made at the Obukhov steel plant originally for the forts of Kronstadt and were transferred from there to Sevastopol. Before the First World War, Battery 16 was one of the two most powerful long-range batteries at Sevastopol. In the early 1920s the guns were moved to Battery 2. By 1923 the battery had three guns, only two of which were operational. A working gun was later added and the battery was temporarily designated Battery 20.

During the Second Defence Battery 16 was completely disarmed and used as an infantry position. It became part of the Belbek Group of defences that included Battery 24 and Fort B. Its role was to repel an amphibious landing. It was provided with a new ditch defended by six pre-cast concrete gun emplacements including four bunkers for 45mm guns. It was surrounded by trenches. In May and June 1942 it housed the 241st Regiment of 95th Rifle Division.

Built between 1912 and 1913, Battery 24 was located 100m north of Battery 16. Its mission was to repel amphibious landings at the mouth of the Belbek and to be able to defend against light enemy vessels. The battery was similar to other batteries of this era with concrete gun platforms and a frontal parapet. The underground area contained magazines, a troop shelter, a power station and rangefinder position on the right flank. Each flank was defended by a Maxim machine gun. The entrances were on the flanks in the form of a chicane.[3] A tunnel passed along the front of the battery but this one was less than 1m wide and it was only used by the crew to move from one area of the underground to another, not for the movement of ammunition. Each gun had two magazines in the flank of each traverse.

During the First World War the battery was armed with 120mm guns. During the Civil War the guns were removed along with the guns of Batteries 23 and 24 and used on armoured trains. No improvements were made to it during the 1920s and during the Second Defence, like its neighbour, it was used as an infantry strongpoint.

The two batteries were linked together to form a common defensive perimeter that included a ditch, outer walls and an iron fence surrounding the entire complex. The defences included Maxim machine guns to repel infantry assaults. The defensive complex was called Fort Khruleva by the Russians and Fort Shishkov by the Germans, after the name of a nearby farm.

Lyubimovka to Hill 104.5

Three lines of defence were built from the coast to the *Ölberg* hill, their main purpose being to protect Battery 30. The Battery 30 strongpoint included reinforced concrete bunkers and pre-cast bunkers. In late December 1941 a new line of defences was built behind Battery 30. From January to March 1942 the Soviets recaptured part of this territory and built another new line in front of the battery which was completed in May 1942. The front line ran along the right bank of the Belbek River to Bunker 5. The second line passed over the heights of Battery 30. It began at the anti-tank ditch next to the coast, passed through the Sophia Perovskoy Farm to the bastion, past the barracks, then on to Hill 104.5. The third line extended from the Battery 16/24 complex along the ridge above Alkadar Valley to the Simferopol Highway behind Hill 104.5.

Most of the fortifications (bunkers and pre-cast bunkers) were built around the Perovskoy Farm and Battery 30. Bunker 80, located in Lyubimovka village, was built from Novem`ber to December 1941 and housed a 100mm B-24 gun. The gun was damaged and put out of commission during the Third Assault. The mission of the bunker was to support troops in the Belbek Valley that were out of the reach of the guns of Battery 30. The bunker was well positioned and could only be attacked from the front. A small anti-tank ditch was added to this sector. An extension of the Belbek River drainage channel, it was widened and deepened from 1941

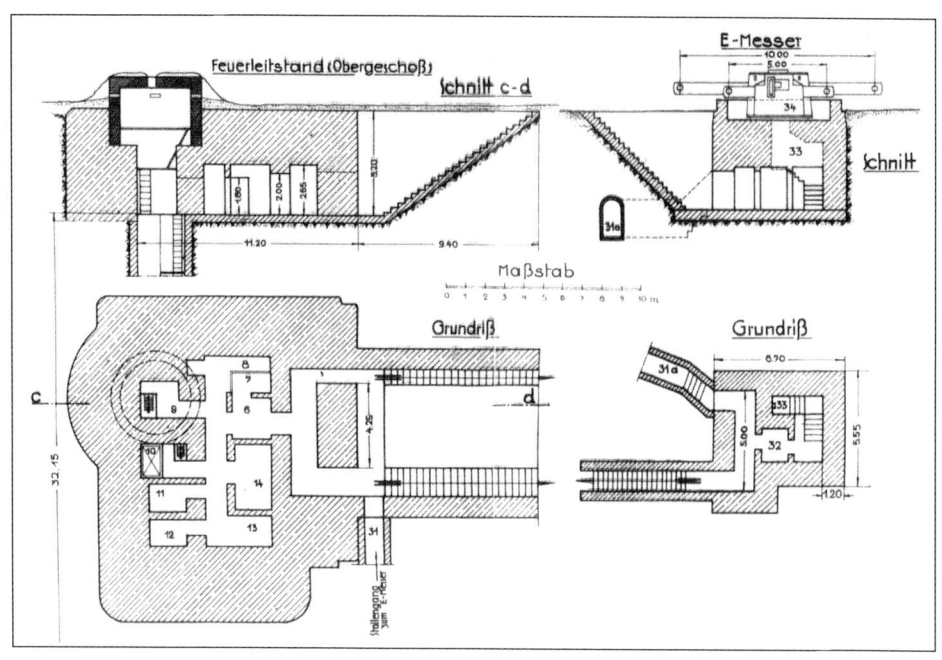

The rangefinder position at Battery 30. (Nachtrag)

to 1942. Battery 30 was defended by six bunkers and six pre-cast bunkers. The Battery 30 defensive zone was surrounded by a number of trenches and small machine-gun emplacements, plus barbed wire and minefields.

Fort Belbek (The Bastion) was located 750m from Battery 30, on the neighbouring height. Originally, the fort and the battery were separate as they performed separate functions. Fort Belbek was built on the hilltop and surrounded by a ditch with two entrances to the interior part of the fort. A shelter for field guns was located along the ditch. Several machine-gun bunkers were placed on the slopes 10–15m below the fort. The outer perimeter was surrounded by three rows of fencing. There were also two semi-underground barracks. An infantry parapet 1m high surrounded the fort. Belbek was originally used as a command post for defence against amphibious attacks beginning in the Soviet era. Later it became the command post for Battery 30, to which it was connected by a tunnel, creating a single complex.

The 161st Rifle Regiment was surrounded at Lyubimovka and attempted to break out of the encirclement. German tanks moved towards the village but ran into a minefield along the road. The 76mm guns of the 97th Anti-Tank Battalion opened fire and several vehicles were damaged. Three tanks nearly broke through to the anti-tank ditch but ran into Bunker 80, which was equipped with a rapid-fire gun. The shells were flying out of the bunker towards the tank every three to five seconds. The Germans moved up 105mm guns to fire on the bunker and cover the advance of pioneers with explosive charges and flamethrowers. The bunker was knocked out by a shot from one of the guns, all but two of the crew being killed. In the evening the 161st was decimated. Only a few dozen men from the regiment made it out of the village to Fort Shishkov.

The remains of the 90th Regiment retreated past Battery 30. Fort Shishkov became the rallying point for what was left of the 241st Regiment and 7th Marine Brigade, a few dozen men of the 161st, the 95th Division artillery units plus a handful of headquarters troops and gunners from the 110th Artillery Regiment. What was left of the 95th Division was surrounded but still fighting at the Sophia Perovskoy Farm.

Fort Molotov was an infantry and anti-aircraft position. It was modified in the early 1930s and served as the command post for the 110th Anti-Aircraft Artillery Regiment. The fort was described by the Germans as a 'two-storey reinforced concrete pillbox with walls of medium thickness'.[4] It had a radius of about 100m and was surrounded by a dense field of barbed wire. The fort had six shelters for the garrison and medical service, plus numerous rifle positions. During the siege its role was greatly reduced but it was originally equipped with a central command post and anti-aircraft defences. Molotov was neither a fort nor even an upland redoubt like its Crimean War neighbours, consisting of the two-storey concrete bunker and some earth-timber bunkers surrounded by barbed wire.

The remaining defenders of Molotov fought well but the position fell to German troops at 1445 hours on 17 June. Despite the capture of this position, the Germans were unable to break through to the bay. They had captured Forts Molotov and GPU and isolated Cheka, 400m southwest of Molotov. Around 1600 hours the Germans advanced towards the coast and the village of Uchkuevki which was captured at 2000 hours. This action cut off Soviet troops in the north and was a direct result of Oktyabrsky's order to hold the line at Lyubimovka and Battery 30 at all costs.

The 132nd Division was occupied with the capture of Battery 30. Around

Identified as Fort Molotov. (NARA)

The Third Assault (3) – 17 to 23 June 1942 – Fall of the North

1330 hours the two gun turrets were hit by Stuka dive bombers. One turret was already completely out of action and the other only had one working gun. A direct hit on the embrasure of the east turret put the last gun out of commission. The storming of the battery was assigned to the 213th Regiment, 132nd Pioneer Battalion and 173rd Engineer Battalion of the 73rd Division. German pioneers moved up from the Belbek Valley to the battery block. They moved from one bomb crater to the next to get closer to the gun turrets.

As the engineers moved towards the battery block, it was necessary to neutralise the flanking threat from the Bastion. The attack on the Battery 30 defensive zone began in the early morning against the anti-tank ditch to the east of the battery. The bunkers defending the ditch were silenced by infantry and artillery. The first and second companies of 132nd Combat Engineer Battalion attacked the Bastion. Around 1430 hours the Germans moved along to the slope of the hill and approached the bastion from the east and west. At 1445 hours the 2nd Battalion of the 213th Regiment attacked the eastern slope and at 1515 hours reached the ruined barracks of the battery below the Bastion, 400m east of the first turret. The first company of the 173rd Combat Engineer Battalion, under cover of infantry fire, attacked the gun turrets. At 1545 hours pioneers with bundles of hand grenades set charges against the turret housing and blasted holes in the concrete. At 1630 hours the western slope of the battery was under German control. The garrison of Battery 30, made up of about 300 men, including Captain Alexander, the battery commander, was trapped inside.

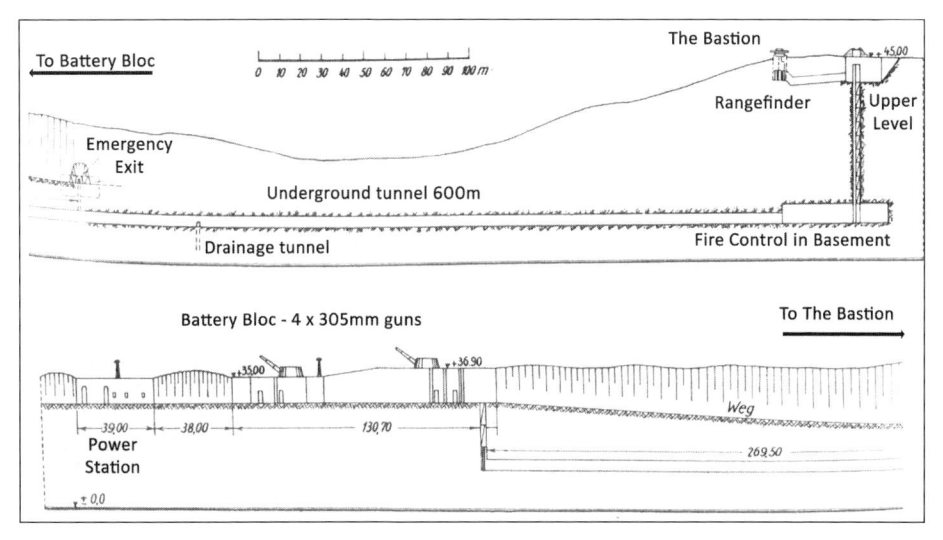

Elevation of the connecting tunnel between Battery 30's command post and the battery block. (Nachtrag)

Battery 30, looking towards the transformer station. (NARA)

The Sophia Perovskoy Farm was 400m to the west of the gun turrets, where the remnants of the 90th Rifle Regiment were holed up. Troops escaping from Battery 30 attempted to break through to the farm but had to cross an open strip of ground to reach the fortified farm. The field was dotted with shell craters that provided enough cover to reach the other side. Around 1500 hours a group of men from the battery escaped, most likely through one of the armoured entrances at the back of the hill between the battery block and the Bastion and reached some outlying farm buildings. There they set up a defensive position in the basement of a stone building located near the road leading to the battery in an attempt to cover the escape of more of their comrades. They waited there until evening but no more men came across the field. Several groups had attempted to escape but were pinned down and had no choice but to return to the battery. One other group of five men escaped at night. The Germans had in the meantime captured the Perovskoy Farm and the Soviets who fled there decided to head for the coast. At night they reached the searchlight station which was still in Soviet hands. The remaining men of 90th Rifle Regiment reached Fort Shishkov around 1600 hours. The troops from 161st Regiment remained holed up in Lyubimovka until they were killed or captured. The main attack on Fort Shishkov began at 2000 hours. The Germans were unable to capture the position that day but cut off the garrison's escape route to the coast.

Desperate fighting continued in the area of the Martynov ravine where the Germans battled the 25th Chapaevsky Division, including 31st Rifle Regiment and 3rd Marine Regiment and several of the bunker crews. Bunker 12 was located on the slope of the Lighthouse Ravine overlooking the Sevastopol-Simferopol Road as it approached Inkerman. Bunker 13, with a 45mm gun, covered the road leading from the Martynov Ravine to the Simferopol Highway. The Germans attempted to break through using tanks but the crew of Bunker 13 knocked out one tank and machine-gunners in pre-cast bunkers on the slope of the ravine halted the German infantry advance.

In Sector 1 the Germans continued to pressure Soviet troops between Kadykova and Chorgun. They broke through between the Fifth Turkish Redoubt (Hill 56.0) and the village of Kadykova. The Soviets brought in the 773rd Rifle Regiment to counter-attack but they came under fire from German guns. The Germans pressed their attack but were shelled by the 3rd Guards Mortar Battalion. With that, the entire 2nd Battalion of 773rd Regiment counter-attacked.

Fighting continued at the junction between Sectors 1 and 2. The withdrawal of Soviet forces on the left and right of the Fedyukhiny Heights exposed the flanks of the Soviet defenders and threatened the command and observation post that served as an excellent vantage point over the entire sector from Balaklava to the Mekenzievy Mountains.

From the Fedyukhiny observation post, the flash of explosions was no longer seen on Chapel Hill and smoke no longer rose from the top of it. Kamary village fell and the Germans now threatened the Fedyukhiny Heights from three sides. They were now only 1km from the Sapun ridge. The Germans attacked Kadykova and troops from the 109th Rifle Regiment and 388th Rifle Divisions were forced to retreat further west. By the end of the day the Grace farm was behind the German lines.

Three German regiments reported they had broken through the junction between Sector 1 and 2 and captured Hills 33.1, the Third Turkish Redoubt, and Hill 56.0, the Fifth Turkish Redoubt. This was not quite true. Hill 33.1 was defended by two artillery and three machine-gun bunkers and held out for at least two more days, allowing the Soviets to cover the interval between Hill 33.1 and the Fedyukhiny Heights. The hills were also covered by the 130mm artillery bunker located above the modern village of Pervomaika. Three bunkers stood at the edge of a field at the foot of the former Fedyukhiny airfield. They entered into battle on the evening of 15 June and wreaked havoc on German forces attempting to pass between them and the Fedyukhiny Heights. In two days the crews deflected nine German attacks. Around 0600 hours on 17 June the Germans launched a new attack, with infantry advancing behind a column of assault guns. The 773rd Regiment of 388th Division retreated towards the bunkers. The 3rd Company of the regiment set up defences along the road from Sevastopol to Balaklava, creating a second line of defence. One battalion of the 9th Marine Brigade moved up from their position in the area of Cape Kaya-Bash. They moved into a pre-fabricated bunker above the village of Karan.

The Germans attacked Hill 33.1 with tanks. The Soviets counter-attacked with a company of the 773rd Regiment and moved forward but came under artillery fire. The company requested artillery support but most of the batteries were running out of ammunition so rocket launchers located near Dergacheva fired on the Germans. The barrage suppressed the German artillery but the counter-attack failed to gain a foothold on the hill. By evening the Germans held Hill 33.1.

The Sevastopol command held a meeting to discuss the situation on the north side and to map out a strategy for the following day. Their exact intentions are unclear and contradictory. General Petrov wanted to launch a counter-attack with the fresh 138th Brigade to release Soviet units trapped in the north. General Morgunov proposed a mission to relieve Battery 30. Vice-Admiral Oktyabrsky wanted the troops to dig in and hold their positions. He ordered the establishment of a line of strongpoints in the remaining bunkers and forts on the north side to keep the Germans from reaching the bay. Engineers on the south side of the bay received the same orders to reinforce existing lines and fighting positions.

Morgunov writes in his book that General Petrov scheduled a counter-attack by the 138th Rifle Brigade and 345th Rifle Division towards the northwest and in the Grafskaya Ravine with a diversionary attack by 79th Brigade and 2nd Perekop Regiment at Martynov. The commanders also discussed General Morgunov's proposal to break the encirclement of Battery 30 to rescue the garrison and sabotage whatever of value was left. The 138th Brigade and 345th Division, with remnants of the 95th Division were selected for the operation. The only other unit on the north side was the Guards Regiment guarding the north shore and the remnants of units which had escaped from the Lyubimovka-Shishkov pocket. All of the long-range coastal artillery was still available for infantry support. The meeting split up after midnight and the various parties went to their respective command posts to plan the operations for the following day.

German attacks on the village of Bartenyevka were repelled by Batteries 79, 552 and 553. These batteries provided cover for transport ships but did not go unnoticed by the Germans. Battery 79 was located on Cape Tolstoy and on 18 June it was a prime target for air and artillery strikes, including the 600mm Karl mortars. When the shelling started the garrison went quickly to their underground shelter. They could feel the earth shake with every shell that landed. One shell hit and the thick metal door to an adjoining room of the shelter blew off, revealing the devastation on the other side and the fact that everyone in the room had been killed. A look on the surface revealed that one gun was upside down and completely wrecked, all of the crew having been killed. The other gun's barrel was damaged. The concrete platform was blown to pieces and several gunners were buried alive under large chunks of concrete. The survivors used crowbars, pickaxes and bayonets to dig out the buried men, the live ones still crying for help. They managed to unearth a few of the men but they were already dead. The battery was completely destroyed. Only Battery 227 remained on the north side. The battery on top of Fort Constantine was silenced.

Battery 30

It took about three days for German pioneers to end the resistance at Battery 30. During the initial attack, they set explosive charges under the turrets to blast their way into the turret housing. The Soviets shot back from inside through embrasures and cracks in the concrete. A second set of charges tore away part of the outer wall, revealing the inside of the huge complex. The pioneers used flamethrowers and smoke to move inside. The turret housing descended three floors. The battery was self-contained, with its own water, power and food supplies. All of the interior rooms contained double steel doors and each door had to be blown off in order to get into the adjacent room. The pioneers worked their way, room by room, into

The transformer station at Battery 30. (NARA)

the bowels of the battery. At each door they set new charges, the explosion blew open the door, the pioneers tossed in grenades and waited for the smoke to clear away. Dead Soviets lay along the hallways, some wearing gas masks because of the smoke and fumes. Once the smoke cleared they rushed into the room only to hear the next door clang shut; over and over again, hour after hour.

The defenders fought almost to the last man. The political commissar allowed no one to surrender. The battery's radio operator in the command post reported back to naval command that the Germans were pounding their way from door to door and that there were only forty-six men left. Half an hour later he reported twenty-two men left. He then said 'Goodbye' and the radio went silent. The battery fell at 1645 hours on 19 June.

On the morning of 18 June a mixed group of stragglers that included Air Force personnel and gunners of the 110th Artillery Regiment who had escaped from Fort Molotov, defended what was left of the line that ran along the north shore of the bay. Another group held the line from St. Michael's Battery where it ran further north, skirted the North Fort and continued to the sea below Uchkuevki. The 345th Rifle Division defended the Grafskaya Ravine. Remnants of the 25th Chapaevsky Division occupied a thin line from Grafskaya to the east of Inkerman lighthouse. The exit from the Martynov Ravine was blocked by Bunker 13, two machine-gun bunkers and a small remnant of 79th Marine Brigade.

The counter-attack in Sector 4 proceeded as planned on the morning of 18 June, but it did not turn out as the commanders had hoped. At 0500 hours, after a short artillery preparation, the 345th Division and the 138th Brigade, supported by the last three tanks of the 125th Tank Battalion, launched an attack in the direction of the Mekenzievy station. The Germans, using their reserves, counter-attacked with the remnants of 47th and 65th Infantry Regiments, forcing the Soviets back to their original positions. Morgunov claimed that the attempt to reach the 95th Division troops and Battery 30 was not successful due to the 'intensive enemy aircraft and artillery'. He was partly correct.

In his memoirs, Admiral Kuznetsov writes about the attack and sheds some light on its failure:

> Two companies of the first battalion of the [138th] brigade were to attack in the direction of the [Perovskoy] farm. A second attack [headed] to the right in the direction of the [Mekenzievy Mountain] station. Third battalion closed a gap in the defences of the right. In reserve were two or three companies of the brigade. The morning was foggy. [The troops headed for an] open field with barbed wire, moved 200 metres, then broke into a run. Suddenly shells came in and the troops ran backwards, stumbling into German bayonets, many taken prisoner.[5]

The Third Assault (3) – 17 to 23 June 1942 – Fall of the North 183

There are clearly some questions to be asked about the 138th Rifle Brigade's failure upon its arrival at Sevastopol. As of 17 June about 5,300 troops of the 138th Brigade (five battalions) were delivered to Sevastopol. They were well trained and had performed well earlier in the war. General Petrov ordered the brigade to move to the north side on the morning of 18 June. Combined with other Soviet units in the north it was a substantial force. Yet, within a short time, the Soviet counter-attack of 18 June was stopped. There are claims that 800 prisoners were taken from the brigade but this does not agree with official records. The numbers taken were a fraction of this, amounting to a few dozen. The official records also reveal something more interesting; that fourteen prisoners were taken and only from 3rd Battalion. Interrogated prisoners revealed the total strength of the Brigade at three battalions, about 3,000 men. What happened to the other 2,000?

The principal mystery remains the missing battalions. The brigade (1st, 2nd and 3rd Battalions) moved out from Suzdal and marched down towards Inkerman where they were met by an unidentified road guide who split up the brigade, sending the battalions in different directions. Two of the battalions came under heavy artillery fire and were unable to move forward. 3rd Battalion was the only unit to reach its assigned location. The 1st Battalion ended up in the Devil's Ravine and the 2nd Battalion near the Inkerman marshes. Still more interesting is the fate of 4th and 5th Battalions. These two battalions arrived late and were sent to become parts of other units. At this time the 79th Brigade and 2nd Perekop Regiment reappear on the roles. The mortar battalion of the 79th, the last remaining unit, had been destroyed in the Martynov Ravine a few days earlier as well as 2nd Perekop Regiment, but these two units reappeared and the 138th was reduced to 1st and 2nd Battalions that fought on the Sapun Ridge. On 30 June a small group of twenty-seven men fought alongside the 79th Brigade at the Kamchatsky Lunette.[6] They identified themselves as from 138th Brigade.[7]

The Germans followed up with their own attacks in Sector 4. Three regiments supported by tanks broke through the Soviet defences and by the end of the day controlled the Fraternal Cemetery and Bartenyevka. Soviet troops were split into three parts: the 345th Rifle Division and 138th Brigade in the area of Grafskaya and Martynov Ravine with whoever may have been left from 2nd Perekop Regiment and 79th Marine Brigade; coastal defence troops, engineers, technical naval aviation staff, the Guards Regiment and the crew of 110th AA Regiment trapped south of Bartenyevka; and the 90th Regiment, with about 300 men, at Fort Shishkov. In Sector 1 the German attack continued in two directions: toward the village of Kadykova to expand the Yalta Highway salient and against the Karagach heights to break the Sapun-Karagach ridge line. In each case the infantry was supported by tanks. The bloody battles along the front lasted for two days, from 18 to 19 June.

Boris Voyetkhov met the commander of a Soviet trench in the Rumanian sector

Before this trench about twenty yards away from this place is a piece of land for the possession of which a battle was fought for seven months and eighteen days. In the messages it was known as a frontline position. Our dead were carefully counted; otherwise you don't get reserves. If you climb up the nearest hill you will see a narrow sector between the German and Russian lines covered with decaying corpses. The bodies are several layers deep and in some places are piled up to a man's height. A corporal estimates the number of attacked by the depth of the unburied dead before the lines. It is impossible to deal with the process of decay. Lime cannot keep up with it. The stench is choking. Nothing can be done about it.

The commander left the dugout to head to the trenches. There was silence, broken by the sound of a Victrola playing in an adjacent trench; the man playing it laughed. The tune was popular among the men. At the same time a chanting was heard from the Rumanian trenches. The Victrola stopped. It was solemn religious chanting; the Rumanians praying for victory. A soldier commented how 'It is a rather jolly religion they have,' as he moved reserve cartridge boxes around his position. The battle would begin momentarily, the soldiers expecting the imminent arrival of German bombers. The sailors awoke, rubbing their eyes, washing up, smoking and eating bread. The trenches were kept neat and orderly, personal gear stowed in niches in the sides carved from rock. The command post of the trench was under camouflage cover. Inside, the commander stood, gazing out over the battlefield through binoculars, a telephone close at hand.

The Russian side of the valley was defended by three lines of trenches covered by minefields and gun positions. Control is centralised. The atmosphere is strange and unpleasant. The German attacks are always preceded by hundreds of shells falling on the position. But today nothing comes from the air. Suddenly tanks are spotted moving out from the left side of the valley, followed by men running, naked to the waste, cotton stuff in their noses to block out the smell of the bodies. The officers are in full uniform. Trumpets blare and Rumanian and German regimental flags appear, moving towards the Russian lines. The tanks move up and come to a stop. The chief artillery officer calls for the guns to fire all calibres without ceasing. Hold machine gun fire until the infantry moves up. Smoke envelops the battle area and all visibility is blocked.

Hours go by and the battle rages in the blinding smoke and dust. Tanks break through the smoke and come near the Russian lines. Molotov cocktails smash and burst into flame against the sides and treads of the tanks. The weight of the explosions presses down on one's head, squeezing one's brains, eyes and eardrums until it seems as though one care bear no more and that one's head will be battered into shapelessness.

The leading tanks reach the trenches. They are stopped there and the next wave of tanks moved past them. The Russian batteries are struck by direct hits from the tanks and more moved forward towards the trenches where they are met by armour-piercing thermite-tipped bullets that burn through the steel and fill the inside with vapour. The tank men jump out and are shot by the sailors. Yet, they keep advancing, new tanks moving up to replace the damaged ones. They are followed closely by German and Rumanian infantry men. The entire forward position is crowded with tanks and infantry. Yet the Germans and Rumanian soldiers are starting to pile up in front of the Russian defences. The Russian long-range and field guns fire non-stop from a battery at the Malakhov Kurgan.

New tanks arrive, using the damaged and abandoned tanks for cover. The infantry move from one cover to the next. Then the Russian marines counter-attack, moving forward over the parapets towards the enemy. Hundreds of men in blue striped jerseys, yelling and cursing loudly, engaged the Rumanians on the left flank. The Rumanians are scattered and begin to move back. Then the sound of German bombers is heard above and the position is struck for the fourth day in a row. The Luftwaffe dive bombers attack the front line. The defenders don't have a chance. The second line holds firm but the Germans move forward. The bombers silence the Russian artillery; anti-aircraft guns, heavy guns, field guns, machine guns. The objective now is to advance to the second line. The Russian continue to fight but the battle is hopeless. About 100 German aircraft circle overhead.

German tanks and infantry assemble and move out from the craters towards the second line. If the Germans break through they will reach the road to Sevastopol. And that breakthrough seemed imminent. The battle raged for two more hours; tanks advancing, aircraft dropped bombs from above, the Germans driving into the three lines of defence. The Germans were just about through when the gunfire ceased. The Germans had paused, waiting for reserves to move up. All seemed to be lost when the commander found an anti-aircraft gun and began to fire it point-blank into the Germans for about 15 minutes. The Germans believed the Russians had received reinforcements and paused to wait for reserves. The commander had been hit and his leg needed to be amputated. It would wait until the next day. And with that he fell asleep for the night.[8]

On the morning of 19 June the Germans redeployed their forces. The 132nd Division, which was moving along the coast, had suffered heavy losses and suspended its operations. The 437th Regiment was sent to Kerch and was replaced by the 72nd Infantry Regiment of 46th Division. The 97th Regiment of 46th Division arrived the previous day along with 88th Pioneer Battalion and they were attached to the 132nd Division. Almost the entire 46th Division was now at Sevastopol. Further east the line was held by 31st Infantry Regiment and 24th Battalion of 24th Division. The 102nd Regiment of the 24th was positioned above Holland Bay. The 65th Regiment of 22nd Division was at the entrances to the Sukharno and Lighthouse ravines. Due to heavy losses the 16th and 47th Regiments withdrew to the second line.

The 50th Division, 4th Rumanian Mountain Division and 18th Rumanian Mountain Division were located near the junction of Sectors 2 and 3. The Rumanian 18th and 1st Rumanian Guards Mountain Divisions were facing Sector 2. The 72nd Infantry Division and 399th and 401st Regiments of the 170th Division had driven a wedge into Soviet forces along the Yalta Highway in Sector 1. The 391st and 420th Regiments (of 125th) Division were in reserve. The 391st was placed under the command of 170th Division. Two regiments of 28th Light Division were holding the extreme left.

German gunners fire on Fort Constantine. (Stanislav Zharkov Collection)

The 399th Regiment, supported by tanks, joined the fighting for the first time on 19 June and broke through the Soviet defences on the outskirts of Kadykova. The Soviets prevented a complete German breakthrough but were forced to retreat to the Sixth Turkish Redoubt (m. Kiev Hussars monument) and the Germans advanced another 800m.

On 19 June Battery 3, the floating battery, was put out of action. A Luftwaffe attack knocked out all of the 76mm guns and two 37mm guns, and 60 per cent of the crew was killed. Prior to the war the Soviets had planned to build up their battleship fleet. Construction was started at the Nikolayev Shipyards. A section of one of the hulls was towed to Sevastopol for testing and was tied up at the Sevastopol Marine Plant. The platform was 44m long, 40m wide and 15m high. When the war approached the Navy did not know what to do with the floating piece of the ship and Captain G. A. Butakov, grandson of the 1876 war hero Admiral G. I. Butakov, proposed that the hull be turned into a floating AA battery. The proposal was accepted and the future crew of the battery started work. The transformation took about seventeen days and included the installation of two 130mm guns to repel enemy ships, three 76mm guns for anti-aircraft coverage and four 37mm guns, plus machine guns and searchlights. The battery commander was Lieutenant-Commander Moshenskiy.

The battery was towed four miles west of Sevastopol harbour on 16 August 1941. The crew consisted of 130 men. The mission of the battery was anti-ship

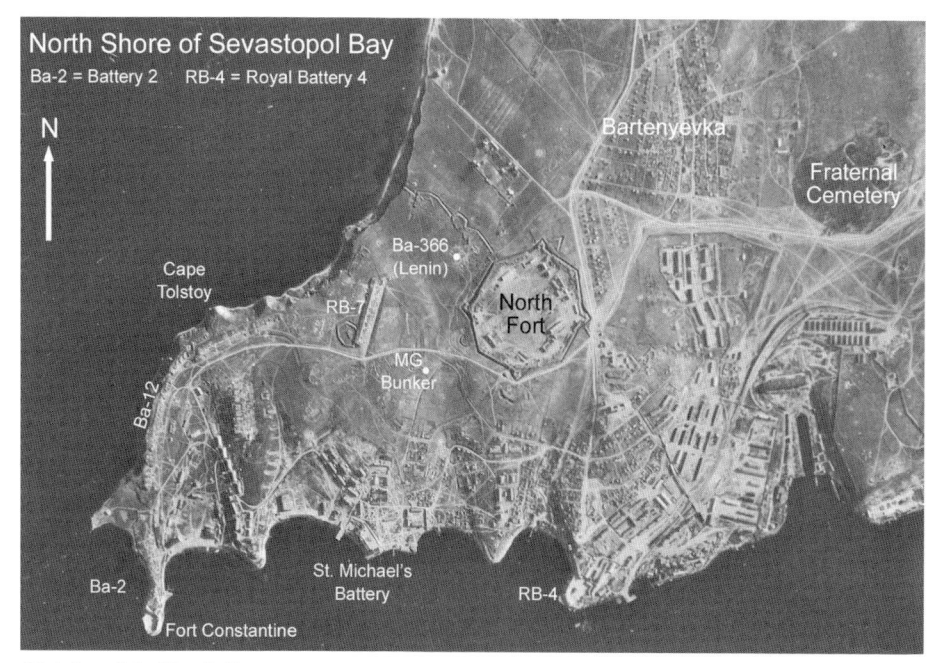

Vicinity of the North Fort. (Author's collection)

and anti-aircraft coverage of the base. On 10 November it was relocated to Cossack Bay for better protection and to provide better stability. The 130mm guns were removed in January 1942 since its anti-ship role was taken over by Battery 35. Commander Moshenskiy only left the battery once in nine months. He was killed on 19 June 1942. By this time the battery was out of ammunition and only had machine guns and anti-aircraft machine gun rounds. It was struck by dive bombers and the command post was destroyed. The survivors fled the battery and joined an Air Force battalion. It was reported the battery shot down a total of thirty-five German aircraft.

Several 'islets' of defence (except for North Fort and Battery 366 – Fort Lenin) remained on the north side. The first zone stretched from Cape Tolstoy down the coast to the battery headland on the bay and included the summer training camp of the VMUBO, the old royal Coastal Batteries 2 and 12, which were used as warehouses of the Black Sea Fleet, Fort Constantine and St. Michael's Battery. The second was further to the west and included the engineering pier and the former Royal 4th battery. And finally, the smallest – a telephone exchange in the Holland Bay staffed by Navy signalmen and Air Force guards of the Black Sea Fleet. Further east the Sukharno Arsenal and small sections of Sukharno and Lighthouse Ravines remained in Soviet hands.

Fort Constantine was guarded by remnants of the 95th Rifle Division and crewmen from Coastal Batteries 2 and 12. The 110th AA Regiment, Coastal Battery 702 and Air Force troops were at St. Michael's Battery. The North Fort was occupied by the 178th Engineering Battalion, the remains of air defence units and more 95th Division soldiers, plus about fifty men from the Guards Regiment. None of the strongpoints ordered by Oktyabrsky were formed until the night of 19/20 June and none had anyone appointed to command them. They were led by the most senior officers and petty officers present. General Morgunov was eventually appointed commander but only at a later time.

Battery 2 was located on a hill above Fort Constantine. It was initially a two-gun battery. In December 1941 a third gun was added and placed on the right wing of the former Royal Battery 3. A fourth gun was added in May from a damaged minesweeper. The battery was re-designated as Battery 2 and Battery 2bis. Two guns were in an upper location and two in a lower position at Fort Constantine. The lower guns were later dismantled and transferred to the south side. On 8 June 1942 the battery was hit by heavy German artillery shells, damaging one of the guns. The final fighting for the battery took place from 20 to 22 June. The gunners of Battery 2 were joined by gunners from Battery 12 and 702 and fought until they were overrun.

Battery 12 was given its number before the war. Its 152mm guns were installed on the former Royal Battery 4 above Fort Constantine, then in August 1941 the

The Third Assault (3) – 17 to 23 June 1942 – Fall of the North   189

guns were removed and sent to Perekop. The battery was not mentioned again until March 1942 when it was manned by gunners of the former Battery 10 near Kacha, commanded by Captain M. V. Matushenko. The guns for the new Battery 12 were taken from two damaged destroyers and installed in new positions. Two 100mm guns were installed at the location of Battery 12 and two 130mm guns placed at the new position on the former Battery 3. Later on a 130mm gun was installed at the former Royal Battery 2.

On the morning of 19 June the North Fort was attacked. The 178th Engineer Battalion was not expecting an attack on the fort. The German 3rd Motorised Company of 88th Pioneer Battalion captured the casemate of the former command post of 1st AA Battalion of 110th Artillery Regiment – the former 7th Royal Battery, located north of the fort. German artillery and small arms fire was extremely heavy. Explosions tore at the concrete of the casemate, breaking through the ceiling which threatened to collapse on the troops sheltered inside. At night the crew withdrew to St. Michael's.

By nightfall the northern Soviet pockets were shrinking. The North Fort was surrounded but there was still a solid defensive line behind the fort from St. Michael's to Fort Constantine including Batteries 2 and 12. Each of these batteries had one gun remaining. Troops of the Guards Regiment (still commanded by Lieutenant-Colonel Baranov) fought off an attack at the engineering pier and at Battery 4. The Germans were moving closer and closer to the bay and could now shell the bay directly. In the afternoon six Soviet ships were turned away and returned to Novorossiysk. The defence of the north end was, for all intents and purposes, finished. In the last couple of days Soviet forces lost 732 killed and 1,317 wounded. However, very difficult mopping-up operations still lay ahead for the Germans.

The North Fort was built in the shape of an octagon 500–600m across, surrounded by a ditch with a scarp and counterscarp 5m wide

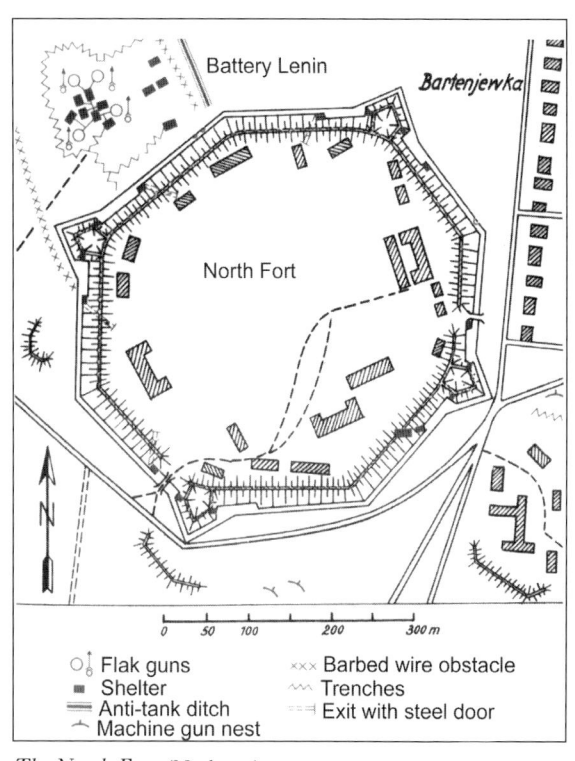

The North Fort. (Nachtrag)

and about 3m deep. Inside the walls were multi-story barracks and underground storage and personnel shelters. The 24th Infantry Division and 3rd Battalion of 31st Regiment moved forward in preparation to attack the fort, which was set for the next day.

Small groups of survivors filtered their way through the hills to the bay and gathered at St. Michael's battery. The two-story casemated stone fort now had four guns set up to face Matyushenko Bay from which direction any armoured attack would come.[9] About 120 infantrymen, artillerymen, signalmen and Air Force personnel from the group were selected to remain and defend the position. The rest were to be moved to the south side by boat to join the defenders of the city. As it turns out there were not enough boats to move large numbers of people and the majority who crossed over were officers. The defences of St. Michael's were quite strong. The defenders were left with three machine guns, two 76mm and two 45mm guns. The fort had three lines of defence. The machine guns were placed inside a large concrete bunker located about 650m north of St. Michael's and 350m south of the North Fort. It was built in August 1941 for defence against amphibious attacks, its outer perimeter surrounded by barbed wire. The second line was the barracks and the outer wall that ran along the barracks. The third line was the walls of the old battery. It was rectangular in shape with three closed sides; the northeast flank was open. Two of the three walls faced the bay. They were very thick and contained firing loopholes.

Troops in Sector 3 held their positions. The front lines of the fight now moved to the underground galleries of the Sukharno ravine. During the night of 19/20 June the remaining ammunition stored at Sukharno, primarily 76mm and 45mm, was moved to other facilities at Inkerman, Sugar Head and the former Battery 24. Some obsolete naval ammunition was left behind. German aircraft had earlier destroyed the bridge over the Black River, but the Soviet engineers built a temporary bridge just below the surface of the water, hidden from spotter aircraft and the trucks travelled up to their wheel hubs in water.

Early in the morning of 20 June the Germans stormed the remaining strongholds on the north side. From 0530 to 0830 hours, heavy 210mm and 305mm mortars struck the North Fort in conjunction with regimental artillery, mortars and air strikes. The main targets were the northern and eastern bastions in an attempt to open a breach in the walls; not too difficult a task against the fort's masonry walls. Attacking units included the 3rd Motorised Company of 24th Engineer Battalion whose mission was to cross the ditch and access the interior of the fort on the right flank of the northern bastion. 2nd Company of 24th Engineer Battalion and 7th Battalion of 31st Infantry Regiment would follow after 3rd Company. 3rd Company of 88th Battalion, reinforced by remnants of 1st Company would move against the eastern flank with 1st Battalion, 24th Engineer Regiment and 5th Company of 31st

The Third Assault (3) – 17 to 23 June 1942 – Fall of the North 191

Infantry Company in reserve. The mission of one platoon of anti-tank guns and one platoon of machine-gunners was to destroy machine-gun casemates on the northern and eastern flanks.

The attack proceeded as follows: at 0830 hours the first pioneer units moved from their starting position to a breach blasted through the northeastern wall according to the plan. Anti-tank guns opened fire on the Soviet machine-gun casemates. A group reached the ditch but came under fire from a gun flanking it. The Soviets launched an unsuccessful counter-attack. Additional German troops moved forward but were unable to get into the fort. Soviet machine-gun and sniper fire poured in from all directions. 3rd Company of 88th Engineer Battalion advanced past the outer wall and reached a group of buildings inside the perimeter. The Soviets counter-attacked again but were forced to retreat further into the fort's interior. 3rd Company of 24th Battalion broke into the fort and became pinned down by Soviet riflemen and machine-gunners. A third Soviet counter-attack attempted to push the pioneers back to the ditch but was repulsed with grenades. The Germans held the position.

A follow-on attack was planned for 1830 hours, and the artillery bombardment continued for several hours. At 2300 hours, a mortar and machine-gun company seized the northern tip of the fort and cleared out Soviet positions, including machine-gun emplacements located in the casemates. Around midnight, with the Germans now in control of the northern part of the fort, the breakthrough was

Casemates inside the North Fort photographed after its capture in late June 1942, showing the destruction caused by the German heavy siege guns. (NARA)

expanded to the northwest and southeast. The troops of 24th Battalion moved into the fort and reached the centre.

On 20 June Battery 2 was attacked and two guns were damaged and the central part of the battery destroyed. The next day, the 31st Infantry Regiment and 24th Infantry Division and a battalion of the 88th Combat Engineer Regiment accompanied by tanks, attacked in the direction of Fort Constantine and Batteries 12 and 2 and also towards St. Michael's Battery south of the North Fort. Heavy fighting broke out and the defenders of the batteries fought until they ran out of ammunition. They retreated towards Fort Constantine with Captain Matushenko.

During the night of 20/21 June two guns (100mm and 130mm) were recovered from Coastal Batteries 2 and 12 and taken by boat to Fort Constantine. In the morning they were set up to fire on German tanks approaching from the north. The small gun crews were commanded by Captain Matushenko. No sooner were they set up when he was summoned to headquarters on the south side to organise the batteries to defend the city. He left the fort with a group of soldiers and wounded and crossed to the south side.

German forces approaching the North Fort also surrounded Battery 366, Fort Lenin. At 0345 hours on 21 June the battery was seized. The Germans moved to the western and southwest bastions of North Fort and seized those positions unopposed. The defenders of North Fort surrendered and about 100 prisoners were taken plus hundreds of rifles, machine guns and mortars, along with their ammunition. According to interrogated prisoners the officers and political commissars committed suicide.

On the morning of 21 June the battle for St. Michael's Battery began. One hundred and thirty men of the 110th Anti-Aircraft Artillery Regiment were inside the fort, plus men of Coastal Battery 702 and some Air Force troops. Overnight a group of thirty men from 90th Rifle Regiment made it to the battery. Fighting broke out around dawn and at that same time a cry came from outside the wall to 'Open up lads!' These were the men of the 90th who had broken through the German lines.[10] The Luftwaffe launched air strikes against the battery. Soviet gunners fired back but the fort's 76mm guns were hit and all three were destroyed one by one. Shelling from the 815th and 857th Howitzer Regiments battered the old fort to pieces. One 210mm shell penetrated to the infirmary in the cellar, killing seventeen men.[11] The eastern wall was destroyed. By mid-afternoon the Germans broke through the second line of defence and crept towards the casemates. The attack slowed down as night approached, but the shelling and destruction continued.

Heavy fighting reached the vicinity of the engineering pier and the docks. The Soviets set up a 122mm howitzer and 152mm gun recovered from Battery 725. The Germans attempted to capture Royal Battery 4 but failed. Fort Constantine, St. Michael's and the shore batteries were not attacked on 21 June but were subjected

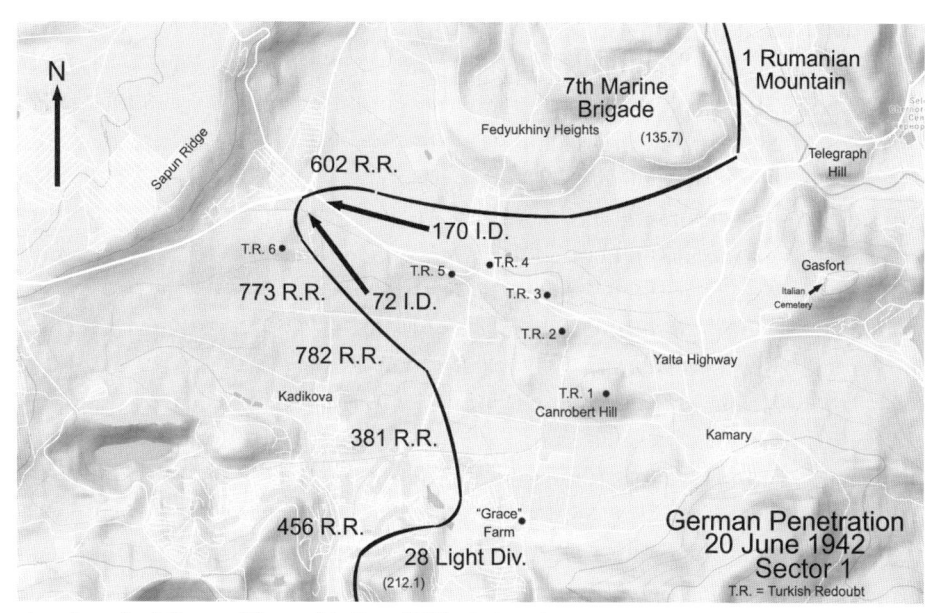

The Third Assault (3) – 17 to 23 June 1942 – Fall of the North 193

Attack on the defences of Sector 1 in June 1942. (© OpenStreetMap contributors, Author's collection)

to heavy bombing and shelling. Fort Constantine's defences were strengthened in anticipation of an infantry assault. At the end of the day Battery 4 and the engineering complex, held by the Guards Regiment, were cut off.

At 0500 hours on 21 June the Germans resumed their offensive in Sectors 1 and 2. A fresh German regiment, the 420th from 125th Infantry Division, was placed under command of the 170th Division. The attack on Sector 1 was carried out in three directions and included nine assault guns and five tanks. The first group attacked towards Kadykova; the second towards Hill 74.0 (Sixth Turkish Redoubt); the third against the southern slopes of the heavily fortified Fedyukhiny Heights. The attack was to be carried out by mixed units of the 170th Division and 420th Infantry Regiment and was planned to begin shortly after midnight to assist in the concealment of the attackers. The former Soviet airfield at the base of the heights, which was visible from the Sapun Heights and covered by Soviet artillery, was the focus of the attack. The 399th Infantry Regiment of 170th Division attacked from the left, the 420th from the right. The battalions penetrated the first line of defence. At 0400 hours the 420th Infantry Regiment reached a point 500m south of the summit of Hill 135.7, one of the two Fedyukhiny Heights. At dawn the attack became visible to the artillery units on the Sapun Heights and the Germans had to seek cover from artillery fire. At 0600 hours German Stukas bombed the Soviet positions, some bombs falling very close to their own men. At 0830 hours the battalions of the 420th Regiment attacked, while the 399th Regiment headed for the top of the heights from the west. German artillery and dive bombers hit the

Sapun Heights artillery positions to keep them from firing on the Germans. The Soviets counter-attacked from Novo Shuli at the foot of the Fedyukhiny Heights, but the two attacks were repulsed and the Germans dug in to the occupied positions. They were now in full control of the Fedyukhiny Heights which offered a commanding view over Sectors 1 and 2. The Germans also captured Hills 25.6 and 29.4 on the outskirts of Kadykova. The remaining Soviet lines held.

On 22 June, around 1800 hours, the Germans captured Battery 12, cutting off Fort Constantine from St. Michael's Battery. Boats were brought in to evacuate troops to the south side. The Germans attempted to clear Soviet troops sheltering in the railway tunnels south of Mekenzievy Station, north of the bay. A series of tunnels was cut into the mountainous area northeast of Sevastopol and also south of the bay, through which the Simferopol-Sevastopol railway line passed. In the nineteenth century six tunnels were cut through the hills: the Suharny (Sukharno) Tunnel – 331m, about 2km south of Mekenzievy Mountain Station, ran under the Sukharno Ravine; Grafskaya Tunnel – 125m, ran below the Serpentine Road through the Grafskaya (Count's) Ravine; White Tunnel – 437m, ran below the ravine between Grafskaya and Martynov Ravines; Romany (Tsyganskiy) Tunnel – 500m, ran between Martynov and Gypsies Ravine; south of bay is Troitskiy (Trinity) Tunnel – 294m, that ran under Trinity hill between Sevastopol Bay and Killen Bay; and finally, Korabelnaya Tunnel – 228m, ran below the naval barracks above Musketeers' Bay.

On the night of 22 June Soviet troops were sheltered in one of the southern tunnels, possibly White or Romany. The German 3rd Company of 22nd Pioneer Battalion was sent in to clear the tunnel by driving the Soviets from the western to the eastern end, where they would be intercepted by other German units. At 0230 hours, two groups of pioneers from 213th Infantry Regiment, dressed in Red Army uniforms, placed 50kg of explosive charges at the western end of the tunnel but they did not go off. The pioneers tried to move inside the tunnel and came under fire from Soviet troops behind a barricade, which, according to German accounts, consisted of boxes of ammunition. The Germans used flamethrowers to ignite the boxes. The contents exploded, along with nearby barrels of fuel and part of the tunnel collapsed, killing the defenders.

Further east, a regiment of the German 50th Infantry Division attacked the Grafskaya Ravine while a second regiment of the 50th attacked the mouth of the Martynov Ravine to flush out the last defenders. 22nd Division sent two battalions towards the Sukharno Ravine. The 25th Chapaevsky Division was pushed back to the railway line. The 345th Division was positioned near the Serpentine Road in the Grafskaya Ravine and further to the left the 138th Brigade covered Sukharno and Lighthouse Ravines.

Fort Constantine. (Nemenko Collection)

St. Michael's Battery and Fort Constantine were in a terrible condition after days of shelling and air strikes. The 210mm mortars had destroyed the walls of St. Michael's Battery and Fort Constantine was in no better state. In some places the walls had collapsed on top of the defenders. The fort was defended by a small number of troops who had escaped from the north. The fort housed a medical team which was caring for several hundred wounded. The garrison held off a much larger German force long enough to complete the evacuation, but many of the defenders were killed. Overnight from 23 to 24 June the majority of troops from St. Michael's, Fort Constantine and Battery 4 were transported to the south side. The garrisons could not find enough boats for all of the men and many of them had to swim for it. Fort Constantine had four boats available but two of them were covered in rubble and one had a hole in it. The evacuation began at midnight and the men queued up for a boat ride to the south side. A small group stayed behind to cover the evacuation of each position and to burn buildings and supplies before they headed across the bay. After the boats left the remaining men swam across the bay to reach the southern coast near Battery 13 at Cape Alexander.

There were no boats available for the garrison of St. Michael's Battery and the survivors swam across, many being lost in the dark waters of the bay. Only thirty-eight men reached the south coast. German documents from the 24th Division show that prisoners were taken from 110th Regiment and 95th Division. Most of the men from the Guards Regiment made it across. Most of the crews of Batteries 79, 219 and 227 were listed as missing.

At 0130 hours on 23 June the German 420th Infantry Regiment captured the village of Novo Shuli at the foot of the Fedyukhiny Heights. Soviet AA batteries located on Sapun Ridge fired on the Germans and at 0400 hours the 7th Brigade counter-attacked and forced the Germans out of the town. At 0530 hours, after heavy air and artillery preparation, the 170th Division launched an offensive against a battalion of the 9th Marine Brigade on Hill 74.0. After heavy fighting and no reinforcements, the battalion was forced back from the Turkish Redoubt.

As a result of the evacuation of the north end, General Petrov adjusted the sector lines and the composition of troops. On the morning of the 24 June the situation was as follows:

- Sector 1 – Major-General Novikov – Balaklava to Hill 113.2 over the Yalta Highway – occupied by 109th and 388th Rifle Divisions and 9th Marine Brigade.
- Sector 2 – Colonel Scutelnic – Hill 113.2 to Hill 75.0 (old French redoubt on the slopes of Sapun Ridge) – occupied by 386th Rifle Division, 7th Marine Brigade, two bunker battalions from 8th Marine Brigade.

The destruction at Battery 30. Exact location unknown. (NARA)

- Sector 3 – Major-General Kolomiec – Hill 75.0 to Novo Shuli – French redoubt – slopes of Mount Kara-Koba – Hill 113.7 – Martynovksy Ravine – Grafskaya Ravine – North Bay – Inkerman – occupied by 25th Infantry Division, 8th Marine Brigade, one bunker battalion and 3rd Marine Regiment.
- Sector 4 – Colonel Kapitohin – Inkerman station – occupied by remains of 79th Infantry Brigade and 2nd Perekop Regiment, plus combined regiments of 95th and 345th Divisions and remnants of 138th Infantry Brigade.

The Germans were now overlooking and in some cases, beside the waters of the bay. It had taken them a long time and many fallen comrades to get this far. They could see the ultimate prize across the bay – the smoking ruins of Sevastopol over which the Hammer and Sickle flag still flew. But it was still out of reach and yet more hard fighting lay ahead.

Chapter 9

The Third Assault (4) – 24 June to 16 July 1942 – The End of the Road

After arriving on the south side of Sevastopol Bay, the evacuees from the north were formed into a composite regiment under the command of Lieutenant-Colonel Baranov, commander of the Guards Regiment since the beginning of the Second Defence. They were ordered to deploy along the south coast from Inkerman Station, on the south side of the Black River at the entrance to the bay, to Quarantine Bay on the Black Sea. The larger units, if they could be so called, retained their numerical designations.

On the morning of 24 June 1942 the Germans attacked from two directions to cut off Soviet forces near Inkerman. One attack was directed at the 386th Division at the foot of Sugar Head while a second attack was against 3rd Marine Regiment

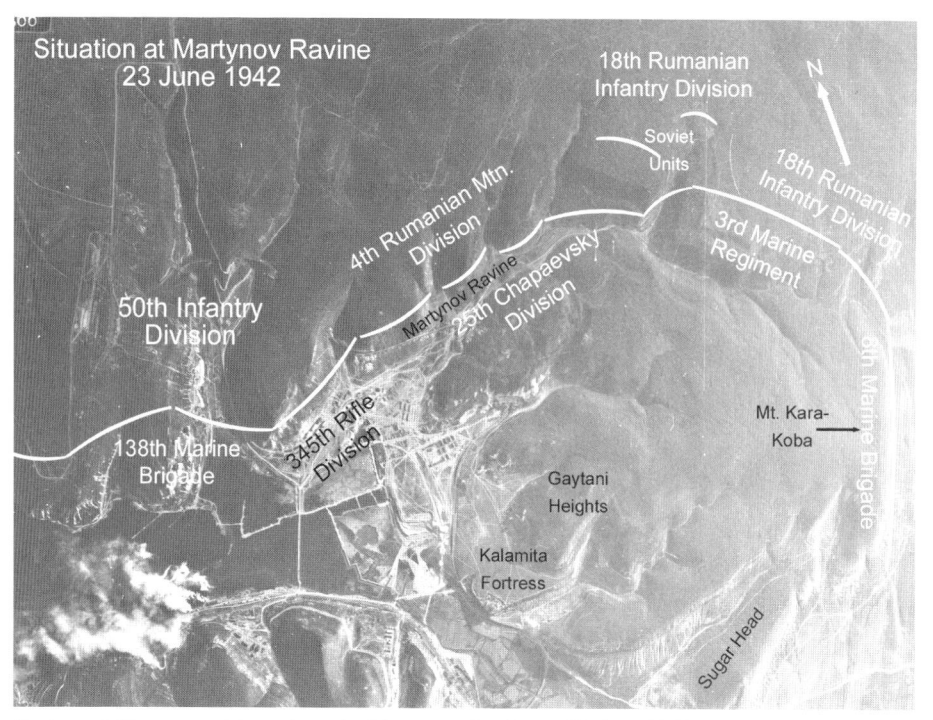

Soviet and German positions along the Martynov Ravine on 23 June 1942. (Author's collection)

which was posted on the southeast side of Martynov Ravine on the right flank of 25th Chapaevsky Division. 8th Marine Brigade was on their right flank. 3rd Regiment made use of the cover of the wooded ravines and retained its position. The Soviets repelled attacks by the Rumanian 18th and 1st Mountain Division.

Soviet troops in Sector 3 moved up to repel a German attack on the 31st Rifle Regiment defending from the East Inkerman lighthouse, but they were thrown back to the Gypsy Ravine. The attacks against 3rd Marine Regiment and 31st Rifle Regiment in the Martynov Ravine were relentless. Bunkers 12 and 13 continued to block the Germans trying to break out of the Ravine. The Germans surrounded Bunker 13 and a nearby group of thirty Soviet troops. By 1800 hours the Germans brought up two 37mm guns and opened fire on the bunker. The 45mm gun inside the bunker damaged one German gun but the Germans fired into the embrasure and the bunker was finally silenced.

The Germans identified three ravines running into the bay on the north side as *Pappelschlucht*, *Gansetal* and *Regensschlucht*. On 17 June the codenames for these ravines were changed to *Drachenschlucht*, *Wolfsschlucht* and *Hollental*. However, operational maps still used the older names. *Pappelschlucht* was Holland Ravine

The attack on the Sukharno Arsenal, 24 to 26 June 1942. (Author's collection)

that emptied into Holland Bay, *Gansetal* was Sukharno Ravine and *Regensschlucht* was the Lighthouse Ravine. Eleven tunnels were dug into the cliffs along the shore between these ravines that served as the main ammunition arsenal at Sukharno and Lighthouse Ravines – the Sukharno Arsenal. Eight storage bunkers were located directly on the water above a concrete pier of the Sukharno docks; the rest were around the bend on the west slope of Sukharno Ravine. The Soviets still held the ammunition bunkers.

When the Germans threatened to break through into the ravines that led to the arsenal the main Soviet defenders withdrew as once the tunnels were destroyed there would be no reason to defend them. Fort Ural and Fort Donets covered the approaches to the ravines leading down to the arsenal. On 24 June Soviet troops withdrew from these forts and the troops at Lighthouse and Sukharno were completely isolated. After the departure of the main force a small garrison stayed behind to cover the withdrawal of the demolitions team and the workers remaining in the tunnels.

Late on the night of 24 June the Soviets were given permission to destroy the tunnels. The demolition team of about twenty men was led by Colonel Donets. The demolition had been scheduled for 24 June but things did not go as planned and the team continued to work throughout the day and into the night of the 24th. The small garrison defended the warehouse alone for an additional day until the galleries were all mined.[1]

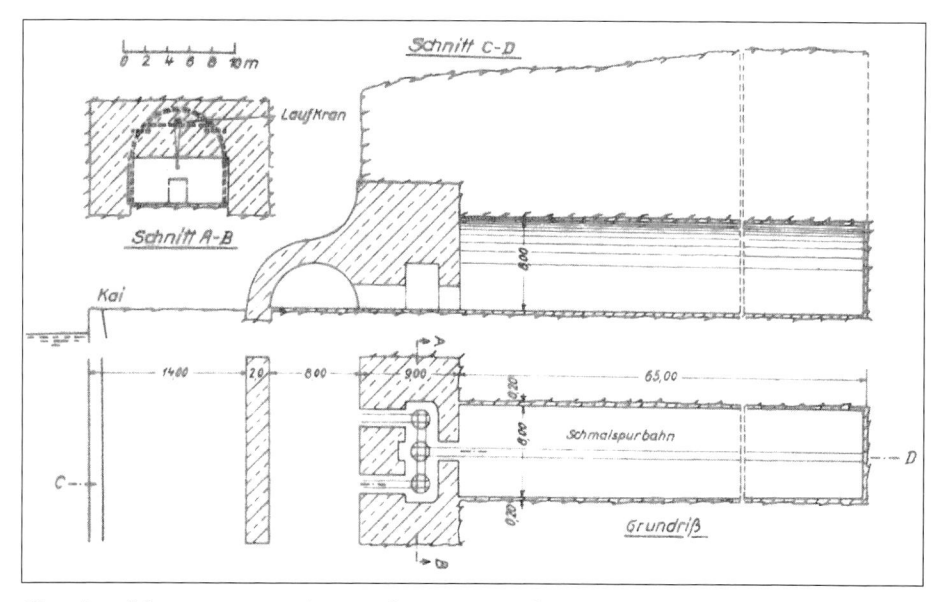

Elevation of the concrete protection over the storage tunnel entrances at Sukharno Arsenal. (Nachtrag)

The Third Assault (4) – 24 June to 16 July 1942 – The End of the Road

On 25 June fierce fighting for the tunnels took place between the Soviet defenders and German pioneers from 16th and 65th Regiments. The Germans broke through to Holland Bay northeast of Sukharno. From this side the approaches to the arsenal were blocked by troops of the Guards Regiment. A squad of defenders moved into one of the arsenal buildings that had been converted into a strongpoint. Another group took up positions at the gate by the Lighthouse Ravine. These were very strong defensive positions. German artillery blasted the defenders and the troops in the guard building fled into the tunnels along the water's edge. The garrison now consisted of about 130 soldiers, plus seventy-six civilian workers. 1st Platoon and a shock platoon of 3rd Company of 22nd Pioneer Battalion attacked the western tunnels and 744th Pioneer Battalion the eastern ones. Around 1000 hours the situation at the main gate became critical as German infantry and tanks appeared. The defenders fled towards Tunnel 11, took up positions behind a wall and threw anti-tank grenades at the attackers, halting the attack for the time being.

The destruction of the other tunnels followed, one by one. The decision had been made to blow the remaining tunnels on the night of 25 to 26 June. They were set to explode automatically every 30 minutes. The engineers did not have the ability to blow the tunnels by remote control, so they had to remain and set the fuzes by hand. Once they were set the engineers and remaining defenders swam

Concrete protection over the entrance to the storage tunnels at Sukharno Arsenal. (Nemenko Collection)

or, if wounded, took a boat to the south side. The Donets group remained behind at Sukharno to finish the job.

Around 1300 hours thirty German pioneers tried to move along the coast by boat to get around the troops guarding the gate and the vicinity of Tunnel 11. The Soviets threw grenades into the boat, ending the sneak attack. The fighting at the gate and the east wall lasted throughout the day. A large group of German soldiers appeared from the Holland Ravine and stormed the platform in front of tunnel 1. Suddenly there was a huge explosion and the tunnel entrance disintegrated, killing and wounding dozens of Germans. In the afternoon of 25 June the Germans decided to storm the remaining tunnels. They approached Tunnel 11, in which the demolition team was finishing their work, fired a shell inside and killed the members of the team.

According to the Report of the Military-Scientific Conference of 1966 (A. P. Protsenko), eight tunnels were mined – 1 to 8. Three tunnels did not have any ammunition stored inside. Tunnel 9 was used as a hospital, and 10 and 11 were shelters. Photos show eight tunnels, two with a semi-circular concrete masking across the front of Tunnels 7 and 8. Galleries 9, 10 and 11 were at another location.

On the morning of 25 June the 72nd Infantry Division attacked the junction of 25th Chapaevsky Division and 3rd Marine Regiment. The Soviets had about 140 defenders against a battalion of Germans who were attempting to move between the two spurs of the Martynov Ravine. The infantry moved through the brush from one hollow to another in the vicinity of the Forest Guard house (Cordon Number 2), firing machine guns and supported by artillery, mortars and aircraft. They had to cross through open areas and when they broke cover many of them were shot down by Soviet riflemen, machine-gunners and from the crews of earth-timber bunkers concealed in the deep cover of the hillsides. German aircraft bombed the grassy slopes for about 30 minutes, reduced them to smoking black craters and leaving the concrete roof of a precast bunker laying on its side. The Germans continued to rush the Soviet position but despite their efforts they could still not dislodge them from the ravine.

The 50th Division had better luck in reaching the marshy area at the mouth of the Black River Valley near Inkerman, the location of the blown bridge. 50th Division troops attacked the 2nd Battalion of 138th Brigade and the remnants of the 345th Division near the bay in the area of the lighthouse. In the evening the Germans captured about 229 soldiers from the 138th and 280 from the 345th. The situation at the junction between 3rd Marine Regiment and 8th Brigade worsened. The Rumanian 4th Mountain and 18th Mountain Divisions, reinforced by two battalions of 2nd Mountain Brigade and 33rd Infantry Regiment, drove 400m into the Soviet line near Mount Kora-Koba. The Rumanians were unable to surround the 3rd Regiment and fighting continued until midnight.

The Third Assault (4) – 24 June to 16 July 1942 – The End of the Road 203

Troops and equipment continued to arrive at Sevastopol. Ships were now being unloaded at Musketeers', Cossack and Reed Bays. On 25 June, 1,100 men of the 142nd Rifle Brigade arrived and 1,245 wounded were evacuated. The 142nd was placed on the Kamezh defensive line, also known as the evacuation covering line. Upon the arrival of the 142nd, two battalions of the 9th Marine Brigade, together with the 778th Rifle Regiment and 81st Tank Battalion, previously covering the evacuation line, were transferred to the front lines.

On 26 June the German 132nd Division, supported by the 4th Rumanian Mountain Division on its left flank, attacked the 25th Chapaevsky Division in Sector 3. Soviet troops located east of the East Inkerman Lighthouse, were forced to abandon Inkerman heights, except for the ruins of the Kalamita fortress on Hill 79.4, overlooking the Inkerman Monastery. By the end of the day the 25th Chapaevsky Division, 8th Marine Brigade and 3rd Marine Regiment were still holding a line that ran along the Black River 500m east of Novo Shuli–across the Black River–Mount Kara-Koba–800m north of Kalamita Fortress and the southern coast near Inkerman at the mouth of the Black River valley. The Rumanians and the 132nd Division, however, had driven a significant wedge into the Soviet line on the Inkerman heights and the situation was dire.

Meanwhile the armoured train *Zhelezniakov* was operating near the mouth of the Trinity Tunnel (on the south side at the tip of Killen Bay). The train made a total of 140 combat runs from 1941 to 1942. Its targets included bunkers, machine

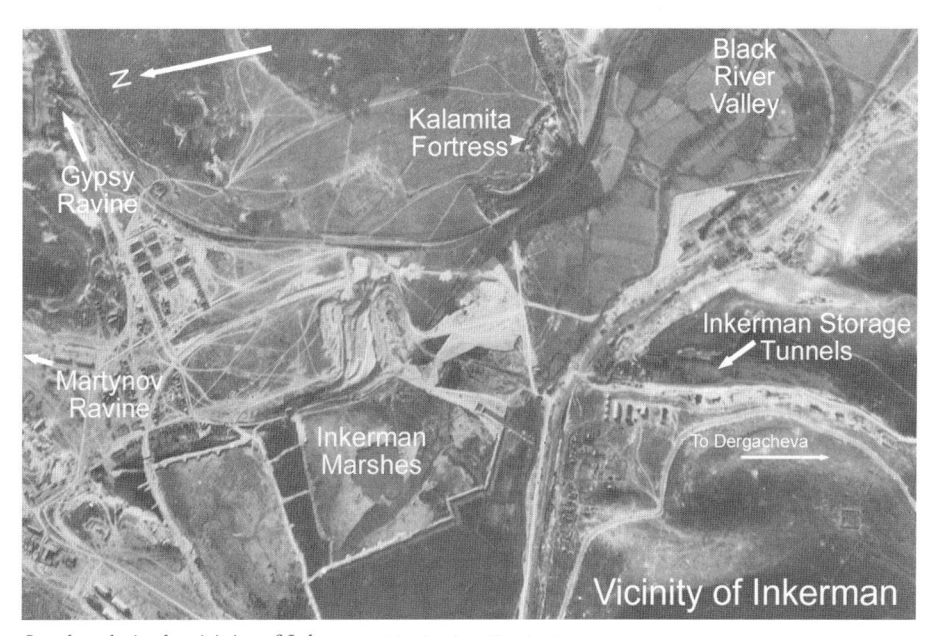

Landmarks in the vicinity of Inkerman. (Author's collection)

The armoured train Zhelezniakov *along the southern coast of Sevastopol Bay.* (Nemenko Collection)

gun nests, heavy gun batteries, aircraft, vehicles and tanks and German infantry. It was now hiding out in the Trinity Tunnel (now the Troitskiy Tunnel). On 26 June the train pulled briefly out of the tunnel mouth to open fire on German troops when the tunnel was attacked by German aircraft. Bombs fell on the tunnel entrance. A massive explosion blocked the mouth of the tunnel and plunged it into total darkness. The exit door from the train was also blocked. Some of the crew climbed out a trapdoor in the floor of the car. It was pitch black inside the tunnel and the air full of smoke. After some time the dust settled and there was a hole in the ceiling of the tunnel through which the men could see the blue sky. The second wagon of the train was completely buried under tons of earth, men trapped inside. The only way inside was to dig through between the wheels and get to the hatch underneath. The rescue party reached the hatch and banged on it but no sound came from inside. They finally pried it open carefully, afraid a man might be lying on it and fall out. Inside it was dark and full of fumes and dead silence. The rescue team dragged the wounded men through the hatch. They worked quickly but had to get out as more rocks and dirt fell on top of the train, leaving twelve men buried inside. It was impossible to get them out. Some of the surviving crew escaped with several mortars and they set these up near the power station. The rest of the crew was trapped in the tunnel and captured on 3 July.[2]

On the night of 26 June about 1,000 more men of the 142nd Brigade were brought in by transport to Sevastopol, plus ammunition and food. At 0015 hours on 27 June, 580 more men arrived. Transport operations were becoming increasingly dangerous, however. During the day the destroyer *Bezuprechnyy* and the submarine *S-32* were sent to Sevastopol but were hit by German bombers and sunk about 60km out to sea. The *Tashkent* was also attacked over a three-hour period and was badly damaged, taking on water. She limped back to Novorossiysk.[3]

Despite the transfer of many of Richthofen's squadrons to the Caucasus to support the German summer offensive, the Black Sea Fleet council reported that the pace of enemy air attacks was still 400 to 600 sorties daily. They dropped 2,500 to 4,000 bombs per day on troops, artillery batteries, docks, etc. Soviet air cover was non-existent. Because of the short period of darkness and good summer weather the Germans found it easier to spot ships at sea. Vice-Admiral Oktyabrsky's report mentioned that food, ammunition and fuel were running out. In some places troops had to be withdrawn for lack of ammunition. There were hints in the report that the Soviets could hold out no more than ten to fifteen days and that they were fighting valiantly, but there was a desperate need for supplies.

Attacks continued in Sector 3. Two battalions of the 72nd Division attacked along the Black River. At the same time the Rumanian 1st Mountain Division and 18th Infantry Division attacked the 8th Marine Brigade at Mount Kara-Koba. 4th Rumanian Mountain, along with parts of 132nd Infantry Division attacked the 25th Chapaevsky Division and 3rd Marine Regiment. The 4th Rumanian Division broke through the junction between 3rd Marine Regiment and 25th Chapaevsky Division to reach Gaytani. This was a tremendous accomplishment and it had serious repercussions on the Soviet situation in the north.

In the early morning hours of 28 June, Sugar Head was captured and Mount Kara-Koba and Hill 119.0, located on the heights south of the valley and held by 8th Brigade, were in danger of being surrounded. The 8th Brigade and 25th Chapaevsky Division were forced to cross over the Black River, abandoning all but a couple of their artillery pieces in the process. The 3rd Marine Regiment fell back to the Inkerman Monastery below Kalamita Fortress and the 25th Chapaevsky moved back between Sugar Head and the Monastery.

The Germans attempted to cross the Black River and cut off the Soviet retreat. The Soviet defences now consisted only of a single line. The 3rd Marine Regiment had two howitzers left and set one up on their last foothold on the Inkerman heights and the other northwest of the Monastery. In that location the gunners had a line of sight to the south that enabled them to cover the river crossing point. The Germans attacked the battery and the guns opened fire at point-blank range. The Germans returned fire on the guns and the gunners moved them to a nearby cave. As soon as the German guns stopped firing the Soviets pulled the guns out of the cave and this routine continued throughout the day but it fulfilled its purpose. By nightfall the whole 25th Chapaevsky Division was on the western shore of the river.

Voyetkhov writes:

> Inkerman finally fell and that action, as with so many others, seemed to signal that the end must now be near. Even the Russians began to admit that the end was near. The mood became grim and angry. There was no thought amongst the Russians that they had been defeated. There was never any talk of surrender. So the fighting went on. The battle became more and more violent and desperate.[4]

The Third Assault had begun on 2 June with five days of heavy bombardment. As the clock ticked past midnight and the 28th day of the assault began, the Germans and Rumanians still looked down on the besieged city, still out of reach. If they thought about past history they would realise that, nearing the end of eight months of fighting, they had not yet reached the lines held by the French and British when they began the siege of Sevastopol in 1854. That siege lasted for 347 days. Nevertheless, as 28 June dawned the Germans had a 4:1 advantage in troops. The Soviets still had no intention of surrendering what was left of Sevastopol. However, by the end of the next day the situation would change drastically and, while it may have been determined a few days before, the fate of Sevastopol was now definitely sealed.

At midnight, the Soviets defended the following lines:

- Genoese tower – bend in the highway 100m west of Hill 99.4 held by 456th Regiment. The 381st Regiment was next to the village of Kadykova. These two groups were opposed by the German 28th Division.
- The 602nd Regiment, 773rd Regiment and the remains of the 782nd Regiment guarded the Yalta Road and faced two regiments of the 170th Division.
- Two battalions of 9th Brigade held the foot of the heights of Karagach (along Yalta Highway at the junction of Balaklava Road). The 72nd Infantry Division faced this position.
- 7th Brigade held the flank of the 9th Brigade against 399th Regiment of 170th Division and 420th Regiment of 125th Division.
- The remnants of 386th Division were positioned 400m south of Hill 75.0 against the 4th and 1st Rumanian Mountain Divisions and 18th Rumanian Mountain Division in reserve.
- The 8th Marine Brigade faced the 132nd Division near the village of Inkerman.
- The 3rd Marine Regiment and remnants of 138th Infantry Brigade occupied the left wing of the ravine below the quarries at Stone Pit Ravine and faced the 22nd Division. The German 22nd and 24th Divisions held the south shore of the bay which was now clear of Soviet troops.

The Third Assault (4) – 24 June to 16 July 1942 – The End of the Road

Three devastating events took place on 29 June. The first was the successful crossing of Sevastopol Bay; second, the assault on Sapun Ridge; and third, the breakthrough along the Yalta Highway.

The final agony began on 29 June, just shortly after midnight. For over a year the Soviet Naval Command feared an amphibious or airborne landing by German troops and their initial strategy was based on defence against such attacks. Ironically the Second Defence of Sevastopol would end, rather than begin, with such an attack.

At 0200 hours the Staff Duty Officer at Fleet Headquarters received a report of enemy ships off of Cape Fiolent. They were Italian torpedo boats plus small German vessels attempting to land troops on the coast between the cape and Cossack Bay. The real purpose of this action was to draw attention away from the main event soon to take place in Sevastopol Bay. The Germans landed four teams at four points along the coast, producing the desired effect of sowing confusion among the Soviet defenders.

Assault across the Bay

German time was one hour behind Soviet time. German reports indicate the time of the launch of the amphibious attack as 0100 hours German time, 0200 hours Soviet time. LIV Corps records show that the troops of 22nd and 24th Infantry Divisions crossed the bay beginning at 0100 hours. The weather was clear and it was necessary to lay down a smokescreen.

General Morgunov wrote that:

> The events of the night of June 29 developed as follows. At 0200 [0100 hours German time] the Nazis opened a massive artillery and mortar fire throughout the area of the southern coast of North Bay[5] from Killen Ravine to the power station. At the same time the area was bombed by enemy aircraft. The weather was not favourable to us – it was relatively quiet, but the wind was blowing from the north and all the south coast in which the enemy was shooting was in the smoke and dust. 2nd and 177th artillery battalions could not see; not only the northern shore, but also the bay. Fortunately, the gunners of the 2nd battalion could view the northern side from Cape Alexander to direct fire at the enemy boats.
>
>   At 0215 the enemy set off a smokescreen to cover the concentration of its crossing equipment. The smokescreen moved very slowly to the southern shore, finally engulfing the entire bay. At 0235 the enemy began forcing the bay, under cover of heavy fire on our coast. The Germans landed at Trinity, St. George and Sushilnaya Ravines. Our coastal artillery and army managed

208   The Defence of Sevastopol 1941–1942

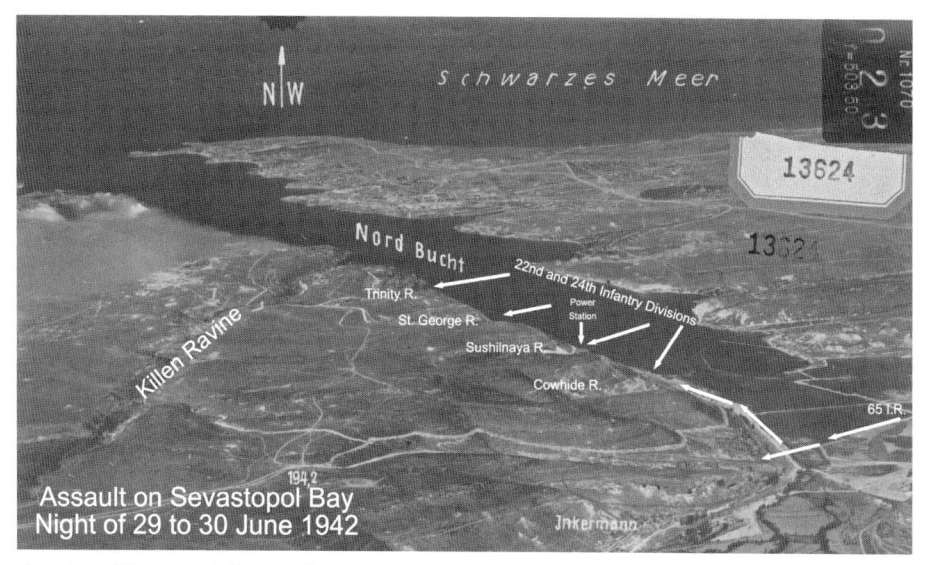

Crossing of Sevastopol Bay on the night of 29 to 30 June 1942. (Author's collection)

to sink a few boats crossing the bay, but most of them had reached the shore. Despite the stubborn resistance of our troops on shore, the enemy still managed to gain a foothold on parts of the coast and quickly consolidated their forces.[6]

I. S. Manoshin states:

> 0200 the enemy opened heavy artillery fire against the southern shore of Sevastopol Bay and at 0235 under the cover of a smoke screen, which was favourable to him and the continuing artillery fire by the 22nd and then and 24th Infantry Divisions, began forcing the bay. They landed in four locations between Killen Bay and the power plant. Our artillery sank seventeen enemy boats. Five boats landed in the vicinity of St. George's Ravine. Counter-attacks were carried out by remnants of our 95th and 345th Rifle Divisions, the 79th Brigade, 2nd Marine Regiment and other units of defence sector 4. The landing in the vicinity of the Cowhide Ravine was secured by the enemy while the other three landings were repelled.[7]

The Soviet accounts claim the operation was preceded by a heavy artillery and mortar bombardment. They also claim that the Germans successfully landed only in one place. However, the Germans claim the landings were secret and carried out without any artillery preparation.

The Third Assault (4) – 24 June to 16 July 1942 – The End of the Road

The remains of Bunker 23's 130mm guns which had been taken from the cruiser Chervona Ukraina. (Nemenko Collection)

Records of the 24th Infantry Division[8] report that just after midnight (0100 hours Soviet time), troops of the 31st Infantry Regiment began to load up the boats. At 0100 hours they began the crossing. The noise of the boats was masked by aircraft engines. The first wave landed without opposition. Soviet deserters stated that the bulk of their troops were in the tunnels and the railway tunnel (Trinity) and caught off guard.

The 22nd Infantry Division Intelligence reported that Soviet artillery fire was negligible and increased only as the night passed into dawn. Particularly heavy fire came from Map Reference 1630[9] (Malakhov Hill). This was followed by heavy mortar fire. The first landing in a small cove met with Soviet resistance. The left flank of the landing party was faced with stiff resistance from the well-fortified position on top of the hill, the old Crimean War redoubts on the south side. Strong counter-attacks took place on the left flank of the 65th Infantry Regiment. 22nd Artillery Regiment reported that at 0130 hours the first group reached the opposite shore and five minutes later the Germans opened fire against 'Area A and B', forty shots on each.

Morgunov continues:

> The soldiers fought bravely, courageously and resolutely counter-attacked the enemy, but were not able to force him back. With large forces, the Germans, continually under cover of a smokescreen and aircraft and artillery, sent

waves of reinforcements to its troops dug in on the south shore. Resistance by remnants of the 95th and 345th Rifle Divisions, the 79th Marine Brigade, 2nd Marine Regiment and other parts, was weak but they showed great courage. Most importantly, our gunners had very few shells. All along the southern shore bloody battles and melees took place. Soviet sailors fought bravely, repeatedly attacking the enemy and firing on the landing parties with mortars and machine guns, but were unable to withstand the onslaught of the superior forces of the enemy and they began to move away. All day the 22nd and 24th Infantry Division attacked the southern shore of the bay. In the afternoon, they launched a decisive attack and began to move to the Killen Ravine and the Suzdal Height, which they were able to capture by the end of the day.[10]

I. S. Manoshin continues:

The Germans quickly shifted their units at each bridgehead. A battalion broke through the Cowhide Ravine to Suzdal. Later an infantry battalion landed at Killen Ravine, St. George's and Sushilnaya Ravines. The 50th and 132nd Infantry Division advanced through Inkerman and towards the Victoria Redoubt. By 1200 hours Soviet forces retreated to the western slopes of Killen Ravine, the Kamchatsky Redoubt and Victoria Redoubt.[11]

These accounts have some flaws. The 345th Division was seeking shelter from German aircraft in the Inkerman tunnels. They in fact 'slept' through the opening phase of the operation and the Germans gained a significant foothold on the south side. The 138th Brigade launched a counter-attack from Suzdal and slowed the Germans but they landed in the rear of Soviet forces near Killen Bay. The landing in the Cowhide Ravine was repulsed and the Germans shifted to the Sushilnaya Ravine, St. George and Trinity. This is the opposite of the Soviet reports and rather shows the Germans successfully landing at three locations and being repelled at only one. By midday on 29 June the Soviets held the Suzdal Heights and the entire line of the Crimean War fortifications along the top but they were partly surrounded by German forces.

At 0400 hours (0500) the 22nd Infantry Division reports state that the regiments captured the northern and northeastern slopes of the 'height to the monument' and a section of the road 400m east of Map Reference 1651 (indicating part of the Serpentine on Sapun Ridge). The report was changed at 1450 hours indicating that the Germans reached the east line of the monument at Map Reference 1650 near the *Grabensystem* (anti-tank ditch) in a group of houses 500m southwest of Map Reference 1615. They ran into tough enemy opposition in the

The Third Assault (4) – 24 June to 16 July 1942 – The End of the Road 211

'height of monuments', especially on the right flank of 50th Division in the area of Map Reference 1653 (the former monastery on the left bank by the modern Inkerman station).

The Germans seized the power plant. The workers inside evacuated because they didn't have authorisation to blow it up. The Germans attempted to damage one of the generators but were repulsed by a counter-attack but at 0700 hours they managed to lay charges and blew up the generator, knocking out the lights and all landline communications. Zhidilov recalls this moment in his memoirs: 'I commanded the first battalion to deploy one rifle company, reinforced by two heavy machine guns and an anti-tank platoon of guns to the Yalta Highway. And then the phone went silent. Wired communication ceased with all battalions and with the headquarters of the army. Attempts to restore it failed. The only communication was via radio.'[12]

From the report of the commander of the 8th Marine Brigade, Colonel P. Gorpishchenko:

> On the morning of June 29, under heavy enemy fire the 775th Regiment began to retreat in disarray on Sapun mountain and on to Dergacheva. They lost contact [with us]. One of our companies near the water tower at Novo Shuli, sent there to prevent the enemy from reaching Sapun Mountain, was surrounded and destroyed. Two battalions of enemy forces followed the retreating troops and moved to the rear brigade. We deployed the 3rd Battalion against them. Wired and wireless communication had been cut.[13]

As if an amphibious landing on the south side of the bay wasn't enough, XXX Corps launched an all-out offensive in the south under cover of darkness. The 170th and 72nd Division attacked towards the Sapun Ridge at Hill 111.0, next to the hairpin turn on the road leading up to the ridge, on the right flank of 7th Brigade at its junction with 769th Regiment of 386th Rifle Division. Also, the 4th Rumanian Mountain Division launched an attack from the direction of Novo Shuli.

XXX Corps' plan was to attack with three regiments of the 170th Infantry Division along a narrow front to gain a foothold on the Sapun Ridge. The 170th had a huge amount of artillery at its disposal, plus the support of the bombers of VIII Air Corps. The 399th Infantry Regiment attacked on the right, the 420th in the centre and the 391st on the left. The overwhelming dawn attack on the Sapun Ridge proved to be a resounding success.

The 7th Brigade was positioned along the edge of the ridge, centred on the winding road, to prevent the enemy from accessing the ridge via the Yalta Highway. The brigade was on the right of the 9th Marine Brigade and to the left of the 769th Rifle Regiment. At 0220 hours the Germans fired artillery and mortars in the area of the 5th Battalion of the 7th Brigade. At 0500 hours the 386th Division retreated in disarray from Sapun Ridge towards the English Victoria Redoubt, and 7th Brigade lost contact with it.

The Rumanian 4th Mountain Division began their attack from Novo Shuli at 0245 hours with an artillery preparation conducted by 1st and 4th Artillery Regiments plus one German anti-aircraft regiment. The attacking units did not wait for the end of the artillery bombardment and moved forward. Around 0420 hours the 7th Brigade began to retreat and the Rumanians moved up to the plateau, the 8th and 9th Battalions, supported by 4th Pioneer Battalion, moving towards the Yalta Highway. The Soviets launched a counter-attack but it failed when the Rumanian 9th Battalion moved in. When the 170th Division stormed the ridge, the Rumanians attacked 2km to the north. Thus, all across the ridge, the Germans broke through the positions of the 775th Regiment of 8th Brigade in the centre and 514th Regiment, all which retreated towards Suzdal and Dergacheva.

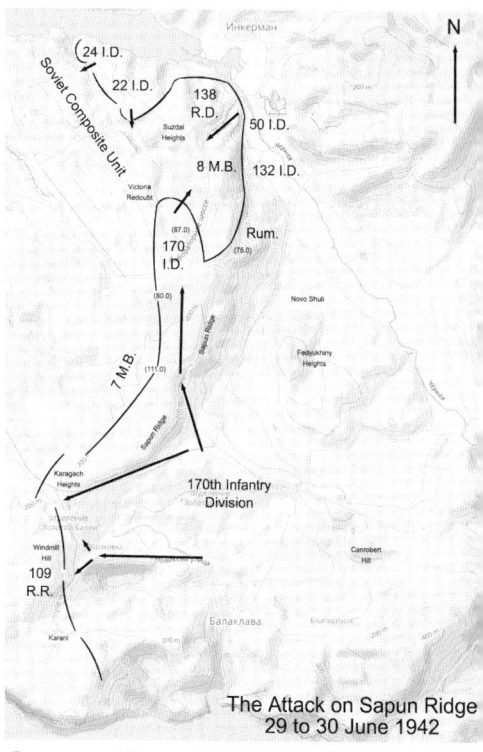

German and Rumanian assault on Sapun Ridge on 29–30 June 1942. (© OpenStreetMap contributors, Author's collection)

Colonel Gorpishchenko, whose troops included the 775th Regiment, were defending the ridge 400m south of hill 75.0, to the left of the 514th Regiment and right of the 386th, reported that the Soviets were retreating from their positions on the ridge towards Dergacheva. The political commissar of the 386th Rifle Division, R. I. Volodchenkova, wrote that, 'At 0315, as dawn approached, the Germans struck all our defences on Mount Sapun [sic]. The mountain slopes burned. The shelling lasted for about 40 minutes before sunrise. Contact with adjoining units was disrupted. At 0350 the offensive began. The Germans turned towards Yalta Highway and broke through the defence on the left flank of our sector on the site of 775th Rifle Regiment.'[14]

The German attack on Sapun Ridge was a complete rout, with the level of success Manstein had hoped for back in October. Black columns of smoke could be seen everywhere, accompanied by flashes of explosions and dirt flying into

The Third Assault (4) – 24 June to 16 July 1942 – The End of the Road 213

the air. The attackers were coming at the Soviets from every direction. Zhidilov described it this: 'The entire front is on fire.'[15] When the Germans approached the top of the ridge, they ran into stubborn Soviet defenders. The Germans hit the lines again with artillery and mortars and this time broke through on the left and surrounded them. The Soviets fell back in two directions, towards Sevastopol Bay and towards the English cemetery. Around 0700 hours the 8th Brigade command post called out on the radio: 'Communication lost all commanders.'[16]

At 1000 hours the 72nd Infantry Division broke through at the junction of the 9th and 7th Marine Brigades. By this time, the 399th Regiment of the 170th Infantry Division had broken through the weakened defences of the 386th Rifle Division at its junction with the 7th Brigade (along the road to Sapun Ridge). By 1200 hours the German troops met in the rear of the 7th Brigade. The brigade was surrounded but Colonel Zhidilov and his staff escaped to the command post at Maximova cottage, where a makeshift battalion was created, along with the remnants of 8th Brigade.

The Germans headed in two directions, towards Hills 80 and 87. A 152mm howitzer battery and troops of the 25th Chapaevsky Division blocked the German/Rumanian advance to the Laboratory Ravine. Crews in Bunkers 20 and 23 stopped the advance on the road from the ridge. Troops of 25th Division launched a counter-attack near Dergacheva, but it failed due to an attack by about a dozen German aircraft that destroyed the barracks at Dergacheva.

Bunker 21 along the Laboratory Ravine. (Nemenko Collection)

On 29 June, the fighting reached Dergacheva. The farm was held by 7th Marine Brigade for twelve hours, allowing the wounded to be removed from the field hospitals. At 1600 hours on 29 June three battalions of the brigade with a total of 150 men moved to Sapun Ridge to mount a final defence.

The Germans broke through on to the Sapun Ridge near Bunkers 27 and 28 and tried to reach the Sapun Highway but encountered the fire of 7th Marine Brigade, supported by Bunkers 18, 23, 24 and 20. During the day the Germans could not break through and retreated back over the top of the Sapun Ridge. The 7th Brigade was forced to move back and Bunker 24 ran out of ammunition, allowing the Germans and Rumanians to get around the defenders near the Maximova Dacha. Bunker 24 continued to fight with machine-gun fire but two hours later the Germans approached from the opposite slope of the hill and scored a direct hit on the bunker, putting it out of action. The crews of the bunkers then withdrew towards the city along the Laboratory Highway. The retreat was covered by the guns of Battery 701 on Malakhov Hill. Bunker 23 also ran out of ammunition but, along with Bunkers 22 and 21 and several pre-cast machine-gun bunkers, covered the retreat of the troops along Laboratory Highway. The fate of their crews is unknown.

On 20 November 1941, Battery 114 was set up on temporary wooden platforms in a position below Dergacheva. It was commanded by Senior Lieutenant Rabinovich who had also commanded the guns when they were aboard the *Chervona Ukraina*. In February 1942 the guns were moved to permanent platforms on the Suzdal Heights. This was due to the change in the lines of defence. The guns could only fire on the Kara-Koba Valley from the former position. From the new location it could sweep the ravines on the north side of the bay and also support troops in Sectors 2 and 3 and also 1 and 4 if necessary. The battery had three magazines. The approaches were covered by Bunkers 15, 16 and 17 and three machine-gun bunkers. Positions for 152mm field howitzer were also located nearby.

The battery was very active from 20 to 29 June 1942 and helped the 138th Brigade and 345th Rifle Division troops to hold on to the Sukharno and Lighthouse Ravines as long as they did. On 29 June the Germans landed on the south coast and pushed up the Trinity Ravine near Killen Bay. In the afternoon they began to penetrate the Killen Ravine. The battery and part of 8th Marine Brigade were surrounded. Battery 703 fought until it ran out of ammunition and then the crew, along with the crews of Bunkers 16 and 17, moved to Victoria Redoubt and then on to Malakhov Hill.

At 1600 hours, the Battle Report of the Maritime Army Staff was issued, detailing the German breakthrough. The northwestern side and northwestern slopes of the ridges leading to Suzdal Heights were captured. 138th Brigade, the residue of 345th Division and 8th Brigade were on the northeastern slopes of

The Third Assault (4) – 24 June to 16 July 1942 – The End of the Road

Battery 114 (703) at Suzdal Heights. The bolts were used to fasten the battery's 130mm guns to the concrete base. (Nemenko Collection)

Suzdal. The front line was held by two battalions of 7th Brigade plus the remnants of 25th Chapaevsky Division and 79th Brigade along the line of Hill 113.2–English Cemetery–Dergacheva–Trinity Hill. The 109th and 388th Divisions and 9th Brigade held the rear lines but there were no reserves behind them. German air and artillery strikes continued non-stop.

Battery 113 (702) was established on 10 December 1941, originally within the English Cemetery near the British Redoubts of the Crimean War. It was 200m from Bunkers 23 and 24, and armed with 130mm guns from the *Chervona Ukraina*. The crew of the battery was also from the ship, including its commander, Lieutenant Denisenko. The battery was under the command of 4th Battalion of 177th Artillery Regiment. In January 1942 the battery was re-designated 702 and was moved to a new location 1.5km to the rear, above the Sarandinakinu (English) Ravine. The guns were installed on permanent concrete platforms with ammunition shelters cut into the rock. The floors were covered with wood due to the lack of concrete. The guns, command post, ammunition and personnel shelters and three machine-gun bunkers were connected by underground tunnels. A dummy battery was located nearby. Major fighting took place around the battery on 29 June 1942. The battery was bombed heavily from the air. Denisenko organised a perimeter defence but when Bunker 29 and the machine-gun bunkers were destroyed the crew blew up the ammunition in the shelters, disabled the guns and withdrew.

The 386th Rifle Division was trapped. The Germans captured the height of Suzdal and were moving towards the bay side along Killen Ravine. The remnants of 772nd and 769th Rifle Regiments were ordered to attack the German flank. They were dug in on the southern slope of Killen Ravine 200–300m from Dergacheva. The remainder of the division waited for orders to break out and retreat but none came. The command staff decided to blow up the command post bunker and all the divisional documents. Soviet troops moved towards the anti-tank ditch that descended from Malakhov Hill and were stopped by German artillery on the south ridge of Killen Ravine.

Hundreds of men from 138th Brigade were hiding out in a cave, a former monastery, on the left bank of the Black River when they were attacked by the 65th Infantry Regiment and 22nd Pioneer Battalion, moving southeast from where they had built a pontoon across the mouth of the Black River. In the evening the 65th Regiment's guns arrived and were set up to fire on the caves. 3rd Marine Regiment's three battalions were reduced to a group of about 200 men. They fell back and made it to the area of the Panorama Museum and then headed towards the bay.

The Sabotage of the Inkerman Galleries

The Inkerman storage tunnels blew up at midday on 29 June, although the date is disputed. Exactly what happened is unclear. Soviet soldiers and civilians were trapped inside the tunnel by German troops. The Soviets decided to proceed with the sabotage of the tunnels, as had been done at the Sukharno arsenal on the north side. The Germans did everything possible to flush out the defenders of the galleries by dropping bombs on top and igniting barrels of gasoline near the tunnel entrances with flamethrowers. The tunnels were mined and fuses were set. A group of about seventy people moved towards the exit from Tunnel 2, one of the soldiers commenting that it was better to go out and get killed by the shells than to be buried alive. The group ran out amidst the German shelling and made it to Dergacheva to a sparkling wine factory and then to the command post in the city to report that the galleries were mined. The technical work was done by men of the 31st Rifle Regiment who planted explosives amongst the old ammunition stored in the tunnels.

Around midday there were two huge explosions. A soldier from 138th Brigade, A. Kolesnikova, wrote in his memoirs[17] that the 1st Battalion was in the caves of the monastery. The Germans were firing at them and they decided to go onto the attack. It was around noon. As soon as he stepped out of his shelter he was 'picked

The Third Assault (4) – 24 June to 16 July 1942 – The End of the Road 217

German aerial photograph showing the complete destruction of the Inkerman tunnel complex on 29 June 1942. (Author's collection)

up from the ground and with great force [thrown] into the swamp'. When he came to he was taken prisoner by the Germans. Another veteran, Evseev[18] describes the explosion:

> It occurred in the afternoon. Suddenly behind us came the strongest explosion and it was followed by another. We stopped and turned to face Sevastopol. The spectacle that I saw still stands before my eyes. Deafening explosions shook the air and followed each other at short intervals. Giant flames rose over Sevastopol and lit the whole area where the city stood.

Another memoir, by Prokhorov who was near Inkerman describes, 'A powerful double explosion. It occurred in the afternoon, on the day when the enemy started to force the Black River [i.e., the 29th] and the sky darkened, turned gray.'[19]

What would cause such a huge explosion that brought down the entire mountain? The Inkerman complex consisted of twenty-seven tunnels, fourteen tunnels on one side used as cellars by the sparkling wine factory and thirteen on the other for the storage of different types of ammunition, mines, gunpowder, etc. The other tunnels were simply large spaces; caverns, with no walls or doors and not adapted for the storage of any kind of military material. Forty-seven men from 25th Chapaevsky Division were in Tunnels 1 and 2; the medics of the 345th Division in 8, 9 and 10; the 1st Soviet hospital in Tunnel 11; a bakery in 6 and 7; a sewing shop plus a school in 12; and a shoe-shop in 13. Shells for 100mm, 130mm and 152mm guns were also stored in the tunnels.

Voyetkhov spent most of the month of June at Sevastopol, writing about the events, remaining until the end of the month. He describes the activity in the Admiralty and the preparations for evacuation:

> Late in the month the Admiralty saw a new type of activity. Radio operators carried their equipment on their shoulders and mechanics ripped wire from the walls. Typewriters were being smashed and a sack of explosives was being carried into the engine room. In every room people were burning documents, smoke spreading through the corridors. The Germans had broken through on the north side and the headquarters was being evacuated and moved to another location. The lights in the corridors began to fail. The walls glistened with damp in the light of the candles. Water dripped somewhere inside the walls.[20]

Soviet submarines arrived in the evening of 29 June and started the evacuation of property and high-ranking personnel from Sevastopol. After delivering supplies in Cossack Bay, the submarine *M-31* loaded money from the State Bank. At midnight the Sevastopol command post staff was ordered to transfer operations to Battery 35. The Black Sea Fleet Chief of Staff, Captain Vasilyeva, was ordered to move immediately to the vicinity of the battery to make preparations for the arrival of the rest of the staff.

The Soviets now created a covering line that ran close to the Crimean War Kamezh lines. It was defended by the 142nd Rifle Brigade; a company of tanks; the 773rd and 782nd Regiments of 388th Division; the 953rd Artillery Regiment and 191st Reserve Regiment. Early in the morning of 30 June, in Sector 1, 142nd Brigade, remnants of 388th Rifle Division and a company of 81st Tank Battalion were placed in reserve and took up defensive positions to cover the approaches to the airfield on Chersonese Peninsula. The 109th Division and 9th Marine Brigade (remnants of 2nd and 4th Battalions) remained in their positions. The 109th withdrew from Balaklava to shorten the line of defence and pulled back to the Karan Valley and Windmill Hill (133.7).

Voyetkhov wrote:

> Now the Russians were leaving the battlefield and the ruins by sea. A number of conferences were held among the command staff. The message was passed on that the aim of the battle ahead was to kill the greatest number of German enemy possible. Only the wounded would be evacuated. The end had come. The city was wracked by huge explosions. Everything that could not be carried away was blown up. Damaged guns were pushed into the sea to prevent them

The Third Assault (4) – 24 June to 16 July 1942 – The End of the Road

Windmill Hill in the Karan Valley. (Nemenko Collection)

falling into German hands to be used as scrap metal. Horses were drowned or shot. Step by step the Russians pulled back – sailors, gunners, cavalrymen, pilots, riflemen, women and young adults. The final battles were bloody and futile. Forced to the sea, they continued to fire on the Germans until their ammunition ran out.[21]

Overnight all vessels remaining in Sevastopol – boats, barges, tugs, trawlers, floating cranes – were destroyed or sunk by a team of naval engineers.

German plans for 30 June called for the 28th Light Division to attack the 109th Rifle Regiment at the fork of the Balaklava/Yalta road at the head of the Karan Valley then capture Maximova, Nikolayevka and the French Cemetery. From there they were to move down the road to Reed Bay, keeping the city on the right. The 170th Infantry Division was to advance along the same road in the direction of Chersonese Lighthouse and Battery 35. The 72nd Division was to move down the same road to Musketeers' Bay. 1st Rumanian Mountain Division was to bypass Balaklava and move to Windmill Hill in the Karan Valley and to St. George's Monastery. 18th Rumanian Mountain Division was to advance in the direction of the English Cemetery. 132nd and 50th Divisions would advance on the road running along Laboratory Ravine to Victoria Redoubt and then to Malakhov Hill and link up with 24th and 22nd Infantry Divisions. 4th Rumanian Mountain Division was in reserve along with 213th and 444th Regiments.

At dawn on 30 June the 28th Light Infantry Division launched an attack on the northern slopes of the Karagach height, bypassing the left flank of 4th Battalion of 9th Brigade. Another attack was launched on Maximova Farm and the Germans moved in behind the 2nd Battalion of 9th Brigade, which was located along Balaklava Highway. The 2nd Battalion broke out of its encirclement and retreated to the southwest towards the 109th Rifle Regiment's position in the direction of the Yuharinaya Ravine. By 1100 hours the Germans headed for the rear defensive lines at the former Kalf farm, which dated back to the eighteenth century.

The Germans approached the 953rd Artillery Regiment in the Yuharinaya Ravine. The battery's supporting infantry fought hard but began to run out of ammunition. The regiment's command post, in a tunnel in the ravine, was in danger of being cut off and the men retreated. Two of the battery's guns (122mm and 76mm) were placed in a hollow near the village of Karani. The remaining shells and guns were blown up and the regiment, pursued by the Germans, moved to Battery 35.

Batteries 19 and 18 were running out of ammunition. They kept firing as long as they could. German tanks broke through onto the ramparts of the former Battery 19. The crew blew up the remaining ammunition and guns and fled towards Battery 18, which continued to fire on the Germans and Rumanians in the Yuharinaya Ravine. Battery 705 was also surrounded and could not fire on the Germans because they were in a defile, out of reach of the guns. Battery 18 was called upon to provide supporting fire and some rounds landed on the Germans. Under covering fire from Battery 18 the guns of Battery 705 were destroyed and the crew headed for Battery 18. When the latter ran out of ammunition both crews withdrew to Battery 35.

Battery 111 was set up on Malakhov Hill in September 1941. Two guns from the damaged destroyer *Bezuprechnyy* were installed on temporary wooden platforms. They were to be returned to the ship after her repair. Their mission was to defend the entrance to Sevastopol Bay after Batteries 12 and 13 were dismantled. On 12 November the *Bezuprechnyy* was again hit by German bombers and completely destroyed, so the guns remained at the battery. Construction of a permanent position began and was completed in February 1942.

The components of the battery were more or less makeshift, combining new construction with that of existing Crimean War elements. The gun platforms were poured in concrete and magazines were created using concrete curbstones. Two small shelters were built on the flanks. The main magazine was in an old Crimean War shelter, and separate ones were built 80m from each of the guns. The guns were on circular platforms and they could fire both towards the land and towards

The Third Assault (4) – 24 June to 16 July 1942 – The End of the Road   221

One of the guns at Battery 111 (701) at Malakhov Hill; present day. (Nemenko Collection)

the sea. However, these guns were not ideal for firing at a flat trajectory so their main mission was to cover the sea. The guns were covered by camouflage nets. The battery was surrounded by trenches and the approaches covered by machine-gun positions. The command post of the battery was located in the old Malakhov Tower and the crews lived in barracks at the foot of the hill. The battery was defended from the air by Battery 54's 85mm AA guns located on the Kamchatsky Lunette. In February the battery was re-designated 701 and was part of 177th Separate Artillery Battalion. The command post of the battalion was in the Victoria Redoubt, 2km from Malakhov Hill. The command post was built in the old British powder magazines. The 177th also included Batteries 702 (113), 704 (115) and 703 (114). On 29 June only Battery 701 remained.

   The German assault reached the area of Victoria Redoubt and the 177th Battalion commander, Major Mozdalevsky decided to withdraw all personnel to Malakhov Hill and reorganise the defence. About forty-five men arrived from Victoria Redoubt on 30 June. Fifteen men of Battery 703 arrived from the vicinity of Suzdal Heights. The fighting for Malakhov Hill lasted throughout the day. The commander of Battery 701 was Captain Matyukhina who organised the perimeter defence. One of the battery's guns had been damaged and was repaired later in the morning. The Germans attacked with tanks and another one of the guns was damaged. Around 1100 hours about fifty more soldiers made it to the hill but by this time German machine-gunners had infiltrated to the rear of the battery and captured the damaged gun. The Soviets counter-attacked and pushed the Germans back, recapturing the gun. Forty more Soviet reinforcements arrived and the fight continued well into the evening. The Germans, using assault guns, finally captured the hill. The survivors fled toward Cape Chersonese. Major Mozdalevsky arrived at Battery 35 on 1 July and set up a field-gun battery nearby. The Major and his crew fought until 5 July when they were finally overrun and Mozdalevsky was killed.

The German 132nd Infantry Division broke through the 79th Brigade positions near Killen Ravine. The brigade was forced to retreat and ended up next to the Malakhov. By 1600 hours the remnants of the brigade defended a semicircle from the sea near Ushakova Ravine to the slopes of Malakhov hill and on to the train station. At the same time troops of 22nd Infantry Division bypassed Kamchatka Lunette and Malakhov Hill and approached the harbour. Part of the 514th and 90th Rifle Regiment retreated along the Laboratory Highway. Despite its efforts the 132nd Infantry Division failed to break through along the Laboratory Highway. General Hansen ordered 4th Rumanian Mountain Division to move that evening towards the Laboratory Highway and at 0200 hours to break through to the city railway station.

The 170th Division captured the Maximova Farm from 9th Brigade and an hour later Mykolaivka. They continued towards the Berman Ravine past the Kalf farm near the upper Turkish Redoubts. Around 1100 hours, the motorcycle company of the division's reconnaissance battalion reached Cape Fiolent. One hundred and fifty Soviet defenders at the dummy Battery 16, about 3.5km from Battery 35 on the beach of Cape Fiolent, fought a short battle then withdrew to Cossack Bay. Around 1600 hours, tanks from 170th Division appeared at the Berman farm. At the same time the Rumanian 1st Mountain Division captured Windmill Hill and moved to St. George's Monastery.

The Germans were now in a position to cut off any remaining Soviet forces in the city. The 95th and 345th Rifle Divisions were ordered to continue fighting. General Petrov ordered all available forces, by 0100 hours on 1 July, to cover the evacuation to Cape Chersonese. Defence of the city was not included in the order. However, if fighting took place it should be in the form of street fighting to inflict maximum damage on the Germans.

In late June 76mm ammunition was moved from the Sukharno arsenal to the magazine of Battery 15. About 100 soldiers put up a last stand there from 30 June to 2 July. Archaeological evidence shows the markings from grenades and bullets on the casemate walls plus fragments of 76.2mm shells and Mosin rifle cartridges.

The Third Assault (4) – 24 June to 16 July 1942 – The End of the Road

Looking towards Battery 35 and Cape Chersoneses, circa 1 July 1942. Destroyed Soviet vehicles. (Bellabs.ru)

The interior walls show evidence of marks from bullets and grenades indicating that the last fight was very fierce. The remaining ammunition was blown up on 1 July 1942.

On the evening of 30 June the Soviets began to move towards Chersonese Peninsula in orderly columns. The Germans fired artillery on the roads but caused only minor casualties. By dawn the troops approached Battery 551 at the Chersonese airfield where they took up defensive positions between Battery 35 and the lighthouse. Sevastopol was left behind. Some pockets of resistance remained, in particular in the vicinity of Cape Fiolent near St. George Monastery and Battery 18; a large group at the Maximova Farm which served as the centre of defence for Battery 702bis. A number of troops fought in scattered strongpoints. The Malakhov was abandoned. Troops that escaped converged around Battery 35.

Evacuation Plans

In the early hours of 30 June the Black Sea Fleet command decided to evacuate Sevastopol. Oktyabrsky reported that Soviet troops were tired but continued to fight heroically. Given the major reduction in firepower the base could hold out for a maximum of only two to three more days. Based on the situation, Oktyabrsky requested permission to evacuate 200 to 250 senior officers by aircraft to the Caucasus. General Petrov would remain behind in command. Oktyabrsky sent telegrams to Admiral Kuznetsov of the Navy and General Budenogo of the Army, requesting permission to evacuate. Budenogo sent a telegram to the Supreme Command (Stavka, i.e., Stalin) describing the danger to ships and that there was now no way to exert any influence on the fate of the Sevastopol Defence Area. Budenogo requested that the Military Council of the Black Sea Fleet, including Vice-Admiral Oktyabrsky, be allowed to fly to Novorossiysk and Major-General Petrov left in command at Sevastopol.

After receiving Oktyabrsky's telegram, Kuznetsov realised the dire urgency of the request. Without the consent of the Supreme Command he replied to Oktyabrsky directly that his proposal 'is fully supported'. However, he had not yet conferred with Stalin and did so soon after, receiving Stalin's support, which he passed on in a subsequent telegram to Oktyabrsky.

At 1900 hours on 30 June the Military Council of the Black Sea Fleet and the Coastal Army gathered at Battery 35 to discuss the current defence situation. It was announced that the evacuation, approved by Kuznetsov, of the council and other high-ranking individuals was to take place. However, the order for evacuation applied only to Navy personnel and not to the Army. The Coastal Army was supposed to wait for permission from Budenogo, but Petrov did not wait. Instead he appointed General Novikov as his replacement and left Sevastopol. Authorisation was obtained from Budenogo the next morning but Petrov had already left, leaving General Novikov behind. The top echelons got away as soon as they knew the base was doomed, leaving the soldiers and sailors to fend for themselves.

The destroyed 305mm turret of Battery 35. The Black Sea is in the background. (Bellabs.ru)

The Third Assault (4) – 24 June to 16 July 1942 – The End of the Road 225

Around 0130 hours on 1 July, Vice-Admiral Oktyabrsky boarded a PS-84[22] aircraft standing by near Battery 35. The rest of the Black Sea Fleet staff followed him into the sky to safety. For the next couple of hours the senior commanders quietly left the battery, following an underground passage to a nearby cove where they boarded submarine *U-209*, which left for Novorossiysk around 0300 hours. Everything went quietly and in an orderly fashion. Prior to his departure Petrov gave his final orders to the army, to continue to fight the enemy and hold the Kamezh defensive line from Cape Fiolent to Musketeers' Bay and to destroy enemy manpower and ensure the evacuation of the greatest possible number of people.

It quickly became clear to the remaining troops that the senior officers had left. What else was there to do but to also get out? Permission was requested and received to send as many ships as possible to evacuate the remaining troops to Novorossiysk and Tuapse. This order came from Marshal Budenogo. As soon as the order went out the ships headed for Sevastopol. At 0130 hours three patrol boats set out, at 0345 hours two groups of minesweepers which were also bringing in ammunition and food, and at 0700 hours a third squadron of about seven patrol boats plus an assortment of tugs, schooners and minesweepers followed. The ships were moored off of the coast near Battery 35 to make the transfers of equipment and personnel. The numbers of those loaded on the ships was pitifully small, however, and most of the troops were left behind. About 600 senior army and navy personnel were evacuated.

General Novikov, the last official commander of Sevastopol, didn't stay very long either. He left for the Caucasus by boat on the night of 1/2 July. What happened to him after that remains a mystery. One Sevastopol veteran, P. A. Vasileva, wrote about him in the memoirs. Vasileva is unsure if he left by boat or was captured near the 35th Battery, 'as many claim'. Eleventh Army capture cards show a P. G. Novikov captured at '*Ssewastopol*'.[23] Regardless, the newly-appointed commander quickly disappeared and was never seen again.

One might assume that chaos reigned afterwards but that is not the case. Another veteran, a gunner from 99th Artillery Regiment of the 25th Chapaevsky Division, Z. Oleynik, writes that people were gathered in groups around Battery 35, trying to organise their troops. All around were scattered broken boxes, suitcases. He saw a group of Soviet officers, ranks no higher than major. Another officer approached Oleynik, Colonel Grossman, who asked where he could find the division headquarters. Oleynik replied that he was also looking for it. Grossman ordered the group of officers to go with him to Battery 35. Upon arrival, it was apparent there was no command structure and no one in particular was giving orders.[24] All command within the remaining combat units rested on the initiatives of the individual commanders. There is little mention of any general orders given by Novikov with the exception of his efforts to create a second line of defence between Kamyshovaya Bay and the coast. Despite the lack of communications, the Soviets established a second line of defence.

Later on, a meeting of senior commanders and political officers was held at the battery. They all agreed to continue the fight and to organise an army command and an orderly evacuation. According to the memoirs of D. I. Piskunova:

> No one wanted to step up and become head of the army, citing their lack of skills and authority to establish a command. Brigade Commissar Aron Khatskevich spoke up and volunteered to head the Coastal Army and to do everything to evacuate the troops. He asked if anyone would join him. Several officers, including Colonel Grossman of the 25th Chapaevsky Division, agreed to help the commissar. The group named themselves the Military Council of the Coastal Army. The remaining officers present at the meeting gave their consent and their word to follow Khatskevich's orders. He was named Chairman of the Military Council and Commander of the Coastal Army.

The council's first list of duties included:

- Find an alternate location for the command post.
- Establish communications with Novorossiysk.
- Leave the communications centre at Battery 35 and ensure its protection.
- Discuss evacuation with Novorossiysk.

Colonel Grossman, commander of the defences, set up his command post in Battery 16. A radio station to establish contact with the troops at the front was set up at Battery 35. Brigade Commissar Khatskevich set up his command post in the tunnels along the western coast at Cape Theophane and established communications with the troops. Just the knowledge that a command-and-control structure was re-established must have been somewhat of a relief for the troops. Up until the point when they started to receive direction from Colonel Grossman, the front was in chaos. The troops desperately needed someone to tell them what to do.

Surprisingly, on 2 July Soviet troops launched an offensive. It was completely accidental. The Germans attacked first in the direction of the Chersoneses Lighthouse. The Luftwaffe and artillery barrage started at 1000 hours. Aircraft bombed Soviet troops and artillery positions at Kamyshovaya and Musketeers' Bays, Battery 35 and Chersonese airfield. The Germans approached the Soviet line and opened fire with mortars on the front line of troops who, instead of running,

The Third Assault (4) – 24 June to 16 July 1942 – The End of the Road

proceeded to rush the Germans. This was a complete surprise and the Germans retreated. Oleynik writes:

> It all happened suddenly and unexpectedly. You can forget its name but the details of the battle are impossible to forget. I remember when we studied the tactics of infantry, I was in various positions and it was my first frontal attack, in which I ran, screaming, shooting, obeying the instinct of self-defence, very little realising what was happening. That's how it was. Enemy fire escalated. Suddenly someone shouted from behind, 'Transporters with infantry! Armoured cars!' We spotted a formation of six armoured cars packed with enemy infantry coming down the hill. The cars did a U-turn and we spotted a 75mm cannon hitched to one of the cars. The soldiers quickly jumped off the armoured cars and some of them disengaged the cannon; the rest took cover, ready to attack. Someone shouted 'Forward for the Motherland! Hurrah!' Our troops rose up in a group, shouting and tore up the hill towards the Germans, who began to turn and run, leaving behind the cannons. I shouted: 'Gunners to the guns!' When I ran to the guns, one of them had already fired at the Germans.[25]

This episode is described by many veterans and clearly indicates the Soviets captured three enemy guns.

On 2 July the Soviets re-established a line covering the evacuation from the coast below Battery 35 to Musketeers' Bay. German records agree, declaring that the Germans used the brief respite to regroup and to suppress pockets of resistance. The 170th Infantry Division continued to battle Soviet remnants in the Yuharinaya ravine and the anti-aircraft batteries. LIV Corps swept through the city. XXX Corps continued to battle resisters north and east of Balosova (m. Victory Park) and on the eastern shore of the bay. They reported that around noon the Soviets launched a surprise attack in Upper Reed Bay and that the 318th Rifle Regiment was forced to withdraw 1.5km. The sweep of Yuharinaya Ravine was completed by the end of the day.

On 3 July Soviet troops were moving to Cossack Bay to await the evacuation ships. At 0300 hours the German 318th and 360th Regiments, along with units of the 170th and 72nd Divisions, approached the bay. German boats armed with artillery and heavy machine guns entered Reed Bay and fired on the flank of Soviet troops defending the centre and left wing, forcing them to pull back. The Soviets counter-attacked but were unable to retake their previous positions. At the same time German tanks advanced on Yuharinaya ravine and broke through the Soviet front, moving on to Reed Bay and, together with German gun boats, defeated Soviet forces operating in Musketeers and Reed Bay. By mid-afternoon the Soviet line ran from the upper reaches of Reed Bay to the coast below Battery 35, the location of the dummy battery. At night Soviet troops attempted to break through to the mountains to join the partisans but most of the attempts were unsuccessful.

On 4 July the 105th Infantry Regiment stormed the dummy Battery 16, 170th Division stormed the former Crimean War line covering Cape Chersonese, and 57th Regiment and 9th Battalion of the 170th took Battery 35. The eight-hour fight for the Chersonese airfield ended at noon. German tanks swarmed across the airfield and German boats moved in on the lighthouse and captured Soviet troops taking refuge there. They then moved along the coast and began to flush Soviet troops out of the caves and crevices in the cliffs. On 5 July the Germans continued their sweep of the area, taking approximately 2,000 more prisoners. The 1st and 4th Rumanian Mountain Divisions launched a major operation against the guerrillas. On 6 July the sweep of the cliffs continued.

On the night of 6 to 7 July two large groups of Soviet troops attempted to fight their way out from Cossack Bay. At midnight, a group composed of men from the 25th Chapaevsky Division attempted to break through to Cape Chersonese and then to Yuharinaya Ravine where they planned to head into the mountains to join the partisans but almost all of them were killed at Cossack Bay.

The Germans continued their sweep of the vicinity of Battery 35 from 9 to 12 July. They also started sending troops to other German fronts. The German heavy guns were dismantled and shipped out. Hundreds of Soviet troops hiding out in

Battery 19 at Balaklava; present day. (Sergey Anaskevitch Collection)

caves ran out of food and water and were forced to surrender. The last mention in the records of a sweep of Cape Chersonese and Fiolent is on 16 July in which twenty-two prisoners were taken. Therefore, out of respect for these twenty-two men, it should be said that the Second Defence of Sevastopol ended on 16 July 1942.

Chapter 10

Conclusions

The Third Assault of Sevastopol lasted for twenty-eight days. It was the greatest battle in terms of the use of destructive material in the Second World War. German artillery fired over 1.6 million shells of all calibres and VIII Air Corps flew 23,751 missions and dropped 21,000 tons of bombs. Over 3,500 permanent or field fortifications (trenches, earth-timber emplacements, bunkers, etc.) were captured.

Captured materiel included 467 guns, twenty-six tanks, eighty-six anti-tank guns and sixty-nine anti-aircraft guns, 758 mortars and an untold number of rifles and other small arms. One hundred and twenty-three Soviet aircraft were shot down and eighteen were destroyed on the ground. The Germans suffered over 27,000 casualties, including 4,327 dead and 1,591 missing. The Rumanians

The buried gun barrels of Battery 30. (NARA)

lost 1,597 dead and 277 missing. Soviet personnel losses were calculated by the Germans to be an approximately equal number.

The attack on Sevastopol was the most difficult one launched against fortified positions in the Second World War, including even the attack on the Maginot Line in 1940. The terrain alone made conditions very favourable for the defence. The Soviets were given several months before and during the battle to prepare their defences, relatively undisturbed, creating a dense and powerful defensive system. Finally, the Soviets were able to deliver supplies and men to Sevastopol by sea, up until the end of June 1942.

Vice-Admiral Oktyabrsky wrote in *The Heroic Defence of Sevastopol, Heroism of a City*: 'On July 3, Soviet troops withdrew from the city. The Germans marched in over mountains of their own dead. It was for them a Pyrrhic victory – they cannot deny that. They lost much and gained a heap of ruins.' He stated that Sevastopol was a naval base built to combat an enemy fleet. Its entire system of defence was based on the ability to counter amphibious landings, but the Soviets were confronted by an enemy fighting mainly with land forces. They only had a short time prior to the arrival of the Germans to prepare their defences. The guns of the heavy, long-range coastal batteries, built to defend against an attack from the sea, were reversed to fire landward. Pillboxes, blockhouses and anti-tank obstacles were built on the approaches to the base. Soviet air forces played a significant factor in the defence, subjecting German troops to heavy bombardment.

Oktyabrsky noted the importance of the 'remarkable' liaison between the army and navy. The defence of the base would have been impossible without the army. It was a 'graphic example of the coordination between the army and navy with its coastal artillery, anti-air defence system, ships, auxiliary units, etc'. From 30 October 1941 to the final day, the Red Army and Black Sea Fleet units disputed every inch of Soviet soil. The Black Sea Fleet took part in repulsing German attacks with the active support of heavy gunfire from the ships. The ships were unable to provide full support during the third assault because of lack of air cover to protect them. The airfields, constantly bombarded and shelled by mortars, were unable to support a large number of aircraft. This gave the Germans command of the air and prevented Soviet ships from taking a more active role.

The Germans assembled a 'colossal' force and counted on capturing Sevastopol in three days. The generals miscalculated and suffered such heavy losses they had to call for reinforcements. The defence was exceptionally stubborn. Anything from fifteen to twenty attacks were repulsed daily. German units quickly became understrength. For example, in 50th Infantry Division the effective strength in officers and men did not exceed two regiments. The Germans had to bring in the two remaining regiments of 46th Infantry Division from Kerch. German soldiers who surrendered to the Soviets testified: 'When we transferred to Sevastopol from the Kerch Peninsula we were in high spirits. Our officers told us: "We'll take Sevastopol in three days." We believed that this would be so, but Sevastopol turned out to be "Journey's End" for most of us and we understood that this was not Belgium, nor was it France.' The German heavy siege artillery fired several hundred thousand shells (37,000 shells in the first two days). The Germans were firmly convinced that their aircraft and artillery fire had 'exterminated every living thing in Sevastopol, but what was their astonishment and alarm when the "dead" trenches came to life and answered the German onslaught with death-dealing fire. They did not enter Sevastopol on 10 June as planned'.

The Admiral believed that, although the Soviets withdrew from Sevastopol, the laurels of victory belonged to them.

> In spite of the fact that we were blockaded from the sea, cut off from overland communications in the rear, confined on a small strip of Soviet territory, small even in comparison with the size of the Crimea, we did not for a second feel alone, cut off from the Motherland or doomed. We were ever conscious of the support of the whole country, conscious of the care and attention of our leader, Comrade Stalin. Our brother's in-arms from the Baltic, the North Sea, the Pacific, the Amur, the Caspian, workers from all districts and regions of the Soviet Union, gave us their moral support and this augmented our strength, increasing it tenfold.

E. Vilensky, a Sevastopol veteran, writes in *Their Fame Will Never Die* that the 'vast and arduous work of directing the military operations of tens of thousands of men devolved on Vice-Admiral Oktyabrsky; the heart and brains of the Sevastopol defence'. He is described as a 'gifted and fiery seaman; excellent organiser and exacting commander'. The defence of Sevastopol, which ranged from Black Sea Fleet warships to infantrymen, was a complex task. Oktyabrsky directed defensive operations 'with the valour of a seaman and the spirit of a patriot'.

Vilensky states that Oktyabrsky and Petrov 'complemented one another perfectly and worked together with rare harmony, making a single powerful team'. There was not a person in Sevastopol who did not know General Petrov. He spent very little time at the command post and at HQ. The rest of the time he was at the front among the men. 'When people asked where Petrov was at the given moment, the answer would invariably be: wherever the fighting is fiercest.' Petrov was very popular among the people of Sevastopol and was respected and loved by all his men, who 'performed truly astounding deeds of heroism'. General Morgunov 'commanded men whom he himself had taken in hand, trained and drilled. A veteran artilleryman, he was like a father to his men, bound to them by the strongest friendship of the service.'

Conclusions 233

Alexei Nikolayevich Tolstoy (no relation to Leo Tolstoy), a Soviet writer, described the end of the fighting and its consequences:

> The flag over Sevastopol was lowered on the night of July 2. During the final days of the defence of the city – a city whose traditions reflect glory on Russia – the garrison, with wrath burning high and utter disregard for death, fought tooth and nail in the suburbs and streets of Sevastopol in order to gain a few more hours in which to evacuate the troops and civilian population and to make the Germans pay still more dearly for the beloved city they were surrendering.

Tolstoy stated that the Germans had every advantage on their side to finish Sevastopol in a few days but had to instead 'scramble over the mountains of their own dead and storm the city or to be mowed down by the machine guns'.

The defenders' task was to divert and tie down as large as possible a force of the enemy, to 'maul them and exterminate them and thus to upset Hitler's plans for a spring offensive'. Tolstoy compares Sevastopol to Verdun in 1916, in which the Germans senselessly sent their divisions to their slaughter. Afterwards the Germans were never able to stop the bleeding.

The destroyed transformer station of Battery 30. (NARA)

What spoils were left to the Germans? Several authors claim that 100,000 prisoners were taken at Cape Chersonese. This was not so, even according to German records. The Germans approached the evacuation line but stopped and waited. The Soviets were finished. There was no sense in losing any more men. There were some Soviet counter-attacks but they had no effect. The 142nd Rifle Brigade and 388th Rifle Division troops maintained their position and were eventually captured. German documents show that about 87,000 people were captured. Of those, about 21,000 were wounded or were local residents. About 16,000 of those reported in the documents were captured on 29 to 30 June, leaving about 50,000 combatants placed into captivity. Of these, several small groups continued to fight in the city and did not evacuate.

The Rumanians report that 9,875 prisoners were captured at Cape Fiolent and Balaklava. About 1,500 were taken in the area of Maximova; 3,500 captured on the slopes of Sapun Ridge; 2,500 in the city; 1,500 at the location of the modern Victory Park around the former Battery 24 and 1,200 in Battery 14. That leaves about 30,000 troops at Cape Chersonese. The documents of 170th Infantry Division indicate 36,000 captives of which 9,000 were civilians. Of the remaining 27,000, 3,500 were officers; most of the rest were from special or artillery units.

Aftermath

Eleventh Army fought its campaign at Sevastopol from early autumn 1941 until mid-summer 1942. It did not take part in *Fall Blau* when Army Group South attacked towards the Caucasus and Stalingrad. Nevertheless Sevastopol was taken. For his achievements in this battle, Manstein was promoted to field marshal. Adolf Hitler also authorised the Crimean Shield to commemorate the efforts of the Eleventh Army. It was a costly victory, however: Eleventh Army's casualties and material losses were so high that it was no longer a viable fighting force in its own right. Manstein recommended that it either cross the straits of Kerch and push into the Kuban area to aid in the capture of Rostov or be placed into Army Group South's reserve. Instead, part of Eleventh Army, along with the heavy siege train, was transferred to Army Group North to oversee the reduction of Leningrad. Manstein went with them. The remainder of Eleventh Army was divided between Army Group Centre and Army Group South. Eleventh Army was officially deactivated on 21 November 1942 and was used to form the newly-created Army Group Don.

This breakup of Eleventh Army had dire consequences for Germany, particularly during the Battle of Stalingrad. Although Sixth Army had managed to capture most of the city, it would have benefitted from the addition of several more infantry divisions to take the city completely. Sixth Army was not reinforced because no troops were available in the region to support them. The Soviets counter-attacked on both sides of Sixth Army and destroyed the Rumanian Third and Fourth Armies. The Soviet armies linked up, surrounding and ultimately destroying the Sixth Army. Had Eleventh Army been available as a reserve, it could have reinforced Sixth Army or at least plugged the gap as soon as the Red Army had broken through the Rumanian lines.

Everything remaining of value at Sevastopol was destroyed by the Soviets. The paraphrased words from the Crimean Guidebook of 1876 seem very fitting once again to describe Sevastopol in July 1942:

> All of Sevastopol's value lay in its historical past. It was once again only famous for its historical ruins. There was almost no population and from many houses gaped broken windows and broken walls. The whole city is littered with new graves; wherever you go, you will stumble on them everywhere. Sevastopol is once again a dead town; a city of the dead.

Notes

Introduction
1. The Light Brigade was ordered to pursue a retreating Russian artillery battery. Due to a miscommunication, the Light Brigade instead was sent to attack a well-prepared, well-defended battery.
2. The invasion of France was called *Fall Gelb* – Case Yellow. It was Manstein's plan.
3. Sevastopol was technically not a siege. That is defined at Dictionary.com as: The act or process of surrounding and attacking a fortified place in such a way as to isolate it from help and supplies for the purpose of lessening the resistance of the defenders and thereby making capture possible.' (Dictionary.com). Sevastopol was not surrounded completely or isolated from help.
4. Several women, especially snipers and machine gunners, are mentioned in Soviet accounts. Maria Baida, a nurse who swapped her medical kit for an automatic rifle, went to fight on the front lines. Sergeant-Major Ludmilla Pavlichenko, one of the Red Army's top snipers, recorded over 300 kills.
5. Hereinafter referred to as 'earth-timber'.

Chapter 1
1. Fuhrer Directives: 21 – Doc ID 1547, German History in Documents and Images – germanhistorydocs.ghi-dc.org/; 33 – Doc # 128, p. 181, Vol XIII, Documents on German Foreign Policy, 1918-1945, Series D, U.S.G.P.O, Washington D.C., 1954; 34 – ibid, Doc # 164 p. 235.
2. Kuznetzov's comment comes from *It Will Never Fade* – Memoirs of Marshal Nikolai I. Krylov – House of USSR Academy of Science, 1963. Taken from militaria.lib.ru/kyrlov1/
3. The Turkish Wall extended from the Gulf of Perekop to the Siwash. It was guarded by three forts, the largest being the Op-Kapu Fortress. It was first built in the fifth century by the Scythians, though some accounts say it was the eleventh century. Its form as it appeared in 1941 was built to protect Russian from raids by the Crimean Tatars in the seventeenth century. Construction began in April 1647 and continued until 1655. It consisted mainly of a ditch, trapezoidal in shape, with an average base of 6m, height of 4.3m and a slope of 25 to 30 degrees. A watchtower was placed every few kilometres. Its depth in some places was as much as 15m and 15m in width. It was repaired by the British and French in 1920 and consisted of three lines of trenches and barbed wire with seventy guns and 150 machine guns. On 8 November 1920 the Red Army crossed through the Litovsky Peninsula. The ditch was flanked and captured.
4. The 'Ziegler Brigade', as it was known, was composed of the motorised elements of German and Rumanian units that had broken through at Perekop. The exact makeup of the brigade is confusing, depending on which account is used. Several historians refer to it as 'hastily assembled', but several of the units were already in existence at the time. It was not much of a 'combined' brigade as the Germans and Rumanians operated independently.
5. LIV Armeekorps Kriegstagebuch, 1 Sep 1 – 31 Oct 1941; National Archives of the United States, Microfilm Item 21711/1, Roll 1339.

Chapter 2

1. 'The Earliest Charts of Akhtiar (Sevastopol)', *Imago Mundi: The International Journal for the History of Cartography*, Vol 52, Issue 1 (2000), pp. 112–23.
2. This is the fifteenth-century Mangup fortress of Kalamita.
3. George Dodd, *Pictorial History of the Russian War 1854-6*, London & Edinburgh: W & R Chambers, 1856, p. 230.
4. Potemkin also claims this distinction for appreciating the quality of the harbour as a fortified place. 'Like a haven', Suvorov wrote, 'Not only in the Crimea but in all of the Black Sea there is none like it'. G. von Fuchs, *Suvorows Korrespondenz, 1799*, Glogan, 1835.
5. The defences were built on the present location of Fort Constantine.
6. *History of the City of Sevastopol*, n.d., p. 27.
7. Ibid, p. 28.
8. John Buchan Teller, *The Crimean Transcaucasia: Being the Narrative of a Journey in the Kouban, in Gouria, Georgia, Armenia, Ossety, Imeritia, Swannety and Mingrelia and in the Tauric Range*, Volume 2, London: H. S. King & Company, 1876.
9. Ibid, p. 202.
10. Named for Colonel V. G. Gasfort, commander of the Kazan Regiment of 16th Infantry Division, who held the hill in the winter/spring of 1855.
11. Named for Marshal Canrobert, commander of French forces at Sevastopol in 1854 to 1855.
12. Named for a mechanical telegraph station during the Crimean War.
13. Florence Nightingale stayed in one of the monastery's apartments during the Crimean War.
14. Named for Lieutenant-General Sir George Cathcart, 45th Division, killed at Inkerman on 5 November 1854. He was buried on the hill.
15. The village of Bartenevkoy was named after Captain Bartenev.
16. A round tower built of masonry. Martello towers were originally built by the Genoese as defensive towers for cannons.
17. Krupp was the primary manufacturer of steel and armaments in Europe, including cannons and gun turrets. Krupp supplied weapons to European and Asian countries from the early 1800s up to the Second World War.
18. Named for Admiral Pavel Nakhimov (1802–55), one of Russia's most famous admirals. He was commander of naval and land forces during the Crimean War. He was shot by a sniper while inspecting Malakhov Kurgan and died two days later.
19. Battery 15 was also known as Fort Strelets.
20. Filipp Sergeyevich Oktyabrsky was the commander of the Black Sea Fleet from March 1939 to April 1943 and again from March 1944 to November 1948.
21. General Morgunov was commander of the coastal defences at Sevastopol.
22. Sevastopol's Guard Regiment 1, numbering 1,595 men, was assigned to defend the main base of the Black Sea Fleet. The Regiment was based in the former Royal Barracks, Battery 4 on the North side.
23. Located at Mykolaivka north of the Alma; technically outside the Sevastopol perimeter
24. Report, Search Group Coastal Defence (2010–2014), litsovet.ru
25. Vaneev provides another figure altogether, stating that, by the beginning of the battle for Sevastopol (30 October 1941), a total of seventy-five artillery bunkers and 232 machine-gun bunkers were built, plus an anti-tank ditch of 32.5km and about 10,000 mines. But in the appendices to his book the numbers are different and indicate twenty-eight bunkers in the forward line, forty-three in the main line and twenty-five in the rear, totalling ninety-six. Historians claim seventy-four bunkers were built at Sevastopol plus eight in Balaklava for a total of eighty-two. If we look at the platoons assigned to defend each bunker group, we come up with the following:

1st Control Group of Bunkers (total twenty)

- 1st Platoon – Bunkers 15, 16, 17, 18, 19 (five)
- 2nd Platoon – Bunkers 20, 21, 22, 23, 24, 25, 26 (seven)
- 3rd Platoon – Bunkers 27, 28, 46 (three)
- 4th Platoon – Bunkers 14, 40, 41, 42, 43 (five)

2nd Control Group of bunkers (total twenty)

- 1st Platoon – Bunkers 1, 2, 35, 36, 37, 45 (six)
- 2nd Platoon – Bunkers 3, 4, 5, 7, 8, 39 (six)
- 3rd Platoon – Bunkers 9, 10, 11, 12, 13 (five)
- 4th Platoon – Bunkers 6, 38, 44 (three)

3rd Control Group of bunkers (total five)

- 1st Platoon – Bunkers 76, 77 (two)
- 2nd Platoon – Bunkers 51, 52, 78 (three)

4th Control Group of bunkers (total ten)

- 1st Platoon – Bunkers 54, 55, 56 (three)
- 2nd Platoon – Bunkers 57, 58, 75 (three)
- 3rd Platoon – Bunkers 53, 59 (two)
- 4th Platoon – Bunkers 60, 61 (two)

5th Control Group of bunkers (total eleven)

- 1st Platoon – Bunkers 64, 65, 66, 67, 68 (five)
- 2nd Platoon – Bunkers 69, 70, 71, 73 (four)
- 3rd Platoon – Bunkers 72, 74 (two)

6th Control Group of bunkers (total six)

- 1st Platoon – Bunkers 29, 30, 31, 32, 33, 34 (six)
- 7th Control Group of Bunkers (Balaklava) – eight bunkers

Grand Total: eighty-four.

Chapter 3

1. Ilya Ehrenburg, 'Sevastopol', published in *The Heroic Defence of Sevastopol*, Moscow: Foreign Language Publishing House, 1942, p. 15. Ehrenburg was a Soviet writer and journalist.
2. Ibid.
3. While Battery 54 was part of a Sevastopol unit, the 1st Separate Artillery Regiment, technically it was outside the Sevastopol defensive zones; yet this particular action is sometimes considered the initial date of the first attack on the naval base. Therefore, 30 October is often cited as the beginning of the First Assault. For our purpose, we will consider the First Assault to have begun on 31 October.
4. Evgeny I. Zhidilova. *We Defended Sevastopol*, 1977.
5. The VMUBO battalion never deployed as far as Aranka, leaving that part of the Kacha Valley undefended.

6. The *Ordzhonikidzevets* was named for Grigory Ordzhonikidze, who organised workers at the Sevastopol Marine Plant. He was later a close associate of Joseph Stalin.
7. A field work used extensively by the Soviets at Sevastopol. It consisted of a dugout into the earth or rock, covered over with wooden beams and then an additional layer of earth or rocks.
8. Soviet sources claim 10th Battery destroyed twenty armoured vehicles, twenty other vehicles and killed 200 German troops. German reports admitted casualties but not on the same scale.
9. Boris Voyetkhov, *The Last Days of Sevastopol*, New York: Alfred A. Knopf, 1943, pp. 77–8.
10. Named for Vasiliy Ivanovich Chapaev, hero of the Civil War, commander of the 25th Rifle Division. He was killed in 1919.
11. Севастопольский оборонительный район (COP) – *Sevastopol'skiy oboronitel'nyy rayon*.
12. Nearby is a grave where the crew was buried.
13. The medieval road, updated by Russian engineers in 1875, is the shortest route from Bakhchisarai to Inkerman. The road was again updated in 1939, but only a 4km stretch to Mackenzie Farm was completed, at the end of which were a small homestead and a watchtower.
14. Coastal Defence Search Group (Sevastopol) Report, 2010, www.litsovet.ru
15. Armistice Day is celebrated in Western countries to signify the end of the First World War One at 1100 hours on 11 November 1918.
16. *The Heroic Defence of Sevastopol, City Nights*, Part III, Chapter 1, p. 99.
17. Ibid.
18. *The Heroic Defence of Sevastopol, The Brave Gunners*, Part I, Chapter 4, p. 28.

Chapter 4
1. Nikolai Krylov, *Never Fade – Memoirs of Nikolai Krylov*, Moscow: Military Publishing, 1984 – militera.lib.ru/krylov1
2. Military Literature Memoirs, T. K. Kolomiec, Major General, Former Commander of the 25th Infantry Division Chapaev, *Chapaevites*, http://militera.lib.ru/memo/russian/sb_ognennye_dni_sevastopolya/31.html]
3. Memoirs, Soviet Archives, Dr. Alexander Nemenko Collection.
4. Ibid.
5. *The Heroic Defence of Sevastopol, City Nights*, Part III, Chapter 1, pp. 99–100.
6. *The Heroic Defence of Sevastopol*, Part I, Chapter 3, *The Brigade of Stout Hearts*, by Captain-Lieutenant Aposhansky, pp. 19–20.
7. The Belbek Valley bunkers were destroyed during the Second Assault and their numbers were used for bunkers on the Suzdal Heights in the spring of 1942.

Chapter 5
1. Zoe Smirnova-Medvedeva, *Scorched Youth*, Moscow: Military Publishing, 1967, cited in Alexander Nemenko, *Chronicle of the Second Defense*, Part 2, Chapter 18 – http://samlib.ru/n/nemenko_a_w/sevas02.shtml, page number unknown.
2. Oberkommando des Heeres, *Nachtrag zu dem Denkschriften über fremde Landbefestigungen*, Berlin, 1943.
3. This presented a problem since the shell casings were collected and reloaded and eventually became worn out from re-use.
4. Voyetkhov, *The Last Days of Sevastopol*, p. 117.
5. *The Heroic Defence of Sevastopol*, Part III, The Besieged Fortress, Chapter 3, The Underground Factory, p. 109.
6. Ibid.
7. P. I. Musyakov, *Feat Thirtieth Battery*, Moscow: Military Publishing, 1961. Cited in Alexander Nemenko, *Chronicle of the Second Defence*, Part 2, Chapter 18 – http://samlib.ru/n/nemenko_a_w/sevas02.shtml, page number unknown.

8. LIV Armeekorps Anlagenteil 3 z. KTB 4, National Archives of the United States Item 21711/16, Microfilm Roll 1344.
9. Report Search Group (Sevastopol) Coastal Defence for 2012, www.litsovet.ru
10. The Soviets claimed that many of the bunkers were blown up after the war to dispose of ammunition left inside but this is only true for about 20 per cent. The rest were destroyed during the assault, a fact the Soviets did not want to publicise.

Chapter 6

1. Some documents say nine batteries, but most likely the figure of seven is correct with Batteries 1, 2, 3, 6, 7, 8 and 9. The report indicates Batteries 4 and 5 were destroyed in the Mekenzievy Mountains.
2. LIV Armeekorps Anlagenteil 3 z. KTB 4, National Archives of the United States Item 21711/16, Microfilm Roll 1344.
3. G. I. Vaneev, *Sevastopol 1941-1942, Chronicle of the Heroic Defence*, Book 1, Kiev: Vydatelstro, 1995. Cited in Alexander Nemenko, *Chronicle of the Second Defence*, Part 3, Chapter 24 – http://samlib.ru/n/nemenko_a_w/sevjanv.shtml, page number unknown.
4. *My Memoirs*, House of U.S.S.R. Academy of Science, 1963.
5. *50 Years in the Ranks*, no further information.
6. Smirnova-Medvedeva, *Scorched Youth*. Cited in Alexander Nemenko, *Chronicle of the Second Defence*, Part 3, Chapter 24 http://samlib.ru/n/nemenko_a_w/sevjanv.shtml, page number unknown.
7. Voyetkhov, *The Last Days of Sevastopol*, p. 146.
8. Ibid, p. 104.

Chapter 7

1. Ehrenburg, 'Sevastopol', p. 15.
2. Ibid, p. 16.
3. Kriegstagebuch 8, Teil I u. II. US National Archives Item No. 21711/32/33, Microfilm Roll 1348.
4. German sources indicate it started at 0600 hours. The German time used was, in fact, daylight-saving time, which explains the difference.
5. Ivan A. Laskin, *On the Way to the Fracture*, Moscow: Military Publishing, 1977. Cited in Nemenko, Alexander, *Chronicle of the Second Defence*, Part 3, Chapter 24 – http://samlib.ru/n/nemenko_a_w/sevjanv.shtml, page number unknown.
6. Ibid.
7. Records of the 22nd German Infantry Division indicate that on 7 June 1942, six prisoners were captured: one lieutenant and five men of the 6th Company, 2nd Battalion of the 514th Rifle Regiment.
8. Upended railway tracks.
9. G. I. Vaneev, *Sevastopol 1941-1942: A Chronicle of the Heroic Defence*, Kiev: Vydatelstro, 1995, Cited in Alexander Nemenko, *Chronicle of the Second Defence*, Part 3, Chapter 24 – http://samlib.ru/n/nemenko_a_w/sevjanv.shtml, page number unknown.
10. Laskin, *On the Way to the Fracture*. Cited in Alexander Nemenko, *Chronicle of the Second Defense*, Part 3, Chapter 24 – http://samlib.ru/n/nemenko_a_w/sevjanv.shtml, page number unknown.
11. Vaneev, *Sevastopol 1941-1942: A Chronicle of the Heroic Defence*. Cited in Alexander Nemenko, *Chronicle of the Second Defence*, Part 3, Chapter 24 – http://samlib.ru/n/nemenko_a_w/sevjanv.shtml, page number unknown.
12. Laskin, *On the Way to the Fracture*. Cited in Alexander Nemenko, *Chronicle of the Second Defence*, Part 3, Chapter 24 – http://samlib.ru/n/nemenko_a_w/sevjanv.shtml, page number unknown.

13. The farm is called *Blagodat* in Russian.
14. Account from a gunner at 80th Battery, name unknown, Nemenko collection.
15. Pyanzin would go on to command Battery 365 when Lieutenant Matveev was wounded.
16. Kolomiec Memoirs, Nemenko collection.
17. Voyetkhov, *The Last Days of Sevastopol*, pp. 58–60.
18. Pairs of 130mm guns from *Chervona Ukraina* were installed in four batteries at Sevastopol. Eight other guns were kept as replacements for worn-out barrels. In fact the barrels held out very well, lasting up to 178 per cent of their expected life. The barrels of Batteries 703 and 704 were replaced in February 1942. Some 750 sailors from the cruiser *Chervona Ukraina* fought in Sevastopol's land batteries. It was an incredible feat.
19. Battery 704 was located in what is now the Mekenzievy Cemetery. The 130mm gun platform is located on a hilltop in the corner of the cemetery. The second gun platform and the underground magazines were 200m away. A mass grave is located a few metres to the southeast. Men from Battery 704, 95th, 345th, 368th and 40th Cavalry Division, plus 79th Brigade, 287th Regiment of 25th Division, 2nd Perekop Regiment, 25th Tank Battalion, 3rd Mortar Battery, 8th and 7th Marine Brigades are buried here.
20. Zhidilova had arrived on the north side with about 1,000 men and on 20 June barely 100 men limped back to the south side.
21. Paul Carell, *Hitler's War on Russia – Hitler Moves East*, London: Little Brown & Company, 1964, p. 225.
22. Prior to the capture of Bunker 55 in the Duvankoi strongpoint the gun was removed during the withdrawal by the 80th Independent Reconnaissance Battalion. Later it was mounted behind Bunker 11 and the position was designated 11A.
23. Forts Siberia, Volga and Stalin were shelled by the heavy gun Dora and not much remains of them today.
24. Kolomiec Memoirs, Nemenko collection.
25. Kriegstagebuch 8, Teil I u. II. US National Archives Item No. 21711/32/33, Microfilm Roll 1348
26. Manstein, *Lost Victories*, p. 250.

Chapter 8
1. Ehrenburg, 'Sevastopol', p. 16.
2. Ibid, pp. 17–18.
3. An entrance to a fortification that, after a few metres, turns at a 90-degree angle. A defensive casemate is located at the point of the turn.
4. *Nachtrag zu dem Denkschriften über fremde Landesbefestigung*, Berlin: 1943, p. 91.
5. Kuznetzov Memoirs, Soviet Archives, Nemenko Collection.
6. The former Crimean War position, Mamelon Hill, located about 1km southeast of Malakhov Hill.
7. While this explanation seems unclear, it is as clear as it gets.
8. Voyetkhov, *The Last Days of Sevastopol*, pp. 154–5, 187–97.
9. The road crossed the top of the ravines past North Fort and swung around to the west, then south across radio hill to the western side of the bay.
10. Memories of P. P. Smetanina, Memoirs, Soviet Archives, Nemenko Collection.
11. Their bodies were found forty years later.

Chapter 9
1. The warehouses at Sukharno and Lighthouse arsenals, as well as other defensive position, such as bunkers and batteries, were mined in March 1942. However, it appears from Soviet records that the galleries at Sukharno were cleared of their charges for fear of sabotage.

242   The Defence of Sevastopol 1941–1942

2. There are several 'tales' about what happened to the train during the German occupation. Some accounts state that parts of the train were restored and it was renamed *Prinz Eugen* and equipped with 105mm howitzers. In 1944 it supposedly participated in fighting at Perekop and Ishun during the Soviet offensive to recapture Crimea. This is unlikely due to the extent of damage to the train cars. Photos exist of cars from an armoured train on a siding at Inkerman, possibly the *Zhelezniakov*. There are also photographs of a second armoured train at Sevastopol, the *Gronyak*, but there is no information about this train.
3. The ship was finished off by German aircraft in the harbour on 2 July.
4. Voyetkhov, *The Last Days of Sevastopol*, p. 216.
5. Sevastopol Bay or Severnaya Bay as translated.
6. Petr A. Morgunov, *Geroicheskii Sevastopol*, Moscow: Nauka, 1979. Cited in Alexander Nemenko, *Chronicle of the Second Defence*, Part 3, Chapter 29 – http://samlib.ru/n/nemenko_a_w/sevjanv.shtml, page number unknown.
7. I. S. Manoshin, *Heroic Tragedy of the Last Days of Sevastopol, June 29 – July 12, 1942*, Simferopol: Tavrida Publishing, 2001.
8. Kriegstagebuch F x. TB, Feindlage, Apr 1 – Jul 10, 1942, National Archives of the United States, Item 21585/1, Microfilm Roll 781.
9. Coordinates from the German tactical map – *Stellungenskarte, Stand vom 17.5.42*, map 864287.
10. Morgunov, *Geroicheskii Sevastopol*. Cited in Alexander Nemenko, *Chronicle of the Second Defence*, Part 3, Chapter 29 – http://samlib.ru/n/nemenko_a_w/sevjanv.shtml, page number unknown.
11. Manoshin, *Heroic Tragedy of the Last Days of Sevastopol*. Cited in Alexander Nemenko, *Chronicle of the Second Defence*, Part 3, Chapter 29 – http://samlib.ru/n/nemenko_a_w/sevjanv.shtml, page number unknown.
12. Evgeny I. Zhidilov, *We Defended Sevastopol*, Moscow: Voenizdat, 1963. Cited in Alexander Nemenko, *Chronicle of the Second Defence*, Part 3, Chapter 29 – http://samlib.ru/n/nemenko_a_w/sevjanv.shtml, page number unknown
13. Gorpischenko memoirs, Soviet Archives, Nemenko collection.
14. Ibid.
15. Zhidilov, *We Defended Sevastopol*. Cited in Alexander Nemenko, *Chronicle of the Second Defence*, Part 3, Chapter 29 – http://samlib.ru/n/nemenko_a_w/sevjanv.shtml, page number unknown.
16. Ibid.
17. Kolesnikova memoirs, Soviet Archives, Nemenko collection.
18. Evseev memoirs, Soviet Archives, Nemenko collection.
19. Prokhorov memoirs, Soviet Archives, Nemenko collection.
20. Voyetkhov, *The Last Days of Sevastopol*, p. 218
21. Ibid.
22. A Soviet version of the Douglas DC-3.
23. Vasileva memoirs, Soviet Archives, Nemenko collection.
24. Oleynik memoirs, Soviet Archives, Nemenko collection.
25. Ibid.

Bibliography

Bidermann, Gottlieb, *As a Deadly Battle – A Soldier's Memoir of the Eastern Front*, Lawrence, KS: University Press of Kansas, 2000.

Clark, Alan, *Barbarossa – The Russian-German Conflict, 1941-1945*, New York: William Morrow & Company, 1965.

Cumins, Keith, *Cataclysm – The War on the Eastern Front 1941-1945*, Solihull: Helion & Co., Ltd., 2011.

Hoyt, Edwin P., *Stalin's War – Tragedy and Triumph 1941-1945*, Washington D.C.: Cooper Square Press, 2003.

Krylov, N. I., *My Memories*, Moscow: House of U.S.S.R. Academy of Science, 1963.

Laskin, Ivan A., *On the Way to the Fracture*, Moscow: Military Publishing, 1977.

Manstein, Erich von, *Lost Victories*, New York: Presidio Press, 1954.

Morgunov, Petr A., *Heroic Sevastopol*, Moscow: Nauka, 1979.

Müller, Rolf-Dieter, *The Unknown Eastern Front – The Wehrmacht and Hitler's Foreign Soldiers*, London & New York: I. B. Tauris, 2012.

Multiple Authors, *The Heroic Defence of Sevastopol*, Moscow: Foreign Language Publishing House, 1942.

Nemenko, Alexander V., 'Sevastopol, Chronology of the Second Defence.' Litsovet.ru, 01/15.

Nemenko, Alexander V., 'The Shadow of the Great Past.' Litsovet.ru, 04/12 to 02/13.

Nemenko, Alexander V., 'Fire Frontiers.' Litsovet.ru, 2007 to 2008.

Nemenko, Alexander V., 'Crimea 1941. Chronology of Defence.' Litsovet.ru, 05/14 to 07/14.

Oberkommando des Heeres, *Nachtrag zu dem Denkschriften über fremde Landbefestigung*, Berlin: 1943.

Seaton, Albert, *The Russo-German War 1941-45*, New York: Praeger Publishers, 1993.

Smirnova-Medveva, Zoe, *Scorched Youth*, Moscow: Military Publishing, 1967.

Sweeting, C. G., *Blood and Iron – The German Conquest of Sevastopol*, Washington D.C.: Potomac Books, Inc., 2004.

Vaneev, G. I., *Sevastopol 1941-1942. Chronicle of the Heroic Defence, Book 1*, Kiev: Vydatelstro, 1995.

Voyetkhov, Boris, *The Last Days of Sevastopol*, New York: Alfred A. Knopf, 1943.

Index

Page numbers in *italics* refer to illustrations.

Akhtiar (Ak-Yar), 23, 24, 237n
Aleksander, Captain G., 79
Alma River, 8, 9, 25, 40, 46, 49, 50, 51, 56, 237n
Alma Station, 52
Altyn-Bair, 48, 87
Arabat, 4, 13, *14*, 17, 18
Aranci Strongpoint, 6, 40, 48, 49, 53–6, 60, 63, 64, 82, 84, 86, 87, 95
Armiansk, 17, 18, 20, 21

Bakhchisarai, 3, 6, 43, 46, 49–53, 59, 102, 105, 116, 239n
Balaclava, 1–3, 6, *7*, 8, 23, 28, 29, 36, 40, 41, 58, 74, 76–8, *78*, 79–82, 108, 117, 118, 120–3, 125, 127, 128, 134, 136, 138, 147, 167, *168*, 169, 179, 180, 196, 206, 218–20, *228*, 234, 237n, 238n
Baranov, Lieutenant-Colonel, 47, 189, 198
Barbarossa, Operation, 10–12, 86, 243n
Bartenyevka, 135, 180, 183
Batov, General Ivan, 14, 15, 17, 57
Bays of Sevastopol:
    Artillery (Artyllereyskaya), 24, 31
    Cossack (Kazachya), 8, 25, 28, 107, 188, 203, 207, 218, 222, 227, 228
    Engineering (Inzhenernaya), 25, 188
    Holland, 25, 27, 31, 186, 188, 200, 201
    Killen (Careenage), 25, *28*, 31, 40, 194, 203, 208, 210, 214
    Musketeer (Streletskaya), 23, 24, 32, 34, 35, 40, *117*, 127, 136, 194, 203, 219, 225, 227, 228
    Quarantine (Karantynnaya), 24, 28, *117*, 138, 198
    Reed (Kamyshovya), 24, 32, 128, 203, 219, 227, 228
    Sandy, 24, 35, *160*
    Sevastopol Bay, 3, 6, 8, 9, 24–6, 29, 72, 74, 83, 86, 89, 98, 105, 113, 132, 165, 194, 198, *204*, 207, 208, *208*, 213, 220, 242n
    Ship (Korabelnaya), 24, 156
    Sukharnaya, 24, 27, 83
Belbek Valley, 6, 9, 26, 27, 34, 36, 40, 56, 59–64, 70–2, 82, 84, 87, 89, 91–6, 101, 102, 106, 115, 135, 141–4, 146, 148, 150, 151, 153, 174, 177, 239n
Black River (Chornaya), 3, 6, 24–7, 29, 66, 72, 73, 76, 77, 82, 89, 96, 107, 117, 118, 121, 124, 132, 190, 198, 202, 203, 205, 216, 217

Canrobert Hill, 28, 29, 82, 125, 126, 132, 147, 166, 167, 237n
Cape Fiolent, 28, 32, 78, 207, 222, 223, 225, 229, 234
Cape Tolstoy, 27, 29, 31, 180, 188
Cherkez-Kerman, 6, 26, 40, 47, 49, 54, 60, 64, *64*, 65, 66, 69, 70, 72, 74, 77, 80, 86, 114
Chersonese, 25, 28, 34, 36, 90, 127, 130, 131, 136, 218, 219, 222, 223, *223*, 226–9, 234
Chongar, 4, 13, *14*, 16–19, 40
Chorgun Strongpoint, 6, 27, 29, 40, 49, 65–7, 72–4, 77, 80, 81, 84, 89, 90, 94, 97, 100, 101, 105, 117, 118, 147, 179
Coastal Army, 8, 17, 22, 45–7, 50, 51, 53, 58, 59, 61, 66, 71, 83, 131, 137, 224, 226
Crimean War, 1, 2, 25, 28–32, 121, 123, 124, 164, 165, 172, 176, 209, 210, 215, 218, 220, 221, 228, 237n, 241n

Dergacheva, 101, 116, 121, 122, 124, 180, 211–16
Djankoi, 16, 21, 44, 45, 130
Dora, railway gun, 116, 129, 139, 241n
Drapushko, Captain Mark Semenovich, 79
Duvankoi Strongpoint, 6, 40, 47–9, 52–4, 57, 57, 59, *60*, 61–4, 66, 68, 71, 82, 88, 92, 241n

English Cemetery, 29, 40, 70, 123, *124*, *125*, *126*, 213, 215, 220

Fedyukhiny Heights, 2, 29, 82, 84, 117, 118, 120, 121, 136, 161, 167, 168, 179, 193, 194, 196
Forsthaus (Mekenzievy Cordon No. 1), 104, 105, 149, 158
forts (German names):
    Cheka, 33, 110, 135, 165, 168, 171, 172, 176
    Donets, 110, 165, 200

Index   245

GPU, 110, 135, 165, 166, 172, 176
Lenin, 110, 162, 165, 188, 192
Maxim Gorki I, 6, *108*, 110, *170*
Maxim Gorki II, 6, 36, 110
Molotov, 98, 105, 110, *129*, 135, 139, 144, 158, 161, 165, 166, 168, 172, 176, *176*, 182, 184
Shishkov, 171, *173*, 174, 176, 178, 180, 183
Siberia, 110, 135, 165, 166, 172, 241n
Stalin, 17, 96, 98, *100*, 110, 148, *155*, 156, 162, 165
The Bastion, 99, 174, 175, 177, 178
Ural, 165, 200
Volga, 165, 166
forts (Soviet names):
  A, 33
  B, 33, 110, 165, 173
  Balaklava (North & South), 28, *75*, 76, 80, 84
  Constantine, 27, 31, 35, 135, 181, *186*, 188, 189, 192–5, *195*, 237n
  Kruhleva, *see* Shishkov *under* forts (German names)
  North Fort, 28–30, 81, 105, 110, 120, 135, 165, 166, 171, 182, *187*, 188, 189, *189*, 190, *191*, 192, 241n
Fraternal Cemetery, 165, 171, 183

Gasfort, Mount, 6, 28, 29, 32, 73, 82, 90, 93, 105, 107, 110, 115, 117, 118, 125, 126, 132, 237n
Gaytani, 26, 132, 133, 135, 136, 205
Genoese Towers, 28, 76, 80, 84, 115, 125, 206, 237n
German Units:
  Corps:
    VIII Air Corps, 5, 116, 134, 211, 230
    XXX Corps, 8, 9, 18, 22, 134, 211, 227
    LIV Corps, 12, 18, 19, 22, 115, 132, 133, 134, 171, 207, 227
  Infantry Divisions:
    22nd, 9, 12, 18, 20, 21, 56, 74, 81, 85, 88–90, 95–7, 100, 105, 107, 133, 140, 141, 146, 153, 154, 157–9, 171, 172, 186, 194, 206–10, 220, 222, 240n
    24th, 9, 21, 84, 88, 89, 96, 114, 133, 152, 154, 167, 172, 186, 190, 192, 196, 200, 206–10, 220
    28th Light, 134, 147, 169, 186, 219, 220
    46th, 18, 19, 21, 22, 171, 172, 185, 231
    50th, 20, 21, 22, 46, 47, 56, 60, 65, 66, 74, 77, 80, 81, 88–90, 94, 95–7, 106, 114, 115, 133, 140, 147, 152, 154, 168, 169, 171, 186, 194, 202, 210, 211, 220, 231
    72nd, 18, 20, 74, 76, 77, 80, 81, 82, 88, 89, 106, 134, 166–8, 186, 202, 205, 206, 211, 213, 219, 227

    73rd, 18, 19, 21, 22, 88, 154, 177
    132nd, 21, 22, 44, 47, 50, 51, 56, 60, 71, 74, 88, 89, 95, 96, 104, 106, 107, 115, 133, 140, 146, 153, 154, 157, 171, 177, 186, 203, 205, 206, 210, 220, 222
    170th, 18–22, 51, 88, 89, 106, 134, 167, 186, 193, 196, 206, 211–13, 219, 222, 227, 228, 234
  Infantry Regiments:
    16th, 114, 141, 143, 144, 146, 149, 158, 162, 237n
    31st, 152, 153, 172, 186, 190, 192, 209
    33rd, 202
    47th, 142, 143, 145, 147, 149, 150, 152, 158, 182, 186
    65th, 114, 144, 146, 149, 150, 182, 186, 201, 209, 216
    105th, 77, 106, 228
    122nd, 21, 152, 153, 169
    161st, 101, 106, 176, 178
    186th, 21, 22
    213th, 19, 20, 21, 22, 133, 154, 177, 194, 220
    399th, 186, 187, 193, 206, 211, 213
    420th, 186, 193, 196, 206, 211
    436th, 95, 115
    437th, 56, 104, 115, 140, 186
    438th, 57, 95, 104, 115, 157
Gorpischenko, Colonel, 211, 212
Grace Farm (Blagodat), 70, 179

Hills (by height no.):
  90.5 (Telegraph Hill), 29, 72, 77, 105, 115
  104.5 (Olberg), 84, 92, 96, 110, 141, 174
  124.5 (Bunkerberg), 92, 141
  126.5 (Stellenberg), 93, 141
  133.1 (Windmill Hill), 127
  137.5 (Machine Gun Hill), 69, 70, 75
  169.4 (Canrobert Hill), 125, 126
  190.0 (Azis-Oba), 40, 48, 49, 56, 90, 91
  192.0 (Trapez), 105, 110, 147, *149*
  209 (Kaya-Bash), 91
  269.0 (Chirish Tepe), 29, 105, 118
Hitler, Adolf, 2, 4, 8, 40, 11, 18, 73, 129, 233, 234, 241n, 243n

Inkerman, 3, 23, 24, 25, 26, 29, 30, 40, 65, 66, 74, 84, 87, *88*, 89, 95, 96, 97, 98, 99, 104, 111, 118, 119, 120, 121, 132, 136, 164, 166, 169, 170, 179, 182, 183, 190, 197, 198, 199, 202, 203, *203*, 205, 206, 210, 211, 216, 217, *217*, 237n, 239n, 242n
Ishun, 4, 9, 17, 18, 20, 21, 22, 52, 66, 158, 242n
Italian Cemetery, 90, 93, 95, 99, 100, 101, 105, 107, 118, 147

Kacha River, 9, 26, 38, 40, 47, 48, 489, 51, 53, 54, 55, 56, 59, 62, 84, 106, 107
Kadykova, 84, 136, 179, 183, 187, 193, 194, 206
Kalamita Fortress, 26, 203, 205
Kamary, 40, 49, 73, 81, 84, 115, 125, 134, 136, 147, 167, 179
Kamyshly Ravine, 26, 52, 71, 84, 89, 90, 92, 94, 95, 105, 114, 115, 135, 141, 144, 147, 148, 149, 154
Kamyshovaya Line (Kamezh), 32, 127, 203, 218, 225
Karagach Height, 29, 127, 183
Karani (Karan Valley), 127, 220, 29, 125, 218, *219*
Kara-Tau Plateau, 8, 26, 47, 48, 49, 56, 57, 60, 70, 82, 90, 92, 95, 141, 144
Karl mortars, 129, 139, 180
Kerch, 8, 13, 23, 68, 80, 85, 86, 87, 88, 94, 97, 101, 102, 103, 104, 105, 106, 107, 113, 114, 115, 116, 128, 171, 172, 186, 231, 232, 234
Khatskevich, Brigade Commissar Aron, 226
Klokacheva, Vice-Admiral Fedota, 23, 24
Kolomiets, Major-General Trofim, 70, 169
Kuznetsov, General F. I., 15, 17, 22
Kuznetsov, Admiral Nikolay, 39, 40, 80, 182, 224

Laskin, Colonel Ivan, 70, 90, 142, 145, 147, 153, 154, 155, 240n, 243n
Leibstandarte SS Adolf Hitler, 18, 20, 21
Levchenko, Vice-Admiral, 22, 46, 57, 58, 61
Litovsky (Lithuanian) Peninsula, 13, 17, 19, 236n
Lower Chorgun, 72, 73, 84, 90, 94
Lyubimovka, 26, 70, 84, 96, 99, 115, 121, 142, 159, 163, 169, 170, 171, 174, 175, 176, 178, 180

Mackenzie, Rear-Admiral Thomas, 24
Mackenzie Farm, 24, 64, 66, 9, 71, 72, 74, 77, 81, 82, 93, 104, 114, 115, 119, 120, 239n
Malakhov, 31, 124, 128, 185, 209, 214, 216, 220, *221*, 221, 222, 223, 237n, 241n
Mamashai, 48, 55, 61, 63, 84, 86, 106, 107
Manstein, General Erich von, vii, 2, 3, 4, 5, 6, 8, 9, 11, 12, 20, 21, 22, 81, 88, 89, 101, 102, 129, 132, 135, 136, 140, 162, 167, 170, 171, 212, 234, 236n, 241n, 243n
Matushenko, Captain M. V., 189, 192
Maximova Farm, 40, 70, 79, 106, 220, 222, 223
Mekenzievy, 3, 24, 26, 27, 40, 48, 69, 70, 82, 84, 88, 89, 92, 93, 95, 96, 97, 98 ,99, 100, 101, *101*, 102, 104, 105, 109, 113, 114, 115, 118, 132, 139, 148, 149, 154, 157, 158, 159, 163, 164, 179, 182, 194, 240n, 241n
Morgunov, General Petr Alekseevich, 5, 9, 38, 39, 40, 41, 42, 46, 47, 49, 58, 61, 69, 108, 180, 182, 188, 207, 209, 232, 237n, 242n, 243n

Mount Kara-Koba, 26, 80, 115, 117, 118, 119, 120, 132, 197, 203, 205

Novikov, Major-General Petr G., 6, 70, 196, 224, 225, 226
Novo Shuli, 66, 116, 118, 120, 194, 196, 197, 203, 211, 212

Odessa, 8, 14, 17
Oktyabrsky, Vice-Admiral Filip Sergeyevich, 5, 8, 9, 17, 28, 46, 49, 58, 70, 80, 87, 94, 99, 100, 102, 105, 116, 146, 159, 163, 166, 169, 170, 176, 180, 188, 205, 223, 224, 225, 231, 232, 237n

Perekop, 4, 8, 9, 13, *14*, 15, *16*, 16, 17, 18, 19, *19*, 20, 21, 22, 31, 40, 47, 59, 66, 77, 80, 81, 82, 88, 92, 94, 98, 114, 115, 149, 150, 158, 163, 169, 180, 183, 189, 197, 236n, 241n, 242n
Petrov, General Ivan, 5, 6, 9, 17, 45, 46, 58, 59, 61, 67, 68, 69, 70, 80, 81, 86, 91, 94, 95, 96, 98, 99, 132, 146, 149, 161, 180, 183, 196, 222, 224, 225, 232
Pyanzin, Lieutenant (Battery 80 and 365), 153, 156, 161, 241n

Richtofen, Baron Wolfram von, 5, 116, 205
Rumanian Units:
 Rumanian Mountain Corps, 13, 132, 133
 1st Mountain Division, 132, 199, 205, 222
 18th Mountain Division, 202

Sapun Ridge, 3, 6, 8, 9, 27, 28, 29, 70, 84, 117, 121, 122, 123, 126, 168, 169, 179, 186, 196, 207, 210, 211, 212, 213, 214, 234
Schobert, General Eugen Ritter von, 4, 11, 12, 13
Sevastopol Ravines:
 Cowhide Ravine, 27, 208, 210
 English Ravine, 28, 215
 Grafskaya (Count's) Ravine, 27, 159, 169, 180, 182, 183, 194, 197
 Gypsy Ravine, 26, 70, 199
 Kamyshly Ravine, 26, 52, 69 71, 84, 89, 90, 92–6, 102, 105, 114, 115, 135, 141, 142, 144, 145, 147–50, 154
 Killen Ravine, 25, 28, 29–31, 40, 124, 161, 194, 203, 207, 208, 210, 214, 216, 222
 Laboratory Ravine (Woronzoff), 28, *110*, 124, 213, *213*, 214, 220, 222
 Lighthouse Ravine, 25–7, 149, 164, 179, 186, 188, 194, 200, 201, 214
 Martynov Ravine, 26, 66, 69, 82, 93, 104, 107, 113, 163, 164, *165*, 169, 179, 182, 183, 194, 197, *198*, 199, 202

Sarandinakinu Ravine, 28, 123, 215
Sukharno (Sukharnaya) Ravine, 27, 33, 78, 113, 157, 159, 162, 164, 166, 169, 172, 186, 188, 190, 194, *199*, 200, *200*, 201, *201*, 202, 214, 216, 223, 241n
Sushilnaya Ravine, 28, 207, 201
Yuharinoy Ravine, 28, 220, 227, 228
Shuli, 6, 27, 40, 49, 64–7, 72–4, 77, 80, 82, 117–19
Simferopol (City, Highway, Railway), *5*, 6, 14, 15, 21, 22, 30, 38, 44–7, 50, 51, 54, 59, 60, 62, 71, 76, 86, 92, 96, 104, 106, 116, 121, 140, 144, 145, 148, 149, 158, 159, 164, 174, 179, 194
Siwash, the, 13, 15, 18, 21, 236n
Sophia Perovskoy Farm, 38, 159, 163, 170, *173*, 174, 176, 178, 182
Soviet Units:
  Corps:
    IX Corps, 2, 14, 15
  Rifle Divisions:
    25th Chapaevsky, 17, 22, 59, 66, 70, 86, 88–90, 94, 105, 113, 115, 131, 149, 159, 161, 163, 169, 179, 182, 186, 194, 197, 199, 202, 203, 205, 213, 215, 218, 225, 226, 228, 239n, 241n
    95th, 17, 22, 65, 69, 88, 90, 94, 101, 105–7, 131, 132, 142, 146, 154, 156, 161, 168, 170, 171, 173, 176, 180, 182, 188, 196, 197, 208, 210, 222, 241n
    106th, 14, 22, 15, 17, 20, 158
    156th, 14, 15, 18–21
    172nd, 59, 67, 70, 78, 88, 90, 92, 106, 107, 113, 114, 132, 137, 141–3, 145–9, 153–6, 158
    271st, 15, 20
    276th, 15, 18, 19
    345th, 96–101, 103–5, 113–15, 131, 153, 156–60, 163, 168, 180, 182, 183, 194, 197, 202, 208, 210, 214, 215, 218, 222, 241n
    386th, 96, 98, 99, 101, 106, 109, 116, 118, 120, 121, 131, 147, 196, 198, 206, 211–13, 216
    388th, 59, 86, 88, 91, 94–6, 126, 127, 131, 132, 147, 152, 166, 167, 169, 179, 196, 215, 218, 234
  Cavalry Divisions:
    40th, 8, 15, 74, 76, 78, 80, 87, 88, 91, 94–7, 99, 101, 113, 115, 241n
    42nd, 15, 20
  Marine Brigades:
    7th, 45–7, 53, 54, 56, 69–71, 75, 77, 81, 90–4, 97–9, 105, 107, 115–18, 121, 132, 147, 159, 161, 168, 176, 196, 206, 211–15, 241n
    8th, 8, 47, 48, 56, 61, 68, 71–2, 86–92, 94–7, 99–101, 105, 107, 116, 118, 132, 161, 168, 180, 182, 183, 194, 196, 197, 199, 202, 203, 205, 206, 210–17
    79th, 95–100, 103, 105, 114, 115, 137, 141–54, 157–9, 161, 163, 168–70, 180, 182, 183, 208, 210, 215, 222, 241n
  Marine Regiments:
    2nd, 49, 66, 81, 89, 90, 93, 94, 208, 210
    3rd, 49, 59, 61, 63, 65, 66, 69, 77, 81, 88, 95, 179, 197–9, 202, 203, 205, 206, 216
  Guards Regiment, 8, 47–9, 54, 56, 61, 88, 97, 180, 183, 188, 189, 193, 196, 198, 201
  Rifle Regiments:
    2nd Perekop, 47, 59, 66, 77, 80, 81, 88, 92, 94, 98, 114, 115, 149, 150, 163, 169, 180, 183, 197, 241n
    31st, 66, 77, 80–2, 90, 93, 100, 105, 114, 179, 199, 216
    54th, 77, 81, 95, 114
    90th, 54, 87, 91, 94, 95, 99, 100, 142, 146, 154, 161, 178, 192, 222
    109th, 167, 179, 219, 220
    161st, 22, 81, 98, 99, 113, 171, 175
    241st, 91, 94, 99
    287th, 94, 97, 105, 138, 149, 153, 154
    514th, 78, 90, 107, 141, 145, 149, 240n
    602nd, 147, 166, 167
    747th, 141, 142, 146, 149–51, 153, 155
    769th, 212, 216
    772nd, 106, 116
    773rd, 91, 96, 179
    775th, 212
    778th, 91, 94, 95, 159, 203
    1163rd, 97, 158
    1165th, 96, 97, 114, 163
    1167th, 115, 156
    1330th, 67, 80, 95, 99, 105
Soviet Anti-Aircraft Batteries:
  Battery 79, 131, 132, 180
  Battery 80, 69, 153, 155, 156
Soviet Armoured Train:
  Zhelezniakov, 42, 51, 52, 68, 88, *88*, 97, 99, 105, 113, 203, *204*, 242n
Soviet Coastal Batteries – Sevastopol:
  Battery 2, 35, 36, 108, 173, 188, 189, 192
  Battery 3, 35, 130, 189
  Battery 4, 31, 108, 188, 189, 192, 193, 195, 237n
  Battery 10, 29, 30, 33, *37*, 38, 42, 54–6, 61, 69, 79, 87, 96, 106, 107, 189
  Battery 12, 16, 188, 189, 194
  Battery 13, 16, 33, 195
  Battery 14, 35, 163, *160*, 234
  Battery 15, 34, 36, 223, 237n
  Battery 16, 34, 172–4, 222, 226, 228

Index 247

Battery 17, 34
Battery 18, 116, 220, 223
Battery 19, *7*, 78, *78*, 79, 169, 220, *228*
Battery 20, 173
Battery 22, 179
Battery 23, 36
Battery 24, 172, 173, 190, 234
Battery 30, 6, 36, 79, 96, 98, 99, 105, 107, 108, *108*, 110, 113, 116, 135, 137, 139, 142, 144, *158*, 159, 161, 163, *164*, 167, 168, 170, *170*, 171, *173*, 174, *175*, 175, 176, 177, *177*, *178*, 180, 181, 181, 182, *196*, *230*, *233*
Battery 35, 6, 36, 77, 90, 107, 108, 110, 188, 219–20, 222, 223, *223*, 224, *224*, 225–9
Battery 54, 15, 42, 43, *43*, 50, 130, 238n
Battery 112 (702bis), 223
Battery 111 (701), 53, 108, 214, 220–2, *221*
Battery 113 (702), 116, 123, 188, 192, 215, 223
Battery 114 (703), 116, 124, 214, 215, 221
Battery 115 (704), 159, 160, 164, 241n
Battery 116 (705), 106, 169, 220
Battery 365, *see* Fort Stalin *under* forts (German names)
Battery 366, *see* Fort Lenin *under* forts (German names)
St. Michael's, 30, 31, 182, 188–90, 192, 194, 195
Soviet Naval Vessels:
Abkhazia, 94, 137, 157, 158
Bezuprechnyy ('Flawless'), 67, 136, 205, 220
Boykiy ('Courageous'), 67
Chervona Ukraina ('Red Ukraine'), 17, 47, 70, 75, 108, 116, 159, *209*, 214, 215, 241n

Kharkov (transport), 86, 95, 113
Krasnyy Kavkaz ('Red Caucasus'), 86, 87
Krasnyy Krim ('Red Crimea'), 137
Molotov, 98, 105, 158, 161, 168
Parizhskaya Kommuna ('Paris Commune'), 98
Soobrazitelnyy, 86, 105
Tashkent, 97, 136, 205
St. George's Monastery, 84, 220, 222
Sugar Head, 26, 84, 117, 118, 120, 134, 190, 198, 205
Suzdal Heights, 29, 40, 101, *123*, 124, 161, 210, 214, *215*, 222, 239n

Trinity (Troitskiy) Tunnel, 28, 194, 203, 204
Turkish Redoubts, 2, 3, 6, 29, 31, 121, 125, 126, 132, 147, 166, 167, *168*, 179, 187, 193, 196, 222
Turkish Wall (Ditch), 15, 16, *16*, *19*, 20, 231n

Upper Chorgun, 29, 65–7, 73, 74

Victoria Redoubt, 29, 32, 70, 121, 124, *125*, 210, 212, 214, 220, 221
Vilshansky, Colonel V. L., 48, 61
Vorobiev, Nikolai (Battery 365), 148, 155
Vorobiev, Major-General V. F., 70, 91

Yalta Highway, 3, 6, 28, 72, 74, 76, 77, 80, 82, 86, 115, 117, 118, 120–3, 125, 127, 132, 134, 166–9, 183, 186, 196, 206, 207, 211, 212

Zhidilov, Colonel Yevgeniy Ivanovich, 44–7, 161
Ziegler Brigade, 22, 44, 50, 52, 56, 60, 64, 236n